CONTEMPORARY THEORY, RESEARCH, AND PRACTICE OF CRISIS AND HOSTAGE NEGOTIATION

THE HAMPTON PRESS COMMUNICATION SERIES
Interpersonal Communication
Don Cegala, series editor

The Biology of Communication: A Communibiological Perspective
Michael J. Beatty & James C. McCroskey

Imagined Interactions: Daydreaming About Communication
James M. Honeycutt

Communication and Personality: Trait Perspectives
*James C. McCroskey, John A. Daly, Matthew M. Martin,
& Michael J. Beatty*

Identity Matters: Communication-Based Explorations and Explanations
Hartmut B. Mokros (ed.)

Conflict and Gender
Anita Taylor & Judi Beinstein Miller (eds.)

Contemporary Theory, Research, and Practice of Crisis and Hostage
Negotiation
Randall G. Rogan & Frederick J. Lanceley (eds.)

CONTEMPORARY THEORY, RESEARCH, AND PRACTICE OF CRISIS AND HOSTAGE NEGOTIATION

edited by

Randall G. Rogan
Frederick J. Lanceley

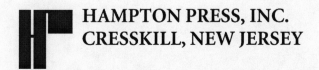

HAMPTON PRESS, INC.
CRESSKILL, NEW JERSEY

Printed in the United States of America

Library of Congress Cataloging-in-Publication Data

Contemporary theory, research, and practice of crisis and hostage negotiation / edited by Randall G. Rogan, Frederick J. Lanceley—1st ed.
    p. cm. — (The Hampton Press communication series)
  Includes bibliographical references and index.
  ISBN 978-1-57273-962-8 (hardcover) — ISBN 978-1-57273-963-5 (paperbound)
  1. Hostage negotiations.   2. Hostage negotiations—Psychological aspects.
3. Crisis management.   I. Rogan, Randall G. II. Lanceley, Frederick J.
  HV6595.C66 2010
  363.2'3—dc22

                                         2010014751

Hampton Press, Inc.
23 Broadway
Cresskill, NJ 07626

Contents

Contemporary Theory, Research, and Practice of Crisis and Hostage Negotiation

An Overview

Randall G. Rogan
Frederick J. Lanceley

The frequency with which crisis and hostage negotiation incidents occur is a rather disheartening statement about human nature and humankind's inability to effectively manage life-stressing events. The most recent statistics from the Federal Bureau of Investigation's (FBI's) Hostage, Barricade, and Suicide (HOBAS) database (Federal Bureau of Investigation, 2007) reveal that, since 1991, nearly 5,100 incidents within the United States have been reported to the FBI. It is important to note that these include *only* those incidents that have been reported to the HOBAS database. These 5,100 incidents translate into an average of nearly 340 incidents per year and almost 1 per day! Undeniably, this frequency of negotiated incidents is significant by any standard.

Yet hostage taking is not a recent phenomenon. History is replete with incidents of crisis and hostage taking, with some authors contending that these incidents date back more than 2,000 years (McMains & Mullins, 2001; Soskis & Van Zandt, 1986). It was not until the 1970s, however, that law enforcement earnestly began to explore strategies for negotiating nonviolent resolutions to hostage and barricade standoffs (Rogan & Hammer, 2006). In fact, various publications cite the Attica prison riot of 1971 and the Munich Olympic Games of 1972 as perhaps the two most pivotal incidents in facilitating the development of law enforcement's implementation of crisis negotiation as an alternative to tactical incident management (e.g., Hammer, 2007; McMains & Mullins, 2001; Poland & McCrystle, 1999). Although approximate in time to these two watershed events, it was psychologist Harvey Schlossberg, then serving with the New York Police Department (NYPD), who began to question the need and desire for a negotiation strategy to crisis and hostage standoffs (Bolz & Hershey, 1979;

Louden, 1998), independent of either the incidents at Attica or Munich. Although he met with some initial resistance, Schlossberg received approval from NYPD commanders to try a "negotiate first" approach to incident resolution. The success of engaging the subject in relational communication quickly proved successful (Louden, 1998). Consequently, Schlossberg's work helped to propel NYPD to the forefront of metropolitan law enforcement for its innovative management of standoff incidents. Schlossberg's "New York Plan" was soon adopted by police departments throughout the United States. The FBI likewise developed its own hostage negotiation unit and training program, building on the basic principles and practices first developed by Schlossberg. Crisis and hostage negotiation is today widely regarded as the primary default strategy for resolving barricade and hostage-taking incidents (Hammer, 2007; Lanceley, 2005; Rogan & Hammer, 2006).

Generally speaking, current crisis and hostage negotiation initiatives are highly effective. The FBI's HOBAS database of 5,071 incidents reveals that 57% of all reported incidents have been resolved through negotiations, and 12% have been resolved by means of an integrated negotiation and tactical approach. In only 20% of the incidents reported was a tactical-only action employed to resolve the event. The remaining incidents were resolved by the suspect's escape (2.7%), suspect suicide/attempted suicide (8.4%), or police disengagement from the incident (.8%). Perhaps the most telling finding that the HOBAS data reveal, however, is that in 97% of all incidents, no injuries or deaths were reported for bystanders or law enforcement officers (Federal Bureau of Investigations, 2007).

Over the years, numerous modifications and refinements have been made to Schlossberg's original model of negotiation. As the number of law enforcement officers engaging in negotiation grew, so did the realization that there was a need for increased knowledge about the myriad dynamics of crisis and hostage negotiations. Although numerous agencies and individuals, including agents of the former Special Operations and Research Unit (SOARU) of the FBI, devoted countless hours to learning about incident type, suspect psychology, motivation, and negotiation strategies, there was a notable paucity of research devoted specifically to crisis and hostage negotiation. Consequently, many of the early principles of negotiation were derived principally from negotiator anecdotal experiences or transferred from such disciplines as clinical psychology (Rogan & Hammer, 2006). This approach generally seemed to prove successful until the death of 83 individuals in Waco, Texas. It was a consequence of the Congressional hearings subsequent to the FBI standoff with David Koresh and the Branch Davidians that Heymann (1993) noted the absence of a dedicated base of social and behavioral science research of crisis negotiations and called for an increased dedication to such initiatives. Since then, a sizeable body of research and literature has developed, both domestically and internationally (see McMains & Mullins, 2006; Rogan & Hammer, 2006, for comprehensive reviews of current research). The purpose of this edited volume is to add to that knowledge base by presenting the work of some of the leading researchers and practitioners of crisis and hostage negotiation.

CONCEPTUALIZING CRISIS
AND HOSTAGE NEGOTIATION

As noted by Hammer (2007) and Rogan and Hammer (2006), most of the literature devoted to crisis and hostage negotiation presumes a shared conceptualization of crisis and hostage negotiation. Yet a variety of definitions have been introduced over the years, with some focusing on the features that distinguish between incident types (e.g., Bolz, Dudonis, & Schulz, 1990; MacWillson, 1992; Maher, 1977; Miller, 1980; Miron & Goldstein, 1979; Ochberg & Soskis, 1982), others emphasizing the confrontational power-based nature of such events (e.g., Cooper, 1981), and still others highlighting the motives of the suspect (Lanceley, 2003; Miron & Goldstein, 1979). Still another cohort of conceptualizations crafted principally by academic researchers tends to emphasize the dynamic nature of the interaction as defined from either a social-psychological or communication-based perspective.

For example, McMains and Mullins (2001) conceptualized crisis and hostage-taking events in terms of the forced detainment of an individual by a suspect and the articulation of some set of demands by said suspect. Lanceley (2003) differentiated between crisis intervention, in which a victim is being held but not for the express purpose of trading, and actual hostage negotiations, in which a person is held against his or her will in order to help the suspect fulfill some substantive demand via trade with the authorities. Donohue and his colleagues (e.g., Donohue, Ramesh, & Borchgrevink, 1991; Donohue & Roberto, 1993, 1996) emphasized the crisis nature that these events constitute for a suspect and conceptualized the objective for law enforcement, regardless of suspect motive, as transforming the interactional dynamics out of crisis bargaining to normative conflict management. Hammer (2001, 2007) has noted that crisis negotiation involves a conflict dynamic centered around perceived goal incompatibilities and interference between the parties involved and that it is this tension that "... gives rise to perceptions of threat and negative emotions" (Hammer, 2007, p. 29). Finally, Rogan and Hammer (2002, 2006) advanced a conceptualization that is grounded in a communication-based perspective in which crisis negotiation is defined in terms of the inherent communicative dynamics and relational interdependencies. Specifically, they define crisis and hostage negotiation as a special context of ... conflict interaction in which law enforcement officers attempt to facilitate a (peaceful) resolution to an incident where an individual barricades him/herself, sometimes with a number of hostages, in an effort to elicit some desired want or to communicate anger and frustration about a personal or social concern. (Rogan & Hammer, 2002, pp. 229–230)

Clearly, there is no one correct conceptualization by which to frame the broad dynamic of crisis and hostage negotiation because definitions vary by the particular foci and lenses by which researchers elect to study these incidents. Nonetheless, we choose to employ the Rogan and Hammer (2002) conceptualization for the general purpose of this book and as a preliminary theoretical heuristic to help

provide clarity to the diverse nature of crisis and hostage negotiation without unnecessarily differentiating it according to incident type, suspect motive, or specific
management approach. Doing so does not negate the importance of suspect psychology, group dynamics, or incident characteristics. Rather, this definition functions as an overarching communication-based conceptualization under which
more incident characteristic-specific differentiations can reside, such as Lanceley's
(2003) bifurcation of incidents as hostage- and nonhostage-taking events. In this
way, the Rogan and Hammer (2002) definition focuses on the *process*, whereas
other conceptualizations define various features of the *event*.

PURPOSE AND PLAN OF THE BOOK

As previously noted, McMains and Mullins (2006) and Rogan and Hammer
(2006) provide perhaps the most comprehensive and systematic reviews of extant practitioner knowledge and scholarly research of crisis and hostage negotiation. McMains and Mullins present a thorough application-based review of research from a variety of disciplinary perspectives as it informs specific topics for
their exemplary text, including bargaining dynamics, stress management, negotiation team structure and command, intelligence gathering, negotiating in correctional facilities, and postincident debriefing, just to name a few.

Comparatively, Rogan and Hammer (2006) provide a cogent summariza-
tion of predominantly scholarly research, with a focus primarily on contemporary social-psychological and communication-based crisis and hostage negotiation-
specific investigations. For example, Rogan and Hammer note the importance
of the various surveys conducted to assess negotiators' needs, the FBI's HOBAS
database as a repository for incident statistics, and the contribution of relatively
nascent social-psychological and communication-based research. Most of this
latter work has involved content and discourse analysis of transcribed negotiation incidents, and it has focused on the three domains of relational development and interdependence, phase modeling, and behavioral model development. Of particular noteworthiness, much of this research has focused on the
dynamic interaction of suspect and negotiator as co-creators of the negotiation event, as opposed to focusing only on the actions of the suspect. As noted
by Rogan and Hammer, most of this work is still in an early stage of development. Nonetheless, researchers have gained substantial insight into various dimensions of the negotiation dynamic as manifested in the participants' communication.

We commend the reader to both the McMains and Mullins (2006) text
and the Rogan and Hammer (2006) chapter for a more complete presentation of
this work because both highlight the significant development of practical and
scholarly-based knowledge of crisis and hostage negotiation since its conception
in the 1970s. The purpose of this book is to build on the existing body of knowledge of crisis and hostage negotiation by providing a forum for the most con-

temporary scholarly thought and research on various aspects of the subject. Toward this end, we have invited several leading academic and practitioner experts to write a chapter presenting their most current thinking and work.

We begin this volume with a chapter by Robert J. Louden (Chapter 1), who presents a comprehensive overview of the genesis and evolution of modern-day crisis and hostage negotiation. His chapter begins with a review of key definitional concepts central to crisis negotiations, thereby laying the foundation for a subsequent discussion about the development of hostage and crisis negotiations by the NYPD in the 1970s. He then offers a brief discussion of practitioner and academic research into the structure and practices of negotiation units within the United States. He concludes with summative comments about the history and evolution of domestic crisis and hostage negotiation and recommendations for future initiatives.

The S.A.F.E. model for negotiating critical incidents is the focus of Mitchell R. Hammer in Chapter 3. In this chapter, Hammer presents an overview to a substantial elaboration of the S.A.F.E. model for negotiating hostage/crisis events. This elaborated model is based on his recent detailed discourse analysis of negotiation dynamics between the perpetrator and the police negotiator in four hostage/crisis incidents. The S.A.F.E. framework identifies key "triggers" and communication strategies for deescalating crisis situations in four areas: Substantive demands, Attunement (trust), Face (an individual's self-image), and Emotion (emotional distress). The chapter concludes with a discussion of current applications of the model in his own work, with an eye toward cross-cultural negotiations and its increasing impact among law enforcement crisis/hostage negotiation teams.

In Chapter 4, Ellen Giebels and Paul J. Taylor explore the interaction patterns of social influence as they occur in crisis negotiations. Building on recent efforts to understand the negotiation process, this presentation considers the role of social influence strategies during hostage crises. Influence strategies are important components of crisis negotiation, representing tangible messages that may be used to influence the way in which an interaction unfolds. The authors unpack the role of influence strategies by introducing the Table of Ten, a theoretical framework for interpersonal influence attempts that distinguishes between relational and content-oriented messages. Giebels and Taylor draw on theory and research using this framework to explore the ways in which cue–response dynamics differ across cultures, time periods, and types of crisis negotiation. For example, they conclude that negotiations with perpetrators from low-context rather than high-context cultures evolve around rational influence strategies. In contrast, affective influence strategies are more central to negotiations with perpetrators from high-context cultures. They end with an example that demonstrates the importance of understanding interaction processes alongside independent variables in negotiators' efforts to resolve conflicts.

In Chapter 5, William A. Donohue explores the effect of coercive relationships that precipitate extortionate transactions in which parties seek their ends through the use of threats, which often take the form of hostages and ransoms. Donohue draws on the work of Muir (1977), who argues that extortionate transactions are organized around a series of paradoxes, and that reconstructing these transactions requires managing the paradoxes. Muir's paradoxes include: The Paradox of Dispossession (The less one has, the less one has to lose), The Paradox of Detachment (The less the victim cares about preserving something, the less the victimizer cares about taking it hostage), The Paradox of Face (The nastier one's reputation, the less nasty one has to be), and The Paradox of Irrationality (The more delirious the threatener, the more serious the threat; the more delirious the victim, the less serious the threat). Thus, the purpose of this chapter is to expand on Muir's paradoxes as a way of understanding how to make the transition from a crisis bargaining to a more normative bargaining mode.

In Chapter 6, Randall G. Rogan presents an investigation of facework in crisis negotiation with a specific focus on implications for predicting suicidality. Specifically, this chapter serves to expand on existing research on facework in crisis negotiation by examining the nature of facework strategies that barricaded individuals and police negotiators use during the course of negotiations, with a particular focus on possible variance in facework maneuvers between incidents concluding in suicide and surrender. Consistent with previous research, the findings indicate that barricaded subjects employ mostly self-directed defending and restoring behaviors, whereas police negotiators use mostly other-directed defending and restoring strategies. Rogan discusses additional findings and their implications for application and future research.

Explicating the dynamics of conflict escalation and deescalation is the focus of Wolfgang Bilsky, Beate Tebrügge, and Denise Weßel-Therhorn in Chapter 7. Specifically, their chapter describes a multilevel analysis of communications between a hostage taker and a negotiator during a single hostage incident. In line with findings from previous conflict research, the authors hypothesized that communications differ substantially depending on whether the respective situation shows features of escalation or deescalation. Four separate studies were conducted, each of them focusing on a different aspect of communicative behavior: emotionality, face issues, motivation and interaction, and tactics. Transcripts of 53 phone calls between hostage taker and negotiator were analyzed by means of content analysis using five different instruments. Emotions (hostility, affect), face concern (support, threat), and goal-directed behavior (distributive behavior, conflict tactics) differed in level depending on the prevailing conflict dynamics as reflected in escalative and deescalative phone calls. The authors discuss their findings and the implications for future research and application.

In Chapter 8, Frederick J. Lanceley presents the findings from a research project that he conducted into the behavior of suicidal persons in the last moments of their lives. Lanceley was concerned about an apparent disparity between what he had been taught in the area of suicide intervention and what law enforcement negotiators were reporting to him during seminars. Specifically, this chapter looks at perturbation, drug and alcohol use, sudden improvements in mood in suicidal persons, and rapport between the negotiator and subject. Lanceley gathered data on 28 suicides primarily by interviewing negotiators who were present when the suicide was committed. Lanceley discusses the differences in presuicidal behavior in the days, weeks, and months before a suicide and presuicidal behavior in the minutes and hours before a suicide.

Drawing on his many years as a psychologist with the Los Angles Police Department, Kris Mohandie provides a thoughtful presentation about the various psychological traits associated with crisis and hostage taking suspects in Chapter 9. Mohandie reviews the essential conditions and characteristics of depression, personality disorders (including antisocial personality, narcissistic personality, paranoid personality, and borderline personality), as well as thought-disordered and psychotic conditions (including schizophrenia, bipolar/manic depressive disorder, and delusional disorder). Mohandie discusses the critical features of each of these various conditions and their implications for negotiators as they strive to manage individuals manifesting these various traits.

We then shift our attention to a focus on terrorism and negotiation. Radical Islamic ideology and its implications for crisis and hostage negotiations are the focus of Chapter 10 by Daveed Gartenstien-Ross and Kyle Dabruzzi. With personal knowledge of Islamic ideology, Gartenstein-Ross and Dabruzzi provide negotiators and researchers with a baseline, yet significant overview to jihadist ideology. The authors review basic tenets of faith for all Muslims and then provide a critical discussion on the theological and philosophical underpinnings of jihadism. They review the teachings of four prominent jihadists in an effort to explicate the worldview of the jihadist. The authors conclude their chapter with a discussion about essential culture norms and mores of which crisis negotiators who confront suspects espousing radical Islamic ideology must be knowledgeable.

In Chapter 11, Wayman C. Mullins and Michael J. McMains provide an equally timely discussion about negotiating with extremists, including terrorists. They contend that it is likely only a matter of time before domestic police agencies have to negotiate with a dedicated terrorist who seeks to achieve certain political goals. They begin their chapter with a definition of terrorism that emphasizes the threat or actual enactment of violence and its implications for negotiators. They further elucidate myriad factors associated with domestic and international terrorist groups and aspects of their psychological and motivational determinants. Mullins and McMains contend that responding to a terrorist negotiation incident requires law enforcement to understand who the suspects are, their motivation for becoming a terrorist, and their psychological characteristics in order to know what negotiation strategies might work in such incidents.

High-reliability organizations (HROs) and their systems for functioning during times of crisis are the focus of Chapter 12 authored by Anthony J. Hare and Karlene H. Roberts. Their chapter reviews HRO theory as a framework for continual performance analysis and practice implementation that has significant application to professionals who work in dangerous or critical environments and its potential for application in crisis and hostage negotiation. The authors note that various researchers and practitioners of HRO report similar conceptual frameworks and procedural practices across diverse technological contexts that arguably enhance practitioner safety and improve performance. Hare and Roberts contend that the application of HRO approaches to critical incident management and hostage and crisis negotiation will be most effectively realized by law enforcement personnel who study and adapt the analyses to their own practice and who work in concert with social scientists and mental health professionals to heedfully evaluate and incorporate innovations into their practice.

Finally, in Chapter 13, Lanceley and Rogan provide a brief commentary on the implications and contribution of each of the chapters to both the practice and study of crisis and hostage negotiation. We also offer some recommendations for future application and research. It is our hope and belief that by working collaboratively, researchers and negotiators can help to continue to enhance the effectiveness of the nonlethal resolution to crisis standoffs, the sole objective of which is to save lives.

REFERENCES

Bolz, F., Dudonis, K. J., & Schulz, D. P. (1990). *The counter-terrorism handbook: Tactics, procedures, and techniques*. New York: Elsevier Science.

Bolz, F., & Hershey, E. (1979). *Hostage cop*. New York: Rawson Wade.

Cooper, H. H. A. (1981). *The hostage-takers*. Boulder, CO: Paladin Press.

Donohue, W. A., Ramesh, C., & Borchgrevink, C. (1991). Crisis bargaining: Tracking relational paradox in hostage negotiation. *International Journal of Conflict Management, 2,* 257–274.

Donohue, W. A., & Roberto, A. J. (1993). Relational development in hostage negotiation. *Human Communication Research, 20,* 175–198.

Donohue, W. A., & Roberto, A. J. (1996). An empirical examination of three models of integrative and distributive bargaining. *International Journal of Conflict Management, 7,* 209–229.

Federal Bureau of Investigations. (2007, April). *HOBAS: Statistical report of incidents.* Quantico, VA: FBI Academy.

Hammer, M. R. (2001). Conflict negotiation under crisis conditions. In W. F. Eadie & P. E. Nelson (Eds.), *The language of conflict resolution* (pp. 57–80). Newbury Park, CA: Sage.

Hammer, M. R. (2007). *Saving lives: The S.A.F.E. model for negotiating hostage and crisis incidents*. Westport, CT: Praeger Publishing.

Heymann, P. B. (1993). *Lessons of Waco: Proposed changes in federal law enforcement*. Washington, DC: U.S. Department of Justice.

Lanceley, F. J. (2003). *On-scene guide for crisis negotiations* (2nd ed.). Boca Raton, FL: CRC Press.

Lanceley, F. J. (2005, August). Twenty-eight suicides: The law enforcement experience. *The Negotiator Magazine*. Retrieved from http://www.negotiator magazine.com/article280_1.html.

Louden, R. (1998). The development of hostage negotiation by the NYPD. In A. Karmen (Ed.), *Crime and justice in New York City* (pp. 148–157). New York: McGraw-Hill.

MacWillson, A. C. (1992). *Hostage-taking terrorism: Incident-response strategy.* New York: St. Martin's.

Maher, G. F. (1977). *Hostage: A police approach to a contemporary crisis.* Springfield, IL: Charles C. Thomas.

McMains, M. J., & Mullins, W. C. (2001). *Crisis negotiations: Managing critical incidents and hostage situations in law enforcement and corrections* (2nd ed.). Cincinnati, OH: Anderson.

McMains, M. J., & Mullins, W. C. (2006). *Crisis negotiations: Managing critical incidents and hostage situations in law enforcement and corrections* (3rd ed.). Cincinnati, OH: Anderson.

Miller, A. H. (1980). *Terrorism and hostage negotiations.* Boulder, CO: Westview.

Miron, M. S., & Goldstein, A. P. (1979). *Hostage.* Elmsford, NY: Pergamon.

Muir, W. K. (1977). *Police: Streetcorner politicians.* Chicago: University of Chicago Press.

Ochberg, F. M., & Soskis, D. A. (Eds.). (1982). *Victims of terrorism.* Boulder, CO: Westview.

Poland, J. M., & McCrystle, M. J. (1999). *Practical, tactical, and legal perspectives of terrorism and hostage-taking.* New York: Edwin Mellen.

Rogan, R. G., & Hammer, M. R. (2002). Crisis/hostage negotiations: Conceptualization of a communication-based approach. In H. Giles (Ed.), *Law enforcement communication, and community* (pp. 229–254). Amsterdam, The Netherlands: John Benjamins Publishing.

Rogan, R. G., & Hammer, M. R. (2006). The emerging field of crisis/hostage negotiation: A communication-based perspective. In J. Oetzel & S. Ting-Toomey (Eds.), *Handbook of conflict communication* (pp. 451–478). Thousand Oaks, CA: Sage.

Soskis, D. A., & Van Zandt, C. R. (1986). Hostage negotiation: Law enforcement's most effective nonlethal weapon. *Behavioral Sciences & the Law, 4,* 423–435.

Hostage/Crisis Negotiation

A Means to an End

Robert J. Louden

Media portrayals in fiction and nonfiction books, feature films, documentaries, on television, in popular magazines, and in the daily press have afforded many an opportunity to learn about and vicariously experience the hostage situation. Such representations, whether they are intended to provide entertainment or education, create an impression and an expectation in the mind of the viewer about what is actually happening and how the "police" should handle it.

Hostage and hostage-type drama has been a reality of life at least since the beginning of recorded history. As the world progressed, it was most often the "police" of the time who became responsible for reacting to and attempting resolution of the most immediate manifestation of the problem. The manner in which the "police" handled such problems had been widely diverse. Egon Bittner (1975) discussed two interrelated aspects of policing that could also be equated to their role in dealing with hostage situations: ". . . the police are nothing else than a mechanism for the distribution of situationally-justified force in society . . . The American city dwellers repertoire of methods for handling problems includes one known as 'calling the cops'" (p. 39). Bittner advances the concept that police are called on to respond to a situation and do something about which something must be done. It has been stated many times in the literature of policing that they are viewed as an immediately available resource in times of emergency and crisis.

To rephrase Bittner: Police are called on to do something about which something must be done and no one else is ready, willing, or able to do it. The "police" were seldom properly prepared for their mission and, in some cases, operated in a confusing and conflicting legal arena, but they did it.

It was not until the second half of the 20th century that many of the challenges presented by hostage-type situations began to be systematically studied by law enforcement agencies and academics and alternative means of resolution were considered and attempted. One innovative approach that resulted from collaboration by traditional law enforcement practitioners and academic contributors is hostage/crisis negotiation.

In a democracy, police work by necessity focuses a great deal of attention on means as opposed to ends, which has an important impact on how the job is to be performed (Kuykendall & Roberg, 1982). Although prepared and justified to use force, a hostage/crisis negotiation posture attempts resolution without resorting to immediate violence. Recurring discussions in policing dealing with concepts such as zero tolerance, pursuit driving, and responding to emotionally disturbed or mentally ill people are largely related to justification for the use of force issues presented in a given incident. In each of these types of incidents, an officer is faced with a choice of means in order to achieve a desired end. The means to an end is the driving force behind hostage/crisis negotiation.

DEFINITIONAL ISSUES IN HOSTAGE/CRISIS NEGOTIATION

Negotiation is a transaction between two parties, representing themselves or others, which is designed to arrive at a mutually agreeable resolution. A dictionary definition of *negotiation* (*American Heritage Dictionary*, 1983) includes, "to confer with another in order to come to terms." Negotiation does not automatically presuppose equality between parties, but does recognize the relative strength or power of each side. Implied in the negotiation process is that each side has something that the other wants, that there is no better mutually acceptable solution immediately available, that there is a willingness to communicate, and that there is a readiness to discuss and consider compromise.

Police officers engage in the practice of negotiation throughout their daily assignments, especially in these times of community policing and collaborative approaches to problem solving. They frequently negotiate about routine events such as noise complaints, neighborhood disputes, situations with disorderly youth, and parking conditions.

The concept of negotiation, which is the subject of this chapter, is somewhat more complex because issues of safety, life, and death are continually and dramatically present. These situations also typically involve the response of a large number of law enforcement personnel, an out-of-the-ordinary if not potentially confusing command structure, and adherence to special procedures that may not be routinely implemented due to the relative rareness of the events. Hostage-type events often result in increased operating cost for the law enforcement agency with simultaneous neighborhood disruption and potential financial loss to affected business. Media attention is a given at virtually every hostage/crisis negotiation scene.

According to Crelinsten and Szabo (1979), "Hostage-taking is a very ancient form of criminal activity. In fact, it was even an accepted tool of diplomacy when used by legitimate authority" (p. ix). Levitt (1988) stated that *hostage taking* is defined by the United Nations as "the seizing or detaining and threatening to kill, injure, or continue to detain another person to compel a third party to do or abstain from doing any act as a condition for the release of the hostage" (p. 14). Rogan, Hammer, and Van Zandt (1997) reported that "hostage takers act to create an extortionate transaction with the police" (p. 3). Hostage/crisis negotiation is a police strategy that consists of responding to a situation that involves imminent danger to the life or limb of a person being held against his or her will. There is not necessarily an immediately apparent connection between captor and victim, as Buhite (1995) noted; individuals are often "taken hostage [only] because they were available and vulnerable" (p. xv).

A law enforcement organization designates an individual as the negotiator to engage the hostage holder in a dialogue in an effort to find a peaceful resolution to the instant problem. The hostage holding may originally be motivated by criminal intent, emotional crisis, or politics. The captor's problems and concerns are often exacerbated by drugs and/or alcohol. The negotiator will attempt to persuade the holder to release the hostage(s) unharmed in return for a pledge that the captor will not be harmed and may even be assisted in resolving his or her immediate problems in a legitimate way. In this way, "negotiation is thought of as the process of discussion engaged in by two or more parties, each of which wants to achieve a desired aim" (Edleman & Crain, 1993, p. xii). For situations where negotiation does not seem to be effective, the process will attempt to facilitate the rescue of the victim and apprehension of the perpetrator by a variety of means, including distracting or attacking the hostage holder. In a discussion on siege management, Bahn (1987) observed that a common element in hostage and barricaded subject incidents is defiance by the subject to orders of the authorities to come out peacefully. He noted that "a standoff develops between the overwhelming power—manpower, firepower and legal authority—of the police, military or other authorities and the defiant, trapped offender" (p. 1).

The negotiation process, which is the subject of this chapter, involves "law enforcement officers who are selected and trained for the task and who are acting on behalf of their employing agency" (Volpe & Louden, 1990, p. 308). For many years, the commonly used term was *hostage negotiation,* and in many jurisdictions it still is. Since approximately 1989 (Kaiser, 1990), the FBI switched to "crisis negotiation," and many agencies have followed suit. The International Association of Chiefs of Police (1992) utilizes the term *hostage communicator.* The term *hostage/crisis negotiation* is utilized throughout this chapter.

Police hostage/crisis negotiators view "the negotiation of substantive and nonsubstantive wants or demands in similar terms: agreement making through bargaining or problem solving, typically via quid pro quo" (Rogan et al., 1997, p. 11). Police hostage/crisis negotiation involves bargaining for the life of an innocent person or may involve dealing with a nonhostage-holding barricaded criminal or dealing with individuals who may be emotionally disturbed or mentally ill. Police generally engage in hostage/crisis negotiation in order to save hostage lives, without unnecessarily endangering the lives of the helpers, including not only law enforcement personnel, but also fire service and emergency medical service (EMS) personnel and third-party intermediaries. Captors and other subjects engage in negotiation for these same hostages for a variety of reasons, initially defined by the original motivation for the event, whether criminal, political, or emotional (see Hacker, 1976).

DEVELOPMENT OF HOSTAGE/CRISIS NEGOTIATION AS A STRATEGY IN U.S. POLICE ORGANIZATIONS

In the late 1960s and early 1970s, Morton Bard (1974) conducted pioneering research that contributed to major shifts in the way police reacted to domestic violence, sexual assault, and hostage holding. Each of these areas involved a wide range of dispute, conflict, and crisis intervention issues. Bard acknowledged that "considerable gaps" still existed between police and academics, but stressed their "commonality of interest." His work sought to establish the "development of a mechanism for coupling the practitioner and the researcher" (Bard, 1974, p. 20). His applied research, from 1967 to 1969, employed crisis intervention techniques for police officers in dealing with domestic violence. He was also a significant contributor to the original application of similar practices for investigators responding to rape and other sexual assault. His work in domestic violence and sex crime was well received by many in the New York Police Department (NYPD). His research findings were integrated into the Police Academy curriculum. Bard's work with sex crime victims was contemporaneous with the development of the new hostage negotiation program in the NYPD. Because both activities were functions of the Detective Bureau, a serendipitous expansion of Bard's interest and techniques was realized. He became an early advocate and adviser of the innovative specialty of hostage/crisis negotiation (Bard, 1975, 1976, 1978; Donovan & Sullivan, 1974).

Two hostage events that occurred in New York State, one in 1971 and the other in 1972, are often referred to in the early literature of hostage negotiation, but did not actually prompt changes in law enforcement policy at the time. The September 1971 Attica prison riot and hostage holding in northwest New York State resulted in death for 28 correction officers and 10 inmates during a rescue attempt. This tragedy prompted controversy in criminal justice and social science circles over force versus restraint in approaching hostage incidents (Garson, 1972; Shelton, 1994; Strollo & Wills-Raftery, 1994; Useem & Kimball, 1989; Wicker, 1975). It did not, however, prompt interest by the NYPD perhaps because it involved convicted prisoners, although many were originally from New York City and because the riot was contained within the walls of a correctional facility located hundreds of miles away. Similarly, almost 1 year later, in August 1972, a bank robbery hostage situation in Brooklyn, New York, which has been perpetuated in a fictionalized account in the popular movie *Dog Day Afternoon* (1975), did not immediately result in a perceived need for a major change in situations involving hostages. However, both Attica and Dog Day, as well as additional examples, were closely examined later, when negotiation came to be seen as a viable strategy for dealing with hostage situations (Bolz & Hershey, 1979; Moorehead, 1980).

It was not until 1975 that the topic of hostage situations was considered separately in standard police texts in the United States. An examination by this author of the indices of numerous textbooks used in criminal justice education programs and for police civil service promotion purposes, published between 1970 and 1980, revealed only one, *Supervision of Police Personnel* (Iannone, 1975), which included a section on hostage situations.

Three early bibliographies published by the U.S. Department of Justice encompassing certain aspects of policing that may be related to hostage negotiation were reviewed for this chapter: *Police Discretion* (1978a) contained 138 items, *Police Management* (1978b) contained 123 items, and *Police Crisis Intervention* (1978c) contained 63 items. These three bibliographies did not contain references on organization and policy issues related to hostage/crisis negotiation team formation. Three additional U.S. Department of Justice bibliographies, each titled *Topical Search: SWAT and Hostage Negotiations* (1983, 1987, 1992), contained 297 entries. Valuable references were obtained, but none of the entries addressed the organization and procedures of hostage/crisis negotiation teams.

Cooper (1985) noted that there was a shift in official responses to hostage situations following the 1972 Munich Olympics incident, and Welch (1984) included in his historical treatment of hostage negotiations a reference to the influence of the crisis at the 1972 Munich Olympics. In the Munich Olympic hostage situation, two members of the Israeli Olympic team were killed in the original takeover. Additionally, one West German police officer, five PLO terrorists, and eight Israeli hostages died during an attempt to free the hostages by force (Moorehead, 1980; Schreiber, 1973; Soskis & Van Zandt, 1986).

The Munich event alerted the NYPD that their jurisdiction could provide a similar opportunity for some group to engage in terroristic diplomacy. The fact that the hostage holding occurred during the International Olympics; involved American allies, Israel, and West Germany; and was broadcast live by the media was enough to prompt an immediate study of the issues (Bolz & Hershey, 1979; Gelb, 1977; Gettinger, 1983).

A literature search consisting of four social science databases, *NCJRS, Criminal Justice Abstracts, Sociofile,* and *PsychLit,* revealed that the first two published articles about police hostage negotiation in the United States were separately authored by two NYPD commanders who had a role in the early formulation of the policy. Donald F. Cawley (1974) was the Chief of Patrol during the post-Munich policy study period and the first field test, albeit spontaneous, of the new *Recommended Guidelines; Incidents Involving Hostages* (1973). These contingency plans stressed that "The primary consideration in such circumstances is to secure the lives and safety of the threatened hostages, the police officers, innocent bystanders, and the criminals themselves" (p. 1). John A. Culley (1974), a Detective Bureau Lieutenant, referring to the same document, noted that Chief Inspector Michael J. Codd had recently "reviewed and approved plans for hostage situations, plans which [Codd] had been working on with various units of the police department since September 1972" (p. 1). This original plan did not specifically mention hostage negotiators.

Once a decision was made in early 1973 to formally select and train hostage negotiators, the challenge to create this then innovative police practice was primarily assumed by two individuals: Frank A. Bolz, Jr., and Harvey Schlossberg. Bolz was an experienced Detective Bureau Lieutenant; among other assignments, he had supervised an undercover investigative unit and a stake-out team. Schlossberg was a patrolman assigned to highway patrol and accident investigation; he had recently earned his PhD in psychology. This dynamic duo pioneered the process in the NYPD and has preached the gospel of police hostage/crisis negotiation worldwide (see Bolz & Hershey, 1979; Schlossberg & Freeman, 1974).

In a then far-reaching review of hostage incident responses, Gettinger (1983) noted that, "Shortly after the Munich incident [1972], Patrick Murphy, then NYPD Commissioner gave the order that New York City should prepare itself for terrorist hostage-taking" (p. 14). His Chief of Special Operations, Simon Eisendorfer, formed a committee consisting of patrol, detective, training, and psychological services representatives. Gettinger further reported that the FBI followed suit in 1973 when it initiated research and training in hostage negotiation. One of the original FBI contributors, Conrad Hassel, noted that this specialty was not even conceived until 1972, and it soon spread across the country (see Gettinger, 1983). Soskis (1983), in an article that discussed behavioral scientists and law enforcement personnel working together, reviewed various possible collaborations and noted that the "new discipline of hostage negotiations . . . had its beginning in the New York City Police Department" (p. 49).

EVOLUTION OF THE DETECTIVE BUREAU HOSTAGE NEGOTIATING TEAM AND ITS RELATIONSHIP TO OTHER NEW YORK POLICE DEPARTMENT UNITS

In January 1973, a significant event in the evolution of hostage negotiation took place over a 2-day period in Brooklyn, New York, at a location known as John & Al's Sporting Goods Store. The local precinct police had responded to a silent alarm call of a possible robbery in progress and were met with gunfire from within the store. Reinforcements arrived, including Emergency Service Unit (ESU) tactical officers, which is the equivalent of SWAT Team personnel in some other jurisdictions. One ESU officer, Steve Gilroy, was killed, and two other officers were wounded in the quickly unfolding event. One of four suspects was also wounded, and eight hostages were held in the store. The new operational plan for incidents involving hostages that Chief Eisendorfer had organized a few months earlier at Commissioner Murphy's direction was implemented for the first time. Its primary concerns were with containment of the scene, control of personnel and resources, and communication with the captors (Cawley, 1974). Forty-seven hours after the incident began, all of the hostages were safe, the four perpetrators were in custody, and there was no further injury to police officers or other responders.

A comprehensive critique of the incident at John & Al's was undertaken. Although, according to Welch (1984), the plan had not been eagerly received throughout the Department, its basic principles were validated by the activities surrounding the 47-hour siege at John & Al's. Although the original plan had stressed the importance of communicating with hostage holders, there had been no prior indication as to who the negotiator would be. The critique made commanders aware of "negotiation deficits" (Welch, 1984, p. 66). A wide variety of police and nonpolice had "negotiated" during the 47 hours, largely without measurable success. As a result of the incident, the idea of having specific individuals designated as hostage negotiators was introduced into the NYPD for the first time. By April 1973, a team of negotiators had been selected from the ranks of the Detective Bureau and put through a 4-week training program (Welch, 1984, p. 66).

Police Commissioner Michael J. Codd (1977) in a report on police preparedness for terrorist events indicated that the hostage situation guide had been designed to "focus on functional team work, effective communications, and skilled coordination of tactics, under the management of a high ranking police commander" (p. 3). A major change to the original draft of the plan, following John & Al's, was the establishment of "a group of specially trained negotiators responsible for communicating with barricaded suspects" in place of "the more traditional response of unconditional assault" (Taylor, 1983, p. 64).

The first formal practice of police hostage negotiation was established in New York City between September 1972 and April 1973 (Bell, 1978; Bolz & Hershey, 1979; Douglas & Olshaker, 1995; Moorehead, 1980; Schlossberg & Freeman, 1974). In 1974, the NYPD received a grant from the New York State Division of Criminal Justice Services to support the efforts that had been initiated post-Munich and revised as a result of John & Al's. A hostage confrontation response system, utilizing Detective Bureau investigators and ESU tactical specialists, was formalized. The investigators and the tactical officers were trained to "meet the problem of hostage negotiating and rescue" under the direction of an incident commander, according to a Police Department document, *Terrorism Control in New York City* (1979). The recommended guidelines had evolved into a *Tactical Manual for Hostage Situations* (1974).

The ESU of the NYPD was a highly diverse mobile force of uniformed officers with full-time citywide responsibility. The members of this all-volunteer group had to have extensive uniformed patrol experience before applying for a transfer into the ESU. The members were rescue-oriented and performed a wide range of specialized tasks. According to their *Operational Policies and Tactics* (1977), among other tasks, they are certified Emergency Medical Technicians, take potential jumpers off bridges and buildings, handle radiation accidents, search for and transport improvised explosive devices, and operate the Emergency Rescue Vehicle (an armored personnel carrier). "They are the [New York City Police] Department's Firearms Battalion. They are the only members qualified to use tear gas. They are also skilled in the use of anti-sniper rifles, carbines, machine guns, and the shotgun, their most basic weapon" (p. 1). One chapter of their *Operational Policies and Tactics* manual was devoted to confrontations, which included "sniper, barricaded criminal/hostage, disorderly group/mob, civilian clothed member [and] dangerous psychotic" (p. 20). The ESU was selected to be the tactical (Special Weapons and Tactics [SWAT]) component of the new hostage confrontation program because of its involvement in closely related activities for many years.

It was an ESU Police Officer, Steve Gilroy, who was killed in the early stages of the siege at John & Al's. It was not surprising that officers assigned to Emergency Service might resent, if not resist, creation of a new team of officers to perform part of their ESU jobs as described by Welch (1984).

It should also be noted that, since the inception of the hostage/crisis negotiation process in New York City, two NYPD officers have been killed in the line of duty at deployments: Steve Gilroy in 1973 at John & Al's and Joe McCormack in 1983 at the scene of a barricaded emotionally disturbed person (EDP) in the Bronx. Both were ESU officers. The subject that shot Joe McCormack was then shot and killed by another ESU officer. Two murdered police officers is two too many, yet countless lives have been saved by the team efforts.

The newly created Detective Bureau Hostage Negotiating Team was an all-volunteer function mostly performed as needed by full-time NYPD Investigators, primarily Detectives and Sergeants. This is an example of a shift to an organic operational function within the context of a primarily mechanistic organization (see Burns & Stalker, 1961; Kuykendall & Roberg, 1982).

The decision to house the negotiator component of the new program in the Detective Bureau rather than Patrol or Special Operations was based on a variety of personnel factors that Schlossberg and Freeman (1974), Bard (1978), and Symonds (1980) had suggested as appropriate criteria for candidates to become successful hostage/crisis negotiators.

Because assignment to the Detective Bureau had been preceded by a range of other policing experiences, the investigator would be chronologically and experientially mature. Investigators worked in civilian clothes, which fit with the crisis intervention notion of nonhostile representation of authority. Detective assignments are normally case-driven as compared with uniformed patrol officers who are often radio-run-incident-driven, so investigators do not have to be readily available for the next routine radio run. Investigators are also expected to be competent in gathering and analysis of intelligence, as well as in conducting interviews and interrogations. These skills were deemed necessary for success in hostage/crisis negotiation.

To have been accepted as a negotiator, the volunteer investigator needed a positive recommendation from his commander, participated in a paper-and-pencil psychological examination and a follow-up interview with a police department psychologist, and had to be favorably interviewed by the Hostage Team Coordinator. Those chosen were then assigned to a 4-week training program designed specifically for the purpose and including psychology, physical fitness, firearms, electronic equipment, and liaison (Culley, 1974, p. 3). Assigned full time in civilian clothes to various Detective Squads, a number of trained negotiators, based on geographic area of assignment, scheduled work time, and any special qualifications, were called together for an incident. After the incident, the negotiators returned to their regular investigative duties. These individuals performed the additional duties of hostage/crisis negotiator, without additional pay, although their base investigator's salary was higher than the base pay of the uniformed Emergency Service Officers.

During approximately the first 10 years of existence, the NYPD Detective Bureau Hostage Negotiating Team was a function without a permanent home. When the hostage confrontation program was formally launched, as a result of the critique of the John & Al's siege, the newly designated Hostage Coordinator, a Lieutenant assigned to the Brooklyn Detective command, was placed in charge and transferred into the Major Crimes Section of the city-wide Special Investigation Division. In 1974, the function was moved to the Office of Chief of Detectives; the coordinator then reported directly to the Deputy Chief of Detectives. One year later, the function and coordinator were shifted to a support staff of the Detective Bureau, the Management Control Division. Approximately 3 years later, the coordinator was promoted to Captain, and the Management Control Division was divided into two functional commands, Management Control and Technical Support, in order to justify retention of the newly promoted Captain in the Detective Bureau. The hostage function became the responsibility of the new Technical Support Unit. In 1979, the Captain and activities related to hostage/crisis negotiation were transferred back to the Special Investigation Division, reporting directly to the Inspector-in-command. Nonhostage-related responsibilities were retained in the reconstituted Management Control Division. In the fall of 1981, the Captain was transferred to a Detective Borough command, but retained as the Department's Senior Hostage Negotiator. The hostage negotiator notation in the transfer order is the first time that this term, *hostage negotiator*, appeared in a personnel order in the NYPD. Command of the Detective Bureau Hostage Negotiating Team was assigned to a Lieutenant, who had been second-in-command of the team since approximately 1978, and the functions remained in the Special Investigation Division. The Lieutenant was also responsible for various aspects of kidnap and extortion investigations.

In 1983, the Lieutenant and the hostage/crisis negotiation function were transferred to a primarily staff unit in the Detective Bureau, the Central Investigation and Resource Division. In addition to coordination of the hostage team, the Lieutenant continued to be responsible for supervision of kidnap and extortion investigations and was also accountable for various other activities, including the unit that provided technical support and surveillance at hostage situations. In April 1983, the then coordinator was formally promoted to Commander of Detective Squad, informally referred to as Detective Lieutenant. That commander, and three subsequent individuals, continued in the multitask role until 2001, when the hostage/crisis negotiation function and current Detective Lieutenant in-command was once again assigned to Special Investigations Division of the Detective Bureau, responsible primarily for hostage-related duties. The other duties that had been assigned as complementary to the hostage function in 1983 had since been assigned to other units and supervisors.

Most of the changes that occurred from 1973 to 1983 were due to resistance or a lack of acceptance on the part of some senior police commanders during a period of adjustment for a new function. The personality of the hostage team coordinator and positive media attention to early successes of the team also created resentment. The original team coordinator was an extremely outgoing individual who was also active in many social organizations within the Department. The New York media provided extensive coverage to the highly successful operational activities of the hostage negotiators, and the coordinator made himself available to a variety of interviewers. This was with the approval of the press office of the Police Department, but yet engendered negative reaction by other commanders. This is consistent with Welch's (1984) observation about organizational resistance in his examination of hostage situations.

Another change that took place during this same time period was in the types of incidents to which hostage/crisis negotiators were dispatched. Originally they responded only to confirmed hostage holdings, and the request for hostage/crisis negotiators was initiated by the ESU supervisor at the scene. Gradually, based on hostage/crisis negotiation success, and accompanying positive media attention, they were dispatched to some nonhostage crisis situation such as barricaded criminals and people threatening suicide. Both of these functions previously had been the exclusive purview of the ESU. Contemporaneous with these expanded duties, hostage/crisis negotiation personnel were also being utilized in kidnap and extortion cases, and in operational planning for high-risk raid and warrant execution. A significant change took place with the publication of the Police Department's *Interim Order No. 51* (1984) when for the first time it was mandated that negotiators be dispatched to certain situations involving nonhostage holding EDPs. These situations were previously handled by the ESU. Likewise, prior to this, calls for the immediate services of hostage/crisis negotiators had been initiated by the ESU Supervisor. However, the new *Interim Order* specified that the requesting authority was to be the Incident Commander, normally the on-scene Duty Captain, who was usually the highest ranking uniformed officer at the incident and ultimately responsible for the outcome.

PREVIOUS RESEARCH ON POLICE
HOSTAGE/CRISIS NEGOTIATION UNITS

Bristow (1977) conducted one of the earliest research projects about police involvement in hostage situations, in connection with curriculum development for a college-level police management course. He examined a 5-year period (1970–1975), using newspaper and periodical indexes, to eventually identify media accounts of 185 cases for examination through content analysis. Bristow's report did not discuss police organizational or management issues, but two of his findings were of interest to this author. In 110 hostage negotiation incidents, 87 (79%) resulted in the unharmed release of the hostages. In 100% (13) of the cases in which trained negotiators were used, no hostages were harmed. Bristow advised that this finding be viewed with caution due to the small number of cases (13) involving trained negotiators.

In June 1983, the Houston, Texas Police Department released the results of a survey of a sample of major police departments throughout the United States regarding hostage negotiation policies and procedures. They had mailed a 31-item questionnaire to 26 agencies during February 1983. Twenty-two (85%) useful responses were received. The report, *Houston Police Department Hostage Negotiation Team Survey* (1983), did not describe the criteria for selection of the sample or characteristics of the agencies. Twenty-one (95%) of the departments reported having a hostage negotiation team. The hostage negotiation function was assigned to the SWAT team in 13 (59%) of the agencies. In addition to hostage negotiation duties, 21 (91%) also responded to barricaded suspects in which no hostages were being held, and 16 (73%) responded to suicide attempts. The median number of years a team had been in existence was 6 years. Three agencies listed 1972 as the year in which their team was formed. Literature reviewed by this author, including follow-up contact with some agencies initially citing pre-1973 as their hostage/crisis negotiation start date, indicates that the first U.S. team was formed in New York City in 1973. The submission to the Houston survey from the NYPD indicated 1973 as the year that their team was formed.

A COP IS MURDERED IN MEMPHIS

In January 1983, a Memphis, Tennessee police officer was held hostage and murdered. Subsequently, the Memphis Police Department mailed a 17-page questionnaire to 230 agencies throughout the United States requesting detailed information about police officers who may have been held hostage in their jurisdiction. They received 156 responses (68%). Neither the original survey nor the results indicated the criteria for selection of the sample or organizational characteristics of the responding agencies. Thirty-one (20%) of the responses contained extensive information about police officers who had been held hostage. There was only one question in the survey about response to these incidents by hostage negotiators, but this item was not tabulated in their *Results of Analysis of Research From Hostage Officer Data* (1983). Two survey items that were included in the summary of the results dealt with hostage negotiation training. Thirteen (41%) of the responses indicated that officers who had been held hostage had received recruit-level academy training about hostage situations. Ten individuals (32%) had received in-service training about hostage situations.

EARLY FBI ANALYSIS OF HOSTAGE DATA

One of the original FBI behavioral scientists and hostage negotiators, Thomas Strentz (1985), reported an analysis of 245 Hostage Incident Reports collected by the FBI from throughout the country concerning incidents that had occurred between 1976 and early 1985. Two of his research questions were of interest: the role of incident commanders and negotiation, and the effect of time in negotiation situations. Strentz found that during incidents in which commanders also decided to negotiate, the subjects were shot 63% of the time. The commanders had themselves negotiated in only 14% of the cases and were accountable for 25 of the subjects being killed or wounded. Strentz also noted that noncommand, untrained negotiators decided to shoot in 27 out of 54 cases (50%). Trained negotiators were credited with taking into custody 193 (85%) of the subjects who were apprehended unharmed. Strentz also reported that there was a correlation between the length of time elapsed and a nonviolent solution to a hostage situation: "The longer a hostage situation continues, the more likely it is that it will be successfully resolved" (p. 13). For example, in 63 cases lasting up to 4 hours, only 36 (57%) of the subjects were negotiated out, whereas in 80 situations lasting between 7 and 9 hours, 76 (95%) ended peacefully.

One of the numerous ways in which the FBI continues to be a valuable primary contributor to the discipline of hostage/crisis negotiation is through the compilation, analysis, and distribution of hostage barricade statistics (HOBAS).

STANDARD OPERATING PROCEDURES (SOPS)
ARE NOT ALWAYS STANDARD

Koleas (1985) conducted an analysis of the SOPs of six police agencies in order to assess their ability to resolve hostage incidents. The agencies were not identified by name. The difference in the length of the published orders received and reviewed from each department ranged from a minimum of 1 page to a maximum of 19 pages; the latter was obtained from an unidentified East Coast department. Only the East Coast department's procedure discussed chain of command sufficiently to determine whether the negotiation function was part of or separate from the SWAT team. In that plan, the hostage and SWAT commanders are separately accountable to the incident commander. Similarly, there was not sufficient information from the six departments to determine common features about selection or training of negotiators. There was a chart comparing the nature of events responded to, which Koleas called Department Adaptability (i.e., political, trapped criminal, mentally disturbed, and domestic). He concluded "that police agency response to hostage incident resolution is not the same everywhere. The Sop's reviewed show a wide range of disparity in terms of specificity, adaptability, and awareness of state of the art techniques" (p. 43).

EARLY ACADEMIC RESEARCH

Head (1989) examined U.S. law enforcement practices about hostage incidents for his doctoral dissertation at the State University of New York at Albany. His research was primarily concerned with characteristics of the situations and their outcomes. He examined 801 cases obtained from various databases over a 10-year period. His analysis utilized 28 independent variables and 3 dependent variables. One independent variable, use of negotiators, revealed that 269 (34%) of the incidents were negotiated by trained law enforcement negotiators, another 70 (9%) were negotiated by untrained law enforcement personnel, and in 270 cases (34%) hostages were released without negotiation. In 192 (23%) of the cases, the use of negotiators was not clearly determined. One dependent variable dealt with the fate of hostages. In those cases in which hostages were safely recovered, 309 (40%) of the releases were with demands not being met, and 192 (24%) were after demands were complied with. Another 82 (10%) were safely rescued during a police tactical assault, 54 (7%) escaped, and 19 (2%) were wounded by their captors. Finally, 50 (6%) were killed by their captors, and six (<1%) were killed or wounded during the police assault to rescue. Another dependent variable, final fate of hostage takers, demonstrated that for the 801 cases, 485 (60%) were arrested, 67 (8%) were killed or wounded by the police, and 16 (2%) committed suicide. The fate of the remaining 233 (30%) was unknown or categorized as other. There was no data or discussion concerning organization, policy, selection, training, and workload or negotiator satisfaction.

For a dissertation submitted to the University of Iowa, Powell (1989) conducted research on the negotiation procedure involved in hostage and barricaded incidents. This was a sociological investigation designed to identify the processes involved in the incidents. His study was concerned with the social conduct of negotiations. Of interest, he noted that:

> In the last fifteen years, police at local, state and national levels have become well-schooled in the techniques of enforcing policy through negotiation. Hostage-takers are met with trained negotiators, and barricaded incidents are almost always resolved by voice appeals alone. Although weapons forces secure the surrounding turf, and tactical solutions are considered necessary under extreme conditions, negotiation is the policy and practice of first resort. (p. 6)

Other areas of research also have relevance for examining diverse aspects of activity likely to have been linked to hostage/crisis negotiation situations. For example, Spunt, Goldstein, Brownstein, Fendrich, and Langley (1994) reported on the nexus between substance abuse and violence; research issues like this informed the development of training topics, the use of third-party intermediaries, and whether it was appropriate to permit negotiators to bargain for alcohol or other drugs.

The first study aimed at "collecting and disseminating information on hostage negotiation team characteristics and crisis incidents" was authored by Hammer, Van Zandt, and Rogan (1994). The authors undertook the task because "little comprehensive data exist concerning crisis negotiation activities in the United States" (p. 8). For their study, a 44-item questionnaire was completed by 100 hostage unit team leaders from across the country in 1992. Among the issues of concern to the researchers were team demographics, selection and training, and workload.

The survey revealed that the majority of negotiators were White, male, and assigned to investigative or patrol duties. Approximately 55% of the teams did not have a written negotiator selection policy. Seventy-four percent stated that initial negotiator training was 10 days or less in duration, and 61% received 5 days or less in-service training. The FBI had provided the initial training for 40% of the teams. During 1991, most teams negotiated less than 10 times in actual situations. The team leaders surveyed also believed that there was a considerable need for additional information about the operations and functions of hostage/crisis negotiation teams.

Rogan, Hammer, and Van Zandt (1994) revised the questionnaire for a follow-up study. They decreased the number of items to 32. The new questionnaire was distributed late in 1992 to 142 individuals from 26 states, each representing a separate hostage/crisis team. The majority (62%) reported that their team did not have written guidelines for selecting team members. They also did not spend much time between incidents involved in coordinating efforts or training with SWAT teams; 90% spent 5 or fewer days in such activities annually. Demographic, training, and workload findings were consistent with their earlier study.

DESCRIPTIVE DATA FROM A LARGER STUDY

During 1998, this author (Louden, 1999) conducted a nationwide study of hostage/crisis negotiation practices of 275 U.S. police departments. Descriptive data obtained from that 1999 study allows for a comparison of selected aspects of the data with some of the earlier research cited in this chapter.

One area for review was whether agencies had written policies specifically related to the selection of personnel for hostage/crisis negotiators. Consistent with the findings of Hammer et al. (1994), which reported that 55% of agencies did not have a written negotiator selection policy, and Rogan et al. (1994), which reported

62% of agencies without such a written policy, this research determined that 56% of the respondents did not have a written policy for selecting hostage/crisis negotiators, although 82% did have a written operational policy for hostage/crisis negotiation. Both of the 1994 studies also reported that most hostage/crisis negotiation commanders were White males; this too was consistent with the findings of this research project. The LEMAS (U.S. Department of Justice, Bureau of Justice Statistics, 1993) data had reported that 90% of sworn officers in their database were male and 80% were White.

The Hammer et al. (1994) study also reported that initial negotiator training was 10 days or less for 74% of the cases studied; 61% received 5 days or less of in-service training. The FBI had provided the initial training for 40% of the agencies. The 1999 study, again consistent with prior research, found a mean of 47 hours, approximately 6 days, for initial negotiator training and 32 hours, approximately 4days, for in-service. The FBI was the initial training provider in 35% of the cases. There is a school of thought that the FBI could be credited with a higher percentage because, during the 1980s and into the 1990s, approximately 75 FBI negotiator trainers provided train-the-trainer hostage/negotiator classes across the country.

Another area of interest involved whether the hostage/crisis negotiation function was part of the SWAT team. The Houston Police Department (1983) study had reported that the hostage negotiation function was assigned to the SWAT team in 59% of the cases. The 1999 research resulted in a similar finding: 56% were part of the SWAT team. Separately, 60% of respondents believe that the hostage/crisis negotiation team should be part of the tactical (SWAT) team.

NEGOTIATOR OPINIONS

The previously noted 1999 study by this author also solicited subjective opinions from negotiators by seeking reaction to a series of items utilizing a 6–point Likert scale. This is one of the few sections of the research questionnaire that received a 100% response ($N = 275$). Because the opinions are reflective of the descriptive data and much of the hostage/crisis negotiator literature does not deal with the personal outlook of the individuals doing the job, it may be appropriate to report on them here.

More than 95% of the contributing negotiators indicated that hostage/crisis negotiation team work is personally satisfying, whereas 57% felt that it enhanced their career and 38% believed that they have received appropriate positive recognition or acknowledgment for their work. Approximately 5% believed that their hostage/crisis negotiation activities had harmed their career, and 78% are of the opinion that hostage/crisis negotiation increases the chance of positive media attention after an incident.

Almost unanimously, 98.9% of the negotiators reported that hostage/crisis negotiation reduces the chance of death or serious physical injury during a con-

tained incident. Similarly, 93.3% acknowledged that hostage/crisis negotiation usually results in resolution through negotiation, rather than a need for a tactical solution. On a related item, 92% believe that there should not be a predetermined time
limit set for negotiating during hostage/crisis situations.

NEGOTIATOR EFFECTIVENESS

Various researchers have reported on the relative effectiveness of negotiation as
a police tactic. Strentz (1985) had reported that 85% of the subjects who had been
taken into custody unharmed were talked out by trained negotiators, whereas
Head (1989) determined that 34% of the cases he studied credited a trained negotiator with peaceful resolution. The 1999 study found that 68% of the 1997
cases reported were concluded through negotiation. Strentz also reported that in
63 cases lasting up to 4 hours, only 36 (57%) of the subjects were negotiated out,
whereas in 80 situations lasting between 7 and 9 hours, 76 (95%) ended peacefully. The 1999 research reported here determined that for almost 3,000 team deployments during 1997, approximately 68% were concluded through negotiation and 32% utilized tactical intervention by a SWAT team after some period of
negotiation. The mean time elapsed in both types of resolutions was 3.5 hours.

The finding that both negotiated solutions and tactical solutions, on average, were accomplished in the same time frame makes it important to consider the
issues of the "means" and "ends" of policing. Emphasis on SWAT tactics after a
given period of time could become a self-fulfilling prophecy. Average time experiences should not become more important than deciding whether negotiation or
SWAT intervention contributes to the safest police response.

A MEANS TO AN END

In the United States, a variety of policing agencies are among the principle elements of government that may legitimately use force to accomplish their mission. This might engender a military mind-set that stressed adherence to a strict
chain of command and the swift use of force as the appropriate means to solve
many problems. The essence of the police function could be reduced to a threat
to use force, not only as an option of last resort (see Kraska & Kappeler, 1997).
Bittner (1975) noted that the police are a mechanism for the distribution of sit-
uationally justified force in society. A skeptical view of this characterization is
that the most expedient police route to solving problems is operationalized only
through military-style tactics, which focus on either the threatened or actual use
of force. A more flexible interpretation might be that the constitutional authority of policing is, in and of itself, a use of force, and from that a continuum is initiated, beginning with presence and verbal suggestion, which may ultimately con-

clude in legally justifiable deadly physical force. This continuum is one way to express the range of actions available to the police when weighing the "means" and "ends" of their activity. Hostage/crisis negotiation is a means to an end.

CONCLUDING REMARKS

This chapter is an account of the adoption and institutionalization of an innovative law enforcement practice—hostage/crisis negotiation. The NYPD is recognized as the first local law enforcement agency in the United States to formally adopt the practice in 1973 when the Detective Bureau, Hostage Negotiation Team (HNT) was formed.[1]

Since that time, the majority of local, county, and state police departments in the United States have adopted or adapted the NYPD plan to fit the operational philosophy and resources reality of their jurisdiction. The FBI, historically the lead federal law enforcement agency for many specialized activities, initiated hostage/crisis negotiation research and practice soon after the NYPD program was launched. Many agencies that do not have the resources to support their own team often enter into agreement with adjoining departments for a regional response scheme.

Because the NYPD was first, and because it is also the largest full-service police department in the United States, it is not surprising that the basic practices followed in routine hostage/crisis negotiation response was expanded to include additional responsibilities over the past 34 years. This was briefly mentioned earlier in the chapter. An elaboration on that expansion is appropriate as this chapter draws to a close.

An important added duty for NYPD negotiators came about in 1984, a little more than 10 years after the team was first formed. This was a new mandate to respond to certain incidents involving nonhostage holding EDPs. The catalyst for this change was well documented by the media, in New York City and elsewhere. An ESU tactical team (SWAT) was requested to assist at the scene of a civil process —the eviction of a tenant for nonpayment of rent from a city-owned housing project. The reluctant individual was an elderly, overweight African-American woman with a history of mental problems. She refused requests to open her door, and ESU was called to force entry. In the process, the woman, armed with a knife, was shot by an ESU officer who believed that his partner was in imminent mortal danger; she subsequently died. The officer who fired that fatal shot was indicted by a Grand Jury and stood trial in Criminal Court for his actions; he was acquitted. Although the legal process was moving slowly, at least 28 months from incident to verdict, the NYPD moved quickly and initiated the new response protocol within less than 60 days.[2]

An additional positive result of the tragedy was the design and adoption of a new police training program for response to EDPs. A short-term program for dealing with mentally ill individuals was designed and presented by the hostage team commander, an ESU commander, the police psychiatrist, and the city commissioner of mental health with the assistance of the FBI. This 1-day program was initially offered within 30 days after the new response plan was put into effect. The need for additional training was evident as the HNT workload increased as a result of the change—from an average of approximately 20 confirmed hostage situation annually to in excess of 200 additional calls for EDPs in the first full year of the change.

A longer training program, which has now been regularly offered for three decades, was later designed and is presented by specialized faculty from John Jay College of Criminal Justice in New York City. Every new ESU officer and HNT member must successfully complete this 40-hour Emergency Psychological Technician training.[3]

Another example of the expansion of HNT duty involves integration into appropriate aspects of high-risk raid and warrant operations. Although this had been an occasional function for the first 10-plus years, the principle was deliberately put into place in another prominent case that received extensive media attention.

During November 1986, a team of detectives and ESU officers were attempting to apprehend a suspect in a murder investigation. Six officers were shot and wounded; the subject escaped. An immediate intense manhunt ensued. While the police were actively pursuing all investigative leads, the subject put the word out on the street that the police had intended to kill him and that he would not be taken alive.[4]

The NYPD countered his claim in the media and designed an elaborate apprehension plan that included the immediate presence of an HNT element to assure the suspect and the general public that, although appropriately upset by the shooting of six officers, the police would act safely and professionally in locating and apprehending the wanted individual. Approximately 3 weeks later, he was located, holding innocent hostages, and safely taken into custody after a several-hour negotiation session.

A final example, again in practice over many years, was evident recently when the president of Iran visited New York City for the UN General Assembly. While he was enjoying the Bill of Rights' guarantee of freedom of speech at Columbia University, an HNT element was among the multitude of police that were deployed to ensure his safety and the safety of the general public. This application of preparedness has been put into practice for a range of dignitaries, including U.S. government officials, foreign heads of state, and the Pope.[5]

The NYPD examples used throughout this chapter, and especially this concluding section, are included to provide a chronicle of how one police agency reacted to an international terrorist incident in Europe and created a plan for preparedness and response that has not only been applied in terror-like events, but also expanded to more mundane but certainly crucial aspects of policing in the

United States, all in the interest of protecting life. Again, hostage/crisis negotiation is a means to an end.

NOTES

1. This author enjoyed the privilege of being a participant observer from 1973 to 1987 and informed observer from 1987 to 2007.

2. The death of Eleanor Bumpurs received extensive media attention. A search of New York-based media outlet websites and Google-type websites will yield extensive references.

3. An interesting aside: There have only been six commanders of the NYPD team from 1973 to 2007. Each has attended one or more training programs at John Jay College, and four of the six have earned undergraduate or graduate degrees there.

4. The shooting by, search for, apprehension of, and subsequent criminal trial of Larry Davis received extensive media attention. A search of New York-based media outlet websites and Google-type websites will yield extensive references.

5. Although not law enforcement-sensitive, this is not common knowledge.

REFERENCES

American Heritage Dictionary (2nd college ed.). (1983). New York: Dell Publishing.

Bahn, C. (1987). *Sieges and their aftermaths.* Unpublished manuscript, John Jay College of Criminal Justice, New York.

Bard, M. (1974, July). Implications of collaboration between law enforcement and the social sciences. *FBI Law Enforcement Bulletin, 43*(7), 25–27.

Bard, M. (1975). *The functions of the police in crisis intervention and conflict management.* Washington, DC: U.S. Department of Justice.

Bard, M. (1976). Role of law enforcement in the helping systems. In J. Monahan (Ed.), *Community mental health and the criminal justice system.* New York: Pergamon Press.

Bard, M. (1978). *Hostage negotiations; Part I, tactical procedures, & Part II, negotiating techniques.* New York: Harper & Row Films.

Bell, J. B. (1978). *A time of terror.* New York: Basic Books.

Bittner, E. (1975). *The functions of the police in modern society.* New York: Aronson.

Bolz, F., & Hershey, E. (1979). *Hostage cop.* New York: Rawson Wade.

Bristow, A. P. (1977, March). Preliminary research on hostage situations. *Law & Order, 25*(3), 73–77.

Buhite, R. D. (1995). *Lives at risk: Hostages and victims in American foreign policy.* Wilmington: Scholarly Resources.

Burns, T., & Stalker, G. M. (1961). *The management of innovation.* London: Tavistock.

Cawley, D. (1974, January). Anatomy of a seige. *The Police Chief, 41*(1), 30–34.

Codd, M. J. (1977). *Police management of terrorist caused crises; a metropolitan perspective.* Unpublished manuscript, New York Police Department.

Cooper, H. H. A. (1985, Winter). Hostage rights—Law and practice in throes of evolution. *Journal of International Law, 15*(1), 7–10.

Crelinsten, R. D., & Szabo, D. (1979). *Hostage-taking.* Lexington: D.C. Heath and Company.

Culley, J. A. (1974, October). Hostage nations. *FBI Law Enforcement Bulletin, 43*(10), 10–14.

Dog Day Afternoon. (1975). Burbank: Warner Brothers.

Donovan, E. J., & Sullivan, J.F. (1974, September). Police response to family disputes. *FBI Law Enforcement Bulletin, 43*(9), 3–6.

Douglas, J., & Olshaker, M. (1995). *Mind hunter.* New York: Simon & Schuster.

Edelman, J., & Crain, M. B. (1993). *The Tao of negotiation.* New York: Harper Business.

Garson, G. D. (1972, October). Force versus restraint in prison riots. *Crime and Delinquency, 18*(4), 411–421.

Gelb, B. (1977, April 17). The cop who saves lives. *New York Times Magazine,* pp. 31–37.

Gettinger, S. (1983, January). Hostage negotiators bring them out alive. *Police Magazine, 6*(1), 10–28.

Hacker, F. (1976). *Crusaders, criminals, crazies: Terror and terrorism in our time.* New York: Norton.

Hammer, M. R., Van Zandt, C. R., & Rogan, R. G. (1994, March). Crisis/hostage negotiation team profile. *FBI Law Enforcement Bulletin, 63*(3), 8–11.

Head, W. (1989). *The hostage response: An examination of U.S. law enforcement practice concerning hostage incidents.* Unpublished doctoral dissertation, The State University of New York at Albany.

Houston Police Department Hostage Negotiation Team Survey. (1983). Unpublished mauscript, Houston Police Department, Houston, TX.

Iannone, N. F. (1975). *Supervision of police personnel.* Englewood Cliffs, NJ: Prentice-Hall.

Interim Order No. 51. (1984). Aided cases, mentally ill or emotionally disturbed persons. New York: NYPD Departmental Order.

International Association of Chiefs of Police. (1992). *Hostage/barricaded subject incidents.* Arlington, VA: International Association of Chiefs of Police National Law Enforcement Policy Center.

Kaiser, N. F. (1990, August). The tactical incident; A total police response. *FBI Law Enforcement Bulletin, 59*(8), 14–18.

Koleas, J. W. (1985). *Variations in police policy relative to hostage incidents.* Unpublished master's thesis, Milwaukee, WI.

Kraska, P. B., & Kappeler, V. E. (1997). Militarizing the American police: The rise and normalization of paramilitary units. *Social Problems, 44*(1), 1–18.

Kuykendall, J., & Roberg, R. R. (1982, August). Mapping police organizational change. *Criminology, 20*(3), 241–256.

Levitt, G. M. (1988). *Democracies against terror: The Western response to state-supported terrorism.* New York: Praeger.

Louden, R. J. (1999). *The structure and procedures of hostage/crisis negotiation units in US police organizations.* Unpublished doctoral dissertation, City University of New York (University Microfilms).

Moorehead, C. (1980). *Hostages to fortune.* New York: Atheneum.

Operational policies and tactics. (1977). Unpublished report, New York Police Department.

Powell, J. O. (1989). *Negotiation processes in hostage and barricade incidents.* Unpublished doctoral dissertation, University of Iowa.

Recommended guidelines: Incidents involving hostages. (1973). Unpublished report, New York Police Department.

Results of analysis of research from hostage officer data. (1983). Unpublished report, Memphis Police Department.

Rogan, R. G., Hammer, M. R., & Van Zandt, C. R. (1994, November). Profiling crisis negotiation teams. *The Police Chief, 61*(11), 14–18.

Rogan, R. G., Hammer, M. R., & Van Zandt, C. R. (1997). *Dynamic processes of crisis negotiation; Theory, research and practice.* Westport, CT: Praeger.

Schlossberg, H., & Freeman, L. (1974). *Psychologist with a gun.* New York: Coward McCann.

Schreiber, M. (1973). *After-action report of terrorist activity; 20th Olympic games Munich, West Germany.* Unpublished manuscript, Federal Bureau of Investigation, Quantico, VA.

Shelton, P. T. (1994). *Attica—1971—LeBastille extraordinaire. History of the New York State Police 1917–1987.* New York: Trooper Foundation of the State of New York.

Soskis, D. A. (1983). Behavioral scientists and law enforcement personnel: Working together on the problem of terrorism. *Behavioral Sciences & The Law, 1*(2), 47–58.

Soskis, D. A., & Van Zandt, C. R. (1986, Autumn). Hostage negotiation: Law enforcement's most effective non-lethal weapon. *Management Quarterly, 6*(4), 1.

Spunt, B., Goldstein, P., Brownstein, H., Fendrich, M., & Langley, S. (1994, Winter/Spring). Alcohol and homicide: Interviews with prison inmates. *Journal of Drug Issues, 24,* 143–163.

Strentz, T. (1985). *A statistical analysis of American hostage situations.* Unpublished manuscript, Federal Bureau of Investigation, Quantico, VA.

Strollo, A. R., & Wills-Raftery, D. (1994). *Four long days: Return to Attica.* Hurley, NY: American Life Associates.

Symonds, M. (1980, June). Victim responses to terror. *Annals of the New York Academy of Sciences, 347,* 129–136.

Tactical Manual for Hostage Situations. (1974). Unpublished manuscript, New York Police Department.

Taylor, R. W. (1983, March). Hostage and crisis negotiation procedures: Assessing police liability. *Trial, 19*(3), 64–69.

Terrorism Control in New York City. (1979). Unpublished manuscript, New York Police Department.

U.S. Department of Justice, Bureau of Justice Statistics. (1993). *Law Enforcement Management And Administrative Statistics (LEMAS)* [Computer file]. Conducted by U.S. Dept. of Commerce, Bureau of the Census. ICPSR ed. Ann Arbor, MI: Interuniversity Consortium for Political and Social Research [producer and distributor], 1996. [paper file, 1995]

U.S. Department of Justice. (1978a). *Selected bibliography—Police discretion.* Washington, DC: National Institute of Justice.

U.S. Department of Justice. (1978b). *Selected bibliography—Police management.* Washington, DC: National Institute of Justice.

U.S. Department of Justice. (1978c). *Selected bibliography—Police crisis intervention.* Washington, DC: National Institute of Justice.

U.S. Department of Justice. (1983, 1987, 1992). *Topical Search—SWAT and hostage negotiation.* Washington, DC: National Institute of Justice.

Useem, B., & Kimball, P. (1989). *States of siege—U.S. prison riots 1971–1986.* New York: Oxford University Press.

Volpe, M. R., & Louden, R. J. (1990). Hostage negotiations: Skills and strategies for third party intervention in high stress situations. In *Dispute resolution and democracy in the 1990's: Shaping the agenda.* Washington, DC: Society of Professionals in Dispute Resolution.

Welch, M. F. (1984). The applied typology and victimology in the hostage negotiation process. *Crime and Justice, 7,* 63–86.

Wicker, T. (1975). *A time to die.* New York: Quandrangle.

3

The S.A.F.E. Model for Negotiating Critical Incidents

Mitchell R. Hammer

A SIMPLE ROBBERY?

On January 31, 2007, at 9:30 p.m., three men brandished a gun and robbed a man in Northeast Washington, DC. They then fled in a red Jeep. Later, police saw the vehicle and gave chase. After cornering the three suspects, the officers were able to arrest two of the men, but a third escaped and commandeered a black Tahoe SUV. A second chase began; this time, however, the suspect hit and critically injured a bicyclist. The pursuit continued to the Capitol Hill area, where the suspect abandoned the Tahoe and broke into a home. The family inside was able to escape, after which the suspect barricaded himself in the house. The police hostage rescue and negotiation teams were called on-scene, and approximately 2 hours later, the tactical unit moved in on the house and was able to arrest the suspect. In a matter of a few short hours, a robbery of a pedestrian turned into a life-threatening car chase, an injured bicyclist, breaking and entering a home (miles from where the initial robbery took place), a terrorized family fleeing their home, and ended up as a critical incident standoff with a barricaded individual (*Robbery Suspects Captured*, 2007).

CRITICAL INCIDENTS

We live in violent times. Each and every day, Internet sites, newspapers, and television and radio stations report the gruesome details of violence run amok. The majority of critical incidents reported by the media are human-made situations (although critical incidents also arise from natural disasters as well). Such human-induced incidents can range from a disgruntled employee barricaded in the lunchroom at work to a cult confrontation such as the tragedy in Waco, Texas, that resulted in the fiery deaths of 81 Branch Davidians. A critical incident can also include a single, suicidal individual with a gun to mass casualty scenarios, such as the calculated and planned bombings on the London mass transit system on July 7, 2006, in which 56 people were killed (including four homicide bombers) and 700 injured, and the terrorist attack on September 11, 2001, on the World Trade Towers in New York City and the Pentagon in Washington, DC, resulting in the deaths of more than 3,000 innocent victims. Critical incidents can be planned to the smallest detail or impulsively ignited (e.g., road rage). They can arise from any type of unsatisfactory encounter, including a robbery, a domestic dispute, an angry confrontation in the workplace, a family argument, and even a casual misunderstanding in a restaurant, bar, or sporting event. A critical incident can involve a subject who is reported to have a weapon and has barricaded him or herself in a room or building. An incident can also be a "hostage" situation, whereby individuals are held against their will in order to attain some identified, instrumental goal, or a "nonhostage" event, in which individuals are held against their will and are victims to the subject's emotional state (Noesner, 1999). Common across this wide variety of incident characteristics, however, is that these potentially deadly situations are often resolved through either negotiation or a tactical solution.

When a crisis incident is resolved tactically, however, there is increased public scrutiny as to whether a tactical assault was necessary to resolve the potentially violent event. With this scrutiny has come increased demands for law enforcement to employ the latest and most effective negotiation approaches for peacefully resolving potentially violent encounters that include prison riots, criminal actions, terrorist acts, suicide attempts, and hostage-taking situations (Hammer, 2007). Yet not all efforts at "negotiating" a crisis situation result in a peaceful surrender of the subject. When negotiation fails, hostages, bystanders, police officers, and the subject are at elevated risk of being injured or killed.

In this chapter, I focus on the role of negotiation in resolving critical incidents. Specifically, I present, in summary form, the S.A.F.E. crisis negotiation model that is grounded in quantitative research (Hammer & Rogan, 2004; Rogan & Hammer, 1994, 1995, 1998) and more recent discourse analytic investigation (Hammer, 2007).[1]

THE S.A.F.E. MODEL OF HOSTAGE/CRISIS NEGOTIATION

When a law enforcement hostage/crisis negotiation team responds to a critical incident, they likely face a situation in which at least one subject has a weapon and has already used it or is threatening to harm others.[2] The subject's stress level often dramatically increases when police cars and incident response vehicles initially arrive, Special Weapons and Tactical (SWAT) officers deploy in full tactical gear, and snipers take up strategic positions. This overwhelming presence of law enforcement induces heightened stress and perceived threat that can compromise the subject's ability to cope with the situation. This can move a subject to view the situation in win/lose terms and increase his or her commitment to violence as a solution to his or her problems (Hammer, 2007). The S.A.F.E. model is developed to assist hostage/crisis negotiation teams more effectively deescalate and peacefully resolve these dangerous events.[3]

A PRACTICAL THEORY

Kurt Lewin stated, "there is nothing so practical as a good theory" (Hunt, 1987). This cogent advice highlights the importance of marrying theory with practice. The "theory" extrapolated in the S.A.F.E. model is an applied framework for critical incident response teams when lives are at stake, and a negotiation strategy is employed to deescalate such crisis events. This model is generated in practice as well as from systematic analysis of actual discourse that emerged among the police negotiator, Third Party Intermediaries (TPIs), the subject, and his or her hostages or victims (Hammer, 2007).

On the one hand, I have been fortunate to be part of hostage negotiation teams in the Washington, DC, area where I helped develop negotiation strategies to deescalate and resolve these violent situations. Thus, every theoretical "concept" of the S.A.F.E. model has had virtually instant "real-world" application and testing of its usefulness to these types of events. In addition, a core group of police crisis negotiators provided continual insights from their own negotiation experiences in real-world incidents that informed the development of the S.A.F.E. framework.[4]

On the other hand, Dr. Rogan and I have conducted social-scientific analyses of audiotaped incidents to generate and refine specific S.A.F.E. concepts and to test in discourse between the police negotiators and TPIs and subjects the viability and applicability of these concepts (Hammer, 2007; Hammer & Rogan, 2004; Rogan & Hammer, 1994, 1998).

In the 1990s, Dr. Rogan and I identified four key "triggers" as a possible line of research for assessing escalation and deescalation patterns in critical incidents. We termed these four "triggers" *F*ace (sensitivity of self-image), *I*nstrumental demands (substantive demands made), *R*elationship (trust/power issues between the police negotiator and the subject), and *E*motion (level of emotional upset experienced by the subject or hostages/victims). We identified this emerging model as the F.I.R.E. approach (e.g., Hammer, 1997, 1999; Rogan, 1999; Rogan, Hammer, & Van Zandt, 1997). As we discussed this F.I.R.E. model with police negotiators, we found the four triggers provided useful explanations of their experiences concerning escalation and deescalation patterns in crisis situations.

One observation made by some police negotiators was that the acronym F.I.R.E. could be misperceived outside law enforcement circles to mean a more aggressive, tactically driven approach for resolving hostage/crisis events, rather than the "negotiation-based" approach advocated by Dr. Rogan and myself. As a result of this practitioner feedback, we changed the acronym of the model to SA.F.E: Substantive demands, Attunement (relational closeness), Face (self-image), and Emotional distress.

A COMMUNICATION APPROACH

Communication approaches for conceptualizing hostage/crisis negotiation dynamics have only emerged since the 1980s (Hammer, 2007; Rogan & Hammer, 2006). This communication approach focuses most directly on the meaning of communication messages as they emerge during interaction between the subject and the hostage/crisis negotiator. A communication approach toward hostage/crisis negotiation is anchored in four key areas. First, microbehavioral analyses of verbal and nonverbal actions are the building blocks through which police negotiators and subjects coordinate their actions and make sense of one another's motivations, intentions, and behavioral acts. Second, a communication approach focuses attention on meaning and how it is socially constructed. Third, discourse characteristics are core competencies for analyzing conflict dynamics and identifying and implementing conflict-resolution practices (Folger & Jones, 2004; Jones, 2006). Finally, police negotiators and subjects construct meaning and enact behavior through core interpretive frames. These frames allow individuals to make sense of and respond to others in situ. Within these core interpretive frames are specific "conflict issues" that are "negotiated" between the parties. The S.A.F.E. model posits that the police negotiator and the subject "negotiate" conflictual issues (topics) that are "framed" in terms of Substantive demands, Attunement, Face, and Emotional distress (Hammer, 2007).

There are identifiable features of how these conflict issues are understood by the subject (and police negotiator) within each S.A.F.E. frame that allows for systematic *tracking* of Substantive demand, Attunement, Face, and Emotional distress issues. The S.A.F.E. model is *strategy* focused and identifies specific Substantive demand, Attunement, Face, and Emotional distress communicative action plans police negotiators may employ to deescalate the situation when interacting with the subject in the identified S.A.F.E. frame of the hostage taker.

Overall, the S.A.F.E. model is designed to aid critical incident management and crisis negotiation. This is done by developing a crisis negotiation strategy to influence the subject to peacefully surrender or assist in a tactical resolution of the incident (Hammer, 2005a). Having a well-developed S.A.F.E. crisis negotiation strategy can (a) increase understanding of the subject's motives, intentions and behavior; (b) identify specific influence strategies to deescalate critical events; (c) assist incident command decision making; and (d) support appropriate responses to various public and legal challenges regarding specific decisions and actions taken toward the subject as an incident unfolds.

THE S.A.F.E. PROCESS

The S.A.F.E. model proposes three interactive steps for law enforcement negotiators to engage.[5] First, police negotiation teams need to identify the predominant S.A.F.E. frame of the subject. Does the subject frame his or her interaction in terms of bargaining or problem solving specific demands (Substantive demand frame), trust issues toward the negotiator or TPIs (Attunement frame), how he or she is being perceived or judged by others (Face frame), or how angry, frustrated, sad, and so on the subject is feeling in the situation (Emotional distress frame)? Also, what is the predominant S.A.F.E. frame of the police negotiator? Second, the police negotiator needs to match his or her communication to the S.A.F.E. frame of the subject. This means that the law enforcement negotiator should interact with the subject within his or her primary S.A.F.E. frame around issues important to the subject. Third, after making some "progress" interacting with the subject in his or her predominant S.A.F.E. frame and deescalating the situation, the police negotiator is more likely to be successful in shifting with the subject to another S.A.F.E. frame. This frame shifting permits the police negotiator to gain influence with the subject and can further deescalate the situation and increase the probability of a peaceful resolution (Hammer, 2001, 2005a, 2005b, 2007).

The notion of an interpretive frame is central to the S.A.F.E. model. Frames are interpretive structures of interaction that enable individuals to define or make sense of one another's behavior. Frames reflect an individual's expectations or viewpoint toward the communicative issues being addressed. Bateson (1954/ 1972) defines a *frame* as " . . . a class or set of messages (or meaningful actions)" (p. 186), which functions as a map providing cues about how the interaction is to be defined and how to interpret the communicative acts within the specific context. Frames are directly connected to how people act in situations. As Gray (2006) points out, "how we frame a situation also affects how we respond to it" (p. 194). Frames, then, are the lenses or interpretive sets through which people perceive and respond to a particular situation, issue, or problem (Hammer, 2007).

Further, frames are set in communicative interaction through which individuals co-create understandings or representations of specific issues (Putnam & Holmer, 1992). Because frames are interactively grounded, they are subject to modification based on the level of synchrony achieved by the interactants (Hammer, 2001; Putnam & Holmer, 1992). Research has shown that individuals who are in conflict and operate from different frames are more likely to engage in win/lose (competitive) behavior and are less likely to achieve resolution compared with parties who operate in convergent frames (Drake & Donohue, 1996). In addition, parties in conflict may shift frames as a result of frame satisfaction during interaction. When applied to critical incident negotiation, these findings suggest that subjects are able to shift frames more easily after some degree of issue resolution has been achieved within the existing discourse frame. In contrast, attempts to shift frames too early can result in conflict escalation (Hammer, 2001).

In tense, potentially violent critical incidents, the police negotiator and the subject interactively shape their negotiation process through the core interpretive frames of Substantive demands, Attunement, Face, and Emotional distress. How issues within these frames are negotiated functions to escalate or deescalate the event. The S.A.F.E. model identifies specific markers for tracking escalation and deescalation and delineates negotiation strategies within each of the four S.A.F.E. frames for deescalating and peacefully resolving the incident.

SUBSTANTIVE DEMAND FRAME NEGOTIATION

In critical incidents, the subject and the police negotiator will often interpret one another's behavior in terms of the substantive demands each other makes. This instrumental frame is consistent with conceptualizations that focus on objective wants, demands, or needs of the parties involved in a conflict (Roloff & Jordan, 1992; Wilson & Putnam, 1990). When the subject and/or the police negotiator is operating within a Substantive demand frame, they are focusing their attention and framing their understanding of one another in terms of whether expressed wants and demands are being acknowledged and "negotiated." Subjects are operating in this frame when they consistently focus on or shift the topic of conversation back to what they want or need. When the subject is operating within a Substantive demand frame, the goal of the police negotiator is to enter into or "match" the substantive frame of the subject and then address the specific "issues" (i.e., demands) made by the subject as well as the claims made by the police negotiator (Hammer, 2005a). Demands refer to statements made by the subject and the police negotiator that request something each wants or needs from the other. There are key markers of conflict escalation and deescalation around substantive demands that are important to track during a critical incident.

The S.A.F.E. model posits two types of wants or demands. Central substantive demands are those statements of want or need made by the subject that are considered most relevant by the subject to his or her current situation. Peripheral substantive demands are wants that are seen by the subject as secondary or less relevant to the situation. As a crisis develops, some demands of the subject may move from being central substantive demands to less important demands (peripheral substantive demands). Listening to the way the demands are presented provides clues as to whether the demand is viewed, from the subject's perspective, as central or peripheral. For example, demands that have a deadline, a threat attached, or increased emotional upset can be considered central at a particular time, compared with demands that do not have these characteristics.

In addition to tracking the type of demands, police negotiation teams are advised to track how the demands are asserted by the subject. Demands should be tracked in terms of whether they are hardening (becoming more positional) or softening and whether they are increasing or decreasing in number. Further, whether a deadline is attached to the demand should also be tracked.

Threats are also important to track within the Substantive demand frame. Threats are messages designed to gain compliance from another party by indicating negative outcomes should the demand not be met (Hovland, Janis, & Kelly, 1953). Threats should be tracked in terms of whether the threat is offensively asserted (expresses intent to harm if the demand is not met) or defensive (intent to harm if the perceived threatening behavior of the other party continues or escalates) (Hammer, 2007). The S.A.F.E. model suggests that any threat to do harm should be taken seriously. However, a defensive threat is considered less potent than an offensive threat insofar as the police have more options at mitigating a defensive threat by discontinuing or lessening a specific behavior. For example, a subject issues a defensive threat when he or she says, "Back up your tactical guys, or I will start shooting!" To this threat, the incident commander has a number of options, including having his tactical unit stop moving closer or moving slightly back, thus deescalating the confrontation.

How the subject responds (considering, accepting vs. ignoring, rejecting) to demands made by the police negotiator should also be tracked. It is possible, for instance, that a situation can deescalate even when a subject does not soften his or her demands. This can occur because the subject expresses more willingness to meet at least some of the demands of the police negotiator while maintaining a more rigid posture regarding his or her own demands. Positively responding to the police negotiator's demands can include, for example, answering the telephone more promptly, talking longer, or releasing hostages.

The S.A.F.E. model identifies a number of Substantive demand frame strategies for deescalating a crisis event. The first and easiest strategy is to simply ignore the demands made by the subject by refocusing the discussion to another topic. This can be done when the subject stops asserting his or her demands or is no longer committed to having his or her demands met by the police negotiator. Police negotiators may respond to deadlines and threats by either talking through the deadline or waiting through the deadline, depending on whether the subject is able to refocus away from the immediate demand and deadline (talk through strategy) or whether the subject is fixated on getting his demand met by the deadline (wait through strategy). Both of these strategies are discussed in greater detail elsewhere (see Hammer, 2005a, 2007; McMains & Mullins, 2006).

Demands may also be downplayed through the strategy of "task breakdown analysis" (Hammer, 2007; McMains & Mullins, 2006). This strategy involves identifying the key tasks that need to be done in order to meet a demand and then reporting progress in accomplishing these specific tasks. This strategy is used when a demand cannot easily be met or the police negotiator is unable to meet the demand. According to McMains and Mullins (2006), this strategy is superior to typical responses of "We are working on it" or "I will have to get my boss to agree to your request." These types of responses communicate stalling and lack of consideration and can therefore escalate the crisis (Hammer, 2007).

A third strategy is to bargain demands. This can be done successfully (from the police negotiator's viewpoint) when the subject is willing to trade a central substantive demand of the police (e.g., release of hostages, surrender) for a peripheral demand of the police (e.g., talking to an attorney once taken into custody). There may be times, however, when central substantive demands of the subject (e.g., release of prisoners, safe passage out of the country) are exchanged for central substantive demands of the authorities (e.g., release of hostages, defusing a bomb). This may be applicable, for instance, to a terrorist incident that involves the threatened use of weapons of mass destruction (Hammer, 2007).

A fourth strategy involves problem solving underlying interests and looking for common goals (Fisher & Ury, 1991; Folger, Poole, & Stutman, 2000; Pruitt & Carnevale, 1993). Problem solving can be effective if either the subject or the police negotiator is not willing to ignore, downplay, or bargain demands. This is accomplished by the police negotiation team identifying common goals and/or interests that underlie the substantive demands made by the subject. For example, a hostage taker may demand a bulletproof vest be delivered to the front door. What is the underlying interest of the subject at this point? It may be that the subject is fearful of being attached by the police and wants the bulletproof vest for safety. Although the police may not wish to bargain with the hostage taker for a bulletproof vest, the police negotiator can negotiate the "safety" concerns (underlying interest) of the subject. In this way, the substantive frame issue is being addressed. By doing this, the situation can deescalate, increasing the probability of a peaceful resolution.

The S.A.F.E. model identifies the following Substantive demand frame patterns. First, the type of demands (central, peripheral), the number of demands, and the relative changes in rigidity (hardening, softening) of demands are related to escalation and deescalation of the event. Second, an increase in the number or positional commitments of the subject to peripheral substantive demands often reflects contention between the subject and police negotiator over issues of power and trust (Attunement). That is, peripheral substantive demands often function as the relational battleground of power/trust between the subject and police negotiator. This can arise when subjects are frustrated with the police negotiator and therefore create additional, peripheral demands in order to reassert power against the police. When this happens, an escalatory pattern emerges. Finally, the Substantive demand frame often stabilizes later in a critical incident in those events that end with a peaceful resolution (e.g., surrender). In these cases, a stable and convergent Substantive demand frame is important insofar as explicit agreements are made by the subject and police negotiator about how the situation can end without violence (i.e., the surrender ritual).

ATTUNEMENT FRAME NEGOTIATION

Attunement is the second core S.A.F.E. frame and has been posited more generally to be a core characteristic of a good or close relationship (Fisher & Brown, 1988). Attunement or trust has been variously defined in terms of a vulnerability that one party extends to another party (e.g., Cupach & Canary, 1997; Rousseau, Sitkin, Burt, & Camerer, 1988) and an "expectation that the other party will cooperate in the future" (Pruitt & Carnevale, 1993, p. 133). Attunement (affiliation) is described by Donohue (1998) as the degree of attraction, liking, respect, trust, and a desire to cooperate with the other party. Overall, attunement is concerned with the quality of the relationship that involves a sense of vulnerability toward the other party, an expectation of cooperation, and a liking toward and consideration for the well-being of the other party (Hammer, 2005a, 2007; Rogan & Hammer, 2006).

Attunement is central to resolution of conflicts and impacts not only ongoing interaction, but future relations as well. As Folger, Poole, and Stutman (2005) point out, "relational communication has its most profound effects through influencing future interaction. How people interact in conflicts is colored by their assessments of others—judgments about things such as the others' trustworthiness, intentions (good or bad), and determination to win" (p. 35). Research suggests that when attunement (trust, affiliation) is present in a relationship, the parties: (a) are less critical of one another, (b) demand less information of one another yet are willing to share more information, (c) engage in more personal disclosure, (d) impute positive motives to the other party's behavior in ambiguous situations, and (e) are able to more easily reach agreements to end their disagreements or conflict (Folger et al., 2005; Kimmel, Pruitt, Magenau, Konar-Goldband, & Carnevale, 1980; Lindskold & Han, 1988).

Attunement is fundamentally grounded in the degree of trust and affiliation experienced between the parties, and it is concerned with the degree of interpersonal closeness and distance between the subject and the police negotiator and/or Third Party Intermediaries (TPIs) (Hammer, 2005a; Rogan & Hammer, 2006). In a crisis event, attunement often becomes a critical consideration for subjects when they are contemplating surrender. For hostage takers to complete the surrender, they typically need to put their weapon away and then leave their (often barricaded) location and walk to an open area where SWAT team members, with weapons drawn, take the subject into custody. What propels a subject to walk out unarmed into a group of armed police officers? Often, the degree of attunement developed with the police negotiator enables a subject to trust that the action taken by the police upon surrender will not be too harmful to him or herself; that is, the surrender will be peaceful (Hammer, 2007).

Attunement is mitigated or enhanced depending on the degree of *competition versus cooperation* between the police negotiator and the parties (Deutsch, 1973). When attunement is being successfully "negotiated" between the police negotiator (and/or TPIs) and the subject, there is often a pattern of movement from more contentious relational communication (competition) to more cooperative interaction. The primary feature of attunement is reciprocal cooperative behavior for deescalating violent situations. Cooperative actions are influential in deescalating crisis situations and building attunement because of the rule of reciprocity. This rule states that competitive behavior breeds competitive actions, and cooperative behavior leads to cooperative reciprocation (McMains & Mullins, 2006).

The S.A.F.E. model encourages police negotiators to frame actions and communication messages with the subject in terms of "cooperative behavior." In this way, the police negotiator earns increased attunement "influence" with the subject. The goal, therefore, of the police negotiator, when the subject is operating within an Attunement frame, is to engage in cooperative behavior in order to gain increased relational closeness with the subject (Hammer, 2005a). This is accomplished through cooperative actions and communicative messages. Building attunement is particularly important as an incident develops because of the typically high levels of mistrust the subject has toward the police negotiator. That is, the subject perceives his or her relationship with the law enforcement negotiator in competitive, relationally distant, threatening terms (Donohue & Roberto, 1993; Hammer, 2007; Rogan, 1990; Rogan, Donohue, & Lyles, 1990).

The S.A.F.E. model recommends police negotiation teams track attunement issues by identifying specific cooperative versus uncooperative acts taken by the subject and by the police SWAT and negotiation units. Cooperative acts can include both behavioral actions (e.g., releasing hostages) and communicative messages ("I appreciate your picking up the telephone and talking to us").

Tracking cooperative and uncooperative actions and communicative messages of the subject and the police negotiator (and Tactical actions) are important insofar as attunement is attained through a reciprocal, step-by-step behavioral process that is framed in cooperative terms. Although attunement is gained incrementally, it can easily be diminished through one uncooperative act. As Johnson (1997) comments, "trust is hard to build and easy to destroy" (p. 75).

Of particular importance is to track the consistency in "message value" of SWAT actions compared with police negotiator assurances. Attunement is next to impossible to build with the subject if Tactical actions contradict cooperative messages of the police negotiator. This was clearly illustrated in the Branch Davidian standoff in Waco, Texas, in 1993. This tragic event was initiated when the Bureau of Alcohol, Tobacco, Firearms, and explosives (ATF) attempted to capture the cult leader of the Branch Davidians in their Mount Carmel compound. Weapon fire was exchanged, resulting in the deaths of 4 ATF agents and the wounding of 16 others. Shortly thereafter, the FBI assumed control of the incident. After 56 days, the standoff ended when the FBI's Hostage Rescue Team (HRT) inserted tear gas into Mount Carmel. Shortly thereafter, fire engulfed the building, resulting in the fiery deaths of 81 Branch Davidian members, including 17 children.

Tactical actions during this siege consistently contradicted the negotiation strategy of the FBI's crisis negotiation unit. The tactical actions were "designed to tighten the perimeter around the compound, to demonstrate to those inside that Koresh was not in full control, to make the lives of those inside increasingly uncomfortable, and to provide greater safety for everyone involved" (Scruggs et al., 1993b, p. 139). Various aggressive, psychological warfare tactics, such as the playing of loud music, noises of dying animals, and Tibetan chants throughout the night, were used to create sleep deprivation among the cult members. In addition, the Special Agent in Charge of the situation shut off electricity to the compound in order to increase physical discomfort. However, this was done without substantial consultation with the crisis negotiators. The result was that the electricity was shut off right after at least two Davidians voluntarily left the compound. Further, the Tactical unit towed the automobiles belonging to Davidian members that were parked in front of the compound. Again, the timing of this action was not fully coordinated with the negotiation team. The result was that the removal of the cars took place right after seven more people exited.

These pressure tactics did not complement negotiation strategy nor were they undertaken to aid in a tactical rescue operation. Rather, these were tactically driven actions designed to force a resolution of the incident irrespective of negotiation strategy (Scruggs et al., 1993a).

Tracking attunement in terms of cooperative (and uncooperative) actions or communication messages can range from noting whether specific actions (e.g., delivery of food) increases relational trust of the subject toward the police negotiator to noting whether expressions of trust/mistrust are made by the subject toward the police negotiator or TPIs.

Strategies to build attunement with the subject can include tactical "containment" actions rather than actions that increase SWAT presence. Engaging the subject in less contentious (e.g., social) topics of conversation, finding commonality in experiences, moving from more formal to informal language, using the language of relational closeness versus distance (e.g., this/these rather than that/those), and using active listening skills can also be effective strategies for building trust (Donohue & Roberto, 1993; Hammer, 2007; McMains & Mullins, 2006).

Crisis negotiation is often begun in situations that can be characterized as low attunement (i.e., a competitive, relational distance frame). This relational distance attunement frame, from the perspective of the subject, involves lack of trust and consideration toward his or her concerns and therefore can escalate conflict between the subject and police negotiator. The S.A.F.E. model suggests that this low attunement frame can remain relatively stable unless specific cooperative actions and communication messages are strategically initiated by the police negotiator and reciprocated by the subject. As attunement increases, there is a greater likelihood that the volatile situation can deescalate. Further, as attunement is developed between the police negotiator and the subject, substantive demands can become more negotiable, and a peaceful resolution of the event is more likely to result.

FACE FRAME NEGOTIATION

The S.A.F.E. model posits "face" as a third trigger of conflict escalation and deescalation in critical incidents. Consistent with Goffman's (1967) seminal conceptualization, *face* can be defined as "a set of coordinated practices in which communicators build, maintain, protect, or threaten personal dignity, honor, and respect" (Littlejohn & Domenici, 2006, p. 228). In essence, face is about how individuals wish to be perceived by others and is grounded in a desire to maintain a positive social expression of themselves. Face is of central concern during conflictual interaction (Donohue & Kolt, 1992; Littlejohn & Domenici, 2006; Northrup, 1989; Ting-Toomey, 1988; Ting-Toomey & Kurogi, 1998). Research suggests that individuals will sacrifice rewards in an effort to maintain face in the eyes of others (Brown, 1977). Face is of central concern in a crisis situation for both perpetrators and police negotiators (Miron & Goldstein, 1979; Rogan, Chapter 6, this volume; Rogan & Hammer, 1994).

The S.A.F.E. model views face as the projected self-image or reputation held by an individual that is grounded in interaction that needs to be validated or acknowledged by others (Hammer, 2007; Hammer & Rogan, 1997; Rogan & Hammer, 1994). Critical incidents, with the visible arrival and presence of the police SWAT and sniper units, are inherently face-threatening to the subject (Rogan, 1990; Rogan & Hammer, 2002). Because of the confrontational nature of interaction between the police and the subject, face remains a consistent focus during a crisis incident. Police negotiators not only need to manage their own face (e.g., self-image, reputation) concerns, but also validate or acknowledge the face needs of the perpetrator (Rogan & Hammer, 1994, 2006).

The goal for the police negotiator in the S.A.F.E. model is to validate the face concerns of the subject (Hammer, 2005a). The S.A.F.E. model posits that face-threatening acts, when reciprocated, escalate conflict, whereas face-honoring acts deescalate conflict. Further, face needs that are not addressed (e.g., ignored) or are perceived to be rejected escalate conflict, whereas face needs that are honored and are perceived to be validated deescalate the situation. In addition, consistent attack self-face acts may be possible indicators of suicidal intentions (Hammer, 2007; Rogan & Hammer, 1994).

Consistent with social identity theory, two types of face are viewed as particularly central to crisis negotiation: social/group identity and individual identity (Tajfel, 1978, 1981). According to Hammer and Rogan (1997), "Personal identity is based on an individual's unique perceptions of his/her own attributes (e.g., strong, weak, intelligent) while social identity consists of those characteristics and their emotional significance that is attached to one's membership in social group(s)" (pp. 15–16).

These types of face can vary both within as well as across incidents. Rogan and Hammer (1994) view personal identity as central in those negotiations involving a suicidal person, whereas social identity characteristics may be more salient in negotiations with certain social groups, cults, or particular national identity organizations (Hammer, 2001). Whether face concerns are more personal identity driven or social identity based, communication that attacks or threatens face tends to escalate conflict, whereas face-honoring messages can deescalate the situation (Hammer, 2007). Overall, then, both individual and/or group face needs can be salient in a crisis situation and, when not validated, equally escalatory.

A subject that is operating within a Face frame during a crisis event engages in behavior that articulates those characteristics of his or her self-image (e.g., an honest person, a drug addict) that is salient to that person. When the subject "explains" his or her situation or problem and highlights key personal or social identity characteristics important to him or her, the subject is, in essence, pleading with the police negotiator to validate (i.e., acknowledge) that the negotiator understands how the subject sees his or her situation and him herself as the crisis incident develops.

Face frame concerns of the subject should also be tracked in terms of the features (positive or negative) of his or her self-image. Further, four specific face behaviors of the subject (and police negotiator) are tracked in the S.A.F.E model: (a) attack self-face behavior (e.g., I really ruined it with my family), (b) attack other face behavior (e.g., you police are idiots if you think I am going to let one of these hostages go), (c) honor self-face behavior (e.g., I have had a responsible job for many years, until now), and (d) honor other face behavior (e.g., yea, you're a good cop).

There are a number of strategies that police negotiators can use to validate the face needs of the subject when the hostage taker is in a Face frame. First, listening skills can be used to encourage subjects to explain their situation and present those qualities of their self-image that need acknowledgment from the police negotiator. Allowing subjects to elaborate "how they got into this situation" often takes the form of justifying or rationalizing their actions and responsibilities. This is communicatively accomplished typically through the use of verbal qualifiers, which linguistically function as markers of Face frame concerns. Verbal qualifiers function for the subject as a way to present his or her self-image in as positive a light as possible and are used as a face-saving mechanism in negotiation (Hammer, 2007). For example, a barricaded subject in an office building, in explaining why he was "unfairly" terminated from his job due, at least in part, to alcoholism, says, "I had a couple of drinks, *people do that. Nothing wrong with that.*" The verbal qualifiers of "people do that" and "Nothing wrong with that" attempt to present the subject's self-image in a positive light—as someone who is not a deviant, but a responsible person.

Subjects do not always attempt to present their self-image in a positive manner, however. In these cases, they often engage in substantial self-face attack behavior and are, in effect, presenting a negative self-image for validation to the police negotiator. When this occurs, it may indicate, according to Rogan and Hammer (1994), an increased likelihood for suicide. Encouraging subjects to talk about themselves is a powerful strategy for validating face concerns. When face needs are validated, a sense of progress in the Face frame arises. When this happens, the situation can de-escalate.

Face frame discourse may likely emerge during the surrender ritual. At this time, subjects may be acutely aware of how they may be perceived by others when they are taken into custody. As a result, they may demand a face-saving exit. For example, a hostage taker may request that he/she not be handcuffed in front of his children. When a subject is focused in the Face frame, the police negotiation team should look to honor face-saving demands made by subject (without compromising safety concerns) (Hammer, 2007).

EMOTIONAL DISTRESS FRAME NEGOTIATION

The fourth S.A.F.E. frame is Emotional distress. Results from a national survey of police crisis negotiators reveals that the two most important needs of negotiators were the assessment of hostage taker's emotionality and improving communication skills (Hammer, Van Zandt, & Rogan, 1994; Rogan, Hammer, & Van Zandt, 1994). The high-stress, potentially life-threatening dynamics involved in hostage/crisis incidents often result in heightened levels of emotional distress experienced by subjects. Hammer (2007) identifies six principals that underlie the Emotional distress frame:

(1) Communication is central in understanding emotion and conflict, and crises are emotional experiences.

(2) Emotions arise from an individual's cognitive appraisal of his or her social situation (Jones, 2001, 2006).

(3) Critical incidents often involve levels of emotional intensity that are more accurately understood in terms of emotional distress (Rogan, 1997).

(4) Emotional distress experiences are most commonly generated from interpersonal communication interactions (Andersen & Guerrero, 1998).

(5) Emotion acts as a barometer of people's social experiences.

(6) Emotional communication involves an interaction of verbal and nonverbal exchanges between individuals that can either intensify or reduce emotional distress (Andersen & Guerrero, 1998).

The S.A.F.E. model defines *emotional distress* as "intense, negative emotions that compromise an individual's coping ability" (Hammer, 2005a, p. 11). Subjects are functioning in this frame when negative emotions dominate their behavior. The police negotiator's goal, when subjects are experiencing emotional distress, is to "help the subject cope with these negative feelings so he/she can re-assess the situation and peacefully surrender" (Hammer, 2005a, p. 11).

The following emotional distress states are identified in the S.A.F.E. model as particularly salient in critical incidents: sadness, fear, disgust, anger, and shame. In addition to these negative emotions, the positive emotional state of joy or happiness is highlighted as the affective alternative to a negatively distressed state. These emotions are posited as central to how humans experience and interact in their social world. The S.A.F.E. model highlights the emotional meaning—what Lazarus (1994) identifies as core relational themes and the action tendencies of these negative emotional experiences (Andersen & Guerrero, 1998; Scherer & Wallbot, 1994; Shaver, Schwartz, Kirson, & O'Connor, 1987).

Sadness is characterized as a sense of loneliness, rejection, and discouragement based on an experience of a significant loss in one's life. The action tendency of sadness is to separate from the identified loss and, more important, to seek help in coping more effectively with the loss. A perceived threat that can psychologically or physically harm oneself generates the emotional distressed state of fear. The action tendency of fear is to avoid or escape from the perceived threat. The emotional meaning of disgust is a sense of distaste or revulsion toward something or someone (including oneself) that is viewed as spoiled or deteriorated. The action tendency of disgust is to get "rid of" or "wash away" the offending emotion. A sense of being physically or psychologically unfairly restrained or contained from pursuing or achieving an important goal generates the emotion of anger. The action tendency of anger is to attack the person or persons who are perceived to be interfering with one's efforts at attaining the targeted goal. Shame is one of the most devastating emotional distressed states because it is experienced as a fundamentally intense, painful feeling of dejection and of being rejected by others. A shame experience views self as inadequate, inferior, and separated from core relationships in one's life (Retzinger, 1993). The action tendency for shame is to hide, disappear, or die. The positive emotional experience of happiness is experienced as elation with being with people, with an action tendency to approach or embrace others who are associated with this joyful experience (Hammer, 2007).

When subjects are in an emotionally distressed state, the S.A.F.E. model identifies tracking protocols for the police crisis negotiation team to observe and confirm possible behavioral patterns associated with the identified emotional distressed state. In critical incident situations, sadness may be indicative of depression and possible suicide. Police negotiators should identify possible suicide intentions of the subject if he or she is experiencing heightened sadness (McMains & Mullins, 2006). Unpredictable and spontaneous actions may be undertaken by subjects or hostages who are experiencing heightened levels of fear. Subjects who are in a disgust emotional distressed state may view themselves as deteriorated, spoiled, or rotten. This sense of self-disgust may be indicative of substance abuse problems. Metaphors often associated with substance abuse, for example, are those that characterize the disgust emotional experience, including "getting clean" and "ridding oneself of the poison inside." The emotional distress state of disgust may also be related to other forms of abuse that is internalized as self-disgust (e.g., sexual abuse). Anger can produce impulsive and explosive violent actions. Subjects may aggressively "take out" their anger (and sense of injustice) by hitting a wall, throwing a telephone, beating a hostage/victim, or shooting at the police. Yet anger often is short-lived (thus someone who has anger problems is also described as operating on a "short fuse"). Once expressed in violent behavior, the subject may regret his or her aggressive behavior. However, the damage may already be done. In contrast to anger, shame is a long-lasting emotionally distressed state. Shame may be experienced as overt shame, where the pain of rejection is more directly felt, but likely misnamed (e.g., I feel awful) or as bypassed shame, where the more direct feeling state of shame is "bypassed" by thinking about "what I should have done or not done" (Retzinger, 1993). When shame becomes salient in a critical incident, it is possible that the hostage taker may have previously been subjected to powerful "shaming" experiences (e.g., sexual or physical abuse). In crisis situations, this sense of shame can blend with a sense of anger and result in a tornado of emotional distress best characterized as "humiliated fury" (Retzinger, 1993). This shame/anger state may behaviorally manifest itself internally, with suicide as a possible outcome, or externally, with aggression and homicide against others or aggression against self in the form of suicide-by-cop (Hammer, 2007).

Although crisis intervention skills (Roberts, 1991) and active listening skills (Noesner & Webster, 1997) provide a foundation for police negotiators to better understand the subject's emotional experience (McMains & Mullins, 2006), they may be inadequate in terms of influencing the subject toward a peaceful resolution.

The Emotional distress frame, as conceptualized in the S.A.F.E. model, both values the use of listening skills and also builds on these skill sets. That is, S.A.F.E. frame insights around emotional distress focus on the emotional meaning, action tendencies, and appraisal processes, such that the police negotiator has a broader set of capabilities to strategically listen and *influence* the subject toward a peaceful surrender.

The S.A.F.E. model emphasizes that police negotiators should respond to the emotional distress state of the subject through supportive communication (Andersen & Guerrero, 1998; Burleson & Goldsmith, 1998; Hammer, 2007; Lazarus, 1991). Briefly, the three key elements of supportive communication incorporated in the S.A.F.E. model are as follows. First, the core feeling state of the subject needs to be attended to by the police negotiator (Hammer, 2005a). As Burleson and Goldsmith (1998) state, "There is evidence that, across a wide variety of situations, focusing on the feelings of the distressed other is consistently evaluated as helpful" (p. 248). Second, the police negotiator should help the subject describe or explain his or her problem or situation. Encouraging the subject to tell "his or her story" should be done by adapting a nonevaluative stance toward the subject's behavior and feelings (Burleson & Goldsmith, 1998). The core emotional reality (distressed state) of the subject can be identified, and encouraging the subject to explain his or her situation can be effectively accomplished by using crisis intervention skills and active listening techniques (Hammer, 2005a). Listening skills such as open-ended questions, paraphrasing, emotional labeling, and offering an explanation of the subject's thoughts, actions, and/or feelings have been identified as particularly supportive and effective in communicating understanding of the subject and his or her emotional experience (Burleson & Goldsmith, 1998; Elliott, 1985; Hill et al., 1988).

Third, after the subject is able to "tell his or her story" and how he or she feels, the S.A.F.E. approach suggests that the police negotiator respond to the *action tendency* of the primary emotion the subject is experiencing. For example, if subjects are experiencing intense sadness, police negotiators can communicate to hostage takers that they are not alone, and they do not have to carry the burden of their perceived loss by themselves. Most important, the police negotiator can emphasize that *help is available.* Because the action tendency of sadness is to seek help, police negotiators are able to gain influence by specifically framing their communication messages in terms of this action tendency of the emotional distressed state of the subject.

Supportive communication aids understanding and helps an individual reappraise his or her situation, enabling more creative problem solving to emerge that can lead to a peaceful resolution, rather than suicide or violent aggression against others. A core aspect of influencing the subject during this reappraisal process is for the police negotiator to frame his or her responses to the subject in terms of the action tendencies of the subject's core emotional distressed state.

A MUSICAL TRAGEDY

Late on a Thursday afternoon, world-renowned pianist Roger Williams telephoned his very good friend, Johnnie Carl, the musical director at the Crystal Cathedral near Los Angeles, California. Carl was an internationally known composer of religious music and recently had a CD "go platinum." Williams became alarmed because Carl's communication was unintelligible. At one point, Johnnie Carl said he was going to kill himself. Following this phone call, Carl walked into the Cathedral and fired four shots from a gun he was carrying. He then barricaded himself in his basement office. Nine hours later, Carl killed himself.

For many years, Johnnie Carl battled with bipolar disorder and severe depression. He had threatened suicide prior to this incident and had been hospitalized for his mental disorder as recently as a month earlier. Although he seemed fine after returning home, he soon became increasingly troubled. While remaining in his basement office, Carl called a number of people, including his wife and psychiatrist. He said he would kill himself if his name was broadcast on the media. Within 45 minutes, the police critical incident unit arrived on-scene. Electricity was shut off in the building, which also prevented direct telephone negotiation to take place. Negotiators had to yell to Carl through his office door. During the incident, police negotiators played a taped message from a friend. Johnnie Carl did not respond to this effort to convince him to surrender. Further, Carl consistently refused to talk to the negotiators. After some time, the tactical unit attempted to open the door and insert a "throw phone" so Carl could talk directly to the police negotiator. Upon seeing the door open, however, Carl ran into the bathroom and locked the door. Shortly thereafter, police heard a single gunshot.

Roger Clarke, a former Los Angeles County Sheriff's Lieutenant, observed following the incident that Carl is "cooped up and there's no way out except to put himself in the hands of officers. You could image the shame. He'd rather be dead" (Gottlieb, Lin, & Hanley, 2004). As this tragic event ended, Roger Williams recalled that "we always said we'd play for each other's funeral" (Gottlieb et al., 2004).

Johnnie Carl's likely emotional distressed state was severe sadness. He probably felt alone and thought ending his internal pain was more important than to continue to live with the anguish he was experiencing. It was a difficult situation to peacefully resolve. The police negotiators were unable to initiate meaningful communication with Carl because the electricity was cut off and Carl refused to talk to the negotiator through the door. When the SWAT team entered the office, Carl may have experienced significant fear—fear that he would be harmed by the police officers. Although this is speculation, his "flight" behavior to the bathroom is consistent with a strong fear response.

From the S.A.F.E. perspective, negotiating with Johnnie Carl likely would have involved entering into this emotionally distressed state of profound sadness (and perhaps shame), validating his feelings, and encouraging him to "tell his story." Appealing to the action tendency to seek help, the police negotiator and TPIs who could directly talk to Carl may have given Johnnie Carl the opportunity to reappraise his situation and perhaps consider the alternative of surrender in order to "live another day." Ultimately, however, whether anyone could have influenced Johnnie Carl is completely dependent on Carl's willingness to accept help. In the final analysis, the decision to kill himself rested solely with Johnnie Carl.

THE S.A.F.E. MODEL ACROSS CULTURES

The crisis/hostage-taking event (in which the threat of internalized [suicide] or externalized homicide) is, unfortunately, found throughout our global community (Hammer, 2007; McMains & Mullins, 2006; Rogan & Hammer, 1997). One question that arises with any "applied" approach for resolving crisis situations is the degree to which the core precepts of the approach generalize to other cultures. The S.A.F.E. model is proposed as an approach that has a reasonable degree of cross-cultural applicability for tracking escalation and deescalation patterns in communication discourse. Further, the strategies identified in the S.A.F.E. framework, it is argued, also possess reasonable generalizability to other cultural contexts.

This sense of reasonable cross-cultural generalizability of the S.A.F.E. framework is grounded in the following observations. First, the pragmatics of human communication meta-theoretical stance (within which the S.A.F.E. model is situated) has a long history of cross-cultural application, including the identification of two universal dimensions of meaning in discourse: the report and command functions of messages (Bateson, 1954/1972; Hammer, 2007; Watzlawick, Bavelas, & Jackson, 1967). Further, the identification of the S.A.F.E. anchors of Substantive demands, Attunement, and Face also have a long and extensive history of investigation and validation across cultural contexts (Putnam & Roloff, 1992). The fourth S.A.F.E. element of Emotion and its conceptualization in the model concerning the core meaning, action tendencies, and functional role in appraisal processes also has an extensive literature that suggests a reasonable universality of these constructs across cultures (Lazarus, 1994; Lewis & Haviland, 1993). Further, current research conducted within other cultural contexts does not contradict the main tenets proposed within the S.A.F.E. model (Giebels & Noelanders, 2004).

Although the S.A.F.E. framework is posited to be a useful "culture-general" approach for negotiating critical incidents, this is not to suggest that cultural differences do not "matter." In the converse, by stating that cultural differences can impact on how escalation and deescalation unfolds in a crisis is also not to imply that the S.A.F.E. approach is, therefore, culturally "biased." To elaborate, there are likely to be specific areas where cultural differences do impact how negotiator's "track" escalation and deescalation and how negotiation strategies are developed. Suggesting that "culture matters" in using the S.A.F.E. (or any other) framework does not imply that these types of culture general approaches are somehow not applicable in other cultures. It only means that the main precepts of the S.A.F.E. approach are not culturally "biased" in ways that would lead to inattentive or inaccurate tracking of escalation/deescalation or inaccurate identification of resolution strategies based on S.A.F.E. analysis. That is, the S.A.F.E. framework is sufficiently interculturally robust, such that patterns of cultural difference can be identified and incorporated in both the tracking of S.A.F.E. issues and the development of negotiation strategies. In short, the S.A.F.E. model represents a reasonable framework for developing negotiation strategies when cultural differences are present.

Attending to cultural differences is central in negotiating critical events. Under conditions of stress and threat, individuals tend to revert to their primary cultural programming (Hammer & Rogan, 1997; Rogan & Hammer, 2006). One area in which I have been developing models and assessment tools concerns the conflict-resolution style people from different cultures rely on in hostage/crisis incidents (Hammer, 2005d; Rogan & Hammer, 2006). In general, cultural differences in conflict-resolution styles have been shown to escalate conflict between parties (Ting-Toomey et al., 2000). More specifically, differences in intercultural conflict styles can have a significant impact on escalation and deescalation processes when negotiating with hostage takers (Rogan & Hammer, 2006).

The Intercultural Conflict Style (ICS) model and assessment inventory identifies ways in which cultural differences influence "how" individuals communicate their concerns and understanding of the other party's concerns/needs. I have identified these different cultural approaches in terms of more direct and indirect patterns for negotiating substantive demands/positions. In addition, the ICS model identifies different cultural approaches, termed *emotionally expressive* and *emotionally restrained*, for how individuals express the level of emotional upset they are experiencing in a conflict/crisis situation (Hammer, 2002b, 2002c, 2003, 2005d). Conflict style is viewed in terms of how individuals communicate about substantive disagreements and how they communicate emotion to one another. The dimensions of direct/indirect patterns for negotiating substantive issues and the emotionally expressive/restrained for communicating emotional experiences have been identified in cross-cultural research as central parameters of cultural differences within our global community (see Hammer, 2003, for a comprehensive review of related literature in this arena).

The ICS model identifies four core intercultural conflict-resolution styles. A more direct, emotionally restrained (controlled) approach is termed a Discussion style. The Engagement style uses more verbally direct strategies that are braided with a more emotionally expressive posture. The Accommodation style employs a more indirect approach for addressing disagreements coupled with a more emotionally restrained approach for dealing with emotional upset. Finally, the Dynamic style involves more indirect strategies along with greater emotional expressiveness.

In crisis/hostage negotiations, differences between these styles can exacerbate tensions and contribute to misunderstandings between the police negotiator and the subject. For example, the "level" of authentic and "in control" emotional expressiveness characteristic of the Engagement conflict-resolution style is likely to be misinterpreted by the more emotionally restrained Discussion approach. The more Discussion-style police negotiator may perceive the increased level of emotional "presence" being communicated by the Engagement subject as indicative of the subject being emotionally "out of control." For the Engagement-style subject, however, this level of emotional expressiveness is comfortable, reasonable, and completely "in control." This misunderstanding concerning the point in discourse when someone may be getting emotionally out of control versus in control of one's emotional experience can lead to a premature tactical intervention when it may not be needed. Similarly, differences in how direct or indirect a subject is in responding to the police negotiator can also fuel misinterpretation and lead to an inaccurate assessment of the motives and intentions of the subject. These and other observed differences in cultural patterns of interpreting a situation or acting in it can be overlaid on the S.A.F.E. model in order to more accurately track S.A.F.E. concerns and identify negotiation strategies to resolve the potentially violent event.

SUMMARY

A core premise of the S.A.F.E. model is that escalation or deescalation of crisis incidents occurs based on whether salient S.A.F.E. frames are addressed; that is, whether Substantive demands are negotiated or ignored, Attunement (relational closeness) enhanced or diminished, Face honored or threatened, and/or Emotional distress empathically transformed or intensified.

The subject and the police negotiator interact with one another through these interpretive frames. As an incident unfolds, there is a fluid movement of the subject and police negotiator into and out of these core interpretive frames. Subjects are more likely to shift interpretive frames when police negotiators enter into or "match" the dominant frame of the subjects. Deescalation is more likely to take place when the police negotiator and subject communicate within the same frame because this allows shared meaning to arise. This shared meaning is experienced as a sense of interactional progress. By "working through" the relevant issues within the dominant frame, the subject can become more willing to shift interpretive frames, with the objective of moving into a Substantive demand frame now focused on the police negotiators' key issues (e.g., release of hostages, surrender), rather than on solely meeting the demands of the subject (Hammer, 2007).

The S.A.F.E. framework suggests that escalation can take place when the police negotiator (or TPIs) and the subject interact with one another in divergent frames. When this occurs, the hostage taker (and negotiator) will likely feel misunderstood and manipulated, resulting in a sense of little "interactional progress." This can stop movement around the salient frame issues and decrease the probability of frame shifting. The situation can also escalate if either the subject or the police negotiator attempts to shift frame before a sufficient sense of interaction progress is attained.

However, conflict can deescalate when both the subject and the police negotiator move to another interpretive frame in a matched, synchronous manner after a sense of negotiated "progress" is achieved within a frame. When this sense of progress is achieved, the police negotiator is better positioned to influence the subject toward moving to the Substantive demand frame for negotiating a peaceful resolution of the crisis event.

NOTES

1. Initial formulation of the S.A.F.E. framework was a joint effort with Dr. Randall Rogan. The current S.A.F.E. model is presented in its most comprehensive form in Hammer (2007), and key aspects are summarized in this chapter. The S.A.F.E. model articulated in Hammer (2007) and this chapter, including additions, elaborations, and/or modifications to the initial concepts of the S.A.F.E. framework, are necessarily my own responsibility.

2. The term *subject* is used to describe the perpetrator or hostage taker in a crisis/hostage situation. The term *hostage* is used to refer to one or more individuals being held against their will by the subject. The term *police negotiator* or *negotiator* is used to refer to the law enforcement personnel who are directly communicating with the subject in order to peacefully resolve the incident.

3. It should be noted that the specific information presented in this chapter on the S.A.F.E. model is not sufficient for law enforcement or other negotiators or crisis interveners to competently implement when a crisis or critical incident arises. Individuals or organizations desiring to learn more about how to use the S.A.F.E. model should contact the author at *www.hammerconsulting.org*.

4. These individuals include Mr. Robert Beach, Mr. William Hogewood, Mr. William Kidd, Mr. Anthony Hare, Mr. Chuck Paris, Mr. Fred Lanceley, and Mr. James Cavenaugh, among many other police officers who worked with the emerging S.A.F.E. framework over a number of years.

5. The discussion of the S.A.F.E. model is presented from the perspective of the law enforcement negotiator who confronts violent subjects. Nevertheless, the S.A.F.E. model equally applies the four frames to the behavior of the police negotiator as well as the subject, although in this chapter the focus is on understanding the behavior of the subject, with less emphasis on the behavior of the police negotiator, except insofar as tactical actions are more directly addressed in this chapter and the model's description (Hammer, 2007).

REFERENCES

Andersen, P. A., & Guerrero, L. K. (1998). Principles of communication and emotion in social interaction. In P. A. Andersen & L. K. Guerrero (Eds.), *Handbook of communication and emotion* (pp. 49–96). San Diego, CA: Academic Press.

Bateson, G. (1954/1972). *Steps to an ecology of mind.* New York: Ballantine Books.

Brown, B. (1977). Face-saving and face-restoration in negotiation. In D. Druckman (Ed.), *Negotiations: Social-psychological perspectives* (pp. 275–299). Beverly Hills, CA: Sage.

Burleson, B. R., & Goldsmith, D. J. (1998). How the comforting process works: Alleviating emotional distress through conversationally induced reappraisals. In P. A. Andersen & L. K. Guerrero (Eds.), *Handbook of communication and emotion* (pp. 245–280). San Diego, CA: Academic Press.

Cupach, W. R., & Canary, D. J. (1997). *Competence in interpersonal conflict.* New York: McGraw-Hill.

Deutsch, M. (1973). *The resolution of conflict: Constructive and destructive processes.* New Haven, CT: Yale University Press.

Donohue, W. A. (1998). Managing equivovality and relational paradox in the Oslo peace negotiations. *Journal of Language and Social Psychology, 17,* 72–96.

Donohue, W. A., & Kolt, R. (1992). *Managing interpersonal conflict.* Newbury Park, CA: Sage.

Donohue, W. A., & Roberto, A. J. (1993). Relational development in hostage negotiation. *Human Communication Research, 20,* 175–198.

Drake, L. E., & Donohue, W. A. (1996). Communication framing theory in conflict resolution. *Communication Research, 23*(3), 297–322.

Elliott, R. (1985). Helpful and nonhelpful events in brief counseling interviews: An empirical taxonomy. *Journal of Counseling Psychology, 32,* 307–322.

Fisher, R., & Brown, S. (1988). *Getting together.* New York: Penguin.

Fisher, R., & Ury, W. (1991). *Getting to yes.* New York: Penguin.

Folger, J. P., & Jones, T. S. (Eds.). (2004). *New directions in mediation: Communication research and perspectives.* Thousand Oaks, CA: Sage Publications.

Folger, J. P., Poole, M. S., & Stutman, R. K. (2000). *Working through conflict* (4th ed.). New York: Addison-Wesley Educational Publishers.

Folger, J. P., Poole, M. S., & Stutman, R. K. (2005). *Working through conflict* (5th ed.). Boston, MA: Pearson.

Giebels, E., & Noelanders, S. (2004). *Crisis negotiations: A multiparty perspective.* Veenendaal, The Netherlands: Universal Press.

Goffman, E. (1967). *Interaction ritual essays on face-to-face behavior.* Garden City, NY: Anchor Books, Doubleday & Company.

Gottlieb, J., Lin, S., & Hanley, C. (2004, December 18). *Mental illness plagued church musical director.* Los Angeles, CA: Los Angeles Times.

Gray, B. (2006). Mediation as framing and framing within mediation. In M. S. Herrman (Ed.), *Handbook of mediation* (pp. 193–216). Malden, MA: Blackwell Publishing.

Hammer, M. R. (1997). Negotiating across the cultural divide: Intercultural dynamics in crisis incidents. In R. G. Rogan, M. R. Hammer, & C. R. V. Zandt (Eds.), *Dynamic processes of crisis negotiations: Theory, research and practice* (pp. 105–114). Westport, CT: Praeger Press.

Hammer, M. R. (1999, February 16–17). *Using the FIRE model in crisis situations.* Paper presented at the Baltimore Hostage Negotiation Conference, Baltimore, MD.

Hammer, M. R. (2001). Conflict negotiation under crisis conditions. In W. F. Eadie & P. E. Nelson (Eds.), *The language of conflict and resolution* (pp. 57–80). Thousand Oaks, CA: Sage.

Hammer, M. R. (2002b). *The intercultural conflict style (ICS) inventory.* Ocean Pines, MD: Hammer Consulting, LLC.

Hammer, M. R. (2002c). *The intercultural conflict style (ICS) inventory: Interpretive guide.* Ocean Pines, MD: Hammer Consulting, LLC.

Hammer, M. R. (2003). *The intercultural conflict style (ICS) inventory: Facilitator's manual.* Ocean Pines, MD: Hammer Consulting, LLC.

Hammer, M. R. (2005a). *S.A.F.E. field guide.* Ocean Pines, MD: Hammer Consulting, LLC.

Hammer, M. R. (2005b). *S.A.F.E. assessment tools.* Ocean Pines, MD: Hammer Consulting, LLC.

Hammer, M. R. (2005d). The intercultural conflict style inventory: A conceptual framework and measure of intercultural conflict approaches. *International Journal of Intercultural Research, 29,* 675–695.

Hammer, M. R. (2007). *Saving lives: The S.A.F.E. model for negotiating hostage and crisis incidents.* Westport, CT: Praeger Publishing.

Hammer, M. R., & Rogan, R. G. (1997). Negotiation models in crisis situations: The value of a communication based approach. In R. G. Rogan, M. R. Hammer, & C. R. V. Zandt (Eds.), *Dynamic processes of crisis negotiations: Theory, research and practice* (pp. 9–23). Westport, CT: Praeger Press.

Hammer, M. R., & Rogan, R. G. (2004). Threats, demands, and communication dynamics: Negotiating the 1991 Talladega prison siege. *Journal of Police Crisis Negotiations, 4*(1), 45–56.

Hammer, M. R., Van Zandt, C. R., & Rogan, R. G. (1994). Crisis/hostage negotiation team profile of demographic and functional characteristics. *FBI Law Enforcement Bulletin, 63,* 8–11.

Hill, C. E., Helms, J. E., Tichenor, V., Spiegel, S. B., O'Grady, K. E., & Perry, S. E. (1988). Effects of therapist response mode in brief psychotherapy. *Journal of Counseling Psychology, 35,* 222–233.

Hovland, C., Janis, I., & Kelly, H. (1953). *Communication and persuasion.* New Haven, CT: Yale University Press.

Hunt, D. E. (1987). *Beginning with ourselves: In practice, theory and human affairs.* Cambridge, MA: Brookline Books.

Johnson, D. W. (1997). *Reaching out* (6th ed.). Boston, MA: Allyn & Bacon.

Jones, T. S. (2001). Emotional communication in conflict: Essence and impact. In W. Eadie & P. Nelson (Eds.), *The language of conflict resolution* (pp. 81–104). Thousand Oaks, CA: Sage.

Jones, T. S. (2006). Emotion in mediation: Implications, applications, opportunities, and challenges. In M. S. Herrman (Ed.), *Handbook of mediation* (pp. 277–305). Malden, MA: Blackwell.

Kimmel, M., Pruitt, D. G., Magenau, J., Konar-Goldband, E., & Carnevale, P. J. (1980). The effects of trust, aspiration, and gender on negotiation tactics. *Journal of Personality and Social Psychology, 38,* 9–23.

Lazarus, R. S. (1991). *Emotion and adaptation.* New York: Oxford University Press.

Lazarus, R. S. (1994). Universal antecedents of the emotions. In P. Ekman & R. J. Davidson (Eds.), *The nature of emotion: Fundamental questions* (pp. 163–171). New York: Oxford University Press.

Lewis, M., & Haviland, J. M. (1993). *Handbook of emotions.* New York: Guilford Press.

Lindskold, S., & Han, G. (1988). GRIT as a foundation for integrative bargaining. *Personality and Social Psychology Bulletin, 14,* 335–345.

Littlejohn, S., & Domenici, K. (2006). A facework frame for mediation. In M. S. Herrman (Ed.), *Handbook of mediation* (pp. 228–246). Malden, MA: Blackwell Publishing.

McMains, M. J., & Mullins, W. C. (2006). *Crisis negotiations: Managing critical incidents and hostage situations in law enforcement and corrections* (3rd ed.). Cincinnati, OH: Anderson Publishing.

Miron, M. S., & Goldstein, A. P. (1979). *Hostage.* New York: Pergamon.

Noesner, G. W. (1999). Negotiation concepts for commanders. *FBI Law Enforcement Bulletin, 68,* 6–14.

Noesner, G. W., & Webster, M. (1997, August). Crisis intervention: Using active listening skills in negotiations. *FBI Law Enforcement Bulletin, 66,* 13–19.

Northrup, T. A. (1989). The dynamic of identity in personal and social conflict. In L. Kriesberg, T. Northrup, & S. J. Thorson (Eds.), *Intractable conflicts and their transformation* (pp. 55–82). Syracuse, NY: Syracuse University Press.

Pruitt, D. G., & Carnevale, P. J. (1993). *Negotiation in social conflict.* Pacific Cove, CA: Brooks/Cole.

Putnam, L. L., & Holmer, M. (1992). Framing, reframing, and issue development. In L. L. Putnam & M. E. Roloff (Eds.), *Communication and negotiation* (pp. 128–155). Newbury Park, CA: Sage.

Putnam, L. L., & Roloff, M. E. (1992). Communication perspectives on negotiation. In L. L. Putnam & M. E. Roloff (Eds.), *Communication and negotiation* (pp. 1–17). Newbury Park, CA: Sage.

Retzinger, S. M. (1993). *Violent emotions: Shame and rage in marital quarrels.* Thousand Oaks, CA: Sage Publications.

Robbery suspects captured after police chase. (2007). Retrieved February 1, 2007, from Nbc4.com.

Roberts, A. R. (1991). *Contemporary perspectives on crisis intervention and prevention.* Englewood Cliffs, NJ: Prentice-Hall.

Rogan, R. G. (1990). *An interaction analysis of negotiator and hostage-taker identity-goal, relational-goal, and language intensity message behavior within hostage negotiations: A descriptive investigation of three negotiations.* Unpublished doctoral dissertation, Michigan State University, East Lansing, MI.

Rogan, R. G. (1997). Emotion and emotional expression in crisis negotiation. In R. G. Rogan, M. R. Hammer, & C. R. V. Zandt (Eds.), *Dynamic processes of crisis negotiation: Theory, research, and practice* (pp. 25–44). Westport, CT: Praeger.

Rogan, R.G. (1999). F.I.R.E: A communication based approach for understanding crisis negotiation. In O. Adang & E. Giebels (Eds.), *To save lives* (pp. 29–45). Amsterdam, The Netherlands: Elsevier.

Rogan, R. G., Donohue, W. A., & Lyles, J. (1990). Gaining and exercising control in hostage taking negotiations using empathetic perspective-taking. *International Journal of Group Tensions, 20,* 77–90.

Rogan, R. G., & Hammer, M. R. (1994). Crisis negotiations: A preliminary investigation of facework in naturalistic conflict. *Journal of Applied Communication Research, 22,* 216–231.

Rogan, R. G., & Hammer, M. R. (1995). Assessing message affect in crisis negotiations: An exploratory study. *Human Communication Research, 21,* 553–574.

Rogan, R. G., & Hammer, M. R. (1998). An exploratory investigation of message affect behavior: A comparison among African-Americans and Euro-Americans. *Journal of Language and Social Psychology, 17*(4), 449–464.

Rogan, R. G., & Hammer, M. R. (2002). Crisis/hostage negotiations: Conceptualization of a communication-based approach. In H. Giles (Ed.), *Law enforcement, communication, and community* (pp. 229–254). Amsterdam, The Netherlands: John Benjamins Publishing.

Rogan, R. G., & Hammer, M. R. (2006). The emerging field of hostage/crisis negotiation: A communication based perspective. In S. T.-T. J. Oetzel (Ed.), *Handbook of conflict communication* (pp. 451–478). Thousand Oaks, CA: Sage.

Rogan, R. G., Hammer, M. R., & Van Zandt, C. R. (1994). Profiling crisis negotiation teams. *Police Chief, 61,* 14–18.

Rogan, R. G., Hammer, M. R., & Van Zandt, C. R. (1997). *Dynamic processes of crisis negotiation: Theory, research and practice.* Westport, CT: Praeger.

Roloff, M. E., & Jordan, J. M. (1992). Achieving negotiation goals: The "fruits and foibles" of planning ahead. In L. L. Putnam & M. E. Roloff (Eds.), *Communication and negotiation* (pp. 21–45). Newbury Park, CA: Sage.

Rousseau, D. M., Sitkin, S. B., Burt, R. S., & Camerer, C. (1988). Not so different after all: A cross-discipline view of trust. *Academy of Management Review, 23,* 393–404.

Scherer, K. R., & Wallbot, H. G. (1994). Evidence for universality and cultural variation of different emotion response patterning. *Journal of Personality and Social Psychology, 66,* 310–328.

Scruggs, R., Zipperstein, S., Lyon, R., Gonzalez, V., Cousins, H., & Beverly, R. (1993a, February 28–April 19). *Report to the Deputy Attorney General on the events at Waco, Texas.* Washington DC: U.S. Department of Justice.

Scruggs, R., Zipperstein, S., Lyon, R., Gonzalez, V., Cousins, H., & Beverly, R. (1993b). *United States Department of Justice report on the events at Waco, Texas.* Washington, DC: U.S. Department of Justice.

Shaver, P. R., Schwartz, J., Kirson, D., & O'Connor, C. (1987). Emotional knowledge: Further explorations of a prototype approach. *Journal of Personality and Social Psychology, 52,* 1061–1086.

Tajfel, H. (1978). Social categorization, social identity, and social comparisons. In H. Tajfel (Ed.), *Differentiation between social groups* (pp. 61–68). London: Academic Press.

Tajfel, H. (1981). Social stereotypes and social groups. In J. Turner & H. Giles (Eds.), *Intergroup behavior* (pp. 144–167). Chicago, IL: University of Chicago Press.

Ting-Toomey, S. (1988). Intercultural conflict styles: A face-negotiation theory. In Y. Y. Kim & W. B. Gudykunst (Eds.), *Theories in intercultural communication* (pp. 213–235). Newbury Park, CA: Sage.

Ting-Toomey, S., & Kurogi, A. (1998). Facework competence in intercultural conflict: An updated face-negotiation theory. *International Journal of Intercultural Relations, 22,* 187–225.

Ting-Toomey, S., Yee-Jung, K. K., Shapiro, R. B., Garcia, W., Wright, R. J., & Oetzel, J. G. (2000). Ethnic/cultural identity salience and conflict styles in four US ethnic groups. *International Journal of Intercultural Relations, 24,* 47–82.

Watzlawick, P., Bavelas, J. B., & Jackson, D. D. (1967). *Pragmatics of human communication: A study of interactional patterns, pathologies, and paradoxes.* New York: W.W. Norton.

Wilson, S., & Putnam, L. L. (1990). Interaction goals in negotiation. In J. Anderson (Ed.), *Communication yearbook* (Vol. 13, pp. 374–406). Newbury Park, CA: Sage.

4

Communication Predictors and Social Influence in Crisis Negotiations

Ellen Giebels
Paul J. Taylor

COMMUNICATION PREDICTORS AND SOCIAL INFLUENCE IN CRISIS NEGOTIATIONS

An observation often made by police officers during their crisis negotiation training is that experienced negotiators have a natural style of interacting that is engaging, reassuring, and difficult to respond to with anger or violence. To the novice, these negotiators are talented in their ability to build rapport, create an atmosphere conducive to cooperation, and present unwelcome messages in a way that minimizes their negative connotations. In part, these abilities are the result of the experienced negotiator's use of techniques such as active listening skills (Rogan, Donohue, & Lyles, 1990; Taylor & Donohue, 2006) and conceptual models such as those that encourage a negotiator to consider emotional, relational, and substantive aspects of the negotiation (Rogan & Hammer, 2002; Taylor, 2002a). However, they are also the result of the negotiator's knowledge about how to present messages in a way that appeals to and persuades the perpetrator. For example, a police negotiator's suggestion to release an elderly hostage is often more effective when it is preceded by conversation about the perpetrator's considerate nature and wish not to harm the hostages. Experienced negotiators have learned that messages presented using known persuasive devices—particular phrases or sequences of arguments—can make them more conducive to compliance or cooperation than would otherwise be the case.

The use of persuasive messages, known in the negotiation literature as influence tactics, is the focus of this chapter. We define the use of influence tactics as deliberate actions by one individual (e.g., police negotiator) directed at another individual (e.g., perpetrator) that seek to alter the attitudes and/or behaviors of the target in a way that would not have otherwise occurred (cf. Gass & Seiter, 1999). We begin the chapter by mapping out the important role of influence tactics in contemporary crisis negotiation research and practice. We then present a theoretically derived set of 10 influence tactics and discuss how and when these tactics can influence the progress of negotiation. We end by outlining how the effectiveness of influence tactics can differ across cultures and negotiation contexts, and we provide some guidelines for negotiators wishing to identify when their messages are having an influence.

UNDERSTANDING NEGOTIATION

In reflecting on what we know about negotiation, it can be useful to divide our understanding into two levels. One level of understanding is focused on the interpersonal factors that fuel crisis negotiation and how changes in these factors allow an interaction to begin, unfold, and resolve. The need to develop affiliation, reduce crisis intensity, and respond to the perpetrator's "face" issues are among the factors that have been shown to play a role in the progress of negotiation (Donohue & Roberto, 1993; Giebels & Noelanders, 2004; Rogan & Hammer, 1994; Taylor, 2002a) and its success (Taylor, 2002b). These factors provide a framework from which a negotiator can begin to understand the issues that drive a crisis negotiation as a whole. By considering these factors, a negotiator is able to construct informed answers to questions such as "What is it I am trying to achieve?," "What factors are making this individual behave this way?," and "How should I approach this interaction to gain trust?" This type of understanding is thus oriented toward enhancing strategic decisions.

The second level of understanding centers on the cues and responses that underlie and give rise to the patterns found at the strategic level (Giebels & Noelanders, 2004; Taylor & Donald, 2003; Weingart, Prietula, Hyder, & Genovese, 1999). The focus here is toward the interconnections among messages, the responses typically elicited by certain cues, and the way in which these cue —response sequences build to move a negotiation down a particular path. For example, messages that draw on rational persuasion and logic are often effective when presented to a Dutch perpetrator, but they can have a very different effect when presented to a perpetrator who was brought up in a collectivist culture such as China. Understanding such cue—response patterns may be thought of as bottom—up or focused on the building blocks of negotiation. An understanding at this level allows negotiators to respond to messages in ways that have been found to increase persuasion; as such, this knowledge may be seen as oriented toward tactical decisions about how to achieve strategic objectives.

The topic of influence tactics fits principally in the second level of understanding. For example, negotiators who want to address the issue of hostage safety may try to elicit a desired response by promising something in return, by referring to their loved ones and their distress, or by warning them of the consequences of not treating the hostage well. These three messages incorporate different types of influence, but each is aimed at achieving the higher level strategic goal of obtaining information and placing the focus of interaction onto the hostages. Thus, strategic goals may be translated into different influence tactics at a microlevel. Tactics are message tools that can be applied at particular times to achieve higher level (sub-) goals of negotiation.

MESSAGES WITH INFLUENCE

A first step in understanding how messages may be designed to influence a perpetrator is to understand the different forms of influence that are available. In the existing literature, three lines of research stand out as relevant to a categorization of influence. The most significant work has been done by experimental social psychologist Robert Cialdini (for a recent discussion, see Cialdini, 2001). Cialdini identifies a number of tactics based on six psychological mechanisms, each of which has been verified through controlled experimental studies. For example, Cialdini showed that people are more likely to take a particular course of action when they believe that others are doing, or would do, the same thing, something he referred to as the principle of social proof. A second area of work stems from communication theory, where researchers have considered influence at the dyadic level, often under the term *compliance-gaining*. For example, in their review of compliance-gaining research, Kellerman and Cole (1994) show that demonstrating some authority on a subject is a good way of encouraging an individual to take your word for it. Finally, organizational psychologists have conducted some research into the effectiveness of different influence tactics on workforce behavior. For example, Higgins, Judge, and Ferris (2003) focus on the relative occurrence and effectiveness of different managerial influence styles in work situations. They find that one effective method of influencing others to work is for the manager to rationalize or rationally persuade the other as to why a particular piece of work is worthwhile.

THE TABLE OF TEN

The three fields of research described earlier propose a range of different influence tactics. Some distinguish as few as 6 types of influence, whereas others distinguish as many as 20 different tactics. Some of these tactics, such as rational persuasion, exerting pressure, and legitimizing, have clear exemplar in the dialogue of crisis negotiations. Others, such as consulting or inspiring, are arguably less applicable to the crisis negotiation context. To determine which influence tactics are most applicable, the first author recently conducted a series of studies involving both interviews with Dutch and Belgian police negotiators and observations of their negotiation behavior in practice (see Giebels & Noelanders, 2004, for details). These analyses suggest that a set of 10 categories of influence behavior are most applicable to crisis negotiation. These tactics, known as the Table of Ten (Giebels, 2002), are outlined in this section.

Table 4.1 summarizes the 10 influence tactics, together with the principles of influence on which they are based. To unpack the tactics presented in Table 4.1, it is useful to distinguish between tactics that are primarily connected with the sender and his or her relationship with the other party (relational tactics) and tactics that are primarily connected with the content of the message and the information conveyed to the other party (content tactics).[1]

More important, this distinction brings to light a fundamental tension that exists in crisis negotiations. On the one hand, police negotiators must work hard to reduce the emotionality of the crisis, which they achieve through empathic, uncritical messages that are supportive of the perpetrator's concerns about issues such as personal safety and self-worth. On the other hand, there is a need for police negotiators to acknowledge the inappropriate actions of the perpetrator and work toward a realistic, substantive resolution. This side of negotiation is inher-

Table 4.1 The Table of Ten Influence Tactics

Tactic	Underlying Principle	Description of Behavior
Being kind	Sympathy	All friendly, helpful behavior
Being equal	Similarity	Statements aimed at something the parties have in common
Being credible	Authority	Behavior showing expertise or proving you are reliable
Emotional appeal	Self-image	Playing on the emotions of the other
Intimidation	Deterrence/fear	Threatening with punishment or accusing the other personally
Imposing a restriction	Scarcity	Delay behavior or making something available in a limited way
Direct pressure	Power of repetition	Exerting pressure on the other in a neutral manner by being firm
Legitimizing	Legitimacy	Referring to what has been agreed on in society or with others
Exchanging	Reciprocity	Give-and-take behavior
Rational persuasion	Cognitive consistency	Use persuasive arguments and logic

ently less empathic and more focused on content, with negotiators often unable to conciliate to the perpetrator's demands and compelled to disagree over the form of a resolution. As Taylor and Donohue (2006) note, police negotiators are required to handle the complexity of expanding the "emotional pie," as well as expanding the traditional "substantive pie." The tactics outlined in Table 4.1 help negotiators achieve both of these objectives.

RELATIONAL TACTICS

Three influence tactics within the Table of Ten may be considered relationally oriented in their focus. These relational-oriented tactics all have more to do with the sender and his or her relationship with the other person than with the substantive content of the message. The first tactic, *Being kind*, refers to a message that presents a willingness to listen to someone and have sympathy for his or her situation. It is based on the psychological principle that people are more open to, and let themselves be influenced by, people whom they like (Karras, 1974). The second tactic, *Being equal*, is based on the well-established principle that the sender of a message has a bigger chance of influencing behavior when the receiver perceives the sender as similar to them in their attitude, background, or viewpoint (Perloff, 1993). This perceived similarity may come from messages that share a common experience, create a mutual external enemy, or emphasize mutual interdependence (Giebels, 2002; McMains & Mullins, 2001). The impact of this inferred common understanding is to increase the perceived similarity and, consequently, the influence that is gained by the message (Byrne, 1971). Finally, the third tactic, *Being credible*, refers to instances in which the sender indicates to the other party that he or she has the position and the capacity to handle a situation and that he or she can be trusted. The credibility of a message source is arguably one of the oldest known methods of social influence. Aristotle, for example, refers to this method as "ethos" in his classical works *The Rhetoric and Poetics* (Aristotle, trans 1954). According to Hovland, Janis, and Kelly (1953), credibility consists of two components: expertise and reliability. A negotiator that conveys both of these facets of credibility typically increases the influence of his or her message.

CONTENT TACTICS

The remaining seven influence tactics of the Table of Ten are geared toward framing the content of the message. By using the tactic *Emotional appeal*, negotiators present messages that play on the other party's personal feelings, values, ideals, and self-image. In *Rhetoric and Poetics*, Aristotle refers to this as "pathos" (Aristotle, trans 1954). A negotiator's messages may appeal to the other's sense of humanity, refer to the positive feeling that the right choice may bring about, or point to the respect that will be gained by choosing the right solution. In contrast, the tactic *Intimidation* involves presenting messages that utilize the power to impose punishments if the request or demand is not met (French & Raven, 1959). This tactic emerges in a range of strongly compelling messages, such as warnings, threats, and personal attacks.

The tactic *Imposing a restriction* is based on the "scarcity principle." According to this principle, people perceive commodities or possibilities as more valuable when they are difficult to obtain or when their availability is likely to be short-lived (Cialdini, 1984). Tactics that impose a restriction include the postponement of certain concessions, but also the association of a time limit or deadline to an offer. The tactic *Direct pressure* refers to direct efforts to persuade or compel the other party to act. These are often repeated so that the other gets used to the idea, and they are presented with reference to reasons as to why the other person should act. Messages that repeatedly issue a demand or deliberately attempt to direct discussions toward an important issue both fall into this tactic category. The tactic *Legitimizing* is an indirect form of influencing, in which the negotiator refers to external actors, events, or issues to illustrate the request as appropriate or common to what others do. To accomplish this, a negotiator may refer to existing rules, laws, or procedures, or he or she may refer to what an influential person (e.g., a religious leader, respected member of the perpetrator's family) thinks about the issue at hand.

The tactic *Exchanging* is based on the "principle of reciprocity" (Cialdini, 2001), the observation that people often feel obliged to respond to a gesture of giving (e.g., compliment, gift) by giving something in return. This sense of obligation is considered by many researchers as universal across cultures (Tinsley, 2001). A negotiator may use this principle by making a concession, but also by asking for something in return (i.e., the "you scratch my back and I'll scratch yours" tactic). Finally, the last tactic of the Table of Ten, *Rational persuasion*, aims at behavioral change through a change of attitude. By means of a logical argument, the negotiator tries to convince the perpetrator that his or her request is reasonable and in accordance with joint goals (Eagly & Chaiken, 1984). This tactic was recognized by Aristotle as "logos," one of the most influential forms of persuasion (Aristotle, trans 1954).

With this approach, because reasoning and arguing are central elements, the negotiator can make use of "the principle of commitment and consistency" (Cialdini, 2001). This principle refers to the need to bring our thoughts or behavior in line with our earlier behavior, attitude, or decision, especially when the early behavior is witnessed by others. An individual is more likely to accept a particular line of argument if to do so would be consistent with what he or she had previously said and done. The following dialogue between a police negotiator and a perpetrator labels the different communicative statements of the police negotiator in terms of influence tactics. To examine the extent to which police negotiators make use of the different influence tactics, and the extent to which the tactics might be considered effective in the various contexts encountered by the police, the next sections draw on findings from ongoing analyses of 35 hostage incidents (Giebels & Noelanders, 2004; Giebels, Noelanders, & Vervaeke, 2005; Giebels & Taylor, 2006, in press). All of the incidents were conducted by phone

Example of Negotiation Interaction: Influence Tactics

Speaker	Message	Influence Tactic
Police negotiator	Marco speaking.	
Perpetrator	Romeo here.	
Police negotiator	Romeo, how are you doing?	*Being kind*
Perpetrator	Do you have the 100,000 in cash ready?	
Police negotiator	I am working on it.	*Imposing an restriction*
Perpetrator	Don't fuck with me!	
Police negotiator	No, I'm not. But it is quite an amount of money, and I have to make sure that people do not react suspiciously.	*Rational persuasion*
Perpetrator	Just 100,000 right away.	
Police Negotiator	I'll do my best. Did I ever let you down before?	*Being credible*
Perpetrator	No, but …	
Police Negotiator	I would like to talk to Cindy when I have the money.	*Exchanging*
Perpetrator	That's ok.	
Police Negotiator	Is she ok? Please take good care of her.	*Emotional appeal*
Perpetrator	Yes.	
Police Negotiator	Thanks. You and I, we are doing great.	*Being equal*

and recorded or transcribed, and they all took place over the past 10 years in either The Netherlands or Belgium. All police negotiators and perpetrators were male. In the following sections, we review the results of these studies in combination with findings from previous research.

USE OF INFLUENCE TACTICS

The Dutch–Belgian research project showed that as much as 70% of the messages that police negotiators convey in crisis negotiations can be characterized as influence tactics (Giebels & Noelanders, 2004). Figure 4.1 presents the frequency of tactic use for the Table of Ten as a function of three types of incidents: sieges, kidnaps, and extortion attempts. Overall, approximately half of the influence tactics could be labeled as relational strategies and the other half as content strategies. As can be seen from Figure 4.1, the frequency with which negotiators use each of the 10 influence tactics differs considerably. Regardless of the type of incident, *Being kind* is the most frequently used influence tactic. This is perhaps not surprising because *Being kind* is at the center of efforts to use empathic and attentive active listening (Vecchi, Van Hasselt, & Romano, 2005). It is also consistent with the finding that nearly 80% of all hostage situations are "relationship-

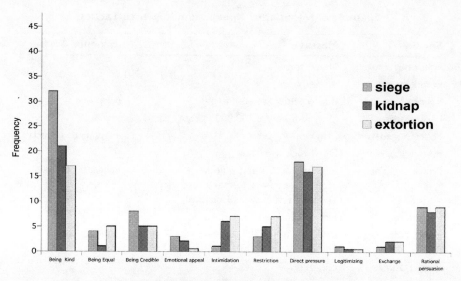

Figure 4.1. Table of Ten influence tactic.

In contrast, other tactics such as *Intimidation* are used sparingly in sieges, but driven" (Van Hasselt, Flood, Romano, Vecchi, de Fabrique, & Dalfonzo, 2005). more frequently in the interactions of extortion incidents. These negotiations are usually about tangible issues and therefore seem to resemble more daily, businesslike negotiations, in which threats are usually considered a central strategy (cf. Giebels, De Dreu, & Van de Vliert, 2003).

It is interesting to note at this point that the pattern of tactic use identified in Figure 4.1 is also found in research with Dutch and Belgian students (asking them to indicate which strategies they consider effective in crisis situations) (Giebels, 2002) and in analyses of influence tactics of Dutch police detectives encountering suspects in police interviews (Beune, Giebels, & Sanders, in press). Although the variation in tactic use might have resulted from the fact that negotiators are more comfortable using some tactics than others, it is also likely to be a reflection of the extent to which negotiators perceive the tactics as useful to the interaction in which they were involved. This raises an important point: Influence tactics vary in their appropriateness and effectiveness according to the circumstances and timing of their use. This notion is well known at the strategic level (Dolnik, 2003; Donohue & Taylor, 2003). For example, phase models of crisis negotiation prescribe a series of changes in the focus of dialogue over time. According to these models, the changes represent the most efficient way of moving a crisis negotiation toward a successful resolution (Donohue, Ramesh, Kaufmann, & Smith, 1991; Holmes, 1992). However, alongside its importance to strategic decisions, the importance of specific circumstances is applicable to our understanding of tactical aspects of crises. Indeed, some of our recent research has shown that the effectiveness of influence tactics is dependent on both the crisis negotiation context and the cultural background of the perpetrator. In the next section, we discuss how the effectiveness of influence tactics has been found to vary across the circumstances of the crisis.

EFFECTIVENESS OF INFLUENCE TACTICS ACROSS INCIDENT TYPE, TIME PERIOD, AND CULTURES

Although an extensive range of influence tactics are documented in the literature, there are surprisingly few studies into their relative effectiveness in different contexts. This means that the choice of a tactic is primarily based on experience and is taken rather intuitively. To support the knowledge learned through experience, we have conducted a series of detailed analyses on the Dutch–Belgium data set that examine both simple cue–response contingencies (Giebels & Noelanders, 2004) and more sophisticated behavioral interrelationships using Taylor's proximity coefficient (Giebels & Taylor, 2006, in press; see also Taylor, 2006; Taylor & Donald, 2007). In the following sections, we review the results of these studies in combination with findings from previous research.

IMPACT OF TYPE OF INCIDENT

An important distinction with regard to crisis situations is between expressive and instrumental crises. In prototypical expressive situations, such as suicide cases and escalated domestic quarrels, the communication is usually intense and emotional, and the interaction may be regarded as synonymous with crisis counseling (Donohue et al., 1991). Typical examples of expressive crises are situations arising from domestic problems or complex suicide attempts. In contrast, instrumental crisis negotiations look much like business transactions because the victim or hostage is used as leverage by the perpetrators. Typical examples of instrumental crises are kidnappings aimed at obtaining money and extortions such as the threat of product contamination (the threat of poisoning retail products and endangering the lives of innocent customers). In Europe, expressive crises represent approximately 60% of the incidents that the police encounter (Giebels, 1999). However, the number of instrumentally oriented negotiation situations is increasing in both Europe and around the world (see Giebels, 1999). In the same way that instrumental and expressive crises are associated with different contextual characteristics, so the interactions that occur during these crises are most influenced by different kind of influence tactics. In comparison with expressive incidents, our analyses show that instrumental incidents are characterized by greater symmetry in the behavior of the negotiator and the perpetrator (Giebels & Noelanders, 2004). This particularly applies to the strategies of *Rational persuasion* and *Exchanging* (Giebels & Taylor, 2006, in press). As such, these negotiations are similar to many day-to-day, businesslike negotiations (e.g., Giebels, De Dreu, & Van de Vliert, 2000; Giebels et al., 2003).

In contrast, perceived relationship difficulties and resentments (e.g., abandonment, rejection) appear to serve as precipitants to a majority of expressive critical incidents (Van Hasselt et al., 2005). For example, Harvey-Craig, Fisher, and Simpson (1997) found that correlates of expressive prison incidents (e.g., those involving suicide threats) were not substantive demands or persuasive discussion, but physical and verbal aggression, and demands to speak with their family. These behaviors are both arguably focused on relational issues, the establishment of relational dominance, and a desire to have contact with a significant other. Consequently, influence tactics that serve to mitigate the aggravating relational factors become primary to negotiation strategy. These tactics, our research suggests, include *Being kind* (i.e., showing sympathy, listening), making an *Emotional appeal* (i.e., asking attention for the victims), and *Legitimizing* (i.e., referring to the external context) (Giebels & Noelanders, 2004).

Finally, some research suggests that expressive situations contain more integrative potential than instrumental situations, which are often win–lose in nature (Giebels & Taylor, in press). That is, although tangible resources are usually the main issue at the table in instrumental negotiations, the co-occurrence of instrumental, social, and relational issues in more expressive crisis situations usually provides opportunities to integrate the interests of the parties involved.

IMPACT OF NEGOTIATION PHASE

Most phase models of negotiation distinguish among three phases (Douglas, 1957, 1962; Holmes, 1992; Putnam, Wilson, & Turner, 1990): the initial crisis phase, the problem-solving phase, and the ending phase. Influence tactics can be used throughout the three phases, but they are most central to the problem-solving phase (cf. Giebels & Noelanders, 2004). The *first phase* is characterized by acute crisis that is dominated by strong competitive behavior, particularly from the side of the perpetrator (Donohue et al., 1991). Police responses that convey a willingness to listen by *Being kind* and a desire to build rapport by *Being equal* (Giebels & Noelanders, 2004) usually prove to be effective in this first stage. Consequently, the interaction patterns are also more asymmetrical in nature.

In the *second phase*, where emotional aspects of the crisis have diminished, negotiations tend to involve less competition and become more dominated by reciprocal behaviour (Giebels & Taylor, 2006). For expressive situations, in particular, we found that the focus of negotiators' attention shifts from their own demands to areas of potential agreement, thereby allowing negotiators to occupy themselves with problem solving. Conversely, for instrumental incidents, this phase is more centered around distributive negotiation behaviors, such as *Rational persuasion* and *Intimidation* (Giebels & Taylor, in press; see also Adair &

Brett, 2004). Also interesting is the finding that, compared with the first phase, the tactic *Being kind* is more immediately followed by the perpetrator's use of *Intimidation*. Although being kind may be important for relationship building in the first stages of an incident, later use may be regarded as more inappropriate and may interfere with the task-related nature of the interaction.

In the third and final phase of negotiation, parties' standpoints come closer together and occupy themselves with the wording of the agreement and its implementation. This dynamic is most evident in the expressive incidents. Moreover, these efforts often occur within a context of the perpetrator becoming increasingly anxious and fearful because he or she perceives him or herself as more vulnerable with the release of the hostages and their eventual surrender. This makes the third phase a critical period for managing both emotionality and substantive issues, and relational- and content-based influence tactics both play a role in bringing the incident to a successful conclusion.

IMPACT OF CULTURAL BACKGROUND

Among the factors that shape crisis negotiations, and one that is becoming increasingly prevalent in applied settings, is the cultural difference between the parties. Police forces in the United States and Europe have reported a significant growth in the cultural diversity of perpetrators, particularly within kidnappings and extortions (Giebels & Noelanders, 2004; Ostermann, 2002; Taylor & Donohue, 2006). Such a trend reasserts the need for scholars to understand intercultural aspects of negotiation. Culture is often defined as the characteristic profile of a society with respect to its values, norms, and institutions (Lytle, Brett, Barsness, Tinsley, & Janssens, 1995). It is an important determinant of people's attitudes, self-construal, and behavior, and hence their strategic choices in conflict situations (cf. Pruitt & Kim, 2004). More specifically, and based on Hall's (1976) distinction between low- and high-context cultures, we distinguish between negotiations with perpetrators from low- and high-context cultures. Most individualistic Western societies, especially in Northern Europe and the Anglo-Saxon world, can be considered low-context cultures, whereas most collectivistic non-Western societies are considered high-context cultures (cf. Gudykunst & Ting-Toomey, 1988; see also Hofstede, 2001).

An important assumption that is characteristic of low-context communication is what Grice (1975; see also Gudykunst & Matsumoto, 1996) labeled the quality maxim: One should state only that which is believed to be true with sufficient evidence. This maxim implies that low-context communication is typically centered around logic and rationality compared with high-context communication (cf. Adair & Brett, 2004). This implication is consistent with research in a number of areas. For example, Ting-Toomey's work on cross-cultural communication (e.g., Ting-Toomey, 1988) suggests that confronting the other party with rational arguments and factual evidence is more central to American than to Chinese conflict environments (see also Fu & Yukl, 2000). Our recent analysis of 25 instrumental crisis negotiations with high- and low-context perpetrators (Giebels & Taylor, in press) shows that low-context perpetrators are found to be more likely to use *Rational persuasion* and reciprocate persuasive arguments of the police negotiator. This relative willingness to engage in rational debate was particularly prevalent for low-context perpetrators during the second half of the negotiation, when the crisis had diminished and more normative interaction had begun to take shape.

Interestingly, we also found significant differences in the immediacy with which negotiators reciprocated *Intimidation*. Although perpetrators form low-context cultures used more intimidation tactics, perpetrators from high-context cultures reciprocated *Intimidation* significantly more often than negotiators from low-context cultures. An explanation for this finding is that intimidation refers to a confrontational and assertive way of handling conflict that is consistent with low-context communication and considered more inappropriate in high-context cultures (Fu & Yukl, 2000). Consequently, high-context negotiators not only use *Intimidation* to a lesser extent, but they are also more likely to "punish" police negotiators who use them with counter-intimidation particularly because crisis negotiation centers on issues of "who is in charge" (Donohue & Roberto, 1993), and high-context negotiators may be more concerned with establishing dominance (Adair & Brett, 2004). This process may be reinforced by the confrontational nature of *Intimidation*, which draws attention to the need to preserve face —something that is considered more important within high-context rather than low-context cultures (Ting-Toomey & Oetzel, 2001).

COMMUNICATIVE DYNAMICS AND EFFICIENCY OF INFLUENCE TACTICS

A question of particular interest to negotiators who wish to use influence tactics in practice is: What tactic(s) is likely to bring about capitulation? This is, of course, a largely unanswerable question because success at any one time depends on a negotiator's goals and the perpetrator with whom he or she is dealing. However, one possible measure of utility is the extent to which different influence tactics were successful at eliciting compromise behavior from the perpetrator. This measure recognizes that an important goal for the police negotiator is to turn the negotiation into a more normative interaction characterized by mutual concession making. It is also consistent with research examining the behavioral correlates of successful win–lose negotiations (De Dreu, 1995; Hornstein, 1965; Michener, Vaske, Shleifer, Plazewski, & Chapman, 1975). The decision to focus on the occurrence of compromising behavior, rather than overall negotiation outcome, is consistent with our focus on cue–response dynamics. However, importantly, the use of an immediate measure of efficiency has value beyond research, providing a negotiator with a way of obtaining more tangible feedback on progress beyond more macrojudgments of success.

In our analyses, low-context negotiators were found to be more likely to respond to *Rational persuasion* in a compromising way (Giebels & Taylor, in press). Interestingly, the effect on compromising behavior occurred irrespective of the negotiation phase. Thus, it seems sufficient to use arguments to elicit cooperation regardless of whether the other party is able to fully process or react to them. The reason for this may be that logic and deductive thinking is generally highly valued in low-context cultures (Gelfand & Dyer, 2000). It may also be seen as an indirect way of showing respect (e.g., "You're an intelligent person, so I want to walk you though my thinking on this topic").

As well as differences in the response to *Rational persuasion*, high- and low-context negotiators also show a difference in their willingness to respond by cooperation following police negotiator *Intimidation*. Specifically, *Intimidation* was found to be more effective at eliciting information sharing in low-context cultures compared with high-context cultures. This is particularly true during early stages of the negotiation. This finding is in line with our previous discussion suggesting that *Intimidation* is more consistent with low-context communication. Thus, our research suggests that both *Rational persuasion* and *Intimidation* seem to be more effective in negotiations with perpetrators from low- rather than high-context cultures. There is also some research and theory suggesting that affective influence tactics, such as an *Emotional appeal*, are likely to be more effective in negotiations with high-context perpetrators (cf. Adair & Brett, 2004).

CONCLUSIONS: PRACTICAL USE
OF THE TABLE OF TEN

The Table of Ten provides a framework for thinking about the ways in which negotiation goals may be presented in a convincing way. In our work, it is providing a basis for constructing research into influence tactics and their effectiveness in helping negotiators achieve their goals at different times and in different contexts. In the work of police negotiators, the framework is providing a systematic way of weighing up different approaches to influence at both planning and delivery stages. Specifically, the framework is useful in at least two ways. First, in a general sense, the Table of Ten has reportedly helped police negotiators in their efforts to diversify their use of influence tactics, and it has facilitated their efforts to switch between different tactics to suit the goal and conditions at hand. This may be especially true during periods of interaction, when negotiators are seeking to make sense of the situation and break through undesirable interaction patterns (Ormerod, Barrett, & Taylor, 2008). The Table of Ten provides a way of monitoring negotiators' use of the available repertoire of influence tactics. If they have inadvertently focused their messages around content-focused persuasion, then this becomes clear in the monitoring process, and the negotiators can consider whether it is worth switching to some of the relational focus influence tactics, such as *Being equal* and *Being kind*. Moreover, by keeping a log of a perpetrator's responses to different influence tactics (either mentally or physically using a chart), negotiators are able to develop a useful portrait of the perpetrator's responses to different attempts at influence.

Second, the Table of Ten framework may help negotiators make a more conscious selection of influence tactic based on what is known about the type of incident, the incident phase, and the cultural background of the perpetrator. By associating research findings with different tactics in the framework, police negotiators are able to bring to their strategies a clear understanding of the complex cue–response relationships that have been identified in the influence literature. For example, one important message from our research is that use of *Rational persuasion* and *Intimidation* is likely to be more effective in negotiations with perpetrators from low- rather than high-context cultures. Thus, when negotiating with a perpetrator from a high-context culture, police negotiators might consider making less use of rational persuasion and more use of affective influence tactics, such as *Emotional appeals*. Our research to date suggests that this approach is likely to receive a more positive response from the high-context perpetrator.

It is important to view the Table of Ten not as an attempt to teach experienced negotiators something that they already know. Rather, the Table of Ten is designed to act as a reference point that facilitates recall and implementation of influence tactics at stressful, time-critical moments. Indeed, the influence tactics identified in the Table of Ten are applicable to other situations that deviate from normative, good-faith interactions. Within daily police practice, one example of where the Table of Ten may play a role is in police interviews. In line with crisis negotiations, these situations are also often characterized by opposing interests and low mutual trust. The police are regularly faced with an aggressive, distrustful interviewee, and the stakes of the interview can create an uncomfortable tension. In such instances, as in the crisis negotiation context, having available a knowledge of proven tactics for presenting messages effectively can bring about the confidence and interaction style needed to achieve a successful conclusion.

ACKNOWLEDGMENTS

This work was supported by a British Council—NWO Partnership Programme in Science grant (No. PS844) awarded to both authors.

NOTES

1. Most of the tactics shown in Table 4.1 may be placed within the five broad categories of conflict behavior and negotiation (i.e., forcing, yielding, compromising, avoiding, and problem solving) found within the conflict management literature (e.g., Rubin & Kim, 2004; Van de Vliert, 1997).

REFERENCES

Adair, W. L., & Brett, J. M. (2004). Culture and negotiation processes. In M. J. Gelfand & J. M. Brett (Eds.), *The handbook of negotiation and culture* (pp. 158–176). Palo Alto, CA: Stanford University Press.

Aristotle. (1954). *The rhetoric and poetics* (W. R. Roberts & I. Bywater, Trans.). New York: Modern Library.

Beune, K., Giebels, E., & Sanders, K. (in press). Are you talking to me? The effectiveness of influencing behaviours while interviewing suspects with different cultural backgrounds. *Psychology, Crime and Law.*

Byrne, D. (1971). *The attraction paradigm.* New York: Academic Press.

Cialdini, R. B. (1984). *Influence: How and why people agree to things.* New York: William Morrow.

Cialdini, R. B. (2001). *Influence: Science and practice* (4th ed.). New York: HarperCollins.

De Dreu, C. K. W. (1995). Coercive power and concession making in bilateral negotiation. *Journal of Conflict Resolution, 39,* 646–670.

Dolnik, A. (2003). Contrasting dynamics of crisis negotiations: Barricade versus kidnapping incidents. *International Negotiation, 8,* 495–526.

Donohue, W. A., Ramesh, C., Kaufmann, G., & Smith, R. (1991). Crisis bargaining in intense conflict situations. *International Journal of Group Tension, 21,* 133–154.

Donohue, W. A., & Roberto, A. J. (1993). Relational development as negotiated order in hostage negotiation. *Human Communication Research, 20,* 175–198.

Donohue, W. A., & Taylor, P. J. (2003). Testing the role effect in terrorist negotiations. *International Negotiation, 8,* 527–547.

Douglas, A. (1957). The peaceful settlement of industrial and intergroup disputes. *Journal of Conflict Resolution, 1,* 69–81.

Douglas, A. (1962). *Industrial peacemaking.* New York: Columbia University Press.

Eagly, A., & Chaiken, S. (1984). Cognitive theories of persuasion. In L. Berkowitz (Ed.), *Advances in experimental social psychology* (Vol. 17, pp. 267–359). San Diego, CA: Academic Press.

French, J. R. P., Jr., & Raven, B. (1959). The bases of social power. In D. Cartwright (Ed.), *Studies in social power* (pp. 150–167). Ann Arbor, MI: Institute for Social Research.

Fu, P. P., & Yukl, G. (2000). Perceived effectiveness of influence tactics in the United States and China. *Leadership Quarterly, 11,* 251–266.

Gass, R. H., & Seiter, J. S. (1999). *Persuasion, social influence and compliance gaining.* Needham Heights, MA: Allyn & Bacon.

Gelfand, M., & Dyer, N. (2000). A cultural perspective on negotiation: Progress, pitfalls, and prospects. *Applied Psychology: An International Review, 49,* 62–99.

Giebels, E. (1999). A comparison of crisis negotiation across Europe. In O. Adang & E. Giebels (Eds.), *To save lives: Proceedings of the first European conference on crisis negotiations* (pp. 13–20). Amsterdam: Elsevier.

Giebels, E. (2002). Beinvloeding in gijzelingsonderhandelingen: De tafel van tien [Influencing in hostage negotiations: The table of ten]. *Nederlands Tijdschrift voor de Psychologie [Dutch Journal of Psychology], 57,* 145–154.

Giebels, E., De Dreu, C. K. W., & Van de Vliert, E. (2000). Interdependence in negotiation: Effects of exit options and social motive on distributive and integrative negotiation. *European Journal of Social Psychology, 30,* 255–272.

Giebels, E., De Dreu, C. K. W., & Van de Vliert, E. (2003). No way out or swallow the bait of shared exit options in negotiations: The influence of social motives and interpersonal trust. *Group Processes and Intergroup Relations, 6,* 369–386.

Giebels, E., & Noelanders, S. (2004). *Crisis negotiations: A multiparty perspective.* Veendendaal, Netherlands: Universal Press.

Giebels, E., Noelanders, S., & Vervaeke, G. (2005). The hostage experience: Implications for negotiation strategies. *Clinical Psychology & Psychotherapy: An International Review, 12,* 241–253.

Giebels, E., & Taylor, P. J. (2006, June). *Cross-cultural differences in patterns of influence.* Presentation at the 19th annual conference of the International Association for Conflict Management, Montreal, Canada.

Giebels, E., & Taylor, P. J. (in press). Interaction patterns in crisis negotiations: Persuasive arguments and cultural differences. *Journal of Applied Psychology.*

Grice, H. P. (1975). Logic and conversation. In P. Cole & J. L. Morgan (Eds.), *Syntax and semantics 3: Speech acts* (pp. 41–58). New York: Academic Press.

Gudykunst, W. B., & Matsumoto, Y. (1996). Cross-cultural variability of communication in personal relationships. In W. B. Gudykunst, S. Ting-Toomey, & T. Nishida (Eds.), *Communication in personal relationships across cultures* (pp. 57–77). Thousand Oaks, CA: Sage.

Gudykunst, W. B., & Ting-Toomey, S. (1988). *Culture and interpersonal communication.* Newbury Park, CA: Sage.

Hall, E. T. (1976). *Beyond culture.* Garden City, NY: Anchor Press/Doubleday.

Harvey-Craig, A., Fisher, N. J., & Simpson, P. (1997). An explanation of the profiling of hostage incidents in HM prison services. *Issues in Criminological and Legal Psychology, 29,* 41–46.

Higgins, C. A., Judge, T. A., & Ferris, G. R. (2003). Influence tactics and work outcomes: A meta-analysis. *Journal of Organizational Behaviour, 24,* 89–106.

Hofstede, G. (2001). *Culture's consequences: Comparing values, behaviors, institutions, and organizations across nations.* Thousand Oaks, CA: Sage.

Holmes, M. E. (1992). Phase structures in negotiation. In L. L. Putnam & M. E. Roloff (Eds.), *Communication and negotiation* (pp. 83–105). Newbury Park, CA: Sage.

Hornstein, H. A. (1965). Effects of different magnitudes of threat upon interpersonal bargaining. *Journal of Experimental Social Psychology, 1,* 282–293.

Hovland, C. I., Janis, I. L., & Kelly, H. H. (1953). *Communication and persuasion.* New Haven, CT: Yale University Press.

Karras, C. L. (1974). *Give and take: The complete guide to negotiate strategies and tactics.* New York: Thomas Y. Crowell Publishers.

Kellerman, K., & Cole, T. (1994). Classifying compliance gaining messages: Taxonomic disorder and strategic confusion. *Communication Theory, 4,* 3–60.

Lytle, A. L., Brett, J. M., Barsness, Z., Tinsley, C. H., & Janssens, M. (1995). A paradigm for quantitative cross-cultural research in organizational behavior. In B. M. Staw & L. L. Cummings (Eds.), *Research in organizational behavior* (Vol. 17, pp. 167–214). Greenwich, CT: JAI Press.

McMains, M. J., & Mullins, W. C. (2001). *Crisis negotiations: Managing critical incidents and hostage situations in law enforcement and corrections* (2nd ed.). Cincinnati, OH: Anderson Publishing.

Michener, H. A., Vaske, J. J., Schleifer, S. L., Plazewski, J. G., & Chapman, L. J. (1975). Factors affecting concession rate and threat usage in bilateral conflict. *Sociometry, 38,* 62–80.

Ormerod, T., Barrett, E., & Taylor, P. J. (2008). Sensemaking in criminal investigations. In J. M. Schraagen, L. Militello, T. Ormerod, & R. Lipshitz (Eds.), *Naturalistic decision making and macrocognition* (pp. 81–102). Aldershot, UK: Ashgate.

Ostermann, B. M. (2002). Cultural differences make negotiations different: Intercultural hostage negotiations. *Journal of Police Crisis Negotiation, 2,* 11–20.

Perloff, R. M. (1993). *The dynamics of persuasion.* Hillsdale, NJ: Lawrence Erlbaum.

Pruitt, D. G., & Kim, S. H. (2004). *Social conflict: Escalation, stalemate, and settlement* (rev. ed.). New York: McGraw-Hill.

Putnam, L. L., Wilson, S. R., & Turner, D. (1990). The evolution of police arguments in teachers' negotiation. *Argumentation, 3,* 129–152.

Rogan, R. G., Donohue, W. A., & Lyles, J. (1990). Gaining and exercising control in hostage taking negotiations using empathic perspective-taking. *International Journal of Group Tension, 20,* 77–90.

Rogan R. G., & Hammer, M. R. (1994). Crisis negotiations: A preliminary investigation of facework in naturalistic conflicts. *Journal of Applied Communication Research, 22,* 216–231.

Rogan, R. G., & Hammer, M. R. (2002). Crisis/hostage negotiations: A communication-based approach. In H. Giles (Ed.), *Law enforcement, communication, and community* (pp. 229–254). Amsterdam: John Benhamin.

Taylor, P. J. (2002a). A cylindrical model of communication behavior in crisis negotiations. *Human Communication Research, 28,* 7–48.

Taylor, P. J. (2002b). A partial order scalogram analysis of communication behavior in crisis negotiation with the prediction of outcome. *International Journal of Conflict Management, 13,* 4–37.

Taylor, P. J. (2006). Proximity coefficients as a measure of interrelationships in sequences of behavior. *Behavioral Research Methods, 38,* 42–50.

Taylor, P. J., & Donald, I. J. (2003). Foundations and evidence for an interaction based approach to conflict. *International Journal of Conflict Management, 14,* 213–232.

Taylor, P. J., & Donald, I. J. (2007). Testing the relationship between local cue-response patterns and global dimensions of communication behavior. *British Journal of Social Psychology, 46,* 273–298.

Taylor, P. J., & Donohue, W. A. (2006). Lessons from hostage negotiation. In A. Schneider & C. Honeymoon (Eds.), *The negotiator's fieldbook* (pp. 667–674). New York: American Bar Association Press.

Ting-Toomey, S. (1988). Intercultural conflict styles: A face negotiation theory. In Y. Y. Kim & W. Gudykunst (Eds.), *Theories in intercultural communication* (pp. 213–235). Newbury Park, CA: Sage.

Ting-Toomey, S., & Oetzel, J. G. (2001). *Managing intercultural conflict effectively.* Thousand Oaks, CA: Sage.

Tinsley, C. H. (2001). How negotiators get to yes: Predicting the constellation of strategies used across cultures to negotiate conflict. *Journal of Applied Psychology, 86,* 583–593.

Van Hasselt, V. B., Flood, J. J., Romano, S. J., Vecchi, G. M., de Fabrique, N., & Dalfonzo, V. A. (2005). Hostage-taking in the context of domestic violence: Some case examples. *Journal of Family Violence, 20,* 21–27.

Vecchi, G. M., Van Hasselt, V. B., & Romano, S. J. (2005). Crisis (hostage) negotiation: Current strategies and issues in high-risk conflict resolution. *Aggression and Violent Behavior, 10,* 533–551.

Van de Vliert, E. (1997). *Complex interpersonal conflict behaviour: Theoretical frontiers.* Hove, UK: Psychology Press.

Weingart, L. R., Prietula, M. J., Hyder, E. B., & Genovese, C. R. (1999). Knowledge and the sequential processes of negotiation: A Markov chain analysis of response-in-kind. *Journal of Experimental Social Psychology, 35,* 366–393.

5

Managing the Paradoxes in Crisis Bargaining

William A. Donohue

In several articles focusing on hostage negotiation, we have explored the concept of paradox in managing the crisis bargaining context (see Donohue & Hoobler, 2002, for a review). The major conclusion of these studies and essays is that crisis bargainers must learn to address, and even make explicit, some inherent paradoxes within the conflict context that work to escalate the cycle of destructive conflict interaction. The purpose of this chapter is to extend our understanding of the kinds of paradoxes that crisis negotiators face in making the transition to normative bargaining and ultimately constructive outcomes.

To begin, it might be useful to review the general frames that participants bring to the hostage negotiation process and then explore Relational Order Theory to better understand the inherent nature of paradox in conflict and how it impacts the bargaining process. The frameworks that will be used to extend the concept of paradox will include Muir's (1977) model of coercive relationships and the development of extortionate transactions to enact those relationships (Holmes, 1990) and work in dialectical tensions (Baxter, 1990; Rawlins, 1989). These frameworks will be integrated to provide a much richer strategy for thinking about how to better approach and manage relationships in crisis negotiations.

CRISIS AND NORMATIVE BARGAINING

In an earlier article, Donohue, Kaufmann, Smith, and Ramesh (1991) make a distinction between crisis and normative bargaining to better understand the general frames that are used to confront the hostage negotiation event. The idea is that crisis bargaining centers on relationship and expressive issues aimed at simply relieving the crisis and placing individuals in a position to focus on substantive issues, or bargaining that is more normative or focused on resolving the crisis. Hammer and Rogan (1997) make a similar distinction in their communication-based negotiation model between instrumental, relational, and identity concerns in a negotiation. These issues are all intertwined, but when they become more balanced, individuals can concentrate on moving toward a negotiated settlement. Situations that stay in crisis have little chance of productive movement because relational and identity concerns dominate. In fact, most of the recommendations that appear in the Rogan, Hammer, and Van Zandt (1997) volume concentrate on how to achieve this transition from a crisis to a normative bargaining mode. This chapter concentrates on how understanding and managing the various paradoxes that present themselves in this context is essential in accomplishing that goal.

RELATIONAL ORDER THEORY AND PARADOX

In a set of articles, Donohue and colleagues (Donohue & Roberto, 1993; Donohue & Hoobler, 2002; Donohue et al., 1991; Donohue, Ramesh, & Borchgrevink, 1991) outlined a theory to account for the dynamic evolution of relationships in conflict. Based on Strauss' (1978) Negotiated Order Theory, Relational Order Theory contends that negotiators continuously create and tacitly negotiate relational limits that serve to constrain the substantive negotiation process. The two main relational parameters or limits that communicators negotiate while they interact are affiliation and interdependence based on the consensus of a variety of articles focusing on the core parameters defining interpersonal relationships (Baxter, 1990; Brown & Levinson, 1978; Burgoon & Hale, 1987; Millar & Rogers, 1976; Rawlins, 1989). The issue of interdependence focuses on the extent to which parties can influence or exert behavioral control over one another in the context of the relationship between them. As parties become more interdependent through increased contact, for example, they expand their rights to demand more and incur more obligations to comply with others' demands. When the interdependence is rewarding, parties acquiesce to one another's demands, and parties focus more on their obligations to, and their investment in, the relationship. When the interdependence is punishing, parties focus more on their individual rights to demand more autonomy.

The relational cluster contributing most to whether parties emphasize rights or obligations in the context of their interdependence is termed *affiliation*, and it focuses on expressions of warmth, friendliness, intimacy, respect, trust, and cooperation (see Winter, 1991, for a review). *Affiliation* is defined as the extent to which individuals communicate attraction, liking, depth, acceptance, and trust. Parties can exchange these messages of affiliation directly, through overt performance, or they can indirectly frame their messages with expressions of approval, liking, and trust. Relational Order Theory positions interdependence and affiliation in relation to one another to define four relational conditions, or contextual orientations, that negotiators create as they continually define and redefine the limits of affiliation and interdependence: collaboration, cooperation, coexistence, and conflict.

COLLABORATION

When parties communicate using expressions of high affiliation and interdependence, they are proposing to become more involved with one another in a collaborative manner. Taking a cue from the Duel Concern Model (Rhoades & Carnevale, 1999), the concept of collaboration is one in which parties seek to help each other accomplish one another's goals. Parties seek to create a relational context that honors role obligations over individual rights. The focus on obligations invests parties in the needs of the relationship over the needs of the individuals. In this sense, the relationship is unconditional. Parties express mutual liking, so they accept their obligations for the sake of solidifying the relationship while paying little attention to their individual rights that might upset the relationship. Because the relationship or other related issues such as face or trust are not the focus of the interaction, parties are free to concentrate on exchanging information, pressing proposals, offering concessions, and so forth to create a mostly issues- or task-focused exchange.

COEXISTENCE

However, when parties communicate with low levels of both affiliation and interdependence, they send messages of separation and isolation. Parties seek to simply coexist by reducing their ties and isolating themselves from the relationship. It is a state of coexistence in the sense that parties are not fighting, but they are not moving forward productively with their substantive agenda. Perhaps they might need time to recover from some incident with the other party. Or, they might need to isolate themselves for a while to save face. Nevertheless, the goal in this condition is to create distance from role obligations and perhaps create new role frameworks to restructure or terminate the relationship. Interaction in this condition might consist of less frequent and superficial information exchange simply to keep up appearances of adhering to old role prescriptions. Or, parties might try to distribute messages supporting their own face to maintain their credibility while they are trying to withdraw from the relationship. Unconditional peace emphasizes constructive processes, whereas isolationist peace emphasizes withdrawal.

Neither of these two relational conditions is paradoxical for participants. When parties communicate within a collaborative frame, they balance their cues of high interdependence with expressions of increased affiliation. When they establish a coexistence frame, a similar match occurs in the opposite direction—that is, parties seek to separate by decreasing both their interdependence and affiliation. That communication in these two conditions is least likely to exhibit paradoxical qualities. Successfully moving toward or away from someone sends a consistent message. Parties establish either an approach-approach, or avoid-avoid context. There are no mixed messages guiding the interaction.

COOPERATION

In this condition of low interdependence and high affiliation, parties exchange messages that work to retain their role autonomy yet demonstrate approval and positive affect for one another. They assert few rights because they are not sufficiently interdependent to demand much. Yet, they remain friendly and polite, generally as an attempt to adhere to socially acceptable norms of interaction. This frame defines the relational condition of cooperation because parties are typically testing one another to decide whether to expand interdependence and role obligations. Parties may be aware of one another's goals, but they are more focused on accomplishing their own as opposed to being committed to both parties achieving goal attainment. A courting relationship might be a useful metaphor here. Individuals send increasing signals toward a desire to encumber the role obligations associated with increased interdependence, but their commitment is conditional. This conditional acceptance is stripped away in a cooperative relational frame. In the collaborative frame, parties have made the commitment to remain highly involved with one another and encumber those role expectations. However, in both cooperation and collaboration, the relationship is generally secondary to each party's substantive agenda. Under both conditions, interactants generally bargain constructively in good faith.

As a result of these mixed messages, cooperation can be labeled the *cooperative paradox* because parties must manage an approach-avoidance frame. On the one hand, parties express attraction while remaining timid about increasing interdependence. This paradox is cooperative in the sense that it sets the stage for collaboration by providing a rationale for becoming more interdependent. However, this condition still provides some tension about the direction of the relationship.

COMPETITION

In this final condition, parties send unaffiliative and disapproving messages in the context of relational dependence. The focus moves away from group or dyadic priorities and toward parties asserting their rights aimed at achieving their own goals while also resisting their group or alliance obligations. Because the emphasis is on asserting rights and resisting obligations, the communication carries almost a moral imperative and authority with it. Parties must resist with all their resources because key, central, and defining rights have been violated. This is the kind of communication that Winter (1991) observed during the first few exchanges between leaders dealing with the Cuban Missile Crisis of 1962. The United States certainly asserted its right to enforce the Monroe Doctrine that seeks to prevent non-Western Hemisphere powers from establishing military dominance in the Western Hemisphere. Yet, as letters from Khrushchev became more conciliatory, the United States altered its focus away from rights and more toward specific substantive issues. The parties moved away from aggression temporarily by agreeing to reduce their interdependence.

This condition can be labeled the *competitive paradox* because parties must manage their avoidance-approach conflict. To defeat their rival, parties must increase interdependence to pull their opponent closer by initiating communication or aggression while also pushing the opponent away through a show of negative affiliation by being unfriendly and untrusting. When parties are in this condition, they communicate directly while showing signs of negative affect (Donohue & Roberto, 1993).

MANAGING THE PARADOXES

The challenge of negotiating in the cooperative paradox is to remain affiliative, but cautious. Achieving this relational goal demands strategic ambiguity (Eisenberg, 1984; Leitch & Davenport, 2002). Parties politely share background information about issues dividing them, but they remain cautious about being too direct or detailed about specific positions. This ambiguity results from remaining cautious about being too interdependent or assuming a role relationship that would allow the other to place demands on the negotiator. This relational state is common in opening remarks in hostage negotiations, for example (Donohue & Diez, 1985). The hostage negotiators remain positive (at least nonthreatening) and even polite by avoiding tasks that might create controversy and decrease affiliation.

Ambiguity works in a different manner as parties seek to resolve the competitive paradox. As parties move deeper into the competitive paradox, affiliation drops and interdependence remains high. When parties violate affiliation parameters, such as trust and attraction, they are more direct with one another as they seek to assert their rights while enforcing the other to fulfill his or her obligations. They may restate positions and even use threats as a way of asserting their rights to make demands while calling in obligations from the other. More demands often result in more resistance, thereby perpetuating the paradox and making it difficult to escape. Relational Order Theory predicts that ultimately parties will find a means of escaping this competition and learn to coexist, which provides some respite from this paradox (Donohue & Roberto, 1993; Donohue & Taylor, 2006).

Research in negotiation using the model (Donohue & Roberto, 1993; Dono-hue & Taylor, 2006) suggests that the most constructive relational frame in a hostage context is collaborative negotiation. Bargaining necessitates interde-pendence because participants must interact to influence one another. When par-ties also create a context of high affiliation, they feel more secure in disclosing information about goals, needs, and fears that figure significantly in building integrative agreements. Negotiators who fail to sustain these relational limits will experience significantly more difficulty reaching satisfying agreements.

What kinds of expressions, performances, or messages do parties exchange to increase or decrease affiliation or interdependence? In a recent article, Taylor and Thomas (2005) examined the linguistic style of hostage takers and hostage ne-gotiators along three dimensions: structural features of language (word count, articles, negations, tense, propositions), social affect (negative and positive emo-tion, relational references), and cognitive contributions (causation, insight, dis-crepancy, certainty, and exclusivity). The hostage takers in these transcripts ranged from criminals caught in the act to domestic disputes to mentally im-paired individuals. The authors found that the hostage negotiator and hostage taker in the successful (a negotiated outcome) condition were synchronous on all but 4 of the 18 categories across these language choices. In the unsuccessful condition (the situation was resolved tactically), the parties were synchronous on only two parameters. Further, when the data were analyzed on a turn-by-turn basis, the hostage negotiator in the negotiation condition drove the frame choices, whereas in the tactical condition, the hostage taker drove the frame choices. In other words, collaboratively resolved negotiations were characterized by more frame coordination and the use of more collaborative frames with fewer transi-tions between frames (Donohue & Taylor, 2006). In comparison with unsuc-cessful negotiations, the dialogue of successful negotiations involved greater co-ordination of turn taking, reciprocation of positive affect, a focus on the present rather than the past, and a focus on alternatives rather than on competition.

This research in hostage negotiation using Relational Order Theory suggests that parties lost within the competitive paradox have greater difficulty reaching a collaborative agreement. However, it is likely that this kind of paradox can be viewed as a broad relational condition that characterizes the greater context. The question is, are there more specific kinds of relational paradoxes that hostage ne-gotiators must confront as they learn to deal with hostage takers? This chapter now turns to the issue of more specific kinds of relational paradoxes that influ-ence hostage negotiation outcomes.

DIALECTICAL TENSIONS AND PARADOX IN HOSTAGE NEGOTIATIONS

The Extortionate Transaction

In a classic book on policing, Muir (1977) describes the kinds of coercive rela-tionships that often emerge in the course of police work. Coercive relationships, or controlling others through threats to harm, precipitate extortionate transactions in which parties seek their ends through the use of threats, which often take the form of hostages and ransoms. Muir argues that extortionate transactions are organized around a series of paradoxes, and that reconstructing these transactions requires managing the paradoxes. Muir's first example is the paradox of Dispossession, or the less one has, the less one has to lose. The idea in this paradox is that the hostage taker is simultaneously powerful and powerless. The hostage taker's power derives from taking something of value from the hostage, but this is an act of a desperately powerless person who must take hostages as a last resort to gain power. If the hostage taker is dispossessed or has the sense that he or she is detached from those things that are valued (even life itself) or has nothing to lose, then the negotiator loses any leverage over the hostage taker. The goal of the negotiator is to find something that the hostage taker values that the negotiator can ultimately control to balance power. This balance is essential in moving from a crisis to a normative bargaining context. When both parties value something, they can bargain in good faith to claim it.

Second, the paradox of Detachment holds that parties are both attached and detached simultaneously to one another and to the situation. They are attached in the sense that they must co-confront a difficult negotiation session, but they are detached in the sense that each party moves back and forth within a frame of indifference. By communicating indifference, the victim can become less valuable to the hostage taker. However, some victims become attached to hostage takers (Stockholm syndrome), thereby increasing their attachment to the situation and their desire to take sides in the conflict. Police might even encourage attachment to improve the hostage's chance for survival resulting from greater personal attachment between the hostage taker and the hostage. The police are somewhat insulated from the situation and experience occasional indifference to various members of the hostage incident depending on their level of professional commitment to the lives of the victims and perpetrators and their ability to focus on the lives of the individuals, as opposed to other priorities, such as resolving the situation because it is becoming expensive or too public. Finally, the hostage taker can be, and often is, indifferent to survival. Many hostage takers try to communicate detachment and dispossession as a means of appearing more reckless and, therefore, more powerful.

Ultimately, the police must learn to maintain sufficient levels of attachment among all parties to move from crisis to normative bargaining. When the hostage taker is attached and values something that the negotiator can control, the negotiator is attached and focused on managing the hostage taker's problem, and the victim and hostage taker are somewhat personally attached to one another, then the bargaining can proceed in good faith. During a prolonged negotiation, managing these values is difficult given the restricted lines of communication and the many sources of interference that may impact the sense of detachment, such as direct communication with family members, for example, or overt signs of threat from police that might cause the hostage taker to become less attached and more desperate.

The Paradox of Face focuses on the broad issue of identity and, often in a hostage situation, the narrower issue of threat. Parties vacillate between communicating both toughness and flexibility and often must do so simultaneously. The professional police identity is rooted in a desire to be both firm and tough, while being tempered with an ability to be understanding and fair. The hostage taker's identity is rooted in being perceived as a credible threat to secure a desired outcome, although not so much of a threat that the police are likely to take tactical action to preserve the lives of the hostages. The hostage taker must strike a balance between being tough, but reasonable, so that negotiation appears more viable as a strategy than tactical action. The hostage's face can shift between being a helpless victim to a hostage taker supporter or even an overt detractor.

Of particular interest in managing this paradox is interpreting threats. In a classic work on threats, Shelling (1956) indicates that for threats to be credible, they must be specific and perceived as within the willingness and capability of the threatener. This threat then binds it to the identity of the threatener and becomes part of their face. In an empirical test of coercive power and concession making in bilateral negotiation, de Dreu (1995) found that balanced power produced fewer threats and demands than unequal power. This result suggests that the role of the police is to manage this paradox by seeking to balance identity issues in such a way as to make threats less necessary so the parties can shift to more of a normative bargaining context and resolve the situation appropriately.

Finally, Muir (1977) identifies the paradox of Irrationality, which focuses on the issue of emotional involvement. In Muir's terms, the more delirious the threatener, the more serious the threat; and the more delirious the victim, the less serious the threat. If the hostage taker is too emotional, he or she may become irrational and incapable of managing the scene or bargaining in any kind of normative manner. If the hostage taker exhibits no emotion or involvement, then it might be a warning sign of detachment, which again removes the possibility of normative bargaining. In his chapter on emotion and emotional expression in crisis bargaining, Rogan (1997) makes the point that it is vital to both understand the kinds of emotional expressions hostage takers are communicating and be able to respond appropriately to them. Muir would argue that the real challenge is to manage the opposing forces of irrationality that intertwine among the hostage taker, hostage negotiator, and the victim. Not only must the police be able to read the hostage taker's emotions, but they must also understand their own emotional conditions. Police can act irrationally when the hostage taker confronts their face or threatens a hostage in some manner. As situations wear on, police might become too emotionally invested in terminating the situation and less invested in concentrating on the welfare of the hostages. Thus, the issue focuses again on the problem of balance. Are the hostage negotiators able to balance the complex set of emotional issues presented by themselves, the hostage takers, and the victims?

Clearly, any negotiation can devolve into an extortionate abyss, in which parties simply try to overwhelm one another with coercive force. That is what war is all about. The declaration of war is an admission that the ability to balance these four paradoxes within the competitive paradox has failed. In a world where all-out war aimed at defeating an enemy into submission is quickly disappearing, the need to understand and manage the extortionate transaction becomes even more imperative. Toward this end, there is one additional set of work that is important to identify that reaches to understand the concept of paradox from the broader perspective of relationships. This chapter now turns to the issue of dialects in managing relationships between parties.

Relational Dialectics

Another approach to the concept of paradox and conflict is found in the work on dialectical tensions proposed by Rawlins (1989) and Baxter (1990). The basic idea of this research is that any relationship must learn to manage three fundamental dialectal tensions: openness/closedness, autonomy/connection, and novelty/predictability. Parties use communication to determine how many secrets to hide or reveal, how much they should be free to express themselves as individuals or be constrained by the corporate relational structure, or how predictable they should be when deciding how to act.

Most recent research examining the issue of relational dialectics is conducted through an interpretive lens by examining how communication processes during negotiation evolve and change over time. It examines how parties develop and enact norms that influence bargaining structures that negotiators co-create. For example, Putnam (2004) examines rhetorical tropes (the use of metaphors, irony, metonymy, and synecdoche) to understand how individuals in bargaining negotiate relational dialectics. She focuses specifically on the use of metonymy (a figure of speech in which a word stands for its constituent parts, such as using the word *culture* to stand for an organization's values, rituals, and myths) and synecdoche (a figure of speech in which the part stands for or symbolizes the whole, such as substituting the word *crown* to stand for the role of the king or queen). In other words, how are people using words in negotiation to conceptualize complex relational dialectics that define the nature of the parties' interdependencies?

In her research, Putnam (2004) focuses on how tropes are used to negotiate autonomy and interdependence in a teacher bargaining context. She found that the term *language* referred to the creation and discussion of policy issues and the term *money* referred to any budget-related items. The bargaining often revolved around who owned the money and the ability to craft the language that would ultimately guide the negotiation. Thus, these concepts were used to negotiate the relationships between the parties.

In hostage negotiations, similar kinds of tropes often emerge. Parties can become fixated on such issues as *cooperation* and use that word to negotiate the level of affiliation and interdependence in the negotiation. For example, a hostage taker might say, "So, you better start cooperating . . ." in reference to fulfilling a demand. In response, the negotiator might try to reframe the concept of cooperating by focusing on how they have complied with a different demand. What these negotiators are doing is managing their relational dialectics by focusing on a specific synecdoche that begins to take on a life of its own and embody a much larger and more important negotiation.

In another study, Jameson (2004) examined how parties negotiated autonomy and connection through politeness in a medical context. She discovered that indirectness and ambiguity are the most common ways of negotiating the autonomy-connection paradox. Ambiguous communication can often take the form of small talk and humor, rather than genuinely self-disclosing true feelings. Jameson examined face-saving strategies as a means of negotiating autonomy and connection. She found that in negotiating treatment options, the medical professionals often emphasized respect for and acknowledgments of the other's competence while also emphasizing solidarity and providing explanations as a means of simultaneously face saving and face supporting. These face strategies acknowledge the other's right to autonomy while carefully framing how parties should be connected.

In the initial stages of a hostage negotiation, the police want to concentrate on relational development and have as a specific goal not threatening the autonomy of the hostage taker or creating the impression of "boxing in" the hostage taker. Many exchanges during these early phases are devoted to the use of small talk and humor, in addition to expressions of support as a means of supporting the hostage taker's face. The goal is to find a balance between autonomy and connection in the development of the relationship that will allow for the transition from a crisis to a normative bargaining mode.

INTEGRATING THE PARADOXICAL PERSPECTIVES

At this point, it is useful to understand how these various approaches to the study of paradox work together to help us understand how hostage negotiators can better manage relationships with hostage takers to begin transforming the negotiation into a more productive form. To summarize the issue of paradox in the context of the extortionate transaction, it appears that parties create and manage relationships by negotiating various paradoxes as they exchange information. The overriding paradox that appears to govern the evolution of the extortionate transaction is the competitive paradox in which parties have to manage the competing forces of affiliation and interdependence. Parties begin to reify their conflict by becoming more interdependent (pulling each other closer and being more direct) and less affiliative (pushing each other away through expressions of mistrust and dislike).

Once parties have begun to understand that they are submerged in conflict and are starting to feel immersed in the competitive paradox, they are faced with two separate issues (which they certainly don't consciously attend to, but evolve over time): their relationship to each other and their position within the context. The challenge with the first problem is that they must begin to build a consensus about the fundamental parameters of their relationship simply as communicators. In this context, they manage the dialectical tensions of connection/autonomy, openness/closedness, public/private, control/yielding, independence/dependence, and so on. They might accomplish this task by focusing on specific rhetorical tropes or by engaging in a variety of face-saving and face-maintaining strategies all aimed at finding a consensus about the relational parameters that simply allow the parties to continue to communicate.

The second issue that the parties must confront deals with their relationship with the context and the problem they are trying to address. This set of paradoxes discussed by Muir (1977) starts to reveal how individuals define their participation in the context or their relationship with the issues and problems. Parties might respond to the context by being more or less dispossessed, detached, nasty, or irrational. They might strategically manage these paradoxical states to create more or less value for their positions, or increase or decrease the nature of their threats. Of course, in the context of managing their threats, parties will also negotiate their relational parameters associated with autonomy or closedness, and so on. Thus, parties can exchange information that simultaneously informs both relational and contextual paradoxes.

For example, a hostage taker might say, "You better start cooperating because I'm gonna strangle her and she's gonna die right here on the floor and then I'm gonna go to the electric chair. So, you better get a gun if you want to save her life" (Holmes, 1990, p. 2). As the hostage taker seeks to detach from both the life of the hostage and his own life, he is also negotiating parameters associated with autonomy and control. In addition, he is using the trope *cooperating* as a means of renegotiating those parameters. This example illustrates that multiple paradoxes are in play at any given point, and the job of the hostage negotiator is to identify those parameters that seem most important to address at the moment. In this example, the detachment issue is clearly apparent, but the control and autonomy issues also bear strategic attention. However, the issue of detachment probably should take priority as a means of persuading the hostage taker to value something, hopefully his own life, to gain leverage in the negotiations. Of course, in this example, the hostage taker is also threatening the negative face of the hostage negotiator that might distract from focusing on the hostage taker and the issue of detachment and value. Negotiators might be aware of these kinds of negotiations to avoid losing the crucial focus on the most important paradox.

MANAGING PARADOX: THE WACO NEGOTIATIONS

At this point, it might be useful to provide a brief transcript of an actual hostage negotiation to explore how parties tacitly bargain these various paradoxes. The

Waco negotiations offer an interesting case study because so much has been written about them, and some examples are readily available. In July 1995, the Justice Department released tapes of negotiations between David Koresh and the FBI during the 1993 Waco standoff. In this transcript recorded in the early morning hours of Friday, April 16, 1993, Koresh and Davidian Steve Schneider discuss surrender terms with the FBI negotiator. In this segment, the surrender terms are revolving around the creation of a set of seals or documents that lays out Koresh's religious perspective:

1. **Koresh:** . . . I say that when I get through writing these, and they're given to my attorney, and my attorney hands them over—What's the two theologians names?
2. **Steve Schneider**: Ah—Philip Arnold and Jim Tabor.
3. **Koresh:** Philip Arnold and Jim Tabor who has shown that they have a sincere interest in these things—you see? Then I can spend all my time in jail, and people can go ahead and ask me all the stupid questions they want—cause they're not gonna ask me about the seals. They're gonna say, "Ah, do you molest young ladies?" "Ah, have you eaten babies?" "Do you sacrifice people?" "Ah, do you make automatic weapons?" "Ah, do you have [unintelligible]." That's what they're gonna be interested in—sensationalism.
4. **FBI:** That's why you need to get it done before you leave there then.

This exchange is interesting because Koresh is responding to the potential criticism that people will think that he is a crazy, irrational freak. Is Koresh trying to exploit the paradox of irrationality as a means of appearing to be a less rational threat or to try to engage in face maintenance to bolster his ability to make a rational deal? Is Koresh asking the negotiator to bolster his positive face to appear less like a freak and more like a religious profit? The FBI focuses on the need to complete the seal as a way of helping Koresh feel better about coming out while ignoring the issue of Koresh's face needs and an opportunity to bolster his face and thus increase the negotiator's value to Koresh:

5. **Koresh:** That's why I'm gonna complete it, because you see, you know as well as I do that people in this world they want something dramatic and sensational. They don't want to have to sit—No one's gonna sit there—and let me sit there in front of a camera and read Psalms 40 to them—to prove the first seal. Dick, it's a real world, and that's why I'm sympathetic with your position. I realize you're frustrated, and I agree with you.
6. **FBI:** I'm not frustrated. I went home and I'm back. I'm no longer frustrated. I never was frustrated.
7. **Koresh:** Did you take a shower for me?
8. **FBI:** Well, yeah. I took a couple of them for you.
9. **Koresh:** Thank you. I appreciate it.

This is also an interesting exchange that appears aimed at enhancing affiliation. Koresh is negotiating the autonomy-connection paradox with humor and perhaps is using the humor to reinforce his autonomy by avoiding the substantive issue of giving up. Notice that the agent picks up on it and reinforces this humorous repartee. Recall that Jameson (2004) points out that ambiguous communication can often take the form of small talk and humor, rather than interactants genuinely self-disclosing true feelings. The agent should recognize that, although the humor appears to reinforce affiliation, it can also be a bid for more autonomy as it looks past the deeper issues. The humor is brief, and, in the next utterance, the agent moves back on task:

10. **FBI:** Now listen. Let's get back to the point in hand. This ah—you know—the writing of the seals. OK. You've got to do that in there, and it's gonna take you x amount of time. But—just tell me this David—are you saying that when you finish that manuscript—
11. **Koresh:** Then I'm not bound any longer [unintelligible]
12. **FBI:** No. But see, that doesn't answer the question.
13. **Koresh:** Then I'll be out—yes—definitely.
14. **FBI:** I know you'll be out, but that could—excuse me I've got a cold. That could mean a lot of things David. That could mean—
15. **Koresh:** I'll be in custody in the jailhouse. You can come down there and feed me bananas if you want.

The banana reference in Koresh's last comment is telling. Again, Koresh appears caught within the detachment and irrationality paradoxes. By referring to himself as a captive crazy sort of monkey in a cage, he is once again pressing the value button in the interaction. Should the FBI raise this issue more explicitly about how Koresh should be more future-focused in terms of his potential impact beyond the hostage incident? Why should he live, and what impact will his life have if he continues to press his message? Instead of offering to probe the value issue and dig more deeply into Koresh's ability to have an impact beyond the event, the FBI chooses to press for a commitment to get a specific time table in place for the surrender process as illustrated in the following exchange:

16. **FBI:** I know—I know that some point in time that's true. But I'm getting from you—I'm asking you, "When that is finished, are you than telling me that you are coming out the next day, or two hours after you send that out or what?"
17. **Koresh:** Oh, I'll probably—when I—when I bring it out—see—my attorney is gonna get the—get to the copy.
18. **FBI:** Right.
19. **Koresh:** OK? And as soon as he hands it over to the scholars—the theologians—right?
20. **FBI:** Um, hm.
21. **Koresh:** That's when—he's gonna come back, and that's when I'm going to go out with him, because he said point blank that—you know—one of the guarantees of me arriving down there is that he is gonna go with me.
22. **FBI:** So you go on paper here and said that David Koresh told me that as soon as he finishes this manuscript—the seven seals—of which you've finished the first chapter dealing with the first seal—
23. **Koresh:** The first seal—right.

24. **FBI:** That you're gonna make that available—
25. **Koresh:** I'll be splitting out of this place. I'm so sick of MRE's—Dick—that ah—
26. **FBI:** Well, I just want to make sure that I have this right—that you're coming out. As soon as that's finished—
27. **Koresh:** That's what—it was said by the attorney's—
28. **FBI:** Well, I know—I know.
29. **Koresh:** That's what I'm saying—
30. **FBI:** OK.

In this exchange, the FBI may not have been listening well to Koresh with respect to processing the paradoxes. Koresh was moving toward expanding both affiliation and interdependence, moving toward collaboration. But the FBI kept Koresh within the cooperative paradox by reciprocating the affiliation and not showing much interest in helping Koresh address the paradoxes within which he was struggling. Koresh made several references to issues related to face, detachment, and irrationality perhaps as a means of extending his autonomy or some ability to balance power with the FBI. Instead of offering to provide additional insight and probe the paradoxes, the FBI presses for specific conditions and details on the surrender sequence. We will never know whether Koresh ever intended to come out, and evidence suggests that he was not so inclined. In the absence of knowing these intentions, all the negotiator can do is work with the information available at the time and process the issues as they present themselves.

LESSONS LEARNED

This analysis raises some potentially useful points for understanding communication in intense conflict situations. The first lesson is that parties will often share fairly specific references about being trapped in paradoxes. Can we notice these references and make good judgments about how they should be processed? In the case of this dialogue, these issues arose in several exchanges, suggesting that they were problematic. However, there are frequently multiple paradoxes that require attention, and perhaps all are important at some point. But, the negotiator must make a judgment about which to raise up that are most critical at that point. Koresh makes several references in this exchange to his incarceration and to being ridiculed as a caged animal. These references may or may not raise issues about being irrational or detached in some way, but the fact that they keep appearing in the context of trying to be cooperative probably rises to the level of importance. That the negotiator ignores them is interesting. I am certainly not criticizing the FBI negotiator because it is easy to second guess an agent in the throws of an actual event, and this transcript is pulled out of context. My only point is to illustrate the importance of understanding paradoxes as they emerge in conflict and the need to sort through potentially competing paradoxes.

A second lesson from this analysis focuses on the police negotiators. Specifically, these police negotiators struggle with paradoxes in the course of dealing with the hostage takers. It is easy to focus exclusively on the hostage taker and not see the kinds of relational traps the negotiators are facing. For example, the paradox of face becomes formidable in the quest to adhere to professional expectations. The negotiator is evaluated in resolving potentially violent situations expeditiously. Keeping this value in perspective is difficult. Delaying a negotiation while attending to other issues that appear like "small talk" might seem counter to those professional values. Indeed, they are not and should be considered when communicating.

A third lesson addresses the issue of relationships. Relationships are always in play in negotiations because participants are continuously exchanging relational messages while they interact. Affiliation messages are often subtle and complex. The slightest change in tone or innocuous word choice can signal a switch in trust, for example. The general rule in guiding this emphasis is that police negotiators must not be afraid to express a broad range of relational messages that hostage takers might use to shape their own talk. The Taylor and Thomas (2005) article clearly indicates that police-guided relational messages are more likely to yield positive outcomes than hostage taker-guided relational messages. When these interactions become synchronous with individuals adopting the same frame, they develop the kind of foundation necessary to make the switch to normative bargaining.

A final lesson for police negotiators that grows increasingly apparent from an emphasis on paradox is the need to listen for tropes—or words and phrases that reappear and are intended to serve as markers for important relational issues. Tropes represent frames for shaping the negotiations. Some of these tropes can be relationally oriented and can become opportunities for disclosing paradoxes. Words such as *cooperation* or even *hostage* can be used by both sides repeatedly to mark a bid for autonomy, for example. Thus, negotiators would be well served to unpack redundant words that gain momentum in a negotiation to help guide police strategy.

STRATEGIES FOR PRACTICE

Sifting through a framework dealing with paradox is difficult because these concepts are fairly abstract and probably difficult to think about in the course of managing an actual hostage scene. Given this challenge, it might be best to identify a few kernels of wisdom that can be used strategically in the field. Perhaps the best place to start is to identify some specific communication skills that are suggested by the focus on paradox. One skill that emerges from this analysis is listening. From the transcripts supplied here and from others that we analyzed, it is clear that few negotiators actively listen to hostage takers. Rather than occasionally repeating back a word or comment or two from the hostage taker, the negotiators appear to press their own agenda, as opposed to actively pursuing thoughts generated by the hostage taker. This process makes it difficult to continue a topic and learn insights from hostage takers about their issues.

A second listening strategy involves comprehending the underlying issue surrounding a comment. Beyond a psychological diagnosis of a specific disorder or pathology, it is important to listen for issues related to face and identity, so many of which deal with the paradoxes discussed here. People label themselves (e.g., "I'm tough" or "You can feed me bananas") all the time, and these labels give insights into how they are viewing themselves in relation to the situation. When Koresh labeled himself as a freak in the transcripts on multiple occasions, he was revealing an important cue concerning how he was viewing his sense of autonomy, his detachment, and his view of the outside world. The point is to listen for the labels that people apply to themselves as cues for how they are likely to respond to various substantive negotiation proposals.

Another important piece of wisdom emerging from this analysis is the issue of code consistency. A communication code is a set of rules for how to conduct an interaction. Interactants form rules about the form of language they will use in sharing thoughts. Certain topics, use of slang or profanity, the presentation of different accents, displays of emotion, and so on define a form. Research indicates that when hostage takers and negotiators match their code and use the same rules, they are more capable of focusing on a substantive agenda. Code consistency is an important marker of increased affiliation. When we use the same codes, it starts to build trust and liking, which begins to move participants away from the competitive paradox and more toward a collaborative frame. Combined with more active listening skills, the development of a more coordinated linguistic code can begin to set the stage for productive negotiation.

REFERENCES

Baxter, L. A. (1990). Dialectical contradictions in relationship development. *Journal of Social and Personal Relationships, 7*, 69–88.

Brown, P., & Levinson, S. (1978). Universals in language usage: Politeness phenomena. In E. Goody (Ed.), *Questions and politeness: Strategies in social interaction* (pp. 256–288). Cambridge, MA: Cambridge University Press.

Burgoon, J. K., & Hale, J. L. (1987). The fundamental topoi of relational communication. *Communication Monographs, 51*, 193–214.

de Dreu, C. K. (1995). Coercive power and concession making in bilateral negotiation. *Journal of Conflict Resolution, 39*, 646–670.

Donohue, W. A., & Diez, M. E. (1985). Directive use in negotiation interaction. *Communication Monographs, 52*, 305–318.

Donohue, W. A., & Hoobler, G. D. (2002). Relational frames and their ethical implications in international negotiation: An analysis based on the Oslo II negotiations. *International Negotiation, 7*, 143–167.

Donohue, W. A., Kaufmann, G., Smith, R., & Ramesh, C. (1991). Crisis bargaining: A framework for understanding intense conflict. *International Journal of Group Tensions, 21*, 133–154.

Donohue, W. A., Armes, C., & Borchgrevink, C. (1991). Crisis bargaining: Tracking relational paradox in hostage negotiation. *International Journal of Conflict Management, 2,* 257–274.

Donohue, W. A., & Roberto, A. J. (1993). Relational development as negotiated order in hostage negotiation. *Human Communication Research, 20,* 175–198.

Donohue, W. A., & Taylor, P. J. (2006, July). *Testing Relational Order Theory in hostage negotiation.* Paper presented to the International Association for Conflict Management, Montreal, Canada.

Eisenberg, E. (1984). Ambiguity as strategy in organizational communication. *Communication Monographs, 51,* 227–242.

Hammer, M. R., & Rogan, R. G. (1997). Negotiation models in crisis situations: The value of a communication-based approach. In R. Rogan, M. Hammer, & C. Van Zandt (Eds.), *Dynamic processes of crisis negotiation* (pp. 9–24). Westport, CT: Praeger.

Holmes, M. E. (1990). *Hostage negotiations and the extortionate transaction.* Unpublished manuscript, University of Minnesota, Minneapolis, MN.

Jameson, J. K. (2004). Negotiating autonomy and connection through politeness: A dialectical approach to organizational conflict management. *Western Journal of Communication, 68,* 257–277.

Leitch, S., & Davenport, S. (2002). Strategic ambiguity in communicating public sector change. *Journal of Communication Management, 7,* 129–139.

Millar, F. E., & Rogers, E. L. (1976). A relational approach to interpersonal communication. In G. R. Miller (Ed.), *Explorations in interpersonal communication* (pp. 55–75). Beverly Hills, CA: Sage.

Muir, W. K. (1977). *Police: Streetcorner politicians.* Chicago: University of Chicago Press.

Putnam, L. L. (2004). Dialectical tensions and rhetorical tropes in negotiations. *Organization Studies, 25,* 35–53.

Rawlins, W. K. (1989). A dialectical analysis of the tensions, functions and strategic challenges of communication in young adult friendships. In J. A. Anderson (Ed.), *Communication yearbook 12* (pp. 157–189). Newbury Park, CA: Sage.

Rhoades, J. A., & Carnevale, P. J. (1999). The behavioral context of strategic choice in negotiation: A test of the dual concern model. *Journal of Applied Social Psychology, 29,* 1777–1802.

Rogan, R. G. (1997). Emotion and emotional expression in crisis negotiation. In R. Rogan, M. Hammer, & C. Van Zandt (Eds.), *Dynamic processes of crisis negotiation* (pp. 25–44). Westport, CT: Praeger.

Rogan, R. G., Hammer, M. R., & Van Zandt, C. R. (1997). *Dynamic processes of crisis negotiation.* Westport, CT: Praeger.

Shelling, T. C. (1956). An essay on bargaining. *The American Economic Review, 46,* 281–306.

Strauss, A. (1978). *Negotiations: Varieties, contexts, processes, and social order.* San Francisco: Jossey-Bass.

Taylor, P. J., & Thomas, S. (2005, July). *Linguistic style matching and negotiation outcome.* Paper presented to the International Association for Conflict Management, Seville, Spain.

Winter, D.G. (1991). Measuring personality at a distance: Development of an integrated system for scoring motives in running text. In A. J. Stewart, J. M. Healy, Jr., & D. J. Ozer (Eds.), *Perspectives in personality: Approaches to understanding lives* (pp. 59–89). London: Jessica Kingsley.

Communication and Crisis/Hostage Negotiation

A Focus on Facework

Randall G. Rogan

Over the span of several months during late 2004 and early 2005, the international community witnessed the horrifying consequences of terrorist-motivated hostage takings. The videotaped broadcasts of the beheading of individuals by anti-coalition insurgents in Iraq revealed, yet once again, the dark side of human behavior. But these were not singular incidents restricted to Iraq. Similar dramatic loss of life occurred in Russia's attempt to resolve a standoff with Chechen rebels in a school in Beslan, Russia, where hundreds of people, many of them children, were killed (BBC News, September, 4, 2004). Few of us could comprehend these brutal acts of violence.

Within the United States, we also have witnessed our share of violent conclusions to hostage taking/barricade standoffs between law enforcement and various individuals and groups. Two such incidents that will forever be etched in our collective psyches are the sieges at Attica Prison in Attica, New York, and the Branch Davidian standoff in Waco, Texas. Both confrontations resulted in a significant and dramatic loss of human life. Fortunately, however, most hostage takings do not end in the violent death of the parties involved (Federal Bureau of Investigation, 2007). Yet when negotiations go bad, they seem to go very bad. Together, the incidents in Iraq and Russia, along with domestic cases of hostage taking in the United States, highlight the need for law enforcement to enhance its understanding of the communicative dynamics of these highly charged interactions as negotiators strive for nonviolent outcome resolutions.

Most practitioner publications dealing with crisis/hostage negotiation emphasize the importance of understanding the nature of the incident in order to effectuate successful resolution. Historically, a number of different, yet overlapping, incident typologies have been advanced. Most of these schemes relied on simple descriptive categorizations that were based on the presumed motive of the suspect, his or her psychological characteristics, specific features of the context in which the incident occurred, or any combination of these factors (e.g., Goldaber, 1979; Hacker, 1976; Schlossberg, 1979). For example, for many years, the Federal Bureau of Investigation (FBI) relied on a four-part classification of hostage takings, including criminal hostage takings (e.g., bank robbery), hostage takings by mentally/emotionally disturbed individuals, terrorist hostage takings, and prison hostage takings (Borum & Strentz, 1992; DiVasto, Lanceley, & Gruys, 1992; Friedland, 1986; Fuselier, 1986; Fuselier & Noesner, 1990; Soskis & Van Zandt, 1986). More recently, the FBI has embraced a two-part Hostage–Non-Hostage typology, whereby an actual hostage situation is one in which a suspect engages in purposeful behavior for the attainment of some instrumental outcome and where hostages function as commodities for bargaining. Comparatively, Non-Hostage incidents are marked by suspects whose behavior and demands are pragmatically unrealistic and where hostages serve no functional value (Noesner, 1999).

Generally speaking, the benefit of such classification schemes is their utility in helping law enforcement officers to understand the types of incidents they encounter and some of the essential conditions associated with the incidents. These typologies have often served as the basis for determining appropriate incident management strategies, with the recommendations gleaned principally from individual negotiators' personal experiences, rather than derived from social and behavioral science research (Heymann, 1993).

Recent data reported in the FBI's Hostage, Barricade, and Suicide (HOBAS) database of 5,100 incidents attests to the effectiveness of negotiation as a strategy for achieving incident resolution (Federal Bureau of Investigation, 2007). According to the database, in 80% of all incidents, no injuries or deaths were reported for bystanders, law enforcement officers, or hostage takers. Further, 58% of all reported incidents were resolved through negotiations, with 11% resolved by a combined negotiation and tactical approach. Comparatively, 20% of all reported incidents were resolved through tactical action only. The remaining 11% of incidents were resolved by the suspect's escape (2.5%), suspect suicide/attempted suicide (8%), or police disengagement from the incident (.5%).

As the HOBAS data indicate, negotiation can often be extremely effective in facilitating nonviolent incident resolution. Yet quite frankly, much is still unknown about the actual communicative dynamics of these negotiations. Nor is there substantial social science knowledge about how participants' linguistic cues might function as possible clues to incident outcome or relate with incident characteristics (Hammer, 2001; Hare, 1997). In recent years, a small number of communication scholars and psychologists have investigated various dynamics of crisis negotiation by conducting content analyses of the discourse of authentic negotiation incidents (e.g., Donohue & Roberto, 1993, 1996; Giebels & Noelanders, 2004; Hammer, 2001; Rogan & Hammer, 1995, 2002, 2006; Rogan, Hammer, & Van Zandt, 1997, Taylor, 2002a, 2002b). Broadly speaking, this work can be grouped into three programmatic areas of research, including (a) relational development and interdependence (Donohue, Ramesh, & Borchgrevink, 1991; Donohue, Ramesh, Kaufmann, & Smith, 1991; Donohue & Roberto, 1993, 1996), (b) phase modeling (Holmes, 1997a, 1997b; Holmes & Fletcher-Bergland, 1995; Holmes & Sykes, 1993), and (c) behavioral model development and testing (Hammer, 1997, 2001, 2007; Hammer & Rogan, 1997; Hammer & Weaver, 1994; Rogan, 1997, 1999; Rogan & Hammer, 1994, 1995, 2002; Rogan, Hammer, & Van Zandt, 1997; Taylor, 2002a, 2002b, 2003, 2004). It is the behavioral models of crisis/hostage negotiation that are of specific interest to this chapter because this line of research focuses on the various communicative dimensions of negotiation and, in particular, highlights the role of face and facework in negotiating barricade standoffs.

COMMUNICATION-BASED MODELS OF CRISIS NEGOTIATION

Currently, there exist two models of crisis negotiation that are grounded in communication theory and constructs. The first is Rogan and Hammer's (2002) four-part behavioral model known as the S.A.F.E. model. Drawing from framing theory (e.g., Bateson, 1954/1972; Dewulf et al., 2005; Putnam & Holmer, 1992; Tannen, 1993), Rogan and Hammer argued that linguistic cues serve as devices by which negotiators and subjects make sense of and define their interaction. According to them, the S.A.F.E. model consists of four communicative dimensions/goals that function as framing mechanisms during negotiation, including: (a) Substantive demands/wants, (b) Attunement, (c) Face, and (d) Emotionality (see Hammer, 2001, 2007; Rogan & Hammer, 2002, 2006, for complete descriptions of this model). Briefly, a Substantive frame denotes concern for instrumentally focused goals; Attunement is concerned with the negotiation of the relational dynamics between the negotiator and subject, including trust, power, and affiliation; and Face denotes individual concern for the self's and others' image and reputation. Emotionality is included as the fourth frame given its significance to conflict interaction (e.g., Adler, Rosen, & Silverstein, 1998; Bodtker & Jameson, 2001; Jones, 2001). Rogan and Hammer (2002) argued that conflict participants make known their dominant/primary individual goal focus concerning the interaction around each of the four frames via their linguistic cues. In this way, insight into participants' framing of themselves and the conflict can be gleaned (see Hammer, Chapter 3, this volume, for an example analysis of framing devices).

The second model is Taylor's (2002a, 2002b) cylindrical model. Drawing in part on Rogan and Hammer's S.A.F.E. framework, general negotiation research, and crisis negotiation literature specifically, Taylor advanced a three-dimensional model of crisis negotiation that melds negotiator behavior on two levels with behavioral intensity. The first level deals with participants' general orientation toward a threefold behavioral scheme of avoidance, integrative, and distributive behavior. The second level focuses on individuals' motivational orientations according to a three-part goal orientation consisting of instrumental, relational, and identity/face goals. Finally, Taylor proposed a third dimension of behavioral intensity, which he defined as a participant's affective state as marked by the use of intense language.

Although these two models delineate multiple dimensions as basic to crisis negotiation, individual concern for face is regarded to be an essential conceptual and operational element of both models and basic to the communicative dynamics of crisis negotiations. Face is likewise noted as a critical functional concern to police negotiators (Davidson, 2002; Fagan & Van Zandt, 1993; Fuselier, Van Zandt, & Lanceley, 1991). Additionally, Rogan and Hammer's (1994) content analysis of actual crisis negotiations concluded that linguistic manifestations of suspects' face concerns, according to particular face-framing devices, may serve as predictive markers for incident outcome. Specifically, they concluded that suspect framing of face in the form of negative self-directed facework was more dominant in suicide than nonsuicide incidents and therefore a possible indicator of suspect suicidal enactment. Unfortunately, their investigation was only based on a single suicide case. It is worthwhile, therefore, to explore further the role of face and facework within crisis negotiation as we strive to increase our understanding about how particular communicative/linguistic mechanisms may serve as predictive clues about incident trajectory. Therefore, the purpose of this chapter is to report the findings of an investigation recently conducted as a follow-up to the Rogan and Hammer (1994) study, in which I principally investigated the potential variability in facework frames between crisis negotiation incidents with suicide and surrender outcomes.

FACE AS A DYNAMIC OF CONFLICT AND CRISIS NEGOTIATION

Conflict scholars agree that face is a key factor in conflict interaction (Cupach & Canary, 1997; Folger, Poole, & Stutman 2005; Northrup, 1989; Ting-Toomey, 1988; Ting-Toomey & Kurogi, 1998; Wilson & Putnam, 1990). In his landmark explication of face in human interaction, Goffman (1967) defined *face* as "the positive social value a person effectively claims for himself by the line others assume he has taken during a particular contact" (p. 5). Broadly speaking, face is an individual's concern for projecting a positive self-expression that is dependent on the dynamics of social interaction. As noted by Goffman, individuals employ various facework strategies to facilitate not only their own face concerns, but also those of the relational partner.

Drawing on the work of Goffman (1955) and Brown and Levinson (1987), Ting-Toomey (1988; Ting-Toomey & Kurogi, 1998) advanced her face-negotiation theory to explain how concern for face varies by culture and how this variability accounts for the variance found in differing conflict management styles and behaviors. Within the context of her theory, Ting-Toomey defined *face* as "the projected and the claimed sense of self-image and self-respect in a relational situation" (Ting-Toomey et al., 1991, p. 278). Further, she conceptualized facework as "the set of interaction strategies used to mitigate face-threatening and/or face-honoring situations" (p. 278). According to her, face concerns include one's personal or self-face needs, other-face needs, and mutual-face concerns.

Over the years, Ting-Toomey and her colleagues have conducted a number of investigations exploring the various ways that culturally grounded face concerns and facework strategies affect conflict management strategies (e.g., Oetzel, 1998; Oetzel, Myers, Meares, & Lara, 2003: Oetzel & Ting-Toomey, 2003; Oetzel, Ting-Toomey, Yokochi, Masumoto, & Takai, 2000; Oetzel et al., 2001; Ting-Toomey & Oetzel, 2001), whereas other scholars explored the role of facework in interpersonal and organizational conflict settings (e.g., Brew & Cairns, 2004; Brown, 1977; Cupach & Messman, 1999; Penman, 1994). In general, research findings suggest that the focus of face concern (self, other, mutual) varies by culture (Ting-Toomey & Oetzel, 2001), and that participants' concern for face often complicates efforts at resolution because the focus of the interaction shifts from an instrumental orientation to one in which parties act to protect, defend, and restore their image or persona. It is this emphasis on face that often makes resolution difficult and elusive to realize (Cupach & Canary, 1997; Folger et al., 2005), as is the case in intractable conflicts (Northrup, 1989).

Within the specific context of crisis negotiation, Rogan and Hammer (1994) posited that facework strategies are manifest in party's linguistic expressions and thereby function as framing devices that represent the individual's definition of the interaction at both the global and regional/episodic levels; Rogan and Hammer contended that these facework frames vary along the three dimensions of (a) locus of concern for self or other, (b) valence of the facework strategy in order to defend, attack, or honor one's own or the relational other's face; and (c) the temporality of the strategy as either proactive, enacted in an attempt to protect against face loss, or retroactive, in order to restore lost face. Integrating these three dimensions produced six types of active facework: (a) Defend Self's Face, (b) Attack Self's Face, (c) Restore Self's Face, (d) Defend Other's Face, (e) Attack Other's Face, and (f) Restore Other's Face. They added a seventh category of "no facework" to account for instances of no discernible active facework (e.g., backchannels: "uh-uh"). Rogan and Hammer used this scheme to code a set of actual crisis negotiation incidents.

According to Rogan and Hammer's (1994) investigation of facework in hostage negotiation, Restore Other's Face was the primary behavior used by negotiators, whereas Restore Self's Face was the principal strategy for suspects. They also noted that Attack Self's Face was a common facework strategy used by suspects in general, and that it was of particular noteworthiness in the suicidal incident. This finding prompted Rogan and Hammer to speculate that certain facework strategies may be associated with particular outcomes (i.e., suicidal vs. nonsuicidal). Unfortunately, however, their study was based on just three incidents, only one of which involved a suicidal resolution.

Given the preliminary findings of the Rogan and Hammer (1994) study, I recently undertook an investigation to explore further the potential variability in facework behavior in crisis negotiations based on incident outcome, as well as other select incident characteristics. The following questions framed this study:

Q1: What facework patterns are present in perpetrators' and negotiators' linguistic communication during crisis negotiation incidents?

Q2: Will perpetrators' and negotiators' facework vary between incidents depending on incident outcome (surrender/nonsurrender)?

Q3: Will perpetrators' and negotiators' facework vary by incident type?

Q4: Will perpetrators' and negotiators' facework vary between incidents in which hostages are held and those in which no hostages are held?

Q5: Will perpetrators' and negotiators' facework vary between incidents in which violence precipitated the event and incidents that did not involve precipitating violence?

CONDUCT OF THE STUDY

Incidents Investigated

Detailed chronological transcriptions of six authentic crisis negotiation incidents conducted by various local law enforcement agencies were obtained from the archives of the FBI's Crisis Negotiation Unit. Each of these incidents was transcribed according to Jefferson's guidelines for audio transcription (Schenkein, 1978) and proofed for accuracy of correspondence with the original audio recording. These incidents were selected for analysis because they were accompanied by some key incident information, including situation outcome, general incident classification by the negotiating agency, basic pre-incident background regarding perpetrator violence preceding the standoff, and information about the presence of hostages. As such, the six incidents consisted of completed suicide and surrender outcomes; Criminal, Mental Instability, and Domestic incidents[1]; incidents in which hostages were held and in which no hostages were held; and incidents in which violence either did or did not precipitate the negotiation. These four incident features served as the bases for comparison of facework behaviors among the six incidents.

OVERVIEW OF THE INCIDENTS

Incident 1 was a criminal incident involving a pre-incident murder by the suspect, with the suspect holding several hostages during the incident and concluding with the release of the hostages unharmed and the suspect's suicide. Incident 2 was also a criminal incident, with a pre-incident shooting of a police officer by the suspect, with several hostages held and released prior to the suspect killing an accomplice to the incident, and concluding in the suspect's suicide. Incident 3 was a domestic dispute with no precipitating violence, with the suspect holding his children hostage in order to address some relationship problems, and concluding with a tactical assault and capture of the perpetrator. Although this incident was resolved by means of a police assault, incident background information suggests that a tactical resolution was employed out of concern for the suspect enacting a homicide-suicide resolution. Incident 4 was likewise a domestic dispute with attempted violence preceding the incident by several weeks, but not immediately prior to the incident, with the suspect holding hostages and ending with the suspect's suicide. Incident 5 was a mental instability situation in which the suspect shot a family member and barricaded himself in a standoff with police prior to surrendering. Finally, Incident 6 was also a mental instability case with no preceding violence, no hostage held, and concluding with the suspect's surrender.

CODING OF THE INCIDENT TRANSCRIPTIONS

Given that this study served as a follow-up to Rogan and Hammer' (1994) investigation, a method similar to that employed by them was used for coding the incidents for possible facework. Briefly, the unit of analysis was the uninterrupted speaking turn (i.e., turn at talk). Individually, Incident 1 was comprised of 227 units ($n = 123$ suspect, $n = 104$ negotiator), Incident 2 accounted for 1,230 units ($n = 718$ suspect, $n = 512$ negotiator), Incident 3 consisted of 893 units ($n = 571$ suspect, $n = 322$ negotiator), Incident 4 had 303 units ($n = 142$ suspect, $n = 161$ negotiator), Incident 5 consisted of 356 units ($n = 187$ suspect, $n = 169$ negotiator), and Incident 6 had 309 units ($n = 148$ suspect, $n = 161$ negotiator).

Rogan and Hammer's (1994) three-dimensional facework model was used for coding each unit of analysis for suspect and negotiator alike. Briefly, their coding metric consists of the following six active types of facework coding categories: (a) Defend Self's Face (DSF), (b) Attack Self's Face (ASF), (c) Restore Self's Face (RSF), (d) Defend Other's Face (DOF), (e) Attack Other's Face (AOF), and (f) Restore Other's Face (RSF). According to Rogan and Hammer, Defend Self's Face acts are proactive, self-focused, face-honoring behaviors that function to protect one's face against possible face loss (e.g., "I'm not certain if I can do what you ask, I'll have to check with my commander"). Likewise, Defend Other's Face acts are proactive attempts to endorse and protect other's face (e.g., "Before we go any further, I just want to say that I think you're handling yourself quite well so far"). Attack Self's Face and Attack Other's Face are simply acts that function to deprecate either one's own or the other's face (e.g., "I'm just a major screw-up, with no reason to go on," and "You're a fool if you think I'm going to buy your crap"). Finally, face restoration behaviors constitute attempts to restore either one's own face (e.g., "What the hell gives you the right to call me crazy?") or to restore other's face (e.g., "Don't talk about yourself that way, you're a good person at heart").

Two research assistants who were blind to the actual purpose of the investigation were trained in the procedure for coding the transcripts according to Rogan and Hammer's (1994) facework metric. In the case where units of analysis reflected more than one possible facework type, coders were instructed to code according to a gestalt impression, or the dominant level of facework manifest in the turn at talk. Following several practice sessions, assistants independently coded 120 practice units extracted from the transcription of another unused crisis negotiation incident. For this pretest, there was an aggregate 79% agreement between the coders, with a Cohen's (1960) kappa (κ) of .76. Each assistant then independently coded each of the six incidents used for analysis. Intercoder reliability was calculated based on 20% of the total units for each incident. For Incident 1, $\kappa = .71$; for Incident 2, $\kappa = .80$; for Incident 3, $\kappa = .78$; for Incident 4, $\kappa = .84$; for Incident 5, $\kappa = .87$; and for Incident 6, $\kappa = .76$. According to Fleiss (1981), and as reported in von Eye and Mun (2005), a κ of .40 to .60 is considered fair, a κ of .60 to .75 is good, and a κ greater than .75 is excellent. Intercoder reliability was therefore considered acceptable for analysis. In cases where the coders disagreed about the type of facework present, they reviewed the transcript and conjointly recoded each unit in order to create a single consensus code for each unit of analysis.

FINDINGS

The first question sought to determine the general facework patterns of suspects and negotiators. Tables 6.1 and 6.2 present the frequency and percentage of facework codes for each type of facework for suspects and negotiators as calculated from the total number of face-only codes for each incident. As can be seen from Table 6.1, suspect facework in Incident 1 was dominated by Attack Self's Face (55%) and Defend Self's Face (27%) behaviors. Similar results were generated for Incident 2 (Attack Self's Face, 28%) and Defend Self's Face, 30%). For Incident 3, Attack Self's Face (35%), Attack Other's Face (21%), and Restore Self's Face (23%) were the dominant face behaviors. Incidents 4 and 5 were each dominated by Restore Self's Face (41% and 43%, respectively), along with Defend Self's facework (29% and 31%). For Incident 6, suspect facework was almost exclusively coded as Attack Other's Face (84%).

Across all six incidents, for suspects' facework, both Attack Other's Face and Restore Self's Face accounted for 25.1% of all facework codes, followed by Defend Self's Face (22.6%), Attack Self's Face (17.5%), Restore Other's Face (5.4%), and Defend Other's Face (4.3%). Yet Attack Self's Face was most common in Incidents 1, 2, and 3, whereas Attack Other's Face was only dominant in Incidents 3 and 6. Defend Self's Face accounted for more than 20% of all facework codes in Incidents 1, 2, 4, and 5, whereas Defend Other's Face accounted for no more than 9% of all facework only in Incident 1. Restore Self's Face accounted for more than 20% of face codes in Incidents 3, 4, and 5; Restore Other's Face accounted for no more than 9% of face codes in Incident 5.

Table 6.1 Frequency and Percent Facework-Only Behavior for Suspect by Incident

Facework Type	One N/%*	Two N/%*	Three N/%*	Four N/%*	Five N/%*	Six N/%*	Sum N/%
Attack Self	6/55	22/28	18/35	1/3.0	2/4.0	0/0.0	49/17.5
Attack Other	0/0.0	2/15	11/21	4/12	2/4.0	41/84	70/25.1
Defend Self	3/27	23/30	9/17	10/29	17/31	1/2.0	63/22.5
Defend Other	1/9.0	3/4.0	0/0.0	3/9.0	5/9.0	0/0.0	12/4.3
Restore Self	1/9.0	14/18	12/23	14/41	24/43	5/10	70/25.1
Restore Other	0/0.0	4/5.0	2/4.0	2/6.0	5/9.0	2/4.0	15/5.4
Total Face Codes	11/8.0	78/10	52/8.3	34/19	55/22.7	49/24.9	279/12.9
No Facework	123/92	718/90	571/91.7	142/81	187/77.3	148/75.1	1,889/87.1
χ	6.1	28.0	12.8	23.5	45.7	90.7	
df	3	5	4	5	5	3	
p	.11	.01	.01	.01	.01	.01	

* Percentage is based on the frequency of each facework type divided by the total facework-only codes for each incident.

103

Table 6.2 Frequency and Percent Facework-Only Behavior for Negotiators by Incident

Facework Type	One N/%*	Two N/%*	Three N/%*	Four N/%*	Five N/%*	Six N/%*	Sum N/%
Attack Self	0/0.0	6/11.5	0/0.0	0/0.0	0/0.0	0/0.0	6/1.7
Attack Other	0/0.0	12/22.5	1/1.1	0/0.0	0/0.0	3/4.3	16/4.5
Defend Self	0/0.0	2/4.0	0/0.0	10/22.2	0/0.0	0/0.0	12/3.4
Defend Other	11/35.5	17/32	4/4.6	13/28.9	30/41.1	13/18.9	88/24.5
Restore Self	0/0.0	2/4.0	0/0.0	9/20.0	0/0.0	0/0.0	11/3.1
Restore Other	20/64.5	14/26	82/94.3	13/28.9	43/58.9	53/76.8	225/62.0
Total Face Codes	31/23.0	53/9.4	87/21.3	45/21.8	73/30.2	69/30.0	358/20.0
No Facework	104/77.0	512/90.6	322/78.7	161/78.2	169/69.8	161/70	1,429/80.0
χ	2.6	23.2	145.5	1.2	2.3	60.9	
df	1	5	2	3	1	2	
p	.11	.01	.01	.77	.13	.01	

* Percentage is based on the frequency of each facework type divided by the total facework-only codes for each incident.

As can be seen from Table 6.2, negotiator facework in Incident 1 was dominated by Restore Other's Face (64.5%) and Defend Other's Face (35.5%). For Incident 2, negotiator facework was comprised mostly of Defend Other's Face (32%), Restore Other's Face (26%), and interestingly by Attack Other's Face (22.5%). Incident 3 facework was almost exclusively coded as Restore Other's Face (94.3%). Incident 4 had the broadest representation of facework behavior, including Defend Other's Face and Restore Other's Face, each accounting for 28.9%, followed by Defend Self's Face (22.2%) and Restore Self's Face (20%). Incidents 5 and 6 were each dominated by Restore Other's Face (58.9% and 76.8%, respectively), with Defend Other's Face also accounting for 41.1% in Incident 5. Across all six incidents, Restore Other's Face accounted for 62% of all negotiator facework, followed by Defend Other's Face (24.5%), Attack Other's Face (4.5%), Defend Self's Face (3.4%), Restore Self's Face (3.1%), and Attack Self's Face (1.7%). Restore Other's Face and Defend Other's Face were clearly the two most dominant types of negotiator facework across all six incidents.

The second question asked whether facework would vary between incidents based on incident outcome. For the incidents used in this investigation, there were essentially two outcomes—Suicide and Surrender. (As noted previously, although Incident 3 actually concluded with a police assault, the dynamics of the incident suggest that a tactical resolution was enacted due to the suspect's apparent expression to commit homicide and suicide.) Thus, Incidents 1, 2, 3, and 4 comprised the "Suicide" outcome, whereas Incidents 5 and 6 comprised the "Surrender" outcome.

Table 6.3 presents the aggregate and mean percentage of facework for suspects according to incident outcome, incident type, the presence of precipitating violence, and the presence of hostages. As can be seen in the first two columns of Table 6.3, Suicide incidents were predominantly characterized by Attack Self's Face (27%), Defend Self's Face (25.6%), and Restore Self's Face (23.4%), although Attack Other's Face did account for 15.4% of all facework. Comparatively, the two Surrender incidents were dominated by Attack Other's Face (41.3%), Restore Self's Face (27.9%), and Defend Self's Face (17.3%). Most notably, an analysis of the difference in proportion (Blalock, 1979) in facework usage between the Suicide and Surrender incidents reveals a significant difference for Attack Self's Face and Attack Other's Face, with Attack Self's Face occurring was most frequently in the Suicide incidents and Attack Other's Face most frequent in the Surrender incidents.

Table 6.4 presents the mean percentage of facework for negotiators according to incident outcome, incident type, the presence of precipitating violence, and the presence of hostages. As can be seen in the first two columns of Table 6.4, Suicide incidents were predominantly characterized by Restore Other's Face (59.7%) and Defend Other's Face (20.8%), whereas the Surrender incidents were likewise dominated by Restore Other's Face (67.6%) and Defend Other's Face (30.4%). Comparatively, negotiators employed Attack Self's Face, Defend Self's Face, and Restore Self's Face in the Suicide incidents, but not at all in the Surrender incidents. An analysis of proportional difference in facework types revealed

Table 6.3 Aggregate Frequency and Mean Percent Facework Behavior for Perpetrator by Incident Outcome, Type, Violence, and Hostage

Facework Type	Suicide N/%*	Surrender N/%*	Criminal N/%*	Domestic N/%*	Mental N/%*	Violence N/%*	No Violence N/%*	Hostage N/%*	No Hostage N/%*
Attack Self	47/27	2/1.9	28/31.5	19/22.1	2/1.9	30/20.8	19/14.1	47/26.9	2/1.9
Attack Other	27/15.4	43/41.3	12/13.5	15/17.4	43/41.3	14/9.7	56/41.5	27/15.4	43/41.3
Defend Self	45/25.6	18/17.3	26/29.2	19/22.1	18/17.3	43/29.9	20/14.8	45/25.7	18/17.3
Defend Other	7/4.0	5/4.8	4/4.5	3/3.5	5/4.8	9/6.3	3/2.2	7/4.0	5/4.8
Restore Self	41/23.4	29/27.9	15/16.9	26/30.2	29/27.9	39/27.1	31/23.0	41/23.4	29/27.9
Restore Other	8/4.6	7/6.7	4/4.5	4/4.7	7/6.3	9/6.3	6/4.4	8/4.6	7/6.7
Total Face Codes	175	104	89	86	104	144	135	175	104
χ	56.7	74.4	36.5	29.0	74.4	48.9	82.9	56.7	74.4
df	5	5	5	5	5	5	5	5	5
p	.01	.01	.01	.01	.01	.01	.01	.01	.01

* Percentage is based on the frequency of each facework type divided by the total facework-only codes for each incident.

106

Table 6.4 Aggregate Frequency and Mean Percent Facework Behavior for Negotiator by Incident Outcome, Type, Violence, and Hostage

Facework Type	Suicide N/%*	Surrender N/%*	Criminal N/%*	Domestic N/%*	Mental N/%*	Violence N/%*	No Violence N/%*	Hostage N/%*	No Hostage N/%*
Attack Self	6/2.8	0/0.0	6/7.1	0/0.0	0/0.0	6/3.8	0/0.0	6/2.8	0/0.0
Attack Other	13/6.0	3/2.1	12/14.3	1/0.8	3/2.1	12/7.6	4/2.0	13/6.0	3/2.1
Defend Self	12/5.6	0/0.0	2/2.4	10/7.6	0/0.0	2/1.3	10/5.0	12/5.6	0/0.0
Defend Other	45/20.8	43/30.4	28/33.3	12/12.9	43/30.3	58/36.9	30/14.9	45/20.8	43/30.3
Restore Self	11/5.1	0/0.0	2/2.4	9/9.8	0/0.0	2/1.3	9/4.5	11/5.1	0/0.0
Restore Other	129/59.7	96/67.6	34/40.5	95/72.0	96/67.6	77/49.0	148/73.6	129/59.7	96/67.6
Total Face Codes	216	142	84	132	142	157	201	216	142
χ	315.6	92.0	68.0	227.7	92.0	205.3	371.2	315.6	92.0
df	5	2	5	4	2	5	4	5	2
p	.01	.01	.01	.01	.01	.01	.01	.01	.01

* Percentage is based on the frequency of each facework type divided by the total facework-only codes for each incident.

107

that negotiators used more Attack Other's Face, as well as more Defend Other's Face in the Suicide incidents than in the Surrender incidents. No other differences were found to be significant.

The third question asked whether facework would vary by incident type. As can be seen in Table 6.3, suspect facework in the Criminal incidents was dominated principally by Attack Self's Face (31.5%) and Defend Self's Face (29.2%), and to a lesser degree by Restore Self's Face (16.9%) and Attack Other's Face (13.5%). Generally, similar results were produced for the Domestic incidents, with Restore Self's Face accounting for 30.2% of all face codes, followed by Attack Self's Face (22.1%), Defend Self's Face (22.1%), and Attack Other's Face (17.4%). Finally, although the Mental Instability incidents were dominated by Restore Self's Face (27.9%) and Defend Self's Face (17.3%), suspects' predominant facework was Attack Other's Face (41.3%). Comparing among the three incident types suggests that they were all characterized by suspects' moderate use of Restore Self's Face, whereas the Criminal and Domestic incidents were marked by a higher proportion of Attack Self's Face and Defend Self's Face.

The most notable distinction for suspects was the predominance of Attack Other's Face in the Mental Instability incidents, accounting for slightly more than 41% of all facework codes. An analysis of the difference in proportion revealed significant differences in facework usage for perpetrators between Criminal and Domestic incidents for Attack Self's Face and Restore Self's Face; between Criminal and Mental Instability for Attack Self's Face, Attack Other's Face, Defend Self's Face, and Restore Self's Face; and between Domestic and Mental Instability for Attack Other's Face.

Referring once again to Table 6.4, negotiators' facework in the Criminal incidents were dominated by Restore Other's Face (40.5%), Defend Other's Face (33.3%), and Attack Other's Face (14.3%). Within the Domestic incidents, negotiators' facework was almost entirely accounted for by Restore Other's Face (72.0%), followed by Defend Other's Face (12.9%). Finally, for the Mental Instability incidents, Restore Other's Face (67.6%) and Defend Other's Face (30.3%) were the two most common types of facework for negotiators.

Comparing again among the three types of incidents for negotiators suggests that all three were dominated by Restore Other's Face, whereas the Criminal and Mental Instability incidents were also marked by Defend Other's Face. The greatest difference was the presence of Attack Other's Face in the Criminal incidents, whereas it was absent in both the Domestic and Mental Instability incidents. An analysis of the difference in proportion revealed significant differences in facework usage for negotiators between Criminal and Domestic incidents for Attack Self's Face, Attack Other's Face, Defend Other's Face, and Restore Other's Face; between Criminal and Mental Instability for Attack Other's Face and Restore Other's Face; and between Domestic and Mental Instability for Defend Self's Face, Defend Other's Face, and Restore Self's Face. All other facework types were used in a proportionally similar manner.

The fourth question asked whether suspect facework would vary by incident according to hostages being held. Table 6.3 shows that suspect facework in the

Hostage incidents involved primarily Attack Self's Face (26.9%), Defend Self's Face (25.7%), and Restore Self's Face (23.4%). Within the Non-Hostage incidents, suspect facework was mostly Attack Other's Face (41.3%) and Restore Self's Face (27.9%). Comparing the two incidents showed that within the Hostage incidents, suspects' facework was essentially self-directed, with a relatively equal distribution among Attack Self's Face, Defend Self's Face and Restore Self's Face, and in the Non-Hostage incidents, suspects tended to use Attack Other's Face and Restore Self's Face. A comparison of usage of each face type between incidents revealed that Attack Self's Face varied by hostage presence, as did Attack Other's Face and Defend Self's Face. There were no significant differences in usage for the other types of facework.

According to Table 6.4, negotiator facework in both Hostage and Non-Hostage incidents involved primarily Restore Other's Face (59.7% and 67.6%) and Defend Other's Face (20.8% and 30.3%), respectively. Comparing the two types of incidents showed that negotiator facework was generally consistent regardless of the presence of hostages. A more specific comparison of the kinds of facework used by negotiators across the two types of incidents revealed that only Attack Other's Face and Defend Other's Face varied by incident; all other facework types were used similarly in each incident.

The fifth question asked whether facework would vary according to whether Violence precipitated the situation. Table 6.3 reveals that suspects' facework in the Violent incidents were primarily Defend Self's Face (29.9%), Restore Self's Face (27.1%), and Attack Self's Face (20.8%). In the No-Violence incidents, suspects' facework was mostly Attack Other's Face (41.5%) and Restore Self's Face (23.0%). In incidents that involved violent precipitating events, suspects' facework was predominately self-directed, including Attack, Defend, and Restore Self's Face, whereas in the No-Violence incidents, suspects tended to use Attack Other's Face and Restore Self's Face. Comparing the types of facework used by suspects across the six incidents, only Attack Other's Face and Defend Self's Face varied by incident; all other facework types did not differ across incident type.

Table 6.4 shows that in the Violence incidents, negotiators engaged in primarily Restore Other's Face (49.0%) and Defend Other's Face (36.9%), whereas in the No-Violence incidents, Restore Other's Face (73.6%) was the predominant type of facework, with Defend Other's Face employed to a much lesser degree (14.9%). Clearly, the negotiator's facework usage in both types of incidents was dominated by other-directed facework. Comparing each type of facework between incidents revealed that negotiators' use of Attack Other's Face, Defend Self's Face, Defend Other's Face, Restore Self's Face, and Restore Other's Face varied by incident.

DISCUSSION OF THE FINDINGS

The study presented in this chapter sought to shed additional light on the dynamics of suspect and negotiator facework in crisis negotiation by building on the earlier work of Rogan and Hammer (1994). The results indicated that, across all six incidents, active facework codes for suspects accounted for just 279 (12.8%) of the total number of speaking units for suspects, whereas facework codes for negotiators accounted for 358 (20.0%) of their total number of speaking units. In general, negotiators appeared to engage in more active facework than do suspects. Further, suspects engaged most frequently in Attack Other's Face and Restore Self's Face, followed by Defend Self's Face and Attack Self's Face. By contrast, negotiators most frequently used Restore Other's Face and Defend Other's Face.

It is clear from the findings that suspects and negotiators differ in their use of facework, with suspects engaging principally in self-directed honoring strategies and some self-directed attacks, as well as attacks against the face of the negotiator. The dominance of self-honoring strategies is consistent with Rogan and Hammer's (1994) claim that the inherent face-threatening nature of crisis/hostage negotiations elicits face-saving efforts by suspects. Negative self- and other-directed acts also seem consistent with Rogan and Hammer's argument that certain incident types and qualities are associated with suspect use of face-attacking behaviors. In contrast, negotiators engaged primarily in other-directed-honoring strategies. Such strategies are typically employed in an effort to bolster the face (identity) of the suspect, most purposively to help calm and stabilize the individual in an effort to reduce the crisis nature of the interaction and to effectuate more normative situation management (Donohue & Roberto, 1993; Lanceley, 2003; Noesner & Webster, 1997).

Although interesting, the aggregate results tend to mask the usage patterns within specific incidents, as well as across different types of incidents. Analysis of facework according to incident outcome (Suicide or Surrender) revealed that suspects engaged mostly in Attack Self's Face, Defend Self's Face, and Restore Self's Face. Of particular interest is the comparison of suspect facework in the Surrender incidents, in which suspects engaged predominantly in Attack Other's Face, followed by Restore Self's Face, with that found in the Suicide incidents, where suspects used mostly Attack Self's Face, Defend Self's Face, and Restore Self's Face. Again, these findings are generally consistent with those reported by Rogan and Hammer (1994) and lend additional support to their conclusions about the self-oriented facework of suicidal suspects. Specifically, they posited that a greater frequency of Attack Self's Face is associated with self-inflicted violent incident resolutions, whereas self-directed face-honoring behaviors are characteristic of negotiated surrenders. These results highlight a pattern of variability in facework behaviors between incidents that conclude with suicide of the suspect and those that end in surrender. In fact, this finding is consistent with results reported by Pennebaker, Mehl, and Niederhoffer (2003), in which they conclude that depression, suicidal ideation, and mania are marked by a high degree of linguistic self-preoccupation as manifest in a frequent use of first-person pronouns.

Taken together, these findings make it reasonable to conclude that a suspect's dominant verbal expression of negative affect directed toward the self, and thereby a placing of blame on the self, is a likely predictor of suicide. Comparatively, attacks directed toward the other, although typically regarded as hostile, aggressive, and confrontational (Cupach & Canary, 1997; Folger et al., 2005), appear to place blame for the situation on the negotiator, rather than the self, thereby sustaining and bolstering the face (projected self-image) of the suspect. Such behaviors ostensibly enable suspects to work through the process of negative emotion management by venting their frustration and ultimately shifting the interaction out of a crisis framework and into more normative problem management (DiVasto, Lanceley, & Gruys, 1992; Donohue & Roberto, 1993; Wind, 1995). Furthermore, it seems likely that these perpetrators did not frame the incident as the consequence of a personal crisis, whereby the standoff was the result of a traumatic precipitating event, but rather as the consequence of having committed an unlawful act to which the police responded. Thus, blame was not self-directed, but rather other-directed.

The facework of negotiators within the Suicide and Surrender incidents was dominated by Restore Other's Face and Defend Other's Face. Negotiators did, however, employ all types of facework within the Suicide situations, as they struggled to establish a baseline rapport with the suspect in the hope of negating the suspect's act of self-destruction. Such efforts are perhaps most evident in the negotiators' use of Attack Self's Face and Attack Other's Face. The former is generally regarded as a mechanism for self-disclosing about personal life challenges and relational problems in an effort to achieve commonality with the suspect, whereas the latter is sometimes recommended as a way to challenge the defeatist thinking of the suicidal suspect when other supportive messages seem to be ineffective (DiVasto, et al., 1992; Noesner, & Webster, 1997). Interestingly, although suspects attacked the face of negotiators within the Surrender incidents, there were no recorded codes for negotiator attempts to defend or restore self-face. It seems that negotiators simply allowed the suspects to vent their anger and frustration in an effort to reduce the overall tension of the situation.

Comparing among the incidents in terms of general type (Criminal, Domestic, and Mental Instability), the most notable finding was that, although suspects engaged in Restore and Defend Self's Face in all three incident types, they employed more Attack Self's Face in the Criminal and Domestic incidents than in the Mental Instability incidents. Attack Other's Face was the third most frequently coded facework in the Mental Instability incidents. Negotiators demonstrated little variability across incidents, engaging mostly in Defend and Restore Other's Face. Surprisingly, the two Mental Instability incidents were not part of the Suicide outcome, as one might anticipate based on the incident moniker. Rather, both Criminal incidents ended in suicide, as did the two Domestic situations. This suggests that the labeling of incidents according to particular a priori categories, such as Criminal, Domestic, and Mental Instability, although functionally useful in establishing broad incident classifications, may fail to offer accurate representations of the actual (communicative) dynamics of such incidents.

Suspect facework in the incidents involving precipitating Violence revealed that Defending and Restoring Self's Face were most the dominant facework types, along with Attack Self's Face. Comparatively, the No-Violence incidents were marked mostly by Attack Other's Face. Suspect's facework in the Hostage incidents was likewise comprised mostly of Attack Self's face, whereas in the No-Hostage incidents, it was predominantly Attack Other's Face. Negotiators' facework was consistent in both Violence conditions, as it was also in the Hostage and Hon-Hostage incidents, comprised predominately of Defend and Restore Other's Face. Of the six incidents, three were marked by violence (Incidents 1, 2, and 4), two of which (Incidents 1 and 2) ended in suicide. These findings suggest that incidents with precipitating Violence "require" the suspect to seek restoration of his or her face as a means of self-justifying the prior action, whereas in the No-Violence incidents, suspects verbalize and articulate their anger and frustration toward the negotiator as the two parties work toward a nonviolent resolution to the standoff.

LIMITATIONS ASSOCIATED WITH THE FINDINGS

Although these findings provide additional insight into the dynamics of facework in crisis/hostage negotiation, the study does suffer from certain weaknesses that limit its general heuristic value. First, operational refinement of Rogan and Hammer's (1994) face-coding metric, in which strict parameters were set on what constituted a face act, resulted in substantially fewer face codes for both suspects and negotiators than in Rogan and Hammer's original study. Specifically, suspect and negotiator face codes accounted for only 12.8% and 20% of possible codable units, respectively. In their investigation, Rogan and Hammer assigned a face code for essentially every unit of analysis. In this study, operationalization of face required an unequivocal face act embedded within the linguistic cue in order to be coded as one of six active face behaviors. This restricted operationalization may have negated more frequent and diverse coding of the different types of facework, thereby skewing the nature of the findings.

A second limitation is the restricted focus on facework-only behavior, as opposed to a more holistic and intergrative analysis of the multiple communicative features that exist in Taylor's (2002a) cylindrical model and Rogan and Hammer's (2002) S.A.F.E. model. As these scholars have argued, crisis communication involves a complex dynamic of communicative interaction among suspect and negotiator focus on instrumental, relational, face, and emotional concerns, as they manifest and consequently impact the integrative, distributive, and avoidant dispositions of the actors. Future research should strive for a more comprehensive analysis of the broader range of communication dynamics and, in particular, focus on the facework behavior among individuals from different cultural groups (Hammer, 1997; Hammer & Weaver, 1994). The work of Ting-Toomey and others (Brew & Cairns, 2004; Brown, 1977 Oetzel, 1998; Ting-Toomey, 1988; Ting-Toomey & Kurogi, 1998) clearly highlights the centrality of face as a central factor influencing the conflict interaction behavior of individuals with different cultural frames. Thus, exploring such patterns can be of significant value for understanding culturally based interaction during crisis conditions. Still, independently, each of the various communicative dimensions delineated in the extant communication-based models of crisis negotiation (Rogan & Hammer, 2002; Taylor, 2002a, 2002b) can provide insight into the link between specific communication acts and particular psychological and dispositional orientations of individual suspects. Taylor (2002a, 2002b) posits that such insight is critical for negotiators as they seek to predict a suspect's future behavior and propensity for violence.

SOME IMPLICATIONS FOR THE FINDINGS

As previously noted, recent incident data reported in the FBI's HOBAS database of 4,067 negotiated barricade situations indicates that 8.2% of all incidents ended with a suspect suicide/attempted suicide. Additionally, Rogan, Hammer, and Van Zandt (1994) reported that their survey of negotiation team leaders revealed that suicides were the most typical incidents to which negotiators responded and for which they sought recommendations for incident resolution. Over the years, much has been written by practitioners and researchers alike about identifying, understanding, and managing suspects with various psychological and emotional disorders (e.g., Borum & Strentz, 1992; Fuselier & Noesner, 1990; Lanceley, 1981; Slatkin, 2003). Specific communication strategies such as active listening, paraphrasing, emotion labeling, and supportive messages were specifically suggested for dealing with suicidal suspects (DiVasto et al., 1992; Noesner & Webster, 1997).

As these findings indicate, a notable difference exists in facework between incidents that conclude in suicide or attempted suicide and those that end in surrender. Suicide outcomes are marked by the suspect's dominant usage of Attack Self's Face, whereas surrender incidents are characterized by Attack Other's Face. Training negotiators to discern the functional value of discrete linguistic expressions for their facework usage could help police more effectively identify and manage suicide incidents by implementing appropriate negotiation tactics that provide expressive support to the suspect. Similarly, knowing that frequent usage of other-directed face attacks are not indicative of suspect violence may provide negotiators with the confidence to work through a suspect's emotional hostility without needing to implement a tactical resolution.

Finally, this study suggests that incident characteristics that serve as a priori taxonomies for identifying and managing standoffs are not necessarily good predictors of outcome. More specifically, the various incident taxonomies that have been advanced by law enforcement and others as a means for defining an incident (e.g., Goldaber, 1979; Hacker, 1976; Miron & Goldstein, 1979; Schlossberg, 1979) actually seem to offer limited insight into the dynamics of such incidents or the likelihood of various outcomes. Historical models that attempt to define incidents according to particular static traits fail to tap into the dynamic communicative nature of these events (Taylor, 2002a). However, a communication-based approach, with particular attention to the locus and valence of facework, provides informative insight into these dynamics and likely outcomes. Being armed with more precise knowledge about the dynamics of facework in crisis/hostage negotiations may enable law enforcement officers to manage these situations more effectively and to achieve nonviolent resolutions more often.

NOTES

1. According to various police negotiation incident classification typologies, Criminal incidents are those in which a suspect is interrupted during the commission of a crime; Mental Instability incidents involve a suspect who is defined as dealing with some sort of psychological or emotional problem; and Domestic incidents involve a suspect whose focus is on a relational issue with a family member, typically a spouse or dating partner.

REFERENCES

Adler, R. S., Rosen, B., & Silverstein, E. M. (1998). Emotions in negotiation: How to manage fear and anger. *Negotiation Journal, 14*, 161–179.

Bateson, G. (1954/1972). *Steps to an ecology of mind.* New York: Ballantine Books.

BBC News. (September, 4, 2004). *High death toll in Russia siege.* Retrieved September 4, 2004, from http://news.bbc.co.uk/1/hi/world/europe/3624024.stm.

Blalock, H. (1979). *Social statistics* (2nd ed.). New York: McGraw-Hill.

Bodtker, A. M., & Jameson, J. K. (2001). Emotion in conflict formation and its transformation: Application to organizational conflict management. *International Journal of Conflict Management, 12*, 259–275.

Borum, R., & Strentz, T. (1992). The borderline personality. *FBI Law Enforcement Bulletin, 61*, 6–10.

Brew, F. P., & Cairns, D. R. (2004). Styles of managing interpersonal conflict in relation to status and face concerns: A study with Anglos and Chinese. *International Journal of Conflict Management, 15*, 27–56.

Brown, B. R. (1977). Face-saving and race-restoration in negotiation. In D. Druckman (Ed.), *Negotiations: Social-psychological perspective* (pp. 275–299). Beverly Hills, CA: Sage.

Brown, P., & Levinson, S. (1987). *Politeness: Some universals in language usage.* Cambridge: Cambridge University Press.

Cohen, J. A. (1960). A coefficient of agreement for nominal scales. *Educational and Psychological Measurement, 20*, 37–46.

Cupach, W. R., & Canary, D. J. (1997). *Competence in interpersonal conflict.* Prospect Heights, IL: Waveland.

Cupach, W. R., & Messman, S. J. (1999). Face predilections and friendship solidarity. *Communication Reports, 12*, 11–19.

Davidson, T. N. (2002). *To preserve life: Hostage-crisis management.* Indianapolis, IN: CIMACOM.

Dewulf, A., Gray, B., Putnam, L., Aarts, N., Lewicki, R., Bowen, R., & van Woerkum, C. (2005, June). *Disentangling approaches to framing: Mapping the terrain.* Paper presented at the International Conflict Management conference, Seville, Spain.

DiVasto, P., Lanceley, F. J., & Gruys, A. (1992). Critical issues in suicide intervention. *FBI Law Enforcement Bulletin, 61,* 13–26.

Donohue, W. A., Ramesh, C., & Borchgrevink, C. (1991). Crisis bargaining: Tracking relational paradox in hostage negotiation. *International Journal of Conflict Management, 2,* 257–274.

Donohue, W. A., Ramesh, C., Kaufmann, G., & Smith, R. (1991). Crisis bargaining in hostage negotiations. *International Journal of Group Tensions, 21,* 133–154.

Donohue, W. A., & Roberto, A. J. (1993). Relational development in hostage negotiation. *Human Communication Research, 20,* 175–198.

Donohue, W. A., & Roberto, A. J. (1996). An empirical examination of three models of integrative and distributive bargaining. *International Journal of Conflict Management, 7,* 209–229.

Fagan, T. J., & Van Zandt, C. R. (1993). Even in non-negotiable situations, negotiation plays a critical role. *Corrections Today, 55,* 132–141.

Federal Bureau of Investigation. (2007, March). *HOBAS: Statistical report of incidents.* Quantico, VA: FBI Academy.

Fleiss, J. L. (1981). *Statistical methods for rates and proportions.* New York: Wiley.

Folger, J. P., Poole, M. S., & Stutman, R. K. (2005). *Working through conflict* (5th ed.). New York: Longman.

Friedland, N. (1986, January). Hostage negotiations: Types, processes, outcomes. *Negotiation Journal,* pp. 57–72.

Fuselier, G. D. (1986). What every negotiator would like his chief to know. *FBI Law Enforcement Bulletin, 55,* 1–4.

Fuselier, G. D., & Noesner, G. W. (1990). Confronting the terrorist hostage taker. *FBI Law Enforcement Bulletin, 59,* 6–11.

Fuselier, G. D., Van Zandt, C. R., & Lanceley, F. J. (1991). Hostage/barricade incidents: High risk factors and the action criteria. *FBI Law Enforcement Bulletin, 60,* 6–12.

Giebels, E., & Noelanders, S. (2004). *Crisis negotiations; A multiparty perspective.* Veenendaal, The Netherlands: Universal Press.

Goffman, E. (1955). On facework: An analysis of ritual elements in social interaction. *Psychiatry Journal for the Study of International Processes, 18,* 213–231.

Goffman, E. (1967). *Interaction ritual essays on face-to-face behavior.* Garden City, NY: Anchor Books, Doubleday & Company.

Goldaber, I. (1979, June). A typology of hostage-takers. *The Police Chief,* pp. 21–23.

Hacker, F. (1976). *Crusaders, criminals and crazies.* New York: W.W. Norton.

Hammer, M. R. (1997). Negotiating across the cultural divide: Intercultural dynamics in crisis incidents. In R. G. Rogan, M. R. Hammer, & C. R. Van Zandt (Eds.). *Dynamic processes of crisis negotiations: Theory, research and practice* (pp. 105–114). Westport, CT: Praeger.

Hammer, M. R. (2001). Conflict negotiation under crisis conditions. In W. F. Eadie & P. E. Nelson (Eds.), *The language of conflict resolution* (pp. 57–80). Newbury Park, CA: Sage.

Hammer, M. R. (2007). *Saving lives: The S.A.F.E. model for negotiating hostage and crisis incidents.* Westport, CT: Praeger.

Hammer, M. R., & Rogan, R. G. (1997). Negotiation models in crisis situations: The value of a communication-based approach. In R. G. Rogan, M. R. Hammer, & C. R. Van Zandt (Eds.), *Dynamic processes of crisis negotiations: Theory, research, and practice* (pp. 9–4).Westport, CT: Praeger.

Hammer, M. R., & Weaver, G. R. (1994). Cultural considerations in hostage negotiations. In G. R. Weaver (Ed.), *Culture, communication and conflict: Readings in intercultural relations* (pp. 499–510). Needham Heights, MA: Ginn Press.

Hare, A. (1997). Training crisis negotiators: Updating negotiation techniques. In R. G. Rogan, M. R. Hammer, & C. R. Van Zandt (Eds.), *Dynamic processes of crisis negotiations: Theory, research, and practice* (pp. 151–160).Westport, CT: Praeger.

Heymann, P. B. (1993). *Lessons of Waco: Proposed changes in federal law enforcement.* Washington, DC: U.S. Department of Justice.

Holmes, M. E. (1997a). Optimal matching analysis of negotiation phase sequences in simulated and authentic hostage negotiation. *Communication Reports, 10,* 1–8.

Holmes, M. E. (1997b). Processes and patterns in hostage negotiations. In R. G. Rogan, M. R. Hammer, & C. R. Van Zandt (Eds.), *Dynamic processes of crisis negotiation: Theory, research, and practice* (pp. 77–94). Westport, CT: Praeger.

Holmes, M. E., & Fletcher-Bergland, T. (1995). Negotiations in crisis. In A. Nicotera (Ed.), *Conflict and organizations: Communicative processes* (pp. 239–256). Albany: SUNY Press.

Holmes, M. E., & Sykes, R. E. (1993). A test of the fit of Gulliver's phase model to hostage negotiations. *Communication Studies, 44,* 38–55.

Jones, T. S. (2001). Emotional communication in conflict: Essence and impact. In W. Eadie & P. Nelson (Eds.), *The language of conflict resolution* (pp. 81–104). Thousand Oaks, CA: Sage.

Lanceley, F. J. (1981). The antisocial personality as hostage-taker. *Journal of Police Science and Administration, 9,* 28–34.

Lanceley, F. J. (2003). *On-scene guide for crisis negotiations* (2nd ed.). Boca Raton, FL: CRC Press.

Miron, M. S., & Goldstein, A. P. (1979). *Hostage.* New York: Pergamon.

Noesner, G. W. (1999). Negotiation concepts for commanders. *FBI Law Enforcement Bulletin, 68,* 6–18.

Noesner, G. W., & Webster, M. (1997). Crisis intervention: Using active listening skills in negotiations. *FBI Law Enforcement Bulletin, 66,* 13–19.

Northrup, T. A. (1989). The dynamic of identity in personal and social conflict. In L. Kriesberg, T. Northrup, & S.J. Thorson (Eds.), *Intractable conflicts and their transformation* (pp. 55–82). Syracuse, NY: Syracuse University Press.

Oetzel, J. (1998). The effects of self-construals and ethnicity on self-reported conflict styles. *Communication Reports, 11,* 133–144.

Oetzel, J., Myers, K. K., Meares, M., & Lara, E. (2003). Interpersonal conflict in organizations: Explaining conflict styles via Face Negotiation Theory. *Communication Research Reports, 20,* 106–115.

Oetzel, J., & Ting-Toomey, S. (2003). Face concerns in interpersonal conflict: A cross-cultural empirical test of the face negotiation theory. *Communication Research, 30,* 599–624.

Oetzel, J., Ting-Toomey, S., Yokochi, Y., Masumoto, T., & Takai, J. (2000). A typology of facework behaviors in conflicts with best friends and relative strangers. *Communication Quarterly, 48,* 397–419.

Oetzel, J., Ting-Toomey, S., Masumoto, T., Yokochi, Y., Pan, X., Takai, J., & Wilcox, R. (2001). Face and facework in conflict: A cross-cultural comparison in China, Germany, Japan, and the United States. *Communication Monographs, 68,* 235–258.

Penman, R. (1994). Facework in communication. In S. Ting-Toomey (Ed.), *The challenge of facework* (pp. 15–46). Albany: State University of New York Press.

Pennebaker, J. W., Mehl, M. R., & Niederhoffer, K. G. (2003). Psychological aspects of natural language use: Our words, our selves. *Annual Reviews of Psychology, 54,* 547–577.

Putnam, L. L., & Holmer, M. (1992). Framing, reframing, and issue development. In L. L. Putnam & M. E. Roloff (Eds.), *Communication and negotiation* (pp. 128–155). Newbury Park, CA: Sage.

Rogan, R. G. (1997). Emotion and emotional expression in crisis negotiation. In R. G. Rogan, M. R. Hammer, & C. R. Van Zandt (Eds.), *Dynamic processes of crisis negotiation: Theory, research and practice* (pp. 25–44). Westport, CT: Praeger.

Rogan, R. G. (1999). F.I.R.E.: A communication-based approach for understanding crisis negotiation. In O. Adang & E. Giebels (Eds.), *To save lives* (pp. 29–45). Amsterdam, The Netherlands: Elsevier.

Rogan, R. G., & Hammer, M. R. (1994). Crisis negotiations: A preliminary investigation of facework in naturalistic conflict. *Journal of Applied Communication Research, 22,* 216–231.

Rogan, R. G., & Hammer, M. R. (1995). Assessing message affect in crisis negotiations: An exploratory study. *Human Communication Research, 21,* 553–574.

Rogan, R. G., & Hammer, M. R. (2002). Crisis/hostage negotiations: Conceptualization of a communication-based approach. In H. Giles (Ed.), *Law enforcement, communication, and community* (pp. 229–254). Amsterdam, The Netherlands: John Benjamins Publishing.

Rogan, R. G., & Hammer, M. R. (2006). The emerging field of crisis/hostage negotiation: A communication-based perspective. In J. Oetzel & S. Ting-Toomey (Eds.), *Handbook of conflict communication.* (pp. 451–478). Thousand Oaks, CA: Sage.

Rogan, R. G., Hammer, M. R., & Van Zandt, C. R. (1994). Profiling crisis negotiation teams. *Police Chief, 61,* 14–18.

Rogan, R. G., Hammer, M. R., & Van Zandt, C. R. (Eds.). (1997). *Dynamic processes of crisis negotiation: Theory, research and practice.* Westport, CT: Praeger.

Schenkein, J. (1978). *Studies in the organization of conversational interaction.* New York: Academic Press.

Schlossberg, H. (1979). Police response to hostage situations. In J. T. O'Brien & M. Marcus (Eds.), *Crime and justice in America* (pp. 209–220). New York: Pergamon.

Slatkin, A. (2003). Suicide risk and hostage/barricade situations involving older persons. *FBI Law Enforcement Bulletin, 72,* 26–32.

Soskis, D. A., & Van Zandt, C. R. (1986). Hostage negotiation: Law enforcement's most effective nonlethal weapon. *Behavioral Sciences & the Law, 4,* 423–435.

Tannen, D. (1993). What's in a frame? Surface evidence for underlying expectations. In D. Tannen (Ed.), *Framing in discourse* (pp. 14–56). New York: Oxford University Press.

Taylor, P. J. (2002a). A cylindrical model of communication behavior in crisis negotiations. *Human Communication Research, 28,* 7–48.

Taylor, P. J. (2002b). A partial order scalogram analysis of communication behavior in crisis negotiation with the prediction of outcome. *International Journal of Conflict Management, 13,* 4–37.

Taylor, P. J. (2003). Foundations and evidence for an interaction-based approach to conflict. *International Journal of Conflict Management, 14,* 213–232.

Taylor, P. J. (2004). The structure of communication behavior in simulated and actual crisis negotiations. *Human Communication Research, 30,* 443–478.

Ting-Toomey, S. (1988). Intercultural conflict styles: A face-negotiation theory. In Y. Y. Kim & W. B. Gudykunst (Eds.), *Theories in intercultural communication* (pp. 213–235). Newbury Park, CA: Sage.

Ting-Toomey, S., Gao, G., Trubisky, P., Yang, Z., Kim, H. S., Lin, S. L., & Nishida, T. (1991). Culture, face maintenance, and styles of handling interpersonal conflict: A study in five cultures. *International Journal of Conflict Management, 2,* 275–296.

Ting-Toomey, S., & Kurogi, A. (1998). Facework competence in intercultural conflict: An updated face–negotiation theory. *International Journal of Intercultural Relations, 22,* 187–225.

Ting-Toomey, S., & Oetzel, J. G. (2001). *Managing intercultural conflict effectively.* Thousand Oaks, CA: Sage.

von Eye, A., & Mun, E. Y. (2005). *Analyzing rater agreement.* Mahwah, NJ: Lawrence Erlbaum Associates.

Wilson, S. R., & Putnam, L. L. (1990). Interaction goals in negotiation. In J. Anderson (Ed.), *Communication Yearbook, 13* (pp. 374–406). Newbury Park, CA: Sage.

Wind, B. (1995). A guide to crisis negotiations. *FBI Law Enforcement Bulletin, 64,* 8–11.

7 Escalation and Deescalation in Hostage Negotiation

Wolfgang Bilsky
Beate Liesner
Denise Weßel-Therhorn

PERSPECTIVES ON HOSTAGE TAKING

Interpersonal conflict has been the focus of numerous theoretical and applied studies during the past decades. Over the wide variety of conflict types, negotiation proved to be a central means for getting the underlying problems under control (Bazerman, Curhan, Moore, & Valley, 2000; Putnam & Roloff, 1992; Rubin, Pruitt, & Kim, 1994). This is especially true for the resolution of crises (i.e., of severe, mostly unforeseen and highly stressful conflicts that are likely to have far-reaching consequences for the parties involved).

The complexity and diversity of cases

Hostage taking is a prototypical type of crisis situation. It requires professional expertise on the part of the negotiator, both with respect to assessing the situation correctly and to guiding the negotiation process in an efficient and responsible way (Gatzke, 1996; McMains & Mullins, 1996; Rogan, Hammer, & Van Zandt, 1997). However, the relevance and impact of negotiations in hostage situations contrasts sharply with the comparatively small range of theoretically founded empirical studies on this topic. Aside from a couple of "how-to" guides to negotiation (e.g., Greenstone, 1995a, 1995b, 2005), only a relatively small group of academics, mostly from communication research and psychology, conducted systematic studies that go beyond occasional research (Donohue, Ramesh, & Borchgrevink, 1991; Donohue, Ramesh, Kaufman, & Smith, 1991; Rogan &

Hammer, 2002; Taylor, 2002; Wilson, 2003). Reasons for this situation are man-
ifold. In addition to the complexity of the problem, two factors complicate research in this domain in particular: the limited number of authentic, easily accessible cases, and the huge variety of crisis incidents. Hence, enlarging the
database and explaining the *between variance* of cases remain permanent and ex-
igent research tasks in hostage negotiation in order to arrive at a better understanding of the diverse relations between case characteristics and negotiation outcomes.

Common features of hostage cases

Although the need for comparative research is beyond doubt, the wide variety of
cases may obscure the fact that hostage incidents, like other conflicts, have a lot in
common. Investigations have shown, for instance, that many, if not most, conflicts pass through several *qualitatively different phases* before arriving at an outcome. Thus, researchers usually differentiate among rapport building, escalation,
stalemate, deescalation, and problem solving as typical constituents of a conflict
(Rubin et al., 1994). Knowing about these regularities means that studying the individual conflict tells us quite a bit about conflicts in general. Assuming that this
holds for hostage negotiation as well, it is both reasonable and necessary to analyze the *individual case* in more detail (i.e., to focus on its *within variance*) in order
to arrive at a better understanding of the dynamics of crisis negotiation in general.

Two of these phases seem to be of particular interest because conflict research
has shown them to have a differential and often even reverse impact on emotions,
cognitions and behavior: escalation and deescalation. *Escalative phases* are usually
characterized by the predominance of demanding, reproachful, aggressive, or
even threatening behaviors. Thus, hostage takers may threaten to hurt or even
kill their hostages in case the authorities are not willing to meet their demands.
Noncompliance by the authorities would cause considerable problems to the
hostage taker, both because of loss of power and loss of face. This may lead to
increased aggression, stress, and negative affect on the part of the hostage taker
and, in turn, result in further escalation of the situation. *Deescalative* phases, in
contrast, are characterized by behaviors that are conducive to cooperation and
problem solving. Striving for compromises or integrative solutions is usually accompanied by a (relatively) lower level of stress and emotional arousal. As a consequence, threats to the health or life of hostages or threats of the hostage taker
to commit (extended) suicide should be less likely in deescalative phases of
hostage negotiation. All in all, escalative and deescalative phases should differ in
many respects and on different levels of analysis.

Our own research starts out from these assumptions about conflict and negotiation dynamics (Rubin et al., 1994) and concentrates on the within variance
of hostage negotiation. However, before outlining our approach, some additional
comments on past and present research seem appropriate.

Research Trends: Past and Present

The appraisal of negotiation and its impact on conflict dynamics and conflict resolution in hostage situations has changed over the years. In retrospect, *instrumental* aspects of communication, mostly related to the perpetrators' demands and their fulfillment, have always been central to hostage negotiation. However, *noninstrumental* aspects gained considerably in importance during the past years (McMains & Mullins, 1996; Rogan, Hammer & Van Zandt, 1997). Problems arising from threatening a hostage taker's self-esteem, for instance, received increasing attention in scientific debate and analysis. Furthermore, diagnosing the emotions of a hostage taker correctly proved to be of vital importance in anticipating possible outcomes of a crisis. Consequently, instrumental and noninstrumental aspects of communication are considered equally important for judging the dynamics of the negotiation process and for risk assessment today.

The importance of issues such as identity and face, emotions, or type of interaction in hostage cases has been stressed by several researchers whose work is directed toward a systematic and comprehensive analysis of crisis negotiation. Thus, Rogan and Hammer (2002) differentiate among four analytical levels—or frames—in their negotiation model: the Substantive (demand), the Attunement, the Face, and the Emotion frames. According to the authors, these analytical levels correspond to interpretative frames through which communicators shape their negotiation discourse. Their model has recently been introduced as the S.A.F.E. model of crisis negotiation in the literature, using the first letters of the analytical levels as an acronym.

Similarly, Taylor (2002, 2003) distinguishes three related analytical levels in his cylindrical model of communication behavior in crisis negotiation. First, his *level of interaction* facet identifies avoidance, distributive, and integrative behavior as three ordered elements that characterize the overall behavioral approach to interaction. Next, his *motivational emphasis* facet distinguishes instrumental, relational, and identity concerns underlying an individual's negotiation approach. Finally, his *intensity* facet is supposed to indicate how negotiators may differ in the extent to which they pursue a certain goal. From this perspective, high intensity relates to less common and more extreme communication.

The Present Approach

Both Rogan and Hammer's S.A.F.E. model and Taylor's facet approach to crisis negotiation serve as theoretical frames for our own analyses. Provided that our considerations with respect to the dynamics and the levels of negotiation apply, diagnostic instruments for assessing *emotionality*, *face related*, and *goal directed (tactical) behavior* should reliably differentiate between escalative and deescalative *phases*. Furthermore, systematic differences with respect to these features should also be found between the *parties* involved (i.e., between hostage taker and negotiator). This additional assumption is grounded in the different roles of the protagonists, their aspirations, anticipated risks, and experiences. If these expectations proved to be true, findings would be informative for both further research and practice. Finding substantial differences for the various variables investigated in our case study would underscore the importance of *further research* into negotiation dynamics (i.e., into the within variance of hostage negotiation). At the same time, this would point to the necessity of sensitizing negotiators for different levels of the negotiation process. Consequently, multilevel analyses of hostage negotiation should become an integral part of *pre- and in-service training programs* for negotiators.

METHOD

Four separate studies were conducted to test the aforementioned assumptions and expectations. Each of them was based on the same hostage taking in a German prison. During this incident, two hostage takers held several hostages in their power, trying to blackmail authorities into guaranteeing ransom, a getaway vehicle, and free passage. They were in possession of a pistol, a knife, and petrol, and they threatened to burn their hostages if authorities were not willing to meet their claims. Four hours of negotiation were tape recorded during this incident, comprising 53 phone calls. Transcripts of the phone calls were scrutinized by three collaborators and assigned to the following categories: escalation, deescalation, and other. Assignments were made consensually by global ratings, applying criteria from both social psychological literature and from interviews with negotiation experts. All in all, 10 phone calls were classified as escalative calls and seven as deescalative. Their content was analyzed in four independent studies using a 2 x 2 design, with *conflict phase* (escalative vs. deescalative) as a first factor and *party* (hostage taker vs. negotiator) as a second factor.

Study 1—Emotionality

Emotion conflict issues relate to the arousal and stress experienced by the negotiating parties. This arousal is supposed to manifest itself in the content of the verbal exchange during negotiation. Initially of little concern in negotiation practice, the emotional state of hostage takers received more attention when the *expressive motivation* of the perpetrator got into the focus of research. Rogan and Hammer (1995), for instance, found in a study on the verbal expression of emotion that verbal cues of affect differ considerably between incidents that end in suicide and those that do not.

Our first study concentrated on differences in emotion as deduced from verbal cues during different phases of negotiation. In this study, we analyzed transcripts of the protagonists' verbal interactions by means of two content analytic measures that are grounded in the conceptual approaches of Rogan and Hammer (1995) and Gottschalk and Gleser (1969), respectively (cf. Bilsky, Müller, Voss, & von Groote, 2005, for a detailed overview).

Measures

Rogan and Hammer distinguish two components supposed to be central for the measurement of emotional arousal—*language intensity* and *valence.* Language intensity reflects the strength of a speaker's affect with respect to a certain topic. It is measured by an overall intensity score assigned to every coding unit of a transcribed verbal interaction. This score depends on the presence of various intensity correlates such as obscure references, qualifiers, general metaphors, sex, profanity, or death references, and it ranges from "nonintensive" to "very intensive." Language intensity reflects the attitudinal deviation from neutrality; it does not assess the positive and negative quality of message content. This is achieved by the second component measure, *message valence*, which ranges from "extremely negative" to "extremely positive." Both components—language intensity and valence—are integrated in one general indicator called *message affect* (Rogan & Hammer, 1995).

Our second indicator is based on the work of Gottschalk and Gleser (Battacchi, Suslow, & Renna, 1996; Gottschalk, 1995; Koch & Schöfer, 1986). It is usually applied to the analysis of standard text probes, mostly in clinical settings, and therefore had to be adapted for coding verbal interactions. The Gottschalk and Gleser approach measures psychological states through the content analysis of verbal behavior at a "molecular" level (i.e., by focusing on themes communicated in the form of a grammatical clause). The relative intensity of different types of affect, experienced during short periods of time, is assessed by referring to directly observable and accessible verbal behavior as recorded by transcripts. Their *hostility scale* is supposed to measure suddenly occurring and changing states of aggressive feelings (i.e., of unstable short-term effects such as those likely to show up during hostage negotiations). Therefore, we considered it a reasonable complement of Rogan and Hammer's measure of message affect.

Hypotheses

Given the 2 x 2 design with *conflict phase* (escalative vs. deescalative) as a first factor and *party* (hostage taker vs. negotiator) as a second factor, the following assumptions seemed reasonable and were tested accordingly:

1. Crisis negotiations are stressful events for both hostage taker and negotiator. However, the risks and negative consequences likely to occur are supposed to be considerably higher for the hostage taker. Consequently, the overall level

of affect and arousal should be higher for the hostage taker compared with the negotiator; this is supposed to be true independently of the respective phase of the negotiation process.

2. The risks of a negative outcome of crisis negotiation are more salient in escalative compared with deescalative phases of a conflict for both the hostage taker and the negotiator. Therefore, the overall level of affect is supposed to be higher in escalative phases than in deescalative phases.

3. It is part of the negotiator's job to control emotionality throughout the negotiation process in order to avoid any escalation that could jeopardize a peaceful and nonviolent end of the incident. In other words, the negotiator should show a professional, emotionally balanced behavior throughout the negotiation. This is not to be expected on the part of the hostage taker. Hence, we expect him to show a more pronounced change in affect from deescalative to escalative phases than the negotiator.

Data Analysis and Results[1]

Transcripts of the 10 escalative and the 7 deescalative phone calls vary considerably in size, ranging from 99 to 1,989 words for hostility and from 73 to 2,033 words for message affect. The slightly different databases for calculating both scores result from the fact that the criteria for specifying the text corpus to be coded are a little different for hostility and message affect.

According to our assumptions about differences in emotionality between hostage takers and negotiators in different phases of the negotiation process, hostility and message affect scores were analyzed within a 2 (hostage taker vs. negotiator) x 2 (escalation vs. deescalation) analysis of variance (ANOVA) design.

A two-factorial ANOVA with *hostility* as a dependent variable revealed significant main effects for the factors person and conflict phase, and a significant person x phase interaction. A graphical summary of these results is given in Figure 7.1.

Message affect was analyzed in the same way as hostility. Again, the two-factorial ANOVA revealed a significant main effect for both the person and the conflict phase; the person x phase interaction, however, proved only marginally significant. Altogether, our data suggest that Gottschalk and Gleser's indicator for hostility and Rogan and Hammer's message affect overlap considerably. This impression was confirmed by correlating both measures: the zero-order correlation coefficient resulted in $r = -.83$.

Despite some conceptual and methodological caveats to be considered in interpreting the previous results (Bilsky et al., 2005), our data show that it is possible to distinguish different levels of affect between escalative and deescalative phases of hostage negotiation and between parties involved; this is possible on the mere basis of verbal transcripts. Interpreting the observed differences as substantial and not as methodological artifacts is backed by the fact that they match our expectations as specified a priori to data analysis. Furthermore, affective dif-

Gottschalk-Gleser-Content-Analysis

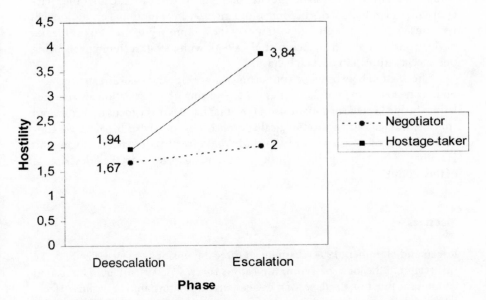

Figure 7.1. Mean Global Hostility scores for party (hostage-taker vs. negotiator) and conflict phase (escalative vs. deescalative).

ferences were identified by means of two instruments that relate to different assumptions and are rooted in different theoretical approaches. Hence, these findings may as well be understood as a mutual validation of research instruments. Finally, these and the following ANOVAs were complemented by nonparametric tests that confirmed the reported effects.[2]

Study 2—Identity/Face

Although the findings of our first study relate to the emotional frame outlined in Rogan and Hammer's S.A.F.E. model, this second study deals with another analytical level discussed by these authors—face concern. Face issues are closely linked to the personal and social identities of individuals. Therefore, people are motivated by the desire to maintain a positive social expression of self. Actions taken by individuals to maintain and support their own or their relational partners' faces are usually called *facework* in literature (Goffman, 1967).

Fear of missing one's goals in social interactions is often associated with an anticipated *loss of face*. When parties understand the other's behavior as a challenge to their own interests and goals, this will probably lead to a conflict. This is supposed to hold for all types of social conflicts, including hostage taking. If a conflict solution is not in sight, the situation is likely to escalate. Under these circumstances, conflict tactics become more intense, and emotional excitation will rise considerably. In addition, parties may show more aggressive and hostile behavior (Bilsky et al., 2005; Rubin et al., 1994), with face-threatening acts being one special expression of such behavior.

The relation between face-supporting (honoring) and face-threatening acts, on the one hand, and conflict dynamics as showing up in escalation and deescalation during hostage negotiation, on the other hand, are the focus of our second study. Although our methodological approach was somewhat broader, we concentrate here on those parts of the study that directly compare to Rogan and Hammer's (1994) research (cf. Bilsky & Kürten, 2006, for a detailed description of this study).

Measures

Rogan and Hammer (1994) distinguish three dimensions of face behavior. The first relates to the locus of a communicator's *concern* (self vs. other). The second denotes the functional *valence* of messages, discriminating among negative (face-attacking), neutral, and positive (face-honoring) acts. The third dimension is called *temporality*. It relates exclusively to face-honoring acts, and it distinguishes more specifically protecting (defending) from mitigating (restoring) acts. Although these authors, in their own study, coded negotiation behavior on all three facework dimensions, we abstained from doing so because of conceptual and methodological reasons. Instead, we concentrated on the analysis of *face valence* (see Bilsky & Kürten, 2006, for more details).

Like Rogan and Hammer, we distinguished three broad categories of face valence: honor face, attack face, and neutral (this latter category also includes statements unrelated to face issues). These categories served for coding uninterrupted verbal behavior of the protagonists, so-called talking turns or macrounits, according to their prevailing content. Finally, relative frequencies of face-supporting and face-threatening acts were computed for every phone call (unit of analysis) and protagonist (i.e., hostage taker and negotiator) to form two broad indicators for facework behavior: Honor Face (HF) and Attack Face (AF).

Hypotheses

Although Rogan and Hammer published their studies on facework more than a decade ago, there is still a considerable lack of substantial findings until today. Consequently, formulating theoretically and empirically well-grounded hypotheses for the present research context is hardly possible. Nevertheless, some tentative suppositions seem justifiable.

If an escalation occurs during negotiation, a prominent task of the negotiator is to calm down the perpetrator and convert the emotionally charged crisis negotiation into a normative interaction (Donohue, Ramesh, & Borchgrevink, 1991). Because an anticipated loss of face on the part of the hostage taker involves the risk of irrational acts and panic reactions, *supporting the perpetrator's face* is one means to avoid disastrous outcomes of negotiation. Apart from this protective function of face-honoring behavior, a negotiator is supposed to show supportive behavior of this kind throughout the negotiation in order to establish a stable rapport with the perpetrator. As regards the hostage taker, less threats and aggressions are expected during deescalative phases. Instead, more self-honoring behavior (i.e., Defend Self's Face and Restore Self's Face) may occur. Overall, however, face-supporting behavior remains a prominent task of the negotiator.

With these considerations in mind, we would expect that (a) negotiators show more face-supporting (honoring) and less face-threatening (attacking) behavior than perpetrators, both in escalative and deescalative phases of negotiation; (b) the overall level of threatening behavior is supposed to be higher in escalative than in deescalative phases; and (c) the verbal behavior of negotiators—whether supportive or threatening—is supposed to be more balanced across different phases of negotiation than that of perpetrators.

Data Analysis and Results

Other than in our study on emotionality, data are based on broader coding units in this second study, so-called talking turns (macrounits). The number of the talking turns per phone call and party varies between 9 and 78 macrounits, reflecting once again the different length of phone calls under study. Apart from these differences, data analyses were accomplished as before, using a 2 (hostage taker vs. negotiator) x 2 (escalation vs. deescalation) factorial design, with face-supporting and face-threatening behaviors as dependent variables.

A two-factorial ANOVA with face-supporting behavior (HF) as a dependent variable revealed significant main effects for the factors person and conflict phases, as well as a significant person x phase interaction (Figure 7.2). Similarly, a two-factorial ANOVA with face-threatening acts (AF) as a dependent variable revealed significant main effects for person and conflict phases and a significant person x phase interaction.

All in all, these analyses confirm our expectations, both with respect to face-supporting and face-threatening acts. First, the negotiator's face-honoring behavior was clearly more pronounced than that of the perpetrator. This holds for escalative and deescalative phases of negotiation. Second, face-threatening acts were less frequently observed for the negotiator than for the perpetrator. This finding is also in line with our assumptions and holds independently of conflict phase. Third, the overall level of threatening behavior was higher in escalative as

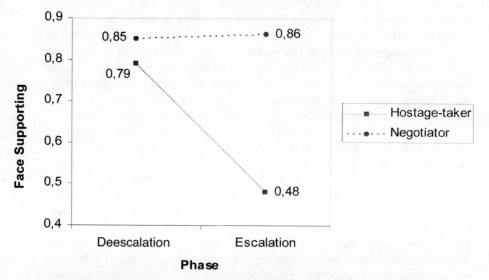

Figure 7.2. Honor Face scores for party (hostage taker vs. negotiator) and conflict phase (escalative vs. deescalative).

compared with deescalative phases, as expected. It should be noted in this context that, on the whole, face-supporting behavior outnumbered face-threatening acts. This result corresponds to those reported by Rogan and Hammer (1994).

Finally, the negotiator's verbal behavior turned out to be more balanced across different phases of negotiation than the perpetrator's. This is evident from the significant person x situation interaction in the ANOVAs. However, with respect to this latter finding, it should be mentioned that these interactions could not be confirmed when analyzing negotiation behavior at a more fine-grained (micro) level (cf. Bilsky & Kürten, 2006). In this case, differences between escalative and deescalative phases proved equally distinct for perpetrators and negotiators. Interpretation of these deviations is not straightforward. Because such interactions are crucial for interpreting negotiation behavior, the choice of adequate coding units and indicators deserves special attention in future research.

Study 3—Motivation and Interaction

While the conceptualization of the first two studies was mainly guided by the work of Rogan and Hammer (1994, 1995), the third one was closely linked to Taylor's (2002) model of communication behavior in crisis negotiations (Bilsky,

2007; Bilsky & Tebrügge, 2006). Two of his three facets—motivation and inter-action—provided the framework for this study. The first facet points to the fact that the (verbal) behavior of parties involved in a crisis may be oriented toward different motivational goals. Taylor distinguishes among *instrumental, identity*, and *relational* motives. This differentiation corresponds essentially to the Sub-stantial (demand), the Face, and the Attunement frames in Rogan and Hammer's S.A.F.E. model. His second facet discriminates among three levels of interaction, characterized by *avoiding, distributive*, and *integrative* behaviors, respectively. It can be understood as a dimension on which elements are ordered by increasing degrees of *cooperation*.

Two goals guided our third study. First, we wanted to verify whether Taylor's (2002, 2003) structural assumptions about communication behavior as specified in his three-dimensional model of crisis negotiation are backed by our data. In terms of data analysis, we wanted to check whether levels of interaction (avoid-ance, distributive, and integrative) and motivational emphasis (instrumental, re-lational, and identity) can be identified as separate facets in multidimensional space by applying the same analytical tools as used by Taylor. Second, we wanted to examine whether and to what extent *distributive (antagonistic) behavior* is sub-ject to variations within our two-factorial research design (i.e., whether it differs substantially between escalative and deescalative phases). Distributive behavior is a core element of Taylor's levels of interaction facet.

Measures

In order to replicate Taylor's (2002, 2003) *structural analysis*, we adopted his transcript-coding procedure as closely as possible (Tebrügge, 2006). Thus, we partitioned the negotiation transcript into episodes of continuous dialogue as a first step. In this context, episodes are understood as coherent periods of inter-action that center around one common theme. Next, we split these episodes into thought units (Krippendorff, 1980). These units served as the actual basis for cod-ing the content of verbal interactions. Finally, we applied an adaptation of Tay-lor's coding scheme to the unitized transcript. All in all, 39 of 41 communication variables from the original study showed up in our data set. The agreement be-tween two independent coders, measured at the thought unit level and using Cohen's (1960) kappa (κ) was .80. The coding procedure outlined thus far re-sulted in a two-way data matrix with 39 communication variables (columns) and 116 episodes (rows). This matrix was the basis for calculating associations (Pear-son correlation coefficients) between variables to be analyzed by means of Small-est Space Analysis (SSA; Borg & Groenen, 2005).

To accomplish our second task, the relative frequency of *distributive acts* was used as a measure of verbal interactions to be analyzed in our 2 x 2 (party x phase) research design. Computations were based on 1,687 coded thought units. Of these, 945 relate to the hostage taker and 596 to the negotiator; the remaining 146 units date from other persons (i.e., from hostages and from the second hostage taker, who was not involved in negotiation).

Hypotheses

Given the *cylindrical structure* of negotiation behavior postulated by Taylor (2002) and confirmed by his data, we expected the level of interaction and the motivational facet to show up on two distinct projections of a three-dimensional, nonmetric, multidimensional scaling (SSA) of our negotiation data. In this analysis, level of interaction was supposed to appear as an axial partitioning of space (Levy, 1985; i.e., as parallel ordered bands of avoidance, distributive, and integrative behavior in a two-dimensional projection of variables). In addition, the motivational facet should pop up on another two-dimensional projection, taking the form of a polar partitioning, thus separating instrumental, relational, and identity in a wedgelike manner.

Our hypotheses with respect to differences in *distributive behavior* were similar to those outlined before. Because distributive behavior is supposed to share several features with aggressive (hostile) behavior, differences in the present context should essentially match those of the first study. Thus, escalation is usually associated with fighting and rigid behavior, whereas deescalation is characterized by more indulgent, compromising behavior. Consequently, we anticipated a higher level of distributive behavior in escalative as compared with deescalative phone calls. With respect to parties, negotiators should show a lower and more balanced level of distributive behavior than hostage takers.

Data Analyses and Results

Our *structural analyses* were conducted by means of the MDS module of the SYSTAT program package. A three-dimensional SSA resulted in plots that basically reflect the expected structures. This is especially true for Taylor's level of interaction facet, which could be identified on dimensions 1 x 2. As can be seen from Figure 7.3, only 3 of 39 variables were misplaced (underlined).

The partitioning of variables according to Taylor's motivational facet was less clear. However, despite a considerable number of misplaced variables, the expected polar structure could be identified along general lines. Figure 7.4 reflects the separation of instrumental, relational, and identity themes on dimensions 2 x 3.

As regards *distributive behavior*, differences between the conditions under study were analyzed in the same way as before. A two-factorial ANOVA with distributive behavior as dependent and party and phase as independent variables revealed a significant main effect for both party and conflict phases. The person x phase interaction, however, was not significant, although our results point toward the expected direction.

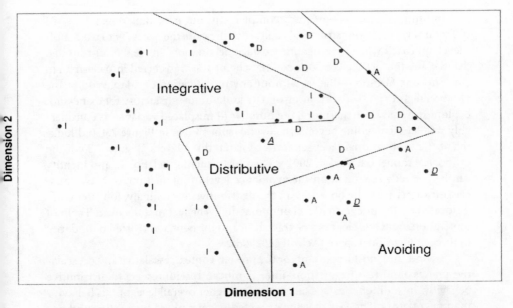

Figure 7.3. Structural analysis (SSA): Levels of interaction facet (A = avoiding, D = distributive, I = integrative).

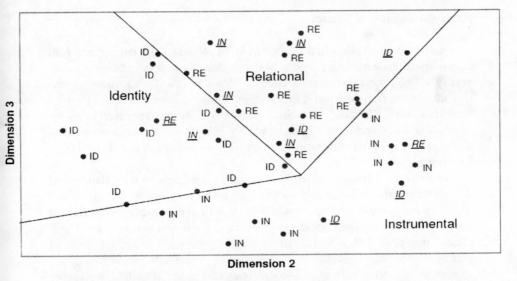

Figure 7.4. Structural analysis (SSA): Motivational emphasis (ID = identity, IN = instrumental, RE = relational).

In summary, the present study complements our preceding research in two different ways. First, our structural analyses underscore the necessity to use a multilevel approach when investigating hostage negotiation. In view of our limited data set and the fact that Taylor's coding scheme was transferred into German in a one-to-one fashion—that is, without any modification or adaptation to the German text corpus—partitioning of data looks quite satisfactory for a one-shot exploratory study. Furthermore, the number of misplaced variables is considerably smaller when going beyond the overall split shown in Figure 7.4 and looking at the motivational facet separately for the three layers (Figure 7.3) of the cylindrical model (cf. Taylor, 2002). Then instrumental, relational, and identity can be perfectly separated on the avoidance level of interaction; only two misclassifications are to be observed on the distributive level; finally, four items are dislocated on the integrative level of interaction. The fact that the overall split of motivation looks less clear can be traced back to the bent and twisted boundaries in three-dimensional space (Tebrügge, 2006).

Second, and most important for the present context, escalative and deescalative phases of hostage negotiation differ significantly with respect to distributive behavior. In addition, hostage takers show a higher overall level of this behavior than negotiators. The fact that the expected party x phase interaction did not reach significance may be due to the index chosen to represent distributive behavior (Tebrügge, 2006). However, this question cannot be answered without further research.

Study 4—Behavioral Tactics

Our fourth and final study had a different focus. When categorizing phone calls into escalating, deescalating, and other, our *global ratings* were based on a diversity of theoretical and applied criteria. Although this was adequate for setting up our research design and for assigning phone calls to different categories according to their level of escalation, cross-validating this approach in an independent study and on the basis of strictly *behavioral criteria* seemed desirable. One central goal of our fourth study was to accomplish just this (Weßel-Therhorn, 2006).

From socioscientific literature on conflicts, we know that escalation and deescalation differ considerably with respect to *strategic choices* and *behavioral tactics*. In this context, strategy usually refers to a set of macroscopic objectives or ends, whereas tactics designate the more microscopic means to these ends (Glasl, 2002; Rubin et al., 1994). Because hostage incidents are considered but a special type of severe conflict, escalative and deescalative phone calls, as analyzed in our studies, should differ with regard to strategies and tactics as well. However, because *tactics* are closer to concrete behavior, they appear more convenient for an empirical analysis of negotiation behavior.

Measures

To realize this analysis, a coding scheme for identifying conflict behavior on different levels of abstractness was developed by closely referring to the conceptual approach of Rubin et al. (1994). Thus, the construction of this scheme was oriented toward four basic *strategies*—contentious behavior, problem solving, yielding, and avoiding—and their accompanying *tactics*. Among the latter, *contentious tactics* deserve special attention because they are assumed to be "more often than not deployed in an escalative sequence, moving from light to progressively heavier" (Rubin et al., 1994, p. 48). Typical tactics of this type are ingratiation, gamesmanship, guilt trips, persuasive argumentation, threats, and irrevocable commitments. For our purposes, each of them was further specified by a varying number of components (subtactics; cf. Weßel-Therhorn, 2006).

Coding of our transcripts was accomplished in a similar way as the Gottschalk–Gleser content analysis in Study 1 (i.e., by focusing on themes communicated in the form of a grammatical clause). However, verbal expressions reflecting different strategies and tactics proved to be quite complex. Therefore, sentences including one or more subordinate clauses were accepted as coding units, if necessary with respect to content. Intercoder agreement for distinguishing coding units and for coding transcripts was checked for two coders, categorizing independently 20 phone calls. Holsti's V_2 Coefficient (Wirtz & Caspar, 2002) was used as a measure for this reliability check. Agreement for both segmentation and coding resulted in coefficients $V_2 > 90\%$. As regards the computation of indices of conflict behavior, we adapted the Gottschalk–Gleser approach as described by Bilsky et al. (2005).

Hypotheses

Given the big gap between the global conflict approach of Rubin et al. (1994), on the one hand, and the concrete negotiation behavior, on the other hand, this analysis was mainly exploratory. Nevertheless, some tentative expectations seemed tenable. Thus, *contentious tactics* were supposed to distinguish best between escalation and deescalation. Furthermore, hostage takers were expected to show more contentious tactics than negotiators. Finally, negotiators were expected to show a more balanced behavior across situations.

Data Analysis and Results

Once again, data were analyzed within our 2 x 2 factorial design by means of a multivariate analysis of variance (MANOVA). Several significant main and interaction effects resulted. As can be seen from Table 7.1, the only behavioral vari-

Table 7.1 MANOVA of Behavioral Tactics (Dependent Variable) With Party and Phase (Independent Variables); Significant Results

Source	Dependent Variable	df	MSQ	F	p
Phase	Ingratiation	1	11.55	10.50	.00
	Threats	1	18.40	33.04	.00
	Irrevocable Commitments	1	1.39	4.71	.04
Party	Gamesmanship	1	16.80	25.51	.00
	Persuasive Argumentation	1	9.20	6.71	.02
	Threats	1	101.47	182.18	.00
	Yielding	1	2.06	5.19	.03
Phase * Party	Guilt Trips	1	3.29	5.36	.03
	Persuasive Argumentation	1	5.59	4.08	.05
	Threats	1	12.36	22.18	.00

able that does not belong to the group of contentious tactics is yielding. It was shown a little more frequently by the hostage taker, who, in addition, expressed more threats. The negotiator, in contrast, scored higher on gamesmanship and persuasive argumentation.

As regards the factor conflict phase, threats and irrevocable commitments were observed more frequently during escalative phone calls, whereas ingratiation prevailed during deescalation. Figure 7.5 illustrates our findings for persuasive argumentation.

In summary, our MANOVA confirmed that *escalation* and *deescalation*, as operationalized in our studies on the basis of phone calls between hostage taker and negotiator, differ with respect to several contentious tactics. In addition, significant main effects for conflict party, as well as phase x party interaction, could be identified.

SUMMARY AND DISCUSSION

In the following, we give a brief synopsis of our research. Then we sketch out the general directions of our prospective research program. This program aims at both additional insight into the dynamics of hostage negotiation and the transfer of research findings into negotiation practice.

The Status Quo

Our investigations started from the assumption that comparative research on hostage negotiation may be complemented efficiently by studies that focus on the within variance of the single case. This assumption was based on findings from

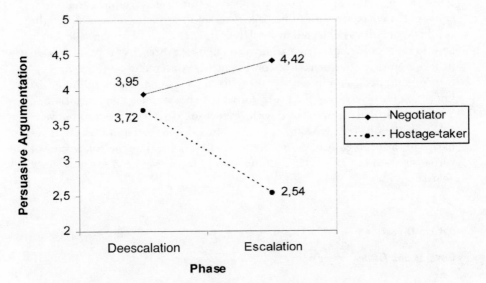

Figure 7.5. **Persuasive argumentation scores for party (hostage taker vs. negotiator) and conflict phase (escalative vs. deescalative).**

conflict research, which suggest that hostage incidents share a lot of characteristics and regularities despite the wide variety of cases. Consequently, in-depth studies of the individual case were supposed to produce insights that are heuristically interesting with respect to a better understanding of hostage negotiation in general.

We concentrated on two phases that are characteristic of conflict dynamics in general—escalation and deescalation. Findings from conflict research have shown that emotions, cognitions, and behaviors of the conflicting parties differ considerably depending on which of these phases prevails. Whether these findings apply to hostage cases as well was tested in four separate studies based on the same hostage incident and centered on emotionality and face issues, motivation and interaction, and behavioral tactics. The selection of these variables was guided by Rogan and Hammer's S.A.F.E. model of crisis negotiation, Taylor's model of communication behavior in conflict negotiations, and Rubin, Pruitt, and Kim's approach toward a theory of conflict. Our analyses were based on transcripts of 53 phone calls between hostage taker and negotiator, and content-analytic data were analyzed in a 2 x 2 design, with conflict phase (escalative vs. deescalative) and conflicting party (hostage taker vs. negotiator) as factors.

In view of the various systematic differences identified in our case study, it seems to be both methodologically possible and theoretically revealing to analyze crisis negotiation with respect to escalation and deescalation against the background of existing models and theories. Based on conceptual approaches from communication research and from social psychology and using five different instruments, we were able to demonstrate variations and differences in the crisis behavior of hostage taker and negotiator depending on the conflict dynamics as reflected in escalative and deescalative phone calls. Thus, emotions (hostility, affect), face concern (support, threat), and goal-directed behavior (distributive behavior, conflict tactics) differed in level between escalation and deescalation. Furthermore, conflict dynamics had a differential impact on the behavior of the protagonists (i.e., hostage taker and negotiator). This is of particular importance with respect to possible differences between role expectations (e.g., vis-à-vis a professional negotiator) and the actual behavior of the protagonists. Altogether, our studies illustrate the *polyvalence* of verbal messages in crisis negotiations and point to the need for multilevel analyses.

Future Directions

Caveats and Future Projects

Despite the encouraging results, some caveats seem appropriate with respect to their interpretation. Thus, all of our instruments had to be modified or (re-) constructed for the special use in our studies. Content categories and coding rules had to be adapted or even constructed from scratch. Because negotiation material is scarce, adapting, testing, and applying instruments to our data could not always be separated in a way desirable for major empirical studies. Consequently, our empirical work resembled sometimes more an iterative and interactive process of instrument construction than a routine application of standard procedures. Although we took considerable precaution not to confound our results with expectations, a blindfold application of instruments to our transcripts could not always be guaranteed. Thus, our findings are still exploratory, although heuristically interesting with respect to the conceptualization of further research.

In order to get beyond mere exploration, we have to cross-validate our findings. To this end, we intend to reanalyze additional hostage cases[3] and consider the *between* variance of cases as well. Furthermore, we plan to revise and simplify our research instruments in such a way that they may be used for both detailed academic research and more topical and practical applications. To accomplish this latter goal, instruments should not only be appropriate for analyzing transcripts; rather, they should allow the analysis of audio recordings and, at best, a well-founded in vivo screening of negotiations, too. This would help considerably in arriving at a theoretically grounded diagnosis of crisis situations.

Transferring theory into practice

In fact, considering the polyvalence of verbal material is important beyond academic multilevel analyses. Negotiators have to decipher and evaluate the verbal messages of their opponent continuously in order to decide on which level of communication to react. Interpreting the other's statements as instrumental, for instance, although meant as a face message, could have detrimental effects and result in an aggravation of the situation. Therefore, available findings from negotiation research deserve careful inspection regardless of whether and to what extent they are of use for improving present practice.

Sensitizing trainees as well as negotiators for the multiple facets of concurrent information contained in verbal messages is an important step toward considerate and responsible negotiation. Even if research on crisis negotiation is still scarce, using the few systematic approaches under discussion as a heuristic or a template for the training of negotiators seems promising.

Due to their professional specialization, a routine exchange of experiences, and regular training, negotiators in North Rhine-Westphalia are familiar with recent developments in negotiation research. Yet transferring abstract knowledge into concrete behavior is a permanent challenge. In this regard, negotiators face the same problems as clinicians, counselors, social workers, or therapists. Hence, discussing and analyzing past or supervising ongoing negotiations is a recurring task for improving professional skills—whether in pre- or in-service training. Valid analytical tools and feedback instruments for assessing the various facets of negotiation behavior are of considerable help in this context. It is a long-term goal of our present activities to develop such instruments. Given the constructive and balanced cooperation between practitioners and researchers in the past, this should be a realistic objective.

NOTES

1. A more complete set of findings, including statistics and figures, can be obtained from the first author.

2. Given the limited database ($n = 1$ case), our analyses pursued mainly descriptive purposes. This applied also to the ANOVAs, which were chosen as a convenient means for summarizing the results of our 2 x 2 design. Taking an inferential perspective, however, the use of an ANOVA in the present context is problematic because independence assumptions are definitely violated. This disadvantage cannot be cured by simply choosing an alternative statistical design. To ensure the significance of our results beyond mere description, we complemented all ANOVAs by Wilcoxon signed-rank tests (Fahrmeir, Künstler, Pigeot, & Tutz, 2003). Thus, for hostility (Figure 7.1), two tests were run on the escalation scores, one for the negotiator and one for the hostage-taker, using the median ($m0$) of the deescalation scores as a reference. The first test checked that for the H0, the $m0$ matched the negotiator's median of escalation, the second that $m0$ matched the hostage-

taker's median of escalation. Although $H0$ was true for the negotiator ($w^+(9) = 31$, *n.s.*), it was rejected for the hostage taker ($w^+(9) = 45$, $p < .01$), confirming our assumptions (according to Gottschalk & Gleser, 1969, only 9 of the 10 escalative phone calls were large enough for computing hostility scores). Analogous tests were run for face (Figure 7.2) and for argumentation issues (Figure 7.5), all of them corroborating the respective ANOVAs.

3. We are grateful to the *Landeskriminalamt* (LKA) of North Rhine-Westphalia, to the *Institut für Aus- und Fortbildung der Polizei* (IAF), and to the *Hostage Negotiation Group* Münster for their interest and support, and for providing authentic material for our analyses.

REFERENCES

Battacchi, M. W., Suslow, T., & Renna, M. (1996). *Emotion und Sprache* [Emotion and language]. Frankfurt/M.: Europäischer Verlag der Wissenschaften.

Bazerman, M. H., Curhan, J. R., Moore, D. A., & Valley, K. L. (2000). Negotiation. *Annual Review of Psychology, 51*, 279–314.

Bilsky, W. (2007). Krisenverhandlungen—Verhandlungen bei Geiselnahmen. Möglichkeiten und Grenzen eines Theorie-Praxis-Transfers [Crisis negotiations—negotiations in the context of hostage takings]. In C. Lorei (Ed.), *Polizei & Psychologie. Kongressband der Tagung "Polizei & Psychologie" am 03.–04. April 2006* (pp. 11–39). Frankfurt/M.: Verlag für Polizeiwissenschaft.

Bilsky, W., & Kürten, G. (2006). "Attack" or "Honour"? Face message behavior in crisis negotiation: A case study. In M. Ioannou & D. Youngs (Eds.), *Explorations in investigative psychology and contemporary offender profiling* (pp. 91–100). London: IA-IP Publishing.

Bilsky, W., Müller, J., Voss, A., & von Groote, E. (2005). Affect assessment in crisis negotiation: An exploratory case study using two distinct indicators. *Psychology, Crime & Law, 11*, 275–287.

Bilsky, W., & Tebrügge, B. (2006, August 26–29). *Theoretical and empirical approaches toward hostage-taking.* Paper presented at the Sixth annual conference of the European Society of Criminology, Tübingen, Germany.

Borg, I., & Groenen, P. J. F. (2005). *Modern multidimensional scaling.* New York: Springer.

Cohen, J. A. (1960). A coefficient of agreement for nominal scales. *Educational and Psychological Measurement, 20*, 37–46.

Donohue, W. A., Ramesh, C., & Borchgrevink, C. (1991). Crisis bargaining: Tracking the relational paradox in hostage negotiation. *The International Journal of Conflict Management, 2*, 257–274.

Donohue, W. A., Ramesh, D., Kaufman, G., & Smith, R. (1991). Crisis bargaining in hostage negotiations. *International Journal of Group Tensions, 21*, 133–154.

Fahrmeir, L., Künstler, R., Pigeot, I., & Tutz, G. (2003). *Statistik* [Statistics]. Berlin: Springer.

Gatzke, W. (1996). Geiselnahmen, Entführungen, Bedrohungslagen [Hostage taking, kidnapping, domestic incidents]. In M. Kniesch (Ed.), *Handbuch für Führungskräfte der Polizei* (pp. 427–449). Lübeck: Schmidt-Römhild.

Glasl, F. (2002). *Konfliktmanagement* [Conflict management]. Bern: Haupt.

Goffman, E. (1967). *Interaction ritual: Essays on face-to-face interaction.* Oxford: Aldine.

Gottschalk, L. A. (1995). *Content analysis of verbal behavior.* Hillsdale, NJ: Lawrence Erlbaum Associates.

Gottschalk, L. A., & Gleser, G. C. (1969). *The measurement of psychological states through the content analysis of verbal behavior.* Berkeley: University of California Press.

Greenstone, J. L. (1995a). Hostage negotiations team training of small police departments. In M. I. Kurke & E. M. Scrivner (Eds.), *Police psychology into the 21st century* (pp. 279–296). Hillsdale, NJ: Lawrence Erlbaum Associates.

Greenstone, J. L. (1995b). Tactics and negotiating techniques (TNT): The way of the past and the way of the future. In M. I. Kurke & E. M. Scrivner (Eds.), *Police psychology into the 21st century* (pp. 357–371). Hillsdale, NJ: Lawrence Erlbaum Associates.

Greenstone, J. L. (2005). *The elements of police hostage and crisis negotiations.* Binghamton, NY: Haworth Press.

Koch, U., & Schöfer, G. (Eds.). (1986). *Sprachinhaltsanalyse in der psychosomatischen und psychiatrischen Forschung* [Content analysis in psychosomatic and psychiatric research]. Weinheim: Psychologie Verlags Union.

Krippendorff, K. (1980). *Content analysis.* Beverly Hills, CA: Sage.

Levy, S. (1985). Lawful roles of facets in social theories. In D. Canter (Ed.), *Facet theory* (pp. 59–96). New York: Springer.

McMains, M. J., & Mullins, W. C. (1996). *Crisis negotiations.* Cincinnati, OH: Anderson Publishing.

Putnam, L. L., & Roloff, M. E. (Eds.). (1992). *Communication and negotiation.* Newbury Park, CA: Sage.

Rogan, R. G., & Hammer, M. R. (1994). Crisis negotiation: A preliminary investigation of facework in naturalistic conflict. *Journal of Applied Communication Research, 22,* 216–231.

Rogan, R. G., & Hammer, M. R. (1995). Assessing message affect in crisis negotiations: An exploratory study. *Human Communication Research, 21*(4), 553–574.

Rogan, R. G., & Hammer, M. R. (2002). Crisis/hostage negotiations: A communication-based approach. In H. Giles (Ed.), *Law enforcement, communication, and community* (pp. 229–254). Amsterdam: John Benjamins.

Rogan, R. G., Hammer, M. R., & Van Zandt, C. R. (Eds.). (1997). *Dynamic processes of crisis negotiation.* London: Praeger.

Rubin, J. Z., Pruitt, D., & Kim, S. H. (1994). *Social conflict.* New York: McGraw-Hill.

Taylor, P. J. (2002). A cylindrical model of communication behavior in crisis negotiations. *Human Communication Research, 28,* 7–48.

Taylor, P. J. (2003). *Intra-individual communication behavior in conflict negotiations.* Unpublished doctoral dissertation, University of Liverpool, UK.

Tebrügge, B. (2006). *Untersuchung authentischer Sprachstichproben einer Geiselnahmeverhandlung auf der Grundlage eines kommunikationswissenschaftlichen Modells von Krisenverhandlungen* [Analyzing an authentic hostage negotiation by using a model from communication research]. Unveröffentlichte Diplomarbeit, Westfälische Wilhelms-Universität, Münster.

Weßel-Therhorn, D. (2006). *Untersuchung zum Einsatz von Konfliktstrategien in einer Geiselnahme* [Investigating conflict strategies in hostage negotiation]. Unveröffentlichte Diplomarbeit, Westfälische Wilhelms-Universität, Münster.

Wilson, M. (2003). The psychology of hostage-taking. In A. Silke (Ed.), *Terrorists, victims and society: Psychological perspectives on terrorism and its consequences* (pp. 55–76). London: Wiley.

Wirtz, M., & Caspar, F. (2002). *Beurteilerübereinstimmung und Beurteilerreliabilität* [Interrater consistency and reliability]. Göttingen: Hogrefe.

8

Completed Suicides

The Law Enforcement Negotiators' Experience

Frederick J. Lanceley

In August 1978, as a member of the Federal Bureau of Investigation (FBI), I was assigned to the Special Operations and Research Unit (SOARU) (now the Crisis Negotiation Unit) at the FBI Academy, which was responsible for all FBI crisis negotiation training and preparedness. The SOARU provided training in programs that included Crisis Management, Hostage, later Crisis, Negotiation, Special Weapons and Tactics, and Major Case Management. My responsibilities fell into three general areas: training, research, and operations in crisis negotiation.

I was the Program Manager for the FBI's Crisis Negotiation In-Service for 13 years. In that position, I developed and taught more than 50 two-week hostage/crisis negotiation in-services at the FBI Academy, and I was responsible for the training and performance of as many as 250 FBI negotiators and negotiation trainers. In addition to crisis/hostage negotiation, I developed and taught seminars on crisis management, kidnap investigation and negotiation, crisis and suicide intervention, abnormal psychology, terrorism, hostage survival, aircraft hijacking, Post-Traumatic Stress Disorder, crisis first response, and kidnap awareness. As a trainer, I conducted or spoke at more than 1,000 seminars worldwide. I worked cases at all levels of law enforcement and government, from patrol officers and dispatchers to ambassadors and national presidents.

Upon notification of a crisis within the FBI's jurisdiction or at the request for assistance from a police department, federal agency, or foreign government, I responded in one of several roles: crisis negotiator, negotiation team leader, or consultant to crisis managers, victim families, and/or negotiators. In these roles, I participated in the resolution of several hundred domestic and international aircraft hijackings, barricade and suicide situations, prison riots, hostage takings, and kidnappings. My experience includes such high-profile cases as those at the Atlanta Penitentiary; the Branch Davidian siege at Waco, Texas; and the Weaver case in Ruby Ridge, Idaho.

In the mid-1970s, the Law Enforcement Assistance Administration (LEAA), a federal agency, funded an FBI component at the FBI Academy that became known as the aforementioned SOARU. The hostage negotiation element of the unit was funded specifically to train nonfederal law enforcement officers in negotiation.

Over time, the SOARU achieved a great deal of success in its training mission, so that when the LEAA funding ended, the FBI maintained the unit and began training FBI Special Agents (SA) and other law enforcement officers in hostage negotiation. Additionally, the SOARU negotiation trainers' role expanded to research and operations.

From 1978 to 1980, I trained primarily police officers and deputy sheriffs in hostage negotiation. When I began to train FBI SAs in hostage negotiation, it became clear that the operational experience of FBI SAs and police officers/deputy sheriffs was different. In general, FBI negotiators were working hostage situations involving hijacked aircraft and failed bank robberies, and local authorities were working domestic situations, barricades, and many suicide threats.

In fact, many negotiations worked by local law enforcement evolved into suicide situations. It was quite common for situations to evolve in a patterned manner as they progressed over time. For example, an incident might typically commence with a husband or boyfriend holding a wife or girlfriend against her will. At this point, officers simply labeled this type of incident a *domestic* situation. After the victim's release was achieved and the subject announced that he was not coming out, the incident had evolved into what is called a *barricade* situation. Not atypically, the subject might then announce his intent to commit *suicide*.

In 1980, when a lieutenant from a major law enforcement agency was asked about his department's negotiation experience, he said that his negotiators worked about three hostage situations a year. He added that the three situations involved a broad definition of the word *hostage*. He went on to say that they also worked about eight suicide incidents per year, but averaged about 50 barricade incidents per year. When asked what percentage of his negotiated barricades involved some discussion of suicide, his reply was, "All of them."

In 1980, a colleague and friend, Gary Noesner, and I were teaching a seminar to about 30 negotiators in California. At the outset of the seminar, we asked, "How many of you have received prior training in hostage negotiation?" Everyone raised their hand. We then asked, "How many of you have negotiated a true hostage situation?" No one raised their hand. We followed with, "How many of you have received prior suicide intervention training?" No one raised their hand. Then, "How many of you have negotiated a suicide incident?" Everyone raised their hand! In my partner's words, it was like a lightening bolt hitting us. We were teaching the wrong topic—hostage negotiation not suicide intervention—to negotiators!

Additionally, I observed that many negotiators were applying hostage negotiation guidelines to domestic, barricade, and suicide situations, and it was not always the best fit. It became increasingly clear that, although I was teaching hostage negotiation, it was only on rare occasions that nonfederal negotiators actually encountered a true hostage situation. As a result, in the early 1980s, I incorporated crisis/suicide intervention, including active listening, into the hostage negotiation course at the FBI Academy.

In preparing to teach the course, I took a lengthy crisis/suicide intervention course, studied many articles, read several books by authorities in the field, and worked some suicide cases. Over the course of several years in teaching suicide intervention to law enforcement negotiators, it became increasingly obvious that there was a disparity between the law enforcement experience and the literature or what others and I were teaching in the classroom.

Of particular concern were the areas of perturbation, drug and alcohol usage, subject/negotiator rapport, and "sudden" improvements in the incident. These topics were of particular concern because over the years negotiators were telling me that the persons they encountered who went on to suicide were not perturbed. Many of the completed suicides were committed by sober subjects. Additionally, there was often good rapport between subject and negotiator, and few negotiators were observing sudden mood changes among those who committed suicide. Let's review the literature in each of those problem areas.

PERTURBATION

Shneidman (1981) described exacerbation of perturbation as one of the four elements of suicide. Shneidman said, "Perturbation refers to how disturbed, "shook up," ill at ease, or mentally upset a person is" (p. 31). Shneidman (1996) argued that when we experience heightened negative emotions, psychological anguish and disturbance follow. We feel upset, disturbed, and perturbed. Perturbation is most often caused by psychological pain, and psychological pain is the basic ingredient of suicide. Shneidman went on to say that the most effective course for defusing a suicide situation is to mollify the kindled emotion or ". . . to do anything (within reason) to make the person less perturbed" (p. 7). Shneidman also urged clinicians to "exercise extreme caution with any patient who is perturbed and has lethal means available" (as cited in Bongar, 1996, p. 94).

Perturbation has been studied and applied in a variety of social contexts. The American Association of Suicidology and the American Foundation of Suicide Prevention both list perturbation as a warning sign of suicide. On the Association web page, the American Association of Suicidology (2007) refers to perturbation when they list rage and uncontrolled anger as warning signs of suicide. Similarly, the American Foundation for Suicide Prevention (n.d.) also lists on their web page "Unexpected rage or anger" as a warning sign of suicide.

Crisis centers as far away as India believe perturbation is a problem with which counselors must contend. For example, Arunkumar and Vadakekara (n.d.) define perturbation at a crisis intervention center in India as the level of stress that a person is experiencing when they telephone the center. At the Thrani Center for Crisis Control in India, counselors are urged to ascertain a caller's level of perturbation early in a telephone conversation. They explain that a perturbed caller is emotionally excited and agitated and, therefore, less likely to think rationally.

Not only has perturbation been investigated among the potentially suicidal, but it has also been studied among inmates, gifted students, and families. For example, Holden's (2003) suicide research in a prison population found that perturbation-based reasons for attempting suicide statistically predicted suicide criteria, including previous attempt, suicide intent, suicidal desire, and suicide preparation. Perturbation appears to have been a factor in a suicide by a gifted student (Cross, Gust-Brey, & Ball, 2002). Shneidman (1981) also reviewed perturbation among gifted persons. McGothlin (2006) has described the assessment of perturbation by the use of scaling questions and the impact of perturbation on the family.

It is the case that much of the literature on perturbation suggests that perturbation is a well-established antecedent to suicide. In fact, perturbation is viewed as a warning sign of suicide by the American Association of Suicidology and the American Foundation of Suicide Prevention. Crisis intervention centers as far away as India view perturbation as an obstacle that must be overcome. Perturbation has also been studied among such disparate groups as gifted students and inmates. Do these studies mean that law enforcement negotiators should be particularly concerned about suicidal individuals who are perturbed? Do these studies mean that negotiators will encounter perturbed suicidal individuals? Do these studies mean, then, that when law enforcement crisis negotiators encounter suicidal persons who *not* are perturbed, these individuals will have a lower risk of suicide?

ALCOHOL AND DRUG USAGE AMONG SUICIDAL PERSONS

Drug and alcohol usage among persons who commit suicide is another much studied topic. Again, the American Association of Suicidology and the American Foundation for Suicide Prevention on their respective web pages indicate that increased substance (alcohol or drug) use is a warning sign of suicide.

Jamison (1999) discussed alcohol and suicide in the psychology of suicide, the role of alcohol in suicide attempts, the treatment and prevention of suicide, and the role of alcohol among those persons with suicidal intentions, to name but a few connections. Colt (1991) refers to alcohol and adolescents and states that attempters and completers have higher rates of drug and alcohol abuse, that a significant percentage of young men who commit suicide are suffering from depression coupled with aggressive behavior complicated by drug or alcohol use, that young people are turning to alcohol at an earlier age, that increased drug or alcohol use is an indicator of possible depression, and so on. Bongar (1996) reviewed a variety of resources for analyzing suicide and its connection to alcohol and alcoholism and does not dispute the idea that alcohol is an antecedent to suicide.

If alcohol abuse is an antecedent to suicide, and from the literature it certainly seems to be, does the fact that alcohol is an antecedent to suicide mean that crisis interveners of all kinds will encounter suicidal persons who are abusing alcohol? More important, do inebriated subjects with whom we are negotiating go on to commit suicide? Roberts and Jennings (2005) point out that there are at least 20 different evidence-based suicide assessment scales available, and many, including their own, include drug and alcohol use as a risk factor. On January 19, 1995, Richard Newman, PhD, a police psychologist, provided me with a document titled "Suicide Assessment Scale." This scale is used on the West Coast to assess suicidal intent and indicates drug and alcohol abuse to be a factor that increases risk. Kaplan and Sadock (1990) warn in their book that alcohol and drug intoxication is a sign of "impending violence" (p. 174). In August 1994, I obtained a form titled "Suicide Lethality Checklist." This form was provided to attendees at a California Suicide Intervention Skills Workshop. The checklist indicated 14 indicators of suicide risk. One of the risk factors was drug and alcohol use. "Drug/alcohol abuse" is a symptom to be looked for when interviewing students with the potential for suicide (University of Technology Sydney, 2007).

Alcohol and/or drug use appears to be an antecedent to suicide. Does this mean then that sober individuals are less of a suicide threat? Does this mean that those persons who are under the influence and with whom we are negotiating will go on to commit suicide? These are important questions that need to be studied and understood.

THE IMPORTANCE OF RAPPORT IN SUICIDE INTERVENTION

The importance of establishing rapport between a crisis negotiator and a suicidal subject is virtually assumed by writers on the topic of suicide intervention. For example, when reviewing the topic of rapport and suicide intervention, one reads advice such as, "To help establish rapport and trust, be non-judgmental" (Justice Institute of British Columbia, 2007). Health workers are advised to, "Confront [suicidal persons] directly in a warm, non-judgmental manner" (University of California Berkeley, 2006). Suicide interveners are advised, "Do try to establish rapport—Try to establish rapport with the potentially suicidal individual so that he or she will be more amenable to referral and follow up" (Carl R. Darnall Army Medical Center, n.d.). First responders are advised, "Establishing rapport with your patient will help you provide effective treatment at the scene and assist the patient and other health care providers in finding appropriate long-term treatment that may prevent another suicide attempt" (Suicide Prevention Resource Center, 2005).

SUDDEN IMPROVEMENTS IN SUICIDE INTERVENTION

The American Association of Suicidology (2007) counsels that "dramatic mood changes" may be a warning sign of suicide. Again, a problem arises over definition. What period of time is "sudden?" Is sudden instantaneously? Is a mood change over 5 hours a sudden, dramatic mood change? What about a subject who is calm, sober, and has good rapport with the negotiator whose mood has seemingly improved over 5 hours? Do these circumstances indicate that an individual will be alive at the end of the incident?

Because of the seeming disparity between what I was taught and read with regard to perturbation, alcohol and drugs, rapport, and sudden improvements and what experienced negotiators were saying, I conducted an informal study that explored the final moments of the suicidal person's life. During my Advanced Crisis Negotiation Seminars, I asked attendees whether any of them had ever been speaking to an individual when they committed suicide. Generally, there were one or two negotiators in each session who had had that experience. I asked the negotiators whether they would be willing to complete a survey form regarding their experience (see appendix). I promised to protect their anonymity if they chose to complete the brief set of questions. Twenty-four negotiators completed surveys for 25 incidents. (One negotiator had experienced two incidents.) Because I had intimate knowledge of three incidents, having acted as an expert witness in lawsuits involving those suicides, I completed the forms for three cases.

FINDINGS

Survey Participants and Subjects

There were 27 negotiators involved in the 28 incidents, with 1 of the negotiators having negotiated two incidents. Negotiators averaged 12.6 years of experience as law enforcement officers. Their average length of service as a negotiator was 4.0 years. Two of the negotiators were women.

The agencies varied greatly in size. One agency had 8 officers, and another national police force had 11,000 officers. Seventeen of the 25 agencies had fewer than 350 officers, and eight agencies had more than 900 officers. Seventeen agencies characterized themselves as police departments. Six organizations were sheriffs' offices, one was a state police agency, and one was a national police force. The 25 agencies represented 17 states and one foreign country.

Twenty-four of the subjects were White, two were of Hispanic ethnicity, and four of the subjects were African American. Twenty-five of the subjects were male (89.3%), and three of the individuals were female (10.7%). The average age of the 25 men at the time of their suicide was 34.9. Of the three women included in the study, two were 35 years of age and one was 49.

Nineteen of the subjects used handguns, two individuals used shotguns, and one used a rifle to commit suicide. One bipolar individual jumped to his death from a bridge, one person died by self-immolation, and four incidents have been described as a suicide-by-cop. Suicide-by-cop is a phrase that I coined in the early 1980s to describe situations wherein a subject uses the authorities as his or her means of suicide. Subjects place law enforcement in such a dangerous situation that deadly force must be employed to stop the subject's actions.

Only two negotiators reported that the subject had a family history of suicide that was known to the authorities. The remaining negotiators answered either "no" or "unknown" to this question. Sixteen negotiators reported that, to their knowledge, the subject had not seen a medical doctor recently. Three negotiators said that the subject had seen a medical doctor, and nine indicated that they did not know. Of the three negotiators who said that the subject had seen a medical doctor recently, only one of the three subjects was taking medication as prescribed by the physician. The one subject who was taking medication as prescribed was suffering from back pain. Another subject had just undergone a bypass operation, but was not taking the prescribed antidepressants. A third subject was described as being terminally ill with cancer, but the negotiation team did not know his medication history. Seven negotiators said their subjects had recently seen a mental health professional, and only three reported that the subject was taking medication as prescribed.

Incident Characteristics

In 10 of the incidents, someone known to the subject called the authorities. In another 10 incidents, a citizen called 911. In four of the incidents, the suicide event was initiated by law enforcement activity (i.e., law enforcement was looking for the subject because of outstanding arrest warrants, the subject was driving erratically, etc.). In four incidents, it was unclear from the participants' responses precisely what precipitated the encounter with the subject. None of the subjects telephoned the authorities and told the authorities of their intent to commit suicide.

The time at which negotiations commenced was relatively evenly distributed throughout the day. Five incidents commenced between midnight and 6:00 a.m., six between 6:01 a.m. and noon, eight between 12:01 p.m. and 6:00 p.m., and six between 6:00 p.m. and midnight. These findings support Jamison's (1999) claim that most suicides occur between 7 a.m. and 4 p.m.

The average duration for incidents was 276 minutes, or just over 4.5 hours. However, the duration of the incident varied significantly from virtually no negotiation to 1,500 minutes of negotiation. Among the lengthier negotiations, one incident lasted 600 minutes, one incident carried on for 660 minutes, two situations lasted 780 minutes, and one incident went on for 1,500 minutes.

Most of the incidents, as one might suspect, took place at the subject's residence, although one of the suicides took place at a victim's residence. The primary means of contact was telephone and direct voice or a combination of telephone and direct voice.

Findings Regarding Perturbation

Based on the writing of Shneidman, in particular, I would have expected our suicidal individuals to be highly perturbed. However, in 17 of the 28 incidents investigated, negotiators explicitly used the word *calm* to describe their subjects.

Two additional negotiators did not use the word *calm*, but described an outwardly calm individual.

In two of the cases described as examples of suicide-by-cop, there occurred an interesting variation on the perturbation theme. In one of the suicide-by-cop cases in this study, the subject was agitated—that is, screaming insults and obscenities. He also fired more than 20 rounds at officers, but when talking to a friend on a cell phone, the friend described him as "calm." In another suicide-by-cop case in this study, the subject was in a moving vehicle until the end of the incident. Because he, too, had fired more than 20 rounds at the police, the authorities felt that they had no option but to stop him before driving through a town. When he was stopped, a gunfight ensued, and the subject was fatally wounded. Later, when questioned, the victims inside the vehicle described the subject as "calm." The victims reported that the subject had reassured them as to their safety and told them that the incident would soon be over because he was running out of ammunition.

Findings for Drugs and Alcohol

Two subjects were using methamphetamine, and one subject was using cocaine during the incident. Two subjects were using prescribed medications (i.e., an unnamed pain medication and Xanax). In 17 incidents, the negotiators reported that no drugs were used. Six negotiators said that they did not know or recall whether drugs were used.

Six negotiators reported that only 6 of the 28 subjects were using alcohol during the incident. Interestingly, two of the six were also using drugs. One of the six was the subject using methamphetamines and the second was the subject using a pain medication. If the presence of drugs was unknown in six of the incidents, it would seem that drugs or alcohol played no part in the negotiation or the subject's behavior. Two of the six individuals drinking alcohol were not intoxicated according to the negotiators; one subject was having a beer, and the other subject drinking champagne.

Findings for Rapport

In this study, despite excellent negotiator/subject rapport or indications of good rapport in several of the cases, people still killed themselves. In one incident, the subject continued to thank the negotiator for helping him before committing suicide. In another incident, the subject said, "Thank you (negotiator by first name) for being so understanding." In a third situation, the subject commented, "Thanks for trying (negotiator by first name)." (Remarkably, he made this comment after he had shot himself.) Another individual, in the moments just before fatally shooting himself, "was telling the negotiator that he (the negotiator) was a good person." Another subject asked the negotiator whether he ever lost anyone. The subject then told the negotiator that he was a good negotiator and that he should not take it personally. One negotiator said that after 13 hours they felt there was good enough rapport for him to come out.

In the moments just before killing themselves, two suicidal persons apologized to the negotiator. One apologized for "causing problems for the police and his grandparents." One subject began breathing heavily and apologizing for his conduct. Still another subject said, "(negotiator's first name), you're good but your not gonna win this one."

Findings With Regard to Sudden Improvements in Suspect Behavior

None of the negotiators reported observing what they considered a sudden improvement over the course of the negotiation. In my personal discussions with the negotiators, many of them were taught to beware of any sudden improvement in an incident with suicidal potential, the concern being that a decision to proceed with the suicide has been made and the decision having been made provides relief to the suicidal individual. This relief may be heard in the voice of the subject. However, 14 of the negotiators reported being surprised by the subject's suicidal act. Because the apparent "improvement" in several of these cases was what the officers considered gradual, the negotiators were hopeful that the negotiation was going well.

A couple of negotiators were surprised when the subjects died because they knew the subject and previous incidents had ended well. Another was surprised because the subject was talking about his children with the negotiator when he committed suicide. Another subject appeared to be considering what the negotiator had said. One individual was talking about surrendering. Three negotiators were surprised by the suicide because they considered the subject to be rational and calm. Another individual was talking about releasing hostages in turn for a pizza delivery.

CONCLUSION

Perturbation

In this study of persons who committed suicide in negotiated incidents, perturbation or agitation was seen in only a small number of cases. Some persons were described by negotiators as confrontational or agitated at the outset, but later calmed down. Two suicide-by-cop subjects were calm when talking to victims or friends, but agitated when interacting with the authorities. From this study, perturbation does not appear to have been present in the minutes or hours immediately prior to the suicidal act. Crisis negotiators or interveners working with suicidal persons should not necessarily view the apparent absence of perturbation or the subject sounding calm as a positive sign during the intervention.

Drugs and Alcohol

A review of the literature indicates that drugs, alcohol, and suicide are inter-related in some fashion. However, because an individual has used or abused drugs and/or alcohol in the past as a means of coping with his or her psychological pain does not mean that he or she will be using either of these substances on the day of his or her suicide. The negotiation scene presents a different picture. The relative absence of drugs and alcohol in this study is striking. The presence of drugs and/or alcohol was specifically noted in only 8 of the 28 cases.

Over the past 15 years, I have asked negotiators at seminars what percentage of their negotiations involved drugs and alcohol. Several negotiators have reported 100%—that is, they have never negotiated with a sober individual. The lowest estimate received, on more than one occasion, was 45%.

Sudden Improvements

From my discussions with negotiators over the years, many negotiators are aware of the following advice from mental health professionals: Beware of "rapid improvements" (i.e., changes in mood with depressed persons over a short period of time). A lifting out of the depression may indicate that they have made a decision to proceed with the suicide. I have been telling negotiators to beware of any improvements, rapid or otherwise.

In this study, 12 negotiators indicated that they were surprised by the subject's decision to commit suicide, especially when the negotiators thought the negotiation was going well. I suspect that the problem is that mental health professionals and police officers have different time frames. Therapists think of improvement in terms of days or even months. Police officers think of improvement in terms of hours. To a law enforcement officer, a gradual change in mood over 5 hours that "gradually" lifts the subject out of an observable depression is a good negotiation. The officer does not view an improvement over 5 hours to be a "rapid" improvement at all. The negotiator just thinks he or she is doing a good job and then to his or her surprise the subject commits suicide. The officer does not see a subject's change of mood over a few hours as a "rapid" change, but I suspect that a therapist would have. To a negotiator, a period of 5 hours is not a rapid change when businesses have been shut down, neighborhoods cordoned off, traffic blocked, a city disrupted, 100 or more officers being paid overtime, and a boss asking, "Why is this taking so long?"

Shneidman (1981) indirectly commented on this problem when he wrote the following:

> . . . the acute suicidal crisis (or period of high and dangerous lethality) is an interval of relatively short duration—to be counted, typically, in hours or days, not usually in months or years. An individual is at peak self-destructiveness for a

brief time and is either helped, cools off, or is dead. Although one can live for years at a chronically elevated self-destructive level, one cannot have a loaded gun to one's head for too long before either bullet or emotion is discharged. (p. 13)

The crisis negotiator's problem is counted in a few hours and, rarely, days. The law enforcement negotiator is there during the "acute suicidal crisis" and there at the "peak of destructiveness," whereas the therapist generally is not. The therapist's problem is long term—that is, one of months and or even years.

My advice to law enforcement negotiators has been to be wary of *any* improvement, sudden or otherwise. If the subject is depressed at the beginning of a negotiation, he or she will be depressed at the end of the negotiation. If mental health professionals could lift people out of a depression merely by talking to them for 4 or 5 hours, it would bankrupt the multibillion dollar drug industry.

I believe that the major difference between the start of a negotiation and the end of a negotiation will be the subject's willingness to accept help and his or her belief that the negotiator can provide that help. By selling the idea that the negotiator can provide help, he or she is also providing hope to the subject.

Rapport

Five years ago, I discussed a suicide case with an experienced crisis negotiator from a large metropolitan area. He told me that at the beginning of the incident the subject was depressed and suicidal. Over a period of 4 to 5 hours, the subject's mood "gradually" improved, as did the negotiator's rapport with the subject. After a while, the subject and negotiator were laughing and joking together. The negotiator said that he was pleased with the progress of the negotiation, and he, in fact, gave a "thumbs up" to his sergeant. A short time after the "thumbs up" gesture, the negotiator heard the subject's self-inflicted, fatal gunshot.

The word *rapport* means different things to different people. To the negotiators in this study, it seems to mean "befriend," but I do not think that the suicidal people in this study needed a friend. In my opinion, what they needed was relief from their psychological pain.

Bongar (1996) wrote, "Arguably, the central issue in suicide is not death or killing; rather, it is the stopping of the consciousness of unbearable pain, which, by its very nature, entails the stopping of life" (p. 2). If we have a toothache, we go to a dentist for relief from the pain. Similarly, if we are experiencing stomach pain, we go to a medical doctor for relief from the pain. In neither case do we go to a friend for pain relief; sympathy, perhaps, but not pain relief. It is my belief that suicidal persons need relief from their psychological pain or the hope of pain relief, not the sympathy of a friendly voice.

The type of rapport that the law enforcement negotiator should be striving to establish is a doctor/patient-type relationship, not a friendship. If a patient has a serious health problem, he or she wants to believe that his or her doctor has the special knowledge, power, and skills to assist him or her with his or her recovery. Mental health professionals and medical doctors do not typically ask or encourage their patients to call them by their first name. The patient experiences a level of comfort and confidence in the formal relationship with their doctor and addresses that professional as "doctor, sergeant, or officer," not "Bill, Bob, or Mary."

Jamison (1999) observed:

... when people are suicidal, their thinking is paralyzed, their options appear spare, nonexistent, their mood is despairing, and hopelessness permeates their entire mental domain. The future cannot be or separated from the present, and the present is painful beyond solace.

Crisis negotiators must sell the idea that, by virtue of their position and authority, not friendship, they can provide options, relieve the despair, and alleviate the hopelessness (i.e., he or she has access to power that can help the suicidal individual). A negotiator can establish rapport and communicate empathy, but still maintain a position of authority, much like a doctor.

FINAL COMMENTS

Law enforcement officers work with agitated persons, substance abusers, and persons who do not like authorities on a daily basis. Over a relatively short period of time, they handle the problem. They calm people down. They take people to jail or mental health centers, and they learn to work with all kinds of people under a wide variety of circumstances. The sample of suicidal persons in this study was generally sober; many had calmed down over a few hours and often became friendly to the negotiator. From their prior experience, it would be difficult to blame negotiators for thinking that this negotiation is an "easy" callout. As a result of this study, my concern is that law enforcement negotiators may view a calm, sober individual with whom they have good rapport and whose mood has seemingly changed for the better over 5 hours as less of a serious suicide threat, when, in fact, those individuals are the persons who went on to commit suicide in this informal study.

This was an informal study, and it was never my intention that the end result should set a standard for crisis/suicide intervention. However, the study does seem to point out some discrepancies between what is being taught to law enforcement officers and what those same officers are actually observing. It is my hope that the academic community and law enforcement officers will work ever closer in resolving some of the questions raised in this study and the myriad of other societal problems.

REFERENCES

American Association of Suicidology. (2007). *IS PATH WARM?* Retrieved April 12, 2007, from http://www.suicidology.org/associations/1045/files/Mnemonic.pdf.

American Foundation for Suicide Prevention. (n.d.). *Warning signs of suicide.* Retrieved April 12, 2007, from http://www.afsp.org/index.cfm?page_id=0519EC1A-D73A-8D90-7D2E9E2456182D66.

Arunkumar, T. S., & Vadakekara, E. (n.d.). *Telephone counselors' manual.* Retrieved April 8, 2007, from http://www.thrani.com.

Bongar, B. B. (1996). *The suicidal patient: Clinical and legal standards of care.* Washington, DC: American Psychological Association.

Carl R. Darnall Army Medical Center. (n.d.). *Medical health services: Suicide prevention.* Retrieved April 8, 2007, from http://hood-meddac.army.mil/default.asp?page=suicide&vi=n&mnu=0.

Colt, G. H. (1991). *The enigma of suicide.* New York: Simon & Schuster.

Cross, T. L., Gust-Brey, K., & Ball, P. B. (2002). A psychological autopsy of the suicide of an academically gifted student: Researchers' and parents' perspectives. *National Association for Gifted Children, 46*(4). Retrieved from http://www.geniusdenied.com/articles/ArticlePrintable.aspx?rid=13961.

Holden, R. R. (2003). Differentiating suicidal motivations and manifestations in a forensic sample. *Canadian Journal of Behavioural Science.* Retrieved from http://www.findarticles.com/p/articles/mi_qa3717/is_200301/ai_n916806/print.

Jamison, K. R. (1999). *Night falls fast: Understanding suicide.* New York: Vintage Books.

Justice Institute of British Columbia. (2007). Suicide-suicide intervention: Tips on what to say and do. Retrieved April 6, 2007, from http://www.jibc.bc.ca./police/main/PIIMIC/2_Suicide/intervention.htm.

Kaplan, H. I., & Sadock, B. J. (1990). *Pocket handbook of clinical psychiatry.* Baltimore: Williams & Wilkins.

McGothlin, J. M. (2006). Assessing perturbation and suicide in families. *The Family Journal, 14*(2), 129–134. Retrieved from http://tfj.sagepub.com/cgi/content/abstract/14/2/129.

Roberts, A. R., & Jennings, T. (2005). *Brief treatment and crisis intervention.* Retrieved from http://brief-treatment.oxfordjournals.org/cgi/content/full/5/3/251.

Shneidman, E. S. (1981). *Suicide thoughts and reflections 1960–1980.* New York: Human Sciences Press.

Shneidman, E. S. (1996). *The suicidal mind.* New York: Oxford University Press.

Suicide Prevention Resource Center. (2005). *First responders: Emergency medical technicians and firefighters.* Retrieved April 12, 2007, from http://www.sprc.org/featured_resources/customized/pdf/first_responders.pdf.

University of California-Berkeley. (2006). *Suicide intervention guidelines for health workers.* Retrieved April 6, 2007, from http://uhs.berkeley.edu/students/healthpromotion/HWSuicideGuidelines.doc.

University of Technology Sydney. (2007). *Suicidality: Policy/guidelines for its prevention, assessment & treatment.* Retrieved April 11, 2007, from http://www2.kumc.edu /people/llong/ccv/lethality/Policy_on_Suicide_Clients.doc.

APPENDIX

Suicide Interview

1. Negotiator rank:
2. Name:
3. Years in law enforcement at time of incident:
4. Years as negotiator at time of incident:
5. Agency:
6. Telephone number:
7. E-mail address:
8. Subject's first name:
9. Race:
10. Gender:
11. Age:
12. Approximate date of incident:
13. Today's date:
14. What brought the incident to law enforcement attention?
15. Means of suicide:
16. Time opened negotiations:
17. Length of negotiation:
18. Location of incident (i.e., residence, car, bridge, etc.):
19. What were the means of communication?
20. If the subject used drugs during the incident, what drugs were used?
21. Did the subject use alcohol during the incident?
22. Did the subject have a family history of suicide, and, if so, who in the family committed suicide?
23. Had the subject seen a medical doctor recently, and, if so, when, and what was the purpose of the visit, diagnosis, and prescribed medication?
24. Was the subject taking the medication as prescribed?
25. Had the subject seen a mental health professional recently, and, if so, when, and what was the purpose of the visit, diagnosis, and prescribed medication?
26. Was the subject taking the medication as prescribed?
27. Did the negotiation team anticipate the subject's actions, and, if so, what were the indicators?
28. Was the negotiation team surprised by the subject's actions, and, if so, what made the team think that it was not going to happen?
29. Summary of events in the subject's life that lead to the incident:
30. What were the last things the subject said to the negotiator?
31. What was his or her emotional state just before the suicide?
32. What were the indicators of that emotional state?
33. What was he or she doing in the moments just before the suicidal act?
34. Were there any indicators that he or she was about to commit suicide, and, if so what were those indicators?
35. *Additional Comments*

The Psychology of Hostage Takers, Suicidal, and Barricaded Subjects

Kris Mohandie

Psychology of the subject is one of several factors—including context of the event (criminal, geographic, cultural), subject agenda (instrumental and expressive), presence of hostages or victims, and crisis management techniques—that affects the dynamics and outcome of crisis negotiation events (Hatcher, Mohandie, Turner, & Gelles, 1998). Roughly 30% of the subjects in a recent Hostage Barricade Database System (HOBAS) data run (Federal Bureau of Investigation, February 27, 2007) have documented mental health histories, including current counseling or therapy attendance, prior mental health commitments, or current residential care. Unfortunately, the HOBAS database does not document specific diagnostic or symptom issues among these subjects.

Personal experience and the work of other authors (McMains & Mullins, 2005) has supported that there are numerous psychological and diagnostic issues among barricaded subjects, jumpers, and hostage takers. Four broad categories of suspects are usually encountered: (a) depressed or despondent individuals, (b) personality-disordered suspects who may be exhibiting one or a combination of distinct patterns of impaired worldview and relational patterns, (c) thought-disordered or psychotic individuals who evidence seriously distorted perceptual processes, and (d) substance-abusing or dependent subjects whose intoxication or use of substances such as alcohol or drugs plays a complicating role in the situation. Past traumatic brain injuries or psychological trauma may also influence subjects. Culture and religious identification and spirituality (beyond the scope of this chapter) add another layer to analysis, as do hierarchies of dominance in multiple hostage-taker scenarios. Suicidal and homicidal states of mind and affective versus predatory violence proclivities are also central to the process.

Crisis management strategies and negotiation themes are initiated based on accurate assessment of the subject's psychology, primary issues, and concerns. The prior list of "usual suspects" is not meant to be exhaustive; rather, it provides a starting point for understanding the more common suspect symptom/behavior patterns and identifying corresponding suggestions and guidelines for intervention. Material here is presented according to diagnostic category; however, observed *behavior* or *symptoms* (which may overlap categories) should drive interventions: Diagnoses are only currently agreed-on labels for commonly co-occurring symptoms patterns.

DEPRESSED/DESPONDENT

Individuals in this general category ordinarily are in crisis, usually over a recent situation involving perceived failure or a series of losses. They may have given up a long-term struggle with deep emotional pain. The symptom pattern is characterized by core themes of hopelessness, helplessness, and worthlessness. Causes range from life events to those depressions that are biologically based. Treatment includes psychotherapy, light therapy, and/or medication with various anti-depressants. Acute depression may result in psychosis—breaks with reality characterized by delusions and hallucinations.

According to the *Diagnostic and Statistical Manual of Mental Disorder, Fourth Edition, Text Revision, Text Revision* (*DSM–IV–TR*; American Psychiatric Association, 2000, p. 356), those experiencing a depressive episode will have five (or more) of the following symptoms that have been present during the same 2-week period and that represent a change from previous functioning; at least one of the symptoms is either (a) depressed mood, or (b) loss of interest or pleasure. Under the formal definition, these symptoms are not due to substance use, a medical condition, or the normal reaction to bereavement.

1. Depressed mood most of the day, nearly every day, as indicated by either subjective report or observation made by others.
2. Markedly diminished interest or pleasure in all, or almost all, activities most of the day, nearly every day.
3. Significant weight loss when not dieting or weight gain, or decrease or increase in appetite nearly every day.
4. Insomnia or hypersomnia (excessive sleep) nearly every day.
5. Psychomotor agitation or retardation nearly every day.
6. Fatigue or low energy nearly every day.
7. Feelings of worthlessness or excessive or inappropriate guilt nearly every day.
8. Diminished ability to think or concentrate, or indecisiveness, nearly every day.
9. Recurrent thoughts of death (not just fear of dying), recurrent suicidal ideation without a specific plan, or a suicide attempt or a specific plan for committing suicide.

Significant to consider is that approximately 15% of individuals with severe depression die by suicide, and there is a fourfold increase in death rates in individuals over age 55 years (American Psychiatric Association, 2000, p. 371). Research indicates that the prevalence of violence among persons who meet criteria for a diagnosis of major depression is five times higher than among the general population and three to four times higher in jail and prison samples than in general population samples (Monahan, 1992). Individuals with depressive symptomatology are at greater risk for violent acting out, whether through suicide, suicide-by-cop, homicide, or homicide/suicide (Mohandie, 2007). Strategies for managing the depressed individual typically involve active listening and crisis intervention to understand and contain crisis, with an emphasis toward counteracting the core themes of the disorder by attempting to instill hope, increase feelings of control, and elevate the person's sense of personal worth. Depressed individuals will often necessitate suicide intervention. Directly ask them about any suicidal thoughts, whether they have already done something self-destructive, what their plans might be, and what they hope to accomplish by the suicidal act. This provides the opportunity to address the reasons for their suicidality, identify flaws in their reasoning, and use "hooks" that can give them a reason to live. Moving the person from abstract depressive thinking ("Everybody has to die sometime") to more realistic thinking ("That's true Joe, but I'm questioning whether now is that time because of everything going on with your kids and it sounds like they need you") is important.

Sometimes the negotiator will attempt to have the person delay his or her actions to some unspecified future point and help the person take immediate steps to reduce his or her lethality ("Joe please take the gun out of your mouth. Try the things we've been talking about for a while and if all else fails you can always consider doing this later, but it would be a waste if these things work to fix your problem and you haven't at least tried them"). Those conversing with depressed individuals may have to be more patient for responses because depression may result in slower cognitive processing.

Other diagnostic labels that are within the spectrum of depressive or "mood disorders" include adjustment disorder with depressed mood, dysthymic disorder, and seasonal affective disorder. Generally, symptom patterns with these various disorders are similar, but causes, course, chronicity, and intensity of impairment may vary.

Case Example I

Two hours after his most recent outpatient therapy session, a 32-year-old male subject climbed over the protective barrier at "Suicide Bridge" and threatened to jump. Responding officers learned that he was severely depressed and had recently been released from a psychiatric hospitalization. The subject's therapist provided important history to the negotiating team. He was apparently upset over his marital separation, the filing of a restraining order by his estranged wife, concerns about her infidelity, and financial problems. His estranged wife had told him that day that there was no hope for reconciliation. Face-to-face negotiations were initiated because of the open air environment and lack of other suitable alternatives, and the subject spoke freely about his hopelessness to the negotiator. The negotiator emphasized active listening and underscored the subject's relationship with his young son. He eventually demanded to talk with his estranged wife. He agreed to surrender after a tape of her was played (content addressing hope for reconciliation), combined with the promise that a supervised visit between the two of them would be facilitated after he surrendered. The negotiation lasted 8 hours and was resolved after playing the tape. Although brief, the supervised visit was facilitated while in law enforcement custody.

Suicidal and Homicidal States of Mind

Shneidman (1996) observes that there are 10 commonalities among suicidal individuals:

1. Solution seeking—a way out
2. Cessation of consciousness
3. Unbearable psychological pain
4. Frustrated psychological needs
5. The common emotion is hopelessness/helplessness
6. Cognitive state is ambivalence
7. Perceptual state is constriction
8. Common action is escape
9. Common interpersonal act is communication of intent
10. Consistency of lifelong styles.

Although a few of these commonalities are self-explanatory, several merit further clarification.

Solution seeking refers to the fact that, although normal people would consider suicide to be dysfunctional, nonetheless it is an attempt by the subject to solve some problem. The negotiator's task is to identify other solutions that the suspect hasn't considered.

Cessation of consciousness means that the person wants to cease to be and no longer wants to be perceive, feel, or think about the circumstances he or she has been dealing with or with which he or she is confronted. The negotiator attempts to convince the person to postpone this objective.

Ambivalence reflects the reality that most suicidal individuals have mixed feelings about living versus dying, and that their suicidal impulses may wax and wane. The person may want to die or simply be ambivalent about living. Negotiators should strive to expand on the reasons that the person wants to continue living.

Constriction means that suicidal subjects have a limited ability to see other options and choices for solving their problem—they often experience some degree of tunnel vision. Buying time and reducing crisis can sometimes help reduce this tunnel vision. Suicide is a form of running from a problem or problems—it is an *action of escape* among several that the subject may use concurrently or have previously exhausted. Other ways to escape may be outlined by the negotiator, or the negotiator may convince the subject that he or she is strong enough to face the feared issue. Most subjects *communicate intent* of suicide prior to actually doing so—Shneidman reported that in 90% of actual suicide cases, people had given verbal or behavioral clues within the week or so before they committed suicide. This provides an important potential intelligence-gathering task.

Consistency of lifelong styles means that people will usually go about their suicide the way they went about their life—if they are impulsive, they will do it impulsively, for example. Learning about the person's personality style may help assess the particular form of suicidality in a given incident and to take appropriate precautions.

Homicidal states of mind seem to parallel the suicidal, with the exception that the violent solution is directed outward, and typically a more angry, blame-consumed, cognitive-emotional state (Meloy, Mohandie, Hempill, & Shiva, 2001). Meloy (2006) distinguishes between violence that is affective versus predatory. Affective violence is reactive to an immediate psychological or actual threat and is defensive in nature, instinctual, and related to a highly aroused emotional state, typically with a time limited period (usually minutes) of arousal. Predatory violence, by contrast, is cold blooded, calculating, driven by fantasy and a cognitive process, and not in reaction to any particular threat. During crises, ongoing violence risk assessment should take into account the subject's likely mode of acting out and be cautious not to omit the predatory form as part of that assessment.

PERSONALITY DISORDERED

These individuals have chronic maladaptive ways of viewing the world and interacting with others, with a strong tendency to blame others for their problems. All people have typical styles of relating; however, in the personality-disordered individual, these traits have evolved to the extent that they are inflexible, maladaptive, and persisting and cause significant impairment and/or distress. According to the *DSM–IV–TR* (American Psychiatric Association, 2000, pp. 685–686), those with personality disorders tend to exhibit an enduring pattern of inner experience and behavior that deviates markedly from the expectations of the individual's culture. The enduring pattern: (a) is inflexible and pervasive across a broad range of personal and social situations; (b) leads to significant distress or impairment in social, occupational, or other important areas of functioning; (c) is stable, in that it traces back to adolescence or early adulthood; and (d) is not caused specifically by something else, such as another disorder, drug use, or a medical condition. This pattern is manifested in two (or more) of the following areas:

1. Cognition (i.e., ways of perceiving and interpreting self, other people, and events),
2. Affectivity (i.e., the range, intensity, lability, and appropriateness of emotional response),
3. Interpersonal functioning, and
4. Impulse control.

The most commonly encountered personality disorders include the antisocial, borderline, narcissistic, and paranoid.

Antisocial Personality

The core themes of the antisocial personality-disordered individual are disregard for rules and violation of the rights of others. Control, power, domination, and sensation seeking may also surface as issues during interactions with such a person. It is not uncommon to encounter antisocial personalities during spontaneous, trapped criminal situations.

These individuals blatantly disregard the rules of society, have little or no empathy for others, and view the world as one "where the strong survive." They tend to crave and seek excitement and have poor impulse control. According to the *DSM–IV–TR* (American Psychiatric Association, 2000, p. 706), those with antisocial personality disorder exhibit a pervasive pattern of disregard for and violation of the rights of others, occurring since age 15 years, as indicated by three (or more) of the following:

1. Failure to conform to social norms with respect to lawful behaviors as indicated by repeatedly performing acts that are grounds for arrest;
2. Deceitfulness, as indicated by repeated lying, use of aliases, or conning others for personal profit or pleasure;
3. Impulsivity or failure to plan ahead;
4. Irritability or aggressiveness, as indicated by repeated physical fights or assaults;
5. Reckless disregard for safety of self or others;
6. Consistent irresponsibility, as indicated by repeated failure to sustain consistent work behavior or honor financial obligations;
7. Lack of remorse, as indicated by being indifferent to or rationalizing having hurt, mistreated, or stolen from another.

Antisocial personalities are self-centered and generally interested in "what's in it for me?" Bargaining strategies that recognize this central theme will often be well received. Because they are impulsive, it is important to keep them occupied so that they do not use idle time to harm hostages or engage in other antisocial acts. They generally blame others when things go wrong, so if they are upset about issues, it may be useful to join with them in their misperception that they are victims. Care should be taken, however, to avoid being too "touchy feely" because they are generally tough-minded. They will often have a realistic concern with jail time—prison or jail may be a familiar place that they can indeed handle. Because of their egos, it may be important to find a face-saving way for them to surrender. Some mistakenly believe that antisocial personalities are not at risk for suicide—on the contrary, they can and do contemplate suicide as an alternative to doing jail time (Lanceley, 1981).

Within the population of antisocial personalities is a recognized subset of individuals who may be considered psychopathic. The psychopath is particularly callous, shallow, manipulative, dishonest, impulsive, and criminally versatile and, when so inclined, can be particularly dangerous (Hare, 2006). Although negotiation teams are cautious with all subjects who create situations, those who are antisocial merit additional attention, and those who are potentially psychopathic should be of even graver concern. This vigilance needs to consider predatory violence potential as well.

Case Example 2

Two armed double homicide suspects on a crime spree (which included robbing a gun store and a carjacking) became trapped inside a county building with a female security guard hostage after a shootout with police at the conclusion of a 60-mile pursuit. Their initial agenda involved a demand for an armored car and money to facilitate escape. The subjects used the hostage to communicate with authorities initially, and it became clear that she was selling herself to them as "on their side." She also apparently downplayed her role as an authority figure and emphasized her similarity as a person of color who had been treated poorly by the American system—the subjects were both Asian immigrants. Near the conclusion of the incident, the lead suspect—the older male—became suicidal and demanded to talk to his common-law wife. He also threatened the younger hostage taker when he decided to surrender. As a former Vietnamese soldier, he had been taught that "soldiers never surrender." It was assessed that he was looking for a face-saving way to give up—if his wife told him to surrender, it would be perceived differently than doing it out of fear or cowardice. A monitored conversation was put into play with this third-party intermediary. He was not sure whether he wanted to do the jail time, and he wanted his wife's input. Negotiators implemented suicide intervention. The hostage would later explain that she also performed a parallel suicide intervention, addressing that he could in fact do the jail time and if he couldn't he could always commit suicide at a later point. Ultimately, the suspects surrendered without further incident. The primary suspect did in fact commit suicide, and the second suspect was executed by lethal injection (Mohandie & Albanese, 2001).

Narcissistic Personality

These individuals feel morally superior to others and vacillate between rage and deflated depression when things do not go their way. They feel entitled to special treatment and are usually encountered in employment and relationship failure situations. According to the *DSM–IV–TR* (American Psychiatric Association, 2000, p. 717), those with narcissistic personality disorder exhibit a pattern of grandiosity (in fantasy or behavior), need for admiration, and lack of empathy, beginning by early adulthood and present in a variety of contexts, as indicated by five or more of the following:

1. Has a grandiose sense of self-importance;
2. Is preoccupied with fantasies of unlimited success, power, brilliance, beauty, or ideal love;
3. Believes that he or she is special and unique and can only be understood by, or should associate with, other special or high-status people (or institutions);
4. Requires excessive admiration;
5. Has a sense of entitlement;
6. Is interpersonally exploitative;
7. Lacks empathy: is unwilling to recognize or identify with the feelings and needs of others;
8. Is often envious of others or believes that others are envious of him or her; and
9. Shows arrogant, haughty behaviors or attitudes.

The task in dealing with a narcissist is to stroke his inflated ego when he acts out in response to his grandiose rage or, if his incident occurs during the throes of depression after experiencing a setback or blow to his ego, to reinflate him. Although egotistical, there is often a brittle surface that masks an underlying and painful sense of inadequacy. Rather than feel that inadequacy, the narcissistic may prefer to quickly launch into empowering rage. If it does not imperil a hostage, it may be useful to side with him in demeaning, for example, the woman who may have left him ("She didn't appreciate what she had . . . you are too good for someone like that"). The negotiator will likely have to practice restraint in dealing with the air of condescension and superiority that may be projected onto the authorities ("You guys are so incompetent. Can't you do anything right!"). Time will also be well spent in active listening and empathy for the subject's favorite person—him or herself. Face saving in surrendering will be an issue with this personality type as well.

Case Example 3

The subject—a former coworker—stalked the victim for 5 years, culminating in a mass murder at her workplace. He believed he was entitled to have a relationship with her and that it was his right to provide her input about how to improve her life—regardless of whether she wanted it—"She didn't want it and it didn't matter, she needed it!" She had recently filed a restraining order triggering his decision to escalate his actions into a planned abduction the day before the hearing for the restraining order. He entered her workplace armed with 95 pounds of ammunition and weapons. When she failed to exit as he had anticipated, he made a violent entry. After killing seven people and wounding three, including his victim, the subject barricaded himself in an office and threatened suicide. Negotiations ensued and the subject, who presented as extremely self-absorbed, strongly contemplated suicide. He was concerned about the kind of life he could lead in prison, wondered whether his mother would forgive him for what he had done, wanted confirmation that his stalking victim would survive the incident and thus suffer with the memory of what she had caused, and demanded a special sandwich and Pepsi from his favorite restaurant after his suicidal impulses diminished. He lacked any concern or empathy for his victims. Negotiators were nonjudgmental, provided hope that he could live a productive life in prison, and suggested adopting a "wait-and-see" attitude regarding his suicidal impulses. They also made small talk. He surrendered after several hours of negotiation, and his food request was granted (Mohandie, 2004).

Stalking

The prior case demonstrates a stalking antecedent. Recent HOBAS data (Federal Bureau of Investigation, 2007) indicate that 5% of the 5,357 subjects in their analysis had an existing restraining order in effect at the time of their incident, and the victim was a current or former significant other in the 22% of the incidents where there was a victim ($N = 1,405$), suggesting that stalking may be a background dynamic preceding and contributing to many scenarios. Mohandie (2004) identified four types of stalkers that can create a hostage or barricade situation: the Intimate stalker, who pursues a current or former intimate; the Acquaintance stalker, who stalks a current or former coworker, care provider, or friend; the Public Figure stalker, who stalks a public figure or celebrity with whom he or she has never had a relationship; and the Private Stranger stalker, who stalks a victim with whom he or she does not have a relationship with, but whom exists in his or her circle of life. Each of these types of cases has its own pursuit patterns and violence risk (Mohandie, Meloy, Green McGowan, & Williams, 2006). Intimate stalkers are most likely to become involved in a crisis event—but all types have been involved in hostage and barricade incidents. Some general points about negotiating with a stalker include: (a) seek the extensive information often available due to the history of stalking; (b) be alert to the true intentions of the subject, particularly if he has taken his target hostage—homicide, homicide-suicide, or suicide could be on his agenda, and the barricade could represent an interrupted planned act of violence; (c) expect that the subject will be highly focused and obsessed on issues related to his victim; (d) be prepared for potential demands involving contact with the victim; and (d) highly controlled TPI interventions might be necessary to consider, even if it means making some false promises. Overall, their tendency to become obsessed with an idea, coupled with hopelessness to choose a method of last-resort problem solving, the presence of a weapon, and the presence of a victim with whom the perpetrator is deeply conflicted, bode poorly for a peaceful outcome (Mohandie, 2004).

Paranoid Personality

These individuals distrust others and often harbor significant grudges, overreact to perceived slights, and read negative intentions into neutral events. They tend to be preoccupied with issues of fairness and often will have a history of filing grievances and frivolous lawsuits. According to the *DSM–IV–TR* (American Psychiatric Association, 2000, p. 694), those with paranoid personality disorder will have a pervasive distrust or suspiciousness of others, such that their motives are interpreted as malevolent, beginning in early adulthood and present in a variety of contexts, as indicated by four (or more) of the following:

1. Suspects, without sufficient basis, that others are exploiting, harming, or deceiving him or her;
2. Is preoccupied with unjustified doubts about the loyalty or trustworthiness of friends or associates;
3. Is reluctant to confide in others because of unwarranted fear that the information will be used maliciously against him or her;
4. Reads hidden, demeaning, or threatening meanings into benign remarks or events;
5. Persistently bears grudges (i.e., is unforgiving of insults, injuries, or slights);
6. Perceives attacks on his or her character or reputation that are not apparent to others and is quick to react angrily or to counterattack has recurrent suspicions, without justification, regarding fidelity of spouse or sexual partner;
7. Has recurrent suspicions, without justification, regarding fidelity of spouse or sexual partner.

With the distrusting personality, it is usually best to avoid saying "trust me." Rather, approach the subject as if it is natural to be tested and that you realize that trust must be earned. Suggestibility techniques that make use of binds and double binds ("You probably won't believe this") are useful prefaces to dialogue. Respect is critical with these types, and they are brittle and sensitive to perceived slights. Avoid laughing and maintain a serious, professional tone and demeanor at all times.

Borderline Personality

These individuals have chronic instability and a history of failure in relationships, career, judgment, and impulse control. These individuals are in chronic crisis and are referred to by some as "emotional hemophiliacs" (M. Webster, personal communication, January 1994). According to the *DSM–IV–TR* (American Psychiatric Association, 2000, p. 710), those with borderline personality disorder exhibit a pervasive pattern of instability of interpersonal relationships, self-image, and affects, as well as marked impulsivity beginning by early adulthood and present in a variety of contexts, as indicated by five (or more) of the following:

1. Frantic efforts to avoid real or imagined abandonment;
2. A pattern of unstable and intense interpersonal relationships characterized by alternating between extremes of idealization and devaluation;
3. Identity disturbance: markedly and persistently unstable self-image;
4. Impulsivity in at least two areas that are potentially self-damaging (e.g., spending, sex, substance abuse, reckless driving, binge eating);
5. Recurrent suicidal behavior, gestures, threats, or self-mutilating behavior;
6. Affective instability due to a marked reactivity of mood (e.g., intense episodic dysphoria, irritability, or anxiety usually lasting a few hours and only rarely more than a few days);
7. Chronic feelings of emptiness;
8. Inappropriate intense anger or difficulty controlling anger (e.g., frequent displays of temper, constant anger, recurrent physical fights);
9. Transient, stress-related paranoid ideation or severe dissociation symptoms.

Borderline individuals are frequently encountered in crisis situations and may be predisposed to engage in repeated crisis events. Their extreme impulsiveness makes them quite unpredictable, and the negotiator needs to be prepared for rapid shifts in the process, which can include a sudden desire to surrender as well as rapid deterioration and escalation. Active listening and sympathy are important, but these individuals usually have so many issues that the negotiator will find it helpful to help the individual talk about one issue or topic at a time, providing structure to the multitude of topics that the borderline individual wallows and gets lost in. A major task is to help him or her control and contain their strong emotions—the negotiator needs to be prepared for an emotional roller coaster. Suicidal thoughts can and do vacillate rapidly. Further complicating the assessment of risk, some of these individuals will engage in self-mutilation—which is not necessarily a precursor to suicide—as a tension-relieving tool.

THOUGHT DISORDERED/PSYCHOTIC

Case Example 4

A disgruntled patient went into the crowded emergency room of a county hospital, shot three male doctors, and took a female physician and clerical worker hostage. He believed that the institution had been conducting illicit medical experiments and had infected him 10 years earlier with an AIDS-like virus that would result in his eventual death. He falsely believed that he was rotting to death and that the stench was going to result in imminent eviction from his apartment. The search warrant uncovered an extensive diary outlining his plan to kill doctors, acquire additional weapons, and then take female hostages to bring attention to his dilemma. His demeanor during the incident was calm, and he ceased threatening behavior, instead talking calmly about his mistreatment by the hospital. During the incident, he complained of pain, and the physician offered to examine him. He apparently bonded with her and indicated that he would surrender at a specific time. He seemed content to talk about his mistreatment by the hospital and system, and the negotiator addressed him respectfully, appeared concerned about his well-being, did not attempt to argue him out of his delusion, listened and empathized with his perceptions and feelings of mistreatment, and focused on what it would take to resolve the incident. The offender surrendered 5 hours later.

The distinguishing feature of this group of subjects is that they have major breaks with reality and serious perceptual problems, which include hallucinations, delusions, thought insertion, ideas of reference, and symptoms that generally can be controlled with medication. These symptoms are referred to as *psychosis*. For a variety of reasons, they may stop taking their medication and become psychotic. Diagnostic labels range from the relatively commonly encountered schizophrenia to brief reactive psychosis and the unusual shared psychotic disorder, the latter which involves more than one person usually living in close proximity sharing a delusional system. In this section, three commonly encountered thought-disordered subjects are described.

Schizophrenia

It is estimated that the prevalence of schizophrenia ranges from .2% to 2% of the population, with a lifetime prevalence estimate of .5% to 1% (American Psychiatric Association, 2000), meaning that at least 1 to 2 persons out of 100 in their lifetime will qualify for this diagnosis at some point in their entire lifespan. There are an estimated 2.5 million Americans who suffer from schizophrenia, and about one third of them are paranoid schizophrenics (Mohandie & Duffy, 1999). According to the *DSM–IV–TR* (American Psychiatric Association, 2000, p. 312), those with schizophrenia will have two or more of the following characteristic symptoms, each of which is present for a significant portion of the time during a 1-month period (or less if successfully treated):

1. Delusions,
2. Hallucinations,
3. Disorganized speech,
4. Grossly disorganized or catatonic behavior, and
5. Negative symptoms (flat or unresponsive affect).

A delusion is an erroneous or false belief that usually involves a misinterpretation of perceptions or experiences. The content of the delusion may be somatic (pertaining to the body), persecutory ("They are trying to poison me"), religious ("I am on a mission for God"), referential ("That actress on TV was sending me a special message"), or grandiose ("I am God"). Most frequently however, the themes are persecutory—hence, the descriptive label *paranoid.* Delusions may range from the bizarre ("I was kidnapped and am now being stalked by aliens") to the nonbizarre ("People at work are conspiring against me").

A hallucination is the perception of a sensory experience in the actual absence of that experience and may occur in any sensory modality. The person senses something that is not there. Most frequent, however, are auditory hallucinations; that is, hearing voices, usually critical, demeaning, or threatening, that are perceived by the subject as distinct from his or her own thoughts. These symptoms cause major social or occupational dysfunction and cannot be explained by some other disorder, such as the use of drugs or a medical condition (American Psychiatric Association, 2000).

There are several subtypes of schizophrenia, and the paranoid type is characterized primarily by delusions or auditory hallucinations in the context of otherwise normal cognitive and affective functioning. Generally, the person's thoughts are well organized, in comparison with other forms of schizophrenia, with the delusion usually being organized around a coherent theme. Anxiety, anger, aloofness, and argumentativeness are common associated features, and the individual will often have a superior or patronizing manner and either a stilted, formal quality or extreme intensity to interpersonal interactions (American Psychiatric Association, 2000, p. 314). The persecutory themes may predispose the individual to suicidal behavior, and the combination of persecutory and grandiose delusions with anger may predispose the individual to violence. The fact that many suffering from paranoid schizophrenia have coherent thinking that accompanies a consistent delusion or delusions is precisely what makes them potentially lethal: They misperceive events, but their behavior is not generally disorganized, making them capable of significant premeditated, goal-directed behavior.

In persons from other cultures, delusions and hallucinations will have content that is consistent with cultural beliefs and practices; for example, a psychotic Russian immigrant may be concerned about the KGB. There is strong evidence that the disorder is a biologically based illness, and many of the available treatments are antipsychotic medications such as the neuroleptics, which include Haldol, Zyprexa, Risperdal, and Thorazine. Many of these medications result in side effects such as involuntary movements of the tongue, jaw, trunk, and extremities (the "Thorazine shuffle"), and additional medications to control these symptoms are often prescribed (Mohandie & Duffy, 1999).

Research demonstrates that the prevalence of violence among those with schizophrenia is five times higher than those with no disorder, and that the prevalence of schizophrenia is three times higher in jail and prison samples than in general population samples (Monahan, 1992). Those who are actively experiencing psychotic symptoms are involved with violent behavior at rates several

times those of nondisordered members of the general population. Alcohol and illicit drug use is fairly common in this group, factors that, if present, elevate risk
of violent acting out.

Several strategies may be useful for dealing with a psychotic individual (Mohandie & Duffy, 1999). First, it is important to seek to *understand the important
issue the subject is trying to communicate.* No matter how bizarre and humorous
the delusion or hallucination may seem, it *is imperative to not laugh, ridicule, or
criticize the person* in any manner. The third-party intermediary issue is also important. Negotiators have found that the use of third parties to negotiate with
suspects has a positive impact on many incidents (Federal Bureau of Investigation, 1998). Due to past negative interactions with the subject and the possibility
that the family member or past treating mental health provider may have been incorporated into any existing delusions as an evil force or imposter, it is *critical to
assess the subject's perceptions about any third parties* being considered for involvement in the process.

It is important to *avoid arguing with the person about the content of his or her
delusions.* There are two schools of thought about whether it is useful to talk with
the subject about the content of them: those that believe it is helpful to understand
the delusion to *avoid law enforcement actions which validate their delusional belief,*
and those who believe it is important to immediately *move to reality—based issues.* Whatever the case, there will be occasions where the person will need to
communicate about their delusion and the negotiator will have to *listen to their
explanation of the world, and side with their perspective without sounding insincere.*
In responding to these kinds of symptoms, it is important to note that, although
we cannot honestly tell the person that we see or believe the things they are reporting, we can honestly communicate to them that we believe they truly believe
these feelings and sensations (Mohandie & Duffy, 1999).

Of critical importance is the *how* of the interaction; that is, the physical
boundaries of the encounter. *Body space, eye contact, and mannerisms of the responding officer or negotiator are perceived in an intensified manner* as potentially
threatening to the subject. These are people who are extremely sensitive to in-
trusions into their body space and may have an expanded sense of personal
boundaries. They may require more physical distance in interactions in order to
feel safe. Further, too much intense eye contact in face-to-face scenarios may
sometimes evoke paranoid fear of aggression or mind control. Similarly, movements by the authorities will often be filtered by the subject through the emotion
of fear and anticipated aggression, and the subject may feel it is important to get
the first punch or shot in order to keep themselves safe. Many of our actions may
be magnified in intensity and significance on the dimension of potential threat,
and the negotiator should *explain as much as possible without compromising the operation prior to doing anything* to prevent unnecessary escalation.

After resolution, it is essential to practice basics learned in negotiation: *fulfill promises as much as possible and attempt to continue to build rapport after arrest or the surrender.* Recognize that this could be a longitudinal problem and

there is a chance that, upon release, there could be another incident. It is important to *share information with any hospital, doctors, and family so that social support is mobilized* in the maximum possible way.

Bipolar/Manic-Depressive

According to the *DSM–IV–TR* (American Psychiatric Association, 2000, p. 362), those who suffer from bipolar disorder will exhibit manic episodes that consist of a distinct period of abnormally and persistently elevated, expansive, or irritable mood, lasting at least 1 week, and during the period of mood disturbance, three to four or more of the following:

1. Inflated self-esteem or grandiosity;
2. Decreased need for sleep (e.g., feels rested after only 3 hours of sleep);
3. More talkative than usual or pressure to keep talking;
4. Flight of ideas or subjective experience that thoughts are racing;
5. Distractibility (i.e., attention drawn too easily to unimportant or irrelevant things);
6. Increase in goal-directed activity or psychomotor agitation;
7. Excessive involvement in pleasurable activities that have a high potential for painful consequences (e.g., spending sprees, sexual indiscretions).

When individuals are in a manic episode, they may be euphoric, coming across as if they are high, yet they have not taken any drugs, and this feeling of euphoria can lead to grandiose delusions. Poor judgment and bad decisions made during an episode can become part of the regret and despair, which may be expressed when the individual shifts to a depressive state, something that often occurs. The name *bipolar disorder* derives from the idea that these people operate at two extremes, sometimes almost simultaneously, shifting from being high to seriously depressed. Research (American Psychiatric Association, 2000, pp. 359–360) indicates that the disorder is likely to be biologically based because there are multiple indicators of "chemical imbalances" in those who suffer from it. Those who suffer from this disorder may take a variety of medications such as Lithium or Depakoate to control it; however, denial is common, and many enjoy the highs, so medication noncompliance often precipitates a rapid return of symptoms. Law enforcement may encounter these individuals during the manic phase when the individual is delusional or in the depressive phase when the person is extremely depressed. Violence and suicide are major concerns with this population.

The prevalence of violence among people who meet criteria for a diagnosis of mania/bipolar disorder is five times higher than in the general population. Further, among jail and prison samples, the prevalence of this disorder is 7 to 14 times higher than in general population samples (Monahan, 1992). Those in an acute manic state may present as psychotic, necessitating strategies as outlined under schizophrenia. However, in the depressed mode, strategies described under the depressed/despondent subject are likely applicable. Suicide risk is a serious concern in this population.

Delusional Disorder

Those with delusional disorder exhibit nonbizarre delusions that involve situations that occur in real life, such as being followed, poisoned, infected, loved at a distance, having a disease, or being deceived by a spouse or lover (American Psychiatric Association, 2000, p. 329). For a person to receive this diagnosis, he or she may, in contrast to those who suffer from schizophrenia, be functioning without obvious impairment apart from his or her behavior related to the delusion. There are a number of subtypes that include: (a) erotomanic type, in which there are delusions that another person, usually of higher status, is in love with the individual; (b) grandiose type, in which there are delusions of inflated worth, power, knowledge, identity, or special relationship with a deity or famous person; (c) jealous type, in which there are delusions that an individual's sexual partner is unfaithful; (d) persecutory type, in which there are delusions that the person, or someone to whom the person is close, is being malevolently treated in some way; and (e) somatic type, in which there are delusions that the person has some physical defect or general medical condition.

Persons with this type of disorder may be lethal, particularly those who are of the persecutory or jealous type. They may strike out against those they believe are causing them harm or even preemptively. They are known to engage in litigious behavior, writing countless letters of protest to city officials and various branches of the government and making many court and other public forum appearances as they try to rectify the conditions they perceive in their delusions. Strategies for dealing with these individuals follow guidelines outlined under schizophrenia.

SUBSTANCE INTOXICATION, ABUSE, AND DEPENDENCY

Subjects often evidence an array of issues with legal, prescription, and illegal substances. Among the 5,357 subjects in the current HOBAS database (Federal Bureau of Investigation, 2007), many had documented substance abuse histories: 29% had a history of alcohol abuse, 18% abuse controlled dangerous substances, 4% abused prescription drugs, and 1% abused nonprescription drugs. HOBAS data also indicated that many were actually under the influence during the incident (although obviously it is not known to what extent because this was not measured): 28% used alcohol, 9% used controlled dangerous substances, 5% used prescription drugs, and 1% used nonprescription drugs. It is likely that the true prevalence of substance use and abuse among subjects is significantly understated given that the HOBAS data in this regard were unknown in more than 40% of their cases. These data support that subjects in crisis negotiation incidents are often acutely intoxicated and may be enmeshed in lifestyles that are dysfunctional due to ongoing abuse of and dependence on these substances.

Substance intoxication refers to the reversible changes that occur to a person as a consequence of his or her ingestion or exposure to a substance—the high affects their feelings, thoughts, and behavior. Each substance has its own typical "syndrome" or common effects. Typically, there are disturbances of perception, wakefulness, attention, thinking, judgment, psychomotor behavior, and interpersonal behavior. It varies significantly due to doses, duration or chronicity of dosing, the ingestion of other substances that may inhibit or exacerbate its effects, the quality or purity of the substance, the person's mental state or expectations at the time, and the environment or setting in which the substance is taken (American Psychiatric Association, 2000, pp. 200–201).

Substance abuse involves one or more of the following occurring within a 12-month period:

1. Recurrent substance use resulting in a failure to fulfill major role obligations at work, school, or home;
2. Recurrent substance use in situations in which it is physically hazardous;
3. Recurrent substance-related legal problems;
4. Continued substance use despite having persistent or recurrent social or interpersonal problems caused or exacerbated by the effects of the substance.

The person in this category has never been diagnosed as substance dependent for the class of substance.

According to the *DSM–IV–TR* (American Psychiatric Association, 2000, pp. 197–198) *substance dependence* is a maladaptive pattern of use that impairs or distresses the person characterized by three or more of the following over a 12-month period:

1. Tolerance;
2. Withdrawal;
3. Taking larger amounts over a longer period than was intended;
4. Persistent desire or unsuccessful efforts to cut down or control substance use;
5. A great deal of time spent in activities to obtain, use, or recover from the effects of the substance;
6. Important social, occupational, or recreational activities are given up or reduced because of substance use;
7. Substance use continues despite knowledge of having a persistent or recurrent physical or psychological problem likely to have been caused or exacerbated by the substance.

Individuals who are substance dependent may or may not have physiological dependence, meaning they evidence tolerance and/or withdrawal. Withdrawal is the development of distressful and impairment-causing symptoms due to cessation or withdrawal of substance use that has been heavy or prolonged—most symptoms are the opposite of those the person experienced while being intoxicated. Drug use patterns that involve more rapid "highs," such as intravenous or smoking, tend to produce a greater likelihood of dependence and withdrawal.

There is an extensive array of substances that subjects use, but several primary drugs will be mentioned here: alcohol, cocaine, methamphetamine, Ecstasy, marijuana, LSD, PCP, heroin and opiate-based prescriptions (Vicodin, Oxycontin, Percoset, Darvon, and other assorted painkillers), and other prescription drugs such as Xanax and Valium. Most of these drugs, with the exception of Ecstasy, marijuana, LSD, and PCP, can have strong physiological addiction potential, although all can have strong psychological addiction components. Opiates in particular are known for their strong withdrawal symptoms. Nicotine—via cigarettes and other tobacco-based products—is yet another substance of abuse well known for its addictive potential and often a point of bargaining during negotiation incidents.

Substance use, intoxication, and dependence are a set of "wild cards" in negotiation. The drunk subject may be difficult, disinhibited, and unpredictable due to his intoxication; but if he is extremely drunk, he may fall asleep and lose his resolve and effectiveness as a potential adversary. Those withdrawing from alcohol may suffer severe withdrawal symptoms, including DTs, depression, agitation, seizures, and even delirium, which can have significant repercussions on the process. This could increase risk for acting out due to the disturbed mood state, whereas it could provide a potential negotiation and tactical strategy. The negotiator might offer to get the person to a more comfortable detox or even consider promising alcohol to them on surrender.

Cocaine and methamphetamine intoxication increase impulsivity, and the excessive use of these substances may increase feelings of paranoia, undermining rapport building and elevating risk of violence. Both substances have a known positive association with violence potential. Negotiation with the subject who abuses or is intoxicated with substances affects the risk assessment. It is well documented that those under the influence of alcohol and drugs evidence a higher risk for violence and suicide (Monahan, 1992).

McMains and Mullins (2005) offer several suggestions for dealing with substance users and abusers, including, most importantly, consideration of "whether to encourage discontinuance or abstinence of the substance during the incident on the basis of anticipated effects of that discontinuance on the person's emotional, mental, and behavioral reaction" (p. 287).

The subject may be interested in discussing the negative consequences of their substance use—a content area for productive dialogue. Many are receptive to framing their problem as an illness ("John I don't hear a bad guy, I hear someone who has what we know is an illness or sickness—you need help!"). This framework may, in fact, move them from the shame that may be precipitating suicidal impulses. If they have sought help before, including rehab and 12-step programs, the biggest hurdle to overcome is their sense of having failed by relapsing. Some familiarity with core 12–step philosophies and jargon may be helpful for the negotiator to know. For example, there are no rules in rehab programs about how much time they have to get sober. Relapses are viewed as part of the process. Twelve-step programs have the following as a core principle: "The only requirement for AA membership is a desire to stop drinking (or in the drug addict situation, stop using)" (Alcoholics Anonymous, 1994, p. 139). The 12-step dropout who has relapsed and is despondent will likely be receptive to this point, which is repeated at the beginning of most 12-step meetings. "Progress not perfection" is another phrase that may be meaningful to the person despondent over his relapse—emphasizing that relapse is a normal part of his or her illness. Twelve-step participants often have sponsors who coach them in their pursuit of sobriety. Accessing these individuals may facilitate intelligence gathering and provide a potentially useful TPI intervention.

Case Example 5

The subject, a 21-year-old gang member with a significant history of violence, became a barricade after a domestic dispute with his estranged girlfriend. She managed to escape, and he proceeded to ingest marijuana, PCP, and alcohol in his parents' house while arming himself with a handgun. He threatened suicide, fastened the handgun to his hand, and tied it so the barrel was pointed at his chin. The subject then turned on the gas in the kitchen and threatened to blow the house up if the tactical team made entry. He demanded a conversation with his girlfriend, who refused to participate in the process other than providing "intelligence." Ultimately, the subject became demanding and controlling with the negotiator, unaware that he really had no bargaining chips once he lost his superficial desire to die. During the passage of time, the tactical team was able to turn off the gas—a most fortunate occurrence because the subject later forgot he had turned it on prior to lighting another marijuana cigarette. He expressed gratitude that the house had not blown up when the negotiator admitted the gas had been turned off to avoid an "accident." A hardball approach was introduced, which included hanging up on the subject—something that was met with some degree of surprise as he demanded to continue his monologue. The threat of force outlined to him was met with profanity and bravado. The negotiator remained firm but apologetic and described the potential impact of tear gas on him and how he could avoid that (it was in his best interest) by surrendering. The subject surrendered just prior to the introduction of tear gas and was amazingly compliant with arresting officers.

CLOSING THOUGHTS

Subject psychology is an important determinant of crisis incident dynamics. Familiarity with the common types and issues identified in this chapter provides an important starting point for initial and ongoing decisions about strategy. The case examples in this chapter make clear that pure types are a rarity—most subjects present an array of symptoms (e.g., depression and substance use, or psychosis and personality disorders). Effective negotiation relies on assessment of salient symptoms/behavior and addressing the themes that underlie those varied issues in a given person. Teams and decision makers should have available to them the current *DSM–IV–TR* (American Psychiatric Association, 2000) as a reference guide when mental health information pertaining to subjects presents itself. Ideally, access to a mental health consultant would be preferred. Unfortunately, many agencies simply do not have this available resource. Recent HOBAS data (Federal Bureau of Investigation, 2007) indicate that mental health consultants were utilized in only 15% of the 5,083 incidents in their most recent data run.

It is important to note that an attitude of respect should be communicated with all types of subjects—thematic content appropriate to a particular individual relies on the stability of this important platform of influence. As with many issues in life, flexibility is also critical—negotiators must be able to think on their feet in order to generate novel solutions to the unusual challenges that hostage takers, suicidal, and barricaded subjects create. Our ability to empathize and understand—although not condone—the worldviews and actions of our adversaries and those needing our assistance provides an extraordinary resource to dangerous and volatile crises.

REFERENCES

Alcoholics Anonymous. (1994). *Twelve steps and twelve traditions.* New York: Alcoholics Anonymous World Services.

American Psychiatric Association. (2000). *Diagnostic and statistical manual of mental disorders, fourth edition, text revision (DSM–IV–TR).* Washington, DC: Author.

Federal Bureau of Investigation. (2007, February 27). *HOBAS data run.* Quantico, VA: FBI Academy.

Federal Bureau of Investigation. (1998, October 5–8). *The police seminar on crisis negotiations.* Burbank, CA: Author.

Hare, R. (2006). Psychopathy: A clinical and forensic review. *Psychiatric Clinics of North America, 29,* 709–724.

Hatcher, C., Mohandie, K., Turner, J., & Gelles, M.G. (1998). An overview of the role of psychologist in crisis/hostage negotiations. *Behavioral Science and the Law, 16,* 455–472.

Lanceley, F. (1981). Antisocial personality and the hostage taker. *Journal of Police Science and Administration, 9,* 28–34.

McMains, M., & Mullins, W. (2005). *Crisis negotiations: Managing critical incidents and hostage situations in law enforcement and corrections.* Cincinnati, OH: Anderson.

Meloy, J. R. (2006). Empirical basis and forensic application of affective and predatory violence. *Australian and New Zealand Journal of Psychiatry, 40,* 539–547.

Meloy, J. R., Mohandie, K., Hemphill, T., & Shiva, A. (2001). The violent true believer: Homicidal and suicidal states of mind (Hassom). *Journal of Threat Assessment, 1,* 1–14.

Mohandie, K. (2004). Stalking behavior and crisis negotiation. *International Journal of Crisis Negotiations, 4,* 23–44.

Mohandie, K. (2007). Forensic psychological issues in officer involved shooting, use of force, and suicide by cop cases. In H. Hall (Ed.), *Forensic psychology and neuropsychology for criminal and civil cases* (pp. 239–262). Boca Raton, FL: CRC Press.

Mohandie, K., & Albanese, M. (2001). Issues to consider in the use of third party intermediaries in the negotiation process. In M. J. McMains & W. C. Mullins (Eds.), *Crisis negotiations* (pp. 310–311). Cincinnati, OH: Anderson Publishing.

Mohandie, K., & Duffy, J. (1999, December). First responder and negotiation guidelines with the paranoid schizophrenic subject. *FBI Law Enforcement Bulletin,* pp. 8–16.

Mohandie, K., Meloy, J. R., Green McGowan, M., & Williams, J. (2006). The RECON typology of stalking: Reliability and validity based upon a large sample of North American stalkers. *Journal of Forensic Sciences, 51,* 147–155.

Monahan, J. (1992). Mental disorder and violent behavior: Perceptions and evidence. *American Psychologist, 47,* 511–521.

Shneidman, E. S. (1996). *The suicidal mind.* New York: Oxford University Press.

10

Abducting Islam

Islamic Extremist Ideology in the Context of Hostage Negotiations

Daveed Gartenstein-Ross
Kyle Dabruzzi

Islamic radicals have taken hostages with disturbing frequency (Ellingwood, 2006; Semple & Filkins, 2006; Struck & Dwyer, 2005). One case that illustrates the importance of understanding Muslim hostage takers' culture and ideology occurred in 1977, when a dozen Hanafi Muslims seized Washington, DC's City Hall building, B'nai B'rith building, and Islamic Center. During a 39-hour stand-off, the Hanafis took 134 hostages, shot city councilman Marion Barry in the chest, and killed a reporter. However, the crisis was successfully resolved after ambassadors from Egypt, Iran, and Pakistan entered the negotiations and re-cited verses from the Qur'an emphasizing compassion and mercy. After the am-bassadors built a rapport with lead hostage taker Khalifa Hamaas Abdul Khaalis, they worked out a face-saving compromise in which Khaalis freed the hostages and agreed to face charges, but was released without bail and allowed to return home before his trial.

Louis Fields, a former State Department lawyer and arms control negotiator, has noted that, "Ambassador [Douglas] Heck's initiative in gathering three Am-bassadors of countries having populations comprising mostly members of the Is-lamic faith was a major contribution to the peaceful resolution of the crisis" (Fields, 1988, p. 281). The negotiators' knowledge of the group's beliefs and val-ues, and the way they employed religious and cultural empathy, helped to resolve the situation peacefully.

Hostage crises involving Islamic militants will undoubtedly arise in the fu-ture. Negotiators likely to face such situations should develop an understanding of Islamic extremists' culture and beliefs. Explaining and predicting behavior is an essential facet of hostage negotiations because it allows negotiators to devise more effective strategies. Gary Weaver (1997), an American University professor who has consulted for the Federal Bureau of Investigation (FBI) and other law enforcement agencies on cross-cultural communication and psychology, writes that, "to explain and predict the behavior of others we must develop *realistic empathy*," which he defines as "the ability to put oneself in another person's psychological shoes" (p. 117). Cultural understanding is an essential part of attaining realistic empathy because "[u]nderstanding a particular culture helps us to explain and predict the behavior of most people in that culture" (Weaver, 1997, pp. 120–121).

This chapter provides negotiators and researchers with a basic understanding of jihadist ideology.[1] It begins by explaining important concepts relevant to all Muslims, and then it turns to the radical worldview. The exposition of radicalism begins by discussing the duty of jihad: the theological and philosophical justifications for undertaking violence against infidels, as well as relevant political grievances. The chapter then examines four critical thinkers—Muhammad ibn Abdul Wahhab, Hassan al-Banna, Sayyid Qutb, and Sayyid Abul A'la Maududi—whose writings and lives may provide insight into Islamic hostage takers' worldview. After explaining how jihadists view their war against the West, the chapter examines specific cultural mores of which negotiators should be cognizant. Finally, because this chapter focuses on Sunni radicalism, a note at the end highlights the differences between Sunni and Shia Islam.

BASICS OF ISLAM

Islam is the Arabic word for "submission," denoting submission to the will of Allah. (*Allah*, Arabic for "the god," is the name that Muslims use to refer to the Creator. It is also a term employed by native Arabic speakers of other religious backgrounds, including Arabic-speaking Christians.) To become Muslim, one must recite the declaration of faith, known as the *shahada*. The *shahada*—which represents Islam's fundamental creed—is spoken in Arabic and translates to: "I bear witness that there is no object of worship except Allah, and I bear witness that Muhammad is the Messenger of Allah." The *shahada* is the first of the five pillars of Islam, the obligatory tenets of the faith. The others are *salat* (five daily prayers), *zakat* (charitable giving), *Hajj* (pilgrimage to Mecca), and *sawm* (fasting during the lunar month of Ramadan).

Muslims believe that Allah sent a series of prophets to the world. These prophets are familiar to Christians and Jews: They include Abraham, Isaac, Jacob, Moses, and Jesus. However, in Islam, Muhammad is considered the last of the prophets. Muslims believe that Muhammad received the direct word of Allah in the form of revelations that were later compiled as the Qur'an, Islam's holy book. Because Islam holds that both the Old Testament and New Testament have been corrupted over time, Muslims believe that today the Qur'an is the only unadulterated divine revelation.

Two complementary bodies of Islamic law stem from Muhammad's life. The first is the Qur'an, and the second is Muhammad's example. Muqtedar Khan of the Center for the Study of Islam and Democracy notes that "the words, deeds and silences (that which he saw and did not forbid) of Muhammad became an independent source of Islamic law. Muslims, as part of religious observance, not only obey, but also seek to emulate and imitate their Prophet in every aspect of life" (Khan, 2003). A critical concept in Muslims' efforts to emulate Muhammad is the *sunna,* which informs them of Muhammad's practices, customs, and traditions. The *ahadith* (singular: *hadith*) are the recorded texts of Muhammad's sayings and doings from which the *sunna* is derived. Although the *ahadith* were primarily compiled by Islamic scholars in the ninth century (about 200 years after Muhammad's death), a complex science has been devoted to determining which prophetic traditions are sound and which are of questionable veracity. Together, the *sunna* and *ahadith* form the second authoritative body of Islamic jurisprudence by providing insight into Muhammad's example.

Islamic tradition holds that Muhammad was born in 570 AD in Mecca, a city located in what is now Saudi Arabia (Hourani, 1991).[2] At the age of 25, Muhammad was hired by Khadijah bint Khuwaylid, a businesswoman (al-Mubarakpuri, 1979). After Muhammad undertook a profitable journey to Syria on her behalf, Khadijah proposed to him. Although she was 15 years older than Muhammad, they married, and Khadijah bore all but one of his children.

Before receiving his first divine revelations, Muhammad had a reputation for being virtuous, chaste, and wise. Islamic legend holds that when he was 35, the tribe of Quraish (a prominent local tribe of traders to which Muhammad's family belonged) decided to rebuild the Kaaba, a large cubical structure where Muslims believe that God asked Abraham to sacrifice his son.[3] When the walls were high enough for the Black Stone (the Kaaba's eastern cornerstone) to be built back into its corner, the clans bickered for some time about who should have the honor of lifting it into its place. Martin Lings writes that the oldest man present proposed that the next man to enter the mosque surrounding the Kaaba should serve as an arbiter. Muhammad was the next to enter, and Lings describes how he managed to break the impasse:

> The sight of [Muhammad] produced an immediate and spontaneous recognition that here was the right person for the task, and his arrival was greeted by explanations and murmurs of satisfaction. "It is al-Amin," said some. "We accept his judgments," said others, "it is Muhammad." When they explained the matter to him, he said: "Bring me a cloak." And when they brought it, he spread it on the ground, and taking up the Black Stone he laid it on the middle of the garment. "Let each clan take hold of the border of the cloak," he said. "Then lift it up, all of you together." And when they had raised it to the right height he took the stone and placed it in the corner with his own hands; and the building was continued and completed above it. (Lings, 1983, p. 42)

Lings (1983) writes that, soon after "this outward sign of his authority and his mission," Muhammad also began "to experience powerful inward signs" (p. 43). He spoke of experiencing visions in his sleep and began to go on spiritual retreats to a cave in Mount Hira, near Mecca's outskirts. During one such retreat, Muslims believe Muhammad received his first revelation from Allah, at age 40. He continued to receive revelations for the rest of his prophethood, which lasted nearly 23 years. After the first 3 years of revelation, Muhammad began to preach openly—and quickly earned the disapproval of Mecca's tribes, notably the Quraish.

The Quraish kept images of the local gods at the Kaaba, and Muhammad's strict monotheism was a direct attack on this practice. The Meccan tribes persecuted Muhammad's followers, and in 622, the Muslims were forced to flee to the settlement of Yathrib, which would later be renamed Medina. This event, known as the *hijra* (flight), not only marks the time when Muhammad began to serve as a military and political leader, but also the beginning of the Islamic calendar.

With the assent of Medina's tribes, Muhammad created a constitution for his city-state. Muhammad Hamidullah (1969) writes: "The document laid down principles of defence and foreign policy.... It recognized that the Prophet Muhammad would have the final word in all differences, and that there was no limit to his power of legislation." This allowed Muhammad to graft his faith to the politics of the state.

After 6 years, Muhammad and his followers gained enough power to face their former persecutors. Their first military encounter with the Quraish came at the legendary Battle of Badr. Islamic tradition holds that 300-strong Muslim forces attacked a Quraishi caravan guarded by a 1,000-soldier army (al-Mubarakpuri, 1979). Although outnumbered, the Muslims won. The victory at Badr made clear that Muhammad was able to openly challenge the Quraish tribes. When Muhammad and his followers eventually returned to Mecca, many Quraishi soldiers deserted and converted to Islam (Lings, 1983). Those who stood opposed were killed. Mecca's pagan idols were destroyed, and Muhammad's rule came to encompass Mecca.

Muhammad died in 632 without naming a successor. Vali Nasr (2007) notes, "Most Muslims at the time (the forebears of the Sunnis) followed the tribal tradition according to which a council of elders would choose the most senior and respected elder to become the head of the Islamic community, or *umma*" (p. 35). This head of the community would be the *caliph*, a term that means "successor" in reference to Muhammad's successor as the Muslims' political leader. The consensus of the group held that Abu Bakr, a close friend of the Prophet as well as his father-in-law, should be the first caliph. Although a small group believed that the Prophet's cousin and son-in-law Ali ibn Abi Talib was more qualified, "[i]n the end consensus prevailed and all dissenters, Ali included, accepted Abu Bakr's leadership" (Nasr, 2007, p. 35).

The controversy concerning Muhammad's successor became more pronounced after the murder of Ali, who was then the fourth caliph, and the caliphate's transformation into a monarchy under the Umayyads. Those who would later be classified as Sunni Muslims (Sunni comes from the Arabic word for "one who follows the traditions of the Prophet") accepted not only Abu Bakr's rise as the first caliph, but also the Umayyads' rule. Not all Muslims did. Nasr (2007) explains:

> Shiism arose in part on the foundation of their dissent. Ali's murder, the transformation of the caliphate into a monarchy, and the de facto separation of religious and political authorities under the Umayyads led a minority of Muslims to argue that what had come to pass was the fruit not of God's mandate but of man's folly. These dissenting voices rejected the legitimacy of the first three Rightly Guided Caliphs, arguing that God would not entrust his religion to ordinary mortals chosen by the vote of the community and that Muhammad's family . . . were the true leaders of the Muslim community. (pp. 36–37)

Thus, the Shias (derived from the *Shi'at Ali*, or Party of Ali) believed that Muhammad's successor should be a blood relative: Ali should have been the first caliph, rather than Abu Bakr, and the Umayyad leadership too was illegitimate.

Because Sunnis are estimated to be 85% to 90% of the worldwide Muslim population today, this chapter focuses on Sunni jihadists. A note at the end discusses the differences between Sunni and Shia Islam.

THE DUTY OF JIHAD

At present, a vigorous debate has gripped both Muslims and non-Muslims concerning the true meaning of jihad and its application to the contemporary world. Some argue that the popular rendering of jihad as "holy war" is misleading and that jihad is less militant than the West fears (Day, 1991; Raza, 1995). For extremist Muslims, however, jihad entails an ongoing obligation to battle nonbelievers. There is both a theological and philosophical basis for this view. This chapter explores both and then examines jihadist political grievances.

The theological case for the radicals' understanding of jihad is exemplified by an essay written by former Saudi Arabian chief justice Sheikh Abdullah bin Muhammad bin Humaid (1996) titled "The Call to Jihad (Holy Fighting in Allah's Cause) in the Qur'an." In it, bin Humaid concisely outlines his view of the three historical phases of jihad in Islamic jurisprudence: "[A]t first 'the fighting' was forbidden, then it was permitted, and after that it was made obligatory— (1) against them who start 'the fighting' against you (Muslims) . . . (2) and against all those who worship others along with Allah" (p. 948).

Bin Humaid's (1996) assertion that warfare was originally forbidden refers to the early part of Muhammad's prophethood, when the Muslims lacked political and military strength. As detailed previously, when Muhammad's followers encountered persecution at the hands of the Quraish tribe during this period, they did not respond militarily. Rather, they fled from Mecca to Medina in the *hijra*.

Bin Humaid (1996) states that the Muslims received further revelations after they relocated to Medina and gained in political and military strength. It is upon these new verses that bin Humaid bases his argument that fighting was later made permissible. Surah 22, ayah 39 of the Qur'an states: "Permission to fight (against disbelievers) is given to those (believers) who are fought against, because they have been wronged, and surely, Allah is Able to give them (believers) victory." The next verse, 22:40, states that fighting is permitted for "those who have been expelled from their homes unjustly only because they said: 'Our Lord is Allah.'" After the revelation of these verses, fighting was permitted for Muslims who were either fought against by unbelievers or who had been expelled from their homes because of their adherence to Islam.

Finally, bin Humaid argues that armed combat was eventually made obligatory for all Muslims, and that the previous strictures delimiting the conditions for battle were broadened. He points to two Qur'anic verses revealed late in Muhammad's life. The first, verse 2:190, enjoins Muslims to "fight in the Way of Allah those who fight you." Verse 9:29 states:

> Fight against those who (1) believe not in Allah, (2) nor in the Last Day, (3) nor forbid that which has been forbidden by Allah and His Messenger . . . (4) and those who acknowledge not the religion of truth (i.e., Islam) among the people of the Scripture (Jews and Christians), until they pay the *Jizyah* with willing submission, and feel themselves subdued.

The language employed by these two later verses is markedly different from that used in Surah 22. The two verses from Surah 22 use permissive language indicating the circumstances in which believers *may* fight against unbelievers—but it is not made obligatory. In contrast, the two later verses are written in the imperative tense. Bin Humaid (1996) argues that this difference in language demonstrates that today believers do not simply have the *option* to fight against unbelievers when the requisite circumstances have been satisfied. Rather, Muslims have the affirmative duty to engage in jihad when unbelievers fight against them (2:190), and when unbelievers refuse to believe in Allah and the Last Day and will not accept Islamic law and pay the *jizya* (9:29). The *jizya* is a special tax that non-Muslims considered to be People of the Book (i.e., Christians or Jews) could pay to continue practicing their religion under Muslim rule. In contrast, those who could not be considered People of the Book (such as polytheists and idolators) enjoyed fewer options: "slavery, conversion to Islam, or death" (Arzt, 2002, p. 27).

The doctrine of abrogation is a principle of Islamic jurisprudence referring to the idea that, where Qur'anic verses conflict, later revelations nullify those that came earlier. Relying on this doctrine, bin Humaid contends that, because the last verses revealed hold that fighting against non-Muslims is obligatory, all Muslims have that obligation today.

Other Islamic scholars have mounted similar theological cases for the obligation of jihad. For example, 20th-century Egyptian thinker Sayyid Qutb concludes from verse 9:29 "that waging jihad against the People of the Book (Jews and Christians) is a permanent, communal obligation upon the Muslims" (Jackson, 2002).

In addition to the theological case, there is a philosophical argument for jihad against unbelievers. Qutb exemplifies the philosophical case. In his famed work,

Milestones, Qutb's (1964) argument for jihad centers around the idea of freedom. He proclaims Islam to be "a universal declaration of the freedom of man from servitude to other men and from servitude to his own desires" (p. 51). To Qutb, Islamic law is the only way to

> bring human beings into submission to God, *to free them* from servitude to other human beings so that they may devote themselves to the One True God, to deliver them from the clutches of human lordship and man-made laws, value systems and traditions so that they will acknowledge the sovereignty and authority of the One True God and follow His law in all spheres of life. (pp. 39–40)

True freedom, according to Qutb, is submission to Allah's will and, by extension, all of Allah's laws. A democratic system like that of the United States—including the right to vote, free speech, and freedom of religion—is servitude because, rather than ruling by Allah's laws, man is in bondage to other men. *Sharia* law is the only way to true freedom.

Qutb develops his justification for jihad from this core principle. He writes that

> [n]o political system or material power should put hindrances in the way of preaching Islam. It should leave every individual free to accept or reject it, and if someone wants to accept it, it should not prevent him or fight against him. If someone does this, then it is the duty of Islam to fight him until either he is killed or until he declares his submission. (Qutb, 1964, pp. 50–51)

But Qutb's justification for jihad does not end with societies that refuse to let individuals preach or accept Islam. He contends that the duty to make war extends even to non-Muslim nations that neither prevent Muslims from preaching Islam nor impede their own citizens' acceptance of the religion. Qutb says there cannot be peace with such countries "unless they submit to [Islam's] authority by paying Jizyah, which will be a guarantee that they have opened their doors for the preaching of Islam and will not put any obstacle in its way through the power of the state" (p. 66). Qutb thus argues that jihad will not cease if Islam is simply left alone. Because Islam is the only path to true freedom, it must be spread through force even if non-Muslim governments do not aggress against the faith.

Although Qutb (1964) thought that jihad should continue even if Islam were left alone, he did not believe this was occurring. He thought Islam was under attack: that the faith was locked in a mortal struggle against disbelief, and only one could survive. Qutb's writings had such an influence on Osama bin Laden (who attended lectures at King Abdul Aziz University in Jeddah by the ideologue's brother, Mohammad Qutb) and other contemporary jihadists that the *9/11 Commission Report* discusses his ideas at some length.

Most jihadist intellectuals derive their argument for the need to battle the West from this general theological and philosophical foundation. In addition to this broad conceptual case, jihadists also harbor particular political grievances.

JIHADIST GRIEVANCES

The previously described theological and philosophical case for warfare against unbelievers is important to understand because jihadists consistently reference it. Likewise, hostage negotiators should understand the set of political grievances articulated by jihadists. Indeed, for some terrorists, political grievances are more important than theology.[4] For example, Lawrence Wright (2006) describes Ramzi Yousef, one of the 1993 World Trade Center bombing plotters, as "not a particularly devout Muslim," and writes that Yousef "was motivated mainly by his devotion to the Palestinian cause and his hatred of Jews" (p. 178).

Osama bin Laden outlined his grievances in his 1996 declaration of war against the United States. The three major grievances he articulated are emblematic of those that were widely shared by jihadists at the time: the U.S. military presence in Saudi Arabia, U.S. support for Israel, and the U.S.-led sanctions against Iraq.

Saddam Hussein's invasion of Kuwait in 1990 prompted the United States to send troops to Saudi Arabia, at King Fahd's request. Bin Laden deplored the presence of American troops on Saudi soil because of a *hadith* where Muhammad, on his deathbed, ordered, "No two religions should coexist in the Arabian Peninsula." To bin Laden, the presence of U.S. troops was an affront that directly contravened this prophetic order. Indeed, in a letter he addressed to Wahhabi clerics in the mid-1990s, bin Laden described the U.S. presence as an "invasion" and wrote:

> This momentous event is unprecedented both in pagan and Islamic history. For the first time, the Crusaders have managed to achieve their historic ambitions and dreams against our Islamic *umma*, gaining control over the Islamic holy places and Holy Sanctuaries, and hegemony over the wealth and riches of our *umma*, turning the Arabian peninsula into the biggest air, land and sea base in the region. (Lawrence, 2005, p. 16)

U.S. support for Israel is a sensitive issue for many Muslims. When Israeli military actions make headlines—for example, the summer 2006 war against Hizballah—reverberations are felt throughout the Islamic world (Kabbani, 2006; MacFarquhar, 2006). To most Islamic extremists, the problem is deeper than perceived Israeli injustices: Israel's very existence is a travesty. Jerusalem is one of Islam's holiest cities. Muslims originally prayed in the direction of Jerusalem, and the Dome of the Rock, built on the same spot as the Jewish Temple, was "Islam's first grand structure" (Pipes, 2001). For many Muslims, the fact that Jerusalem is now in non-Muslim hands is appalling—but even worse is the fact that it rests in Israel, the home of the Jewish people. Moreover, classical Islamic jurists divided the world into two separate spheres that were in conflict: the *dar al-Harb* (abode of war) and the *dar al-Islam* (abode of Islam). The *dar al-Islam* "describes those places in the world where the Shari'ah, the corpus of Islamic law, prevails and is enforced" (Freamon, 2003, p. 300). Classical jurists believed that once land became part of the *dar al-Islam*, it could not return to being part of the *dar al-Harb*. For this reason, bin Laden's mentor, Abdullah Azzam, wanted to reconquer not only Israel, but also "Bokhara, Lebanon, Chad, Eritrea, Somalia, the Philippines, Burma, Southern Yemen, Tashkent, and Andalusia [southern Spain]" (Bergen, 2001, p. 53).

Most jihadists will be satisfied by nothing less than Israel's destruction. In a tape released in December 2006, al-Qaeda deputy leader Ayman al-Zawahiri said that, "as Muslims, we cannot possibly concede to Israel so much as a hand-span of Palestine, and there is no difference as far as we are concerned between Palestine 1948 and Palestine 1967: all of it is Palestine and all of it belongs to the Muslims" (al-Zawahiri, 2006).

The third grievance that bin Laden outlined in his declaration of war was the U.S.-led sanctions that the United Nations imposed on Iraq. Bin Laden (1996) claimed that "[m]ore than 600,000 Iraqi children have died due to lack of food and medicine and as a result of the unjustifiable aggression (sanction) imposed on Iraq and its nation. . . . You, the USA, together with the Saudi regime are responsible for the shedding of the blood of these innocent children." Although these sanctions were lifted when Saddam Hussein's regime was toppled, the war in Iraq has now replaced them as a grievance. In 2004, bin Laden warned that "[t]he occupation of Baghdad is only one practical stage in what the United States has already thought through and planned. The entire region was targeted in the past, it is being targeted now, and will remain targeted in the future" (Lawrence, 2005, p. 215). Moreover, bin Laden has identified numerous other grievances rooted in U.S. foreign policy. In his October 2002 "letter to the American people," bin Laden stated: "You attacked us in Somalia; you supported the Russian atrocities against us in Chechnya, the Indian oppression against us in Kashmir" (Lawrence, 2005, p. 163).

A fourth grievance of no less significance than the previous three can also be seen in bin Laden's public statements: the fall of the caliphate. This is in fact so significant to jihadists that it is the first complaint listed in al-Qaeda's training manual: "After the fall of our orthodox caliphates on March 3, 1924 and after expelling the colonialists, our Islamic nation was afflicted with apostate rulers who took over in the Moslem nation. These rulers turned out to be more infidel and criminal than the colonialists themselves" (*The Al Qaeda Manual*, n.d.). In the jihadist view, European imperial powers dismantled the caliphate because of their hatred for Islam. Some jihadist thinkers even argue that Islam cannot truly be practiced without a caliphate unifying the Muslim world and implementing *sharia* (Qutb, 1964). Virtually all jihadist intellectuals agree that the Islamic world can only return to its former glory through the reestablishment of a " 'pious caliphate' that would be governed by Islamic law and follow Islamic principles of finance and social conduct" (Blanchard, 2004, p. 3).

A fifth grievance is rooted in culture. When Sayyid Qutb lived in America, he was struck by what he regarded as its perversity. During his boat ride from Egypt to the United States, a young woman whom Qutb described as thin, tall, and "half-naked" asked to share his room for a night. When Qutb said that his room had only one bed, the woman replied: "A single bed can hold two people" (Wright, 2006, p. 10). He was further appalled by the overt sexuality that he glimpsed in New York City. Qutb saw licentiousness even in the church dances he encountered in Greeley, Colorado. "The dancing hall was decorated with yellow, red and blue lights," Qutb recalled. "The room convulsed with the feverish music from the gramophone. Dancing naked legs filled the hall, arms draped around the waists, chests met chests, lips met lips, and the atmosphere was full of love" (Wright, 2006, p. 22).

Today, American culture is more dominant throughout the globe than it was in Qutb's time. Television and cinema are edgier and more sexually charged. The United States is perceived to be forcing such values as secularism, feminism, and gay rights on the rest of the world. Many people from traditional cultures—and from the Islamic world in particular—feel that the moral fabric of their society is under attack.

This description of jihadist grievances is, of course, not exhaustive. Bin Laden's October 2002 "letter to the American people," which ranges far and wide in its complaints, provides some idea of the scope of his attacks on the West. His justifications for fighting America include its support for Middle Eastern regimes that prevent the implementation of *sharia* law; its theft of "our wealth and oil at paltry prices" (Lawrence, 2005, p. 163); American laws that allow "the immoral acts of fornication, homosexuality, intoxicants, gambling, and usury" (Lawrence, 2005, p. 166); the fact that American law is based on the U.S. constitution, rather than "the *sharia* of God" (Lawrence, 2005, p. 167); and even America's refusal to sign the Kyoto protocol on climate change. But the five grievances outlined earlier are frequently cited by jihadist intellectuals and also the foot soldiers in their war.

In the jihadist worldview, these grievances form a compelling portrait of a world that has conspired to topple Islam from its past glory, leaving it subjugated and powerless. Where the Islamic world was once united by a caliphate that ruled according to Allah's dictates, it has now been carved into nominally Muslim states according to a map devised by European colonialists. The Muslim world is now dominated by authoritarian kleptocracies. It is not just radicals who are disturbed by this state of affairs; but to the radicals, it constitutes a *casus belli*.

THE INFLUENCE OF JIHADIST IDEOLOGUES

This section examines four significant jihadist ideologues: Muhammad ibn Abdul Wahhab, Hassan al-Banna, Sayyid Qutb, and Sayyid Abul A'la Maududi. Their teachings and writings provide a richer understanding of the jihadist worldview. All four thinkers helped shape the outlook of such leaders as Osama bin Laden and Ayman al-Zawahiri. Even when contemporary jihadist leaders do not cite directly to these thinkers, they have often been influenced by their ideas (Habeck, 2006).

Muhammad ibn Abdul Wahhab

Muhammad ibn Abdul Wahhab, the intellectual progenitor of the modern-day Wahhabi sect, was born in 1703 in the Uyaina region of what is now Saudi Arabia. Abdul Wahhab preached against the anti-Islamic practices of "ignorance, *shirk* [association of partners with Allah], and innovation" (Algar, 2002, p. 13). He believed that such practices could cast other Muslims out of the faith, after which "warfare against them became not simply permissible but obligatory: their blood could legitimately be shed, their property was forfeit, and their women and children could be enslaved" (Algar, 2002, p. 34).

Although Abdul Wahhab's scholarly output was meager, he was effective at forming alliances with Arabian political leaders. His first patron was the ruler of Uyaina, Uthman ibn Muammar, who allowed Abdul Wahhab to put his strict religious ideas into practice politically. After Abdul Wahhab personally stoned an adultress, ibn Muammar succumbed to popular pressure and expelled the theologian. Thereafter, Abdul Wahhab forged a new, fateful alliance with the ruler of Diriyah, Muhammad ibn Saud (founder of the first Saudi state). Abdul Wahhab's theological ideas provided ibn Saud with a rationale not only for his rule, but also for the conquest of non-Wahhabi Muslims.

As a thinker, Abdul Wahhab was greatly influenced by Ahmad ibn Abdal-Halim ibn Taymiyya, a Sunni jurist who lived from the mid-13th century to the early 14th century. At this time, the Mongols had conquered a broad stretch of Muslim lands, but claimed that they had converted to Islam. Ibn Taymiyya was asked whether it was permissible to declare a jihad against them. A strong Sunni tradition militated against doing so, as the Sunni position is encapsulated in the saying: "Better sixty years of tyranny than a single day of civil strife" (Nasr, 2007, p. 36). But ibn Taymiyya argued that Islam required state power, and that the Muslims had a duty to fight to ensure that the state was governed according to Islamic principles. Because the Mongols ruled according to Genghis Khan's *yasa* legal code, rather than the *sharia*, ibn Taymiyya declared them to be infidels who should be fought.

Abdul Wahhab believed that the era in which he lived was analogous to ibn Taymiyya's. The Ottomans governed the Muslim world, and Abdul Wahhab believed that their governance contributed to "the spiritual decline and moral laxity of his society" (Esposito, 2002, p. 47). He saw their rule as illegitimate and believed it necessary to undertake jihad against them.

Abdul Wahhab's argument for jihad centers on the notion of *tawhid*, Islamic monotheism. This concept is central to Islam, denoting that Allah is the supreme power with no partners or associates. To Abdul Wahhab, there were three aspects of *tawhid*: the uniqueness of Allah's lordship (that all lawmaking is reserved for Allah alone), the uniqueness of Allah's names and attributes, and the uniqueness of Allah's worship (Philips, 1990). He held that the uniqueness of Allah's worship was violated "whenever an act of devotion involves, in any fashion at all, an entity other than the worshipper and God" (Algar, 2002, p. 32). So Abdul Wahhab regarded it as an abominable act of *shirk* if Muslims invoked saints in their prayers or supplicated at the site of a grave. Under this view, Shias are seen as heretics because of their high regard for the Prophet's family and their belief in the supplication of saints.

The Wahhabi disdain for Shia practice is reflected in their massacres of thousands of Shias in southern Iraq in the early 19th century (Gold, 2003). This disdain is also seen today, reflected in the targeting of Shias by Abu Musab al-Zarqawi and other Sunni extremists.

Hassan al-Banna

Three 20th-century ideologues have had a major impact on jihadist thought. The first is Hassan al-Banna, who founded the Muslim Brotherhood, an underground movement designed to counter the growing Western influence in Egypt and, more ambitiously, to create a caliphate that would rule the Muslim world (Lia, 1998; Mitchell, 1969).

Al-Banna was born in 1906 in Mahmudiyya, Egypt. In 1923, he moved to Cairo, where he saw Western values and cultural mores taking root. While in college, al-Banna was influenced by Muhammad Rashid Rida, a Syrian who demanded that Muslims stop imitating Western ways and instead rediscover their Islamic values. Rida taught al-Banna that the Muslim world's decline could only be reversed by returning to the practice of Islam as it existed during Muhammad's time. To accomplish this, al-Banna believed that grassroots movements needed to suppress Western values, replacing them with Islamic education. Al-Banna summarized his goal as "stand[ing] against the flood of modernist civilization overflowing from the swamp of materialistic and sinful desires" (Yakan, n.d., p. 21).

Al-Banna believed that Western culture and values were in fact so harmful that retarding their spread was only a half-measure. He wrote that Muslims should "pursue this evil force to its own lands, invade its Western heartland, and struggle to overcome it until all the world shouts by the name of the Prophet and the teachings of Islam spread throughout the world" (Yakan, n.d., p. 21).

In other words, al-Banna believed that not only Muslim lands, but also Muslim hearts and minds, had been colonized. In his estimation, the critical tool for returning his coreligionists to the religious practice of Muhammad's day was *dawah*, Islamic missionary work. He believed that once enough Muslims returned to this form of Islam, they could spread the faith through jihad. To al-Banna, jihad was obligatory for all Muslims. He wrote that his followers should "always intend to go for jihad and desire martyrdom. Prepare for it as much as you can" (al-Banna, n.d.).

In his quest to revive Islam, al-Banna formed the Muslim Brotherhood in 1928. The Brotherhood created charitable institutions to help it gain support at the grassroots level. But the Brotherhood was not all charity. Its militant side is reflected in the group's motto: "Allah is our objective. The Prophet is our leader. The Qur'an is our Law. Jihad is our way. Dying in the way of Allah is our highest hope."

In December 1948, Egyptian Prime Minister Nuqrashi Pasha was assassinated by a member of the Muslim Brotherhood. In retaliation, Egyptian police killed Hassan al-Banna, and the government officially dissolved the Brotherhood. However, by the time of al-Banna's assassination, the Brotherhood had 2,000 branches throughout Egypt (Gold, 2003). Al-Banna's death did not destroy the group, and today Brotherhood members regard him as a martyr.

Sayyid Abul A'la Maududi

A second significant 20th-century jihadist ideologue is Sayyid Abul A'la Maududi, who was born in what is now Maharashtra, India, in 1903. Like al-Banna, Maududi wanted to revive Islam in the face of pervasive Western influence. He thought "it would be possible to revive Islam gradually and peacefully through an ideological party, . . . but he asserted as well that jihad was absolutely essential for the religion and that sooner or later open warfare would come between the believers and the infidels" (Habeck, 2006, p. 37).

Maududi (1959) wrote that jihad was "as much a primary duty of the Muslims concerned as are the daily prayers or fasting. One who avoids it is a sinner. His very claim to being a Muslim is doubtful" (p. 106). He disregarded those scholars who tried to distinguish between offensive and defensive modes of fighting, writing that jihad is "both offensive and defensive at one and the same time" (Maududi, 1939, pp. 18–19). Undertaking combat, Maududi explained, is offensive because a Muslim "attacks the rule of an opposing ideology," but is defensive at the same time because by mounting such an attack, a Muslim can "protect the principles of Islam in space-time forces" (Maududi, 1939, p. 19).

Maududi wrote that the goal of such an attack was to entirely "abolish the government" that sustains non-Islamic principles (Maududi, 1939). He wanted to do away with all governments not ruled by *sharia*. "Islam requires the earth," Maududi wrote, "not just a portion, but the entire planet" (Maududi, 1939, p. 7).

Maududi was also one of the first thinkers to revive the idea of *jahiliyya*, the condition of ignorance that Muslims believe characterized pre-Islamic Arabia. He believed that Muslim societies had regressed back to this state, largely because Western notions of modernity and liberalism had undermined the Muslim population's devotion to Islamic values. Maududi's revival of the idea of *jahiliyya* had a tremendous impact on Sayyid Qutb's writings.

Sayyid Qutb

The third of the significant 20th-century jihadist ideologues is Sayyid Qutb, who was born in Egypt in 1906. Although he grew up in "a mud-walled village in Upper Egypt," his mother, Fatima, sent him to Cairo to pursue his studies (Wright, 2006). In 1948, as Qutb began to gain recognition as an important Islamic thinker, he traveled to the United States on a scholarship to pursue graduate education. Instead of liberalizing him, Qutb's experiences in the United States produced a loathing toward the country. He was incensed by what he saw as the immorality of American culture, including racism and overt sexuality.

On his return to Egypt, Qutb became a leader of the Muslim Brotherhood. When Gamal Abdul Nasser plotted his military revolution, he frequently coordinated with the Brotherhood, and Qutb hoped he would be given a cabinet position in Nasser's government. The two factions soon realized that their visions for society were irreconcilable: Nasser favored pan-Arab socialism, while the Muslim Brotherhood wanted to impose "Islamic values on all aspects of life" (Wright, 2006, p. 27). Eventually, Nasser imprisoned Qutb, which more deeply radicalized him.

Although Qutb's first stint in prison lasted only 3 months, he would face more time in incarceration—and harsher conditions—after a Muslim Brotherhood member attempted to assassinate Nasser. Thereafter, Nasser conducted a massive roundup of the group's members, including Qutb. Wright (2006) notes that "[s]tories about Sayyid Qutb's suffering in prison have formed a kind of Passion play for Islamic fundamentalists" (p. 28). The imprisoned Muslim Brothers were subjected to torture. At one point, a number of them were fired on after staging a strike in which they refused to leave their cells, and 23 members were killed (Wright, 2006).

While imprisoned, Qutb wrote his famous commentary, *In the Shade of the Qur'an*. Mary Habeck (2006) elucidates four central themes in Qutb's writings. First is the importance of *tawhid*, where Qutb echoes the thoughts of earlier ideologues such as Abdul Wahhab: he argues that, because dominion belongs only to Allah, all non-Islamic governance, including liberal democracy, is fatally flawed. Muslims have to reject democracy as not only a false political idea, but also a false religion. Second, true freedom can only be found in Islamic law. Non-Islamic systems of government, including liberal democracy, are in fact servitude to other men. Third, the world is beset by *jahiliyya*, the ignorance characteristic of pre-Islamic Arabia. There is no middle ground between Islam and *jahiliyya*, and Muslims who did not agree with Qutb's view of the struggle were complicit in *jayiliyya*'s spread. Indeed, if a Muslim disagreed with Qutb's understanding of this global struggle, Qutb believed that he could be declared an unbeliever and thus fought. The concept of declaring another Muslim an apostate or unbeliever is known as *takfir*.

The fourth significant theme is jihad. Qutb (1964) argued that jihad could be undertaken:

> to establish God's authority in the earth; to arrange human affairs according to the true guidance provided by God; to abolish all the Satanic forces and Satanic systems of life; to end the lordship of one man over others since all men are creatures of God and no one has the authority to make them his servants or to make arbitrary laws for them. These reasons are sufficient for proclaiming Jihad. (p. 63)

JIHADIST CULTURAL MORES

We now turn from the ideological underpinnings of the jihadist worldview to jihadist cultural mores. Negotiators should understand hostage takers' likely cultural mores in order to understand areas of particular sensitivity, and thus control the introduction of emotion into negotiations. They should also understand the impact that jihadists' differing notions of time and history may have on their mindset. Finally, one critical question that negotiators must face is the hostage takers' intentions: whether they want to barter or simply kill their captives.

Areas of Sensitivity

At the outset, it is worth noting that Muslims involved in hostage situations designed to advance radical Islamic causes will not always be particularly religious. This chapter has already addressed Ramzi Yousef, who was motivated more by his strong feelings about the Israeli–Palestinian conflict than by religious sentiment. Wright (2006) describes Yousef's uncle, terrorist mastermind Khaled Sheikh Mohammed, as "pious but poorly trained in religion; an actor and a cutup; a drinker and a womanizer." This caveat aside, negotiators should be aware of the cultural mores that often dominate among radical Muslims—because those involved in the war against the West are often quite religious.

Indeed, religion is a sensitive topic for jihadists. Any extensive conversation that invokes theology may produce aggressive or confrontational reactions. For this reason, any hostage-taking situation should be carefully assessed before a Muslim negotiator is introduced. Muslim negotiators have proved to be assets in some situations, such as the 1977 negotiations with Hanafi Muslims. (The Hanafi case, however, wasn't a jihadist hostage-taking situation: The hostage takers wanted to avenge the killing of Khalifa Hamaas Abdul Khaalis's children.) The danger is that introducing a Muslim negotiator could trigger a religious debate. Jihadist hostage takers may even regard the negotiator as an apostate.

To determine whether a Muslim negotiator is appropriate, it is necessary to make preliminary contact with hostage takers to assess their temperament, demands, and grievances. Introducing a Muslim negotiator may pose a greater risk when the hostage takers appear unstable and prone to overreaction.

Two other kinds of negotiators may also spur emotional reactions in jihadist hostage takers. First, because many jihadists oppose allowing women to serve in professional roles and believe in strict separation of the sexes (Al-Musnad, 1996; Khan, 1995), female negotiators may be an emotional trigger. Second, because of the virulent anti-Semitism that pervades in Islamic extremist circles, the same may be true of Jewish negotiators.

Many jihadist hostage takers will agree with the movement's major ideologues that Islamic law is the only proper source of judgment. If negotiators enter into discussions with hostage takers about morals or ethics, they should be aware that jihadist morals and ethics are often derived from their view of Islamic law. Thus, for example, a jihadist's notion of freedom will likely be markedly different than Western ideas of freedom.

Many jihadists' strict religious worldview will also cause them to regard certain activities as offensive. For example, one Wahhabi scholar described drinking alcohol, smoking, gambling, watching television or movies, and listening to music as sinful acts (Zino, 1996). It thus may be ineffective or inappropriate to ask a jihadist hostage taker if he wants a cigarette or to try to engage him in small talk about popular entertainment.

The fact that some jihadists have lived impure lives should not lead us to conclude that they lack religious devotion. Although the frequency with which jihadists have been found engaged in hedonistic activities has puzzled some analysts, there are three explanations for the apparent incongruity. First, some jihadists engage in un-Islamic behavior for strategic reasons, to avoid suspicion. A European terror expert told *Time Magazine* in 2002 that bin Laden aide Abu Zubaydah instructed recruits in training camps "to shave their beards, adopt Western clothing and 'do whatever it takes to avoid detection and see their missions through' " (Calabresi & Ratnesar, 2002). A second explanation is that humans are fallible and often fall short of their ideals. Even the most devoted believers find themselves unable to adhere constantly to every religious stricture, and it is not uncommon for people to preach obedience to religious doctrine while breaking the rules they advocate. This does not necessarily make them hypocrites, but merely humans. Third, there is a theological justification: "[A]s entry to paradise is guaranteed to martyrs, there is little cost to sinning one last time" (Sageman, 2004, p. 94).

Ultimately, hostage takers claiming radical Islamic ideology should be evaluated as individuals—but it is worth knowing the strict lifestyle to which they may adhere.

Differing Concepts of Time and History

Another consideration for negotiators is that Westerners often have a different concept of time and history than those from the Islamic world. Sunni Muslims tend to focus on the past, looking to the practices of Muhammad and the earliest generations of Muslims as guides to their own religious life. Most Sunni extremists believe that Islam has fallen from its past glory, and that it is necessary to "purify" the faith by stripping out all deviation that has been introduced over the centuries.

Moreover, for many from the Muslim world, the past has not passed, but continues in the present day. This tendency can be seen in the major jihadist ideologues. For Maududi and Qutb, *jahiliyya* is not simply an analogy to a bygone era, but a contemporary existential threat to Islam.

Seeing history as a series of repeating patterns, many prominent jihadists model themselves after Muslim historical figures. For example, U.S. intelligence likely could have undermined Abu Musab al-Zarqawi's al-Qaeda in Iraq terror network more effectively had it understood his role model, Nur al-Din Zanki (Miniter & Gartenstein-Ross, 2006). Zanki was a 12th-century Arab fighting king whose twin missions were to drive the Crusaders from Arab lands and overthrow the Shia Fatimid caliphate. In a book about Zarqawi, Jordanian journalist Fouad Hussein noted that Zanki was Zarqawi's ideological guiding star and wrote that "one cannot understand Zarqawi and cannot attempt to predict the future of his organization and the next steps that it will take without being familiar with Nur al-Din Zanki" (Hussein, 2005). Hussein claimed that Zarqawi made strategic decisions based on his devotion to Zanki. He argued that understanding Zarqawi's fascination with Zanki:

> enables us to answer the proverbial question of why Zarqawi, of al-Qaeda leaders, specifically chose to settle in Iraq after the American military occupied Afghanistan. Perhaps he wants to begin liberating Iraq from Mosul and to spread the *tawhid* in Syria, Northern Iraq and Egypt as a preliminary step before liberating Jerusalem. Perhaps it is possible for us to adopt the theory that says that those who closely study history sometimes take on their heroes' roles and follow their footsteps in order to reshape the course of history. (Hussein, 2005)

The legendary Saladin, who battled Richard the Lionhearted and recaptured Jerusalem for the Muslims, served as Zanki's general in his military campaigns against the Fatimid empire—but ultimately robbed Zanki of his opportunity to be remembered as the man who reconquered Jerusalem. When Zanki tried to organize campaigns to take Jerusalem, Saladin offered excuses about why it could not be accomplished then. Only after Zanki died did Saladin mount an attack on Jerusalem; he now enjoys a sainted place in Islamic history.

This represents a missed opportunity for U.S. intelligence, which was largely unaware of Zanki's importance to Zarqawi. Not only could Zanki's prominence in Zarqawi's imagination have provided clues about where he intended to strike next, but it also could have produced a promising psy-ops campaign. Because Zarqawi was doubtless aware of why his role model failed to retake Jerusalem, the United States could have embarked on a "Project Saladin" to make Zarqawi suspect that his closest lieutenants' ambitions would produce similar betrayal.

For negotiators, the ability to call on experts or advisors who are conversant in Islamic history could be a great asset. This knowledge of history can shed light on hostage takers' likely goals and motivations and can help to identify such subtle weaknesses as Zarqawi's probable fear of betrayal.

HOSTAGE TAKERS' INTENT FOR THE HOSTAGES

A negotiator's overriding objective is securing the release of hostages. Unfortunately, many jihadist abductors have killed their captives without entering negotiations—shown, for example, by the grisly beheadings of *Wall Street Journal* reporter Daniel Pearl (Pearl & Crichton, 2004) and American contractor Nicholas Berg (Dao, 2004). Negotiators will have to confront the question of whether the hostages will be used to barter or whether they were only taken as a sign of power and control. Is the hostages' killing a foregone conclusion?

Absent an attempted rescue, hostage negotiations have three potential outcomes: The hostages may be freed with no demands met, the hostages may be freed with some or all demands met, or the hostages may be killed.

In several cases involving Islamic captors, hostages have been freed without either a settlement or military incursion. In August 2006, an obscure Palestinian group calling itself the Holy Jihad Brigades captured Fox News journalists Steve Centanni and Olaf Wiig and demanded that the United States "release all 'Muslim prisoners' in American jails within 72 hours in exchange for the abducted journalists" (Westervelt, 2006). After 2 weeks of captivity, during which they "converted" to Islam at gunpoint, Centanni and Wiig were released. When terror groups release captives without having any demands met, the captors are frequently a startup group similar to the Holy Jihad Brigades, whose hostage taking was intended to either win a hefty ransom or gain prestige. The groups that release hostages without having their demands met tend to be inexperienced and do not know what to do when their demands are not satisfied. Negotiators should thus try to determine whether the captors are connected to an experienced terror group. Newer groups that lack experience operate from weaker negotiating positions.

Sometimes jihadist hostage takers release their captives after some or all of their demands are satisfied. In March 2007, Taliban hostage takers in southern Afghanistan agreed to release journalist Daniele Mastrogiacomo from *La Repubblica* after Italy convinced the Afghan government to release five Taliban prisoners (Fisher, 2007). Another example came on New Year's Eve in 1999. Indian Airlines Flight 814 was hijacked out of Kathmandu just before Christmas. The hijackers forced a landing in Kandahar and eventually agreed to release the passengers and crew (with the exception of one passenger whom they murdered) in exchange for the Indian government's release of three jailed militants (Spaeth, 2000).

Sometimes jihadists execute their captives, often in a sensationalistic fashion. The Daniel Pearl and Nicholas Berg beheadings are examples of this. Often when jihadists kill their hostages, they are part of an established group with a record of brutality.

SHIA ISLAM

Although this chapter has focused on Sunni radicalism, it is worth noting the distinctions between Sunni and Shia Islam in case the hostage takers are Shia. As political science professor Ahmed Nizar Hamzeh (2004) notes, Shia Islam's legacy is one of "martyrdom, persecution, torment, suffering, powerlessness, and insecurity, resting on a religiously sanctioned belief that Islamic history was derailed when political power passed from the hands of the family of the Prophet Muhammad in the seventh century" (p. 7). Shias believe that only Prophet Muhammad's blood relatives are fit to lead the unified Muslim community:

> Shias believe that the Prophet possessed special spiritual qualities, was immaculate from sin (*ma'soum*), and could penetrate to the hidden meaning of religious teachings. Shias further believe that Ali and his descendants had these special spiritual qualities too. They bore the light of Muhammad (*nur-e Muhammadi*). They were his "trustees" (*was*) and were privy to his esoteric and religious knowledge. They could understand and interpret the inner meaning of Islam, as opposed to merely implementing its outward manifestations. (Nasr, 2007, p. 39)

Shias thus hold that Ali, Muhammad's cousin, was the only legitimate ruler among the four caliphs believed to be "rightly guided" by Sunnis. After Ali became caliph in 656, he was opposed both by Muawiya ibn Abi Sufyan, the leader of the Umayyad dynasty, and by the Kharijites, a puritanical movement that denounced both Ali and Muawiya as unfit leaders. In 661, the Kharijites assassinated Ali, and Muawiya became the caliph. Nasr notes that this series of events gave rise to Shiism:

> Ali's murder, the transformation of the caliphate into a monarchy, and the de facto separation of religious and political authorities under the Umayyads led a minority of Muslims to argue that what had come to pass was the fruit not of God's mandate but of man's folly. They saw the roots of the problem going back to the choice of the first successor to the Prophet. Muslims had erred in choosing their leaders, and that error had mired their faith in violence and confusion. The dissenting voices rejected the legitimacy of the first three Rightly Guided Caliphs, arguing that God would not entrust his religion to ordinary mortals chosen by the vote of the community and that Muhammad's family—popularly known as the *ahl al-Bayt* (people of the household)—were the true leaders of the Muslim community. (Nasr, 2007, pp. 36–37)

Muawiya had Ali's son Hassan poisoned, while Muawiya's son, Yazid, had Ali's second son, Hussein, killed in 680. The feelings of persecution triggered by the killings of Ali, Hassan, and Hussein are still deeply felt by Shias today. These feelings are reflected in the Shia observance of the Day of Ashura, a somber occasion meant to commemorate Hussein's martyrdom.

Because Shias refused to recognize the legitimacy of the Umayyad and Abbasid caliphs, both dynasties "imprisoned and killed Shia imams and encouraged Sunni ulama to define Sunni orthodoxy and contain the appeal of Shiism" (Nasr, 2007, p. 53).

Shia cultural mores are similar to Sunni mores, but not identical. Shia Islam historically has not been as legalistic as the Sunnis' practice. In fact, Nasr (2007) describes the "excessive legal-mindedness" of the ayatollahs in Iran as "in some ways a 'Sunnification' of Shiism" (p. 58). Regardless, today many Shia scholars offer legalistic outlooks. For example, the website of Grand Ayatollah Ali al-Sistani, Iraq's leading Shia cleric (who on balance has been a force for stability in that country), declares non-Muslims to be ritually unclean and has a strident approach to homosexuality. Just as there may be particular emotional triggers in negotiations with Sunni extremists, such triggers may also exist in negotiations with Shia hostage takers.

HIZBALLAH

Hizballah is the most prominent Shia terrorist group. Until 9/11, Hizballah was responsible for more American deaths than any other terrorist organization. The group was created in the early 1980s in response to a number of factors, including "the Lebanese civil war, the marginalization of the Lebanese Shiite community, the Islamic revolution in Iran, and the 1982 Israeli invasion of Lebanon" (Jorisch, 2004, p. 6).

Hizballah's ideology and goals were expressed in a manifesto released in 1985 titled "The Open Letter Addressed by Hizballah to the Oppressed in Lebanon and the World." The manifesto outlines three primary objectives. The group's first goal was "to expel the Americans, the French, and their allies definitely from Lebanon, putting an end to any colonialist entity on our land" (Alagha, 2006, p. 227). Second, the group wanted to bring the Phalangist Christians of Lebanon "to justice for the crimes they have perpetrated against Muslims and Christians" (Alagha, 2006, p. 227). Its third goal was to allow the people of the Middle East "to determine their future," while pointedly calling on them "to pick the option of an Islamic state, which alone, is capable of guaranteeing justice and liberty for all" (Alagha, 2006, p. 227).

Hizballah's most dramatic attack was its 1983 bombing of the U.S. Marine barracks in Beirut, which killed 241 American servicemen and caused the United States to disengage from Lebanon. The group has also waged a long military campaign against Israel. Since the 1990s, it has gained more of an international reach. American and Israeli officials believe that Hizballah orchestrated 1992 and 1994 attacks against the Israeli embassy and Jewish cultural center in Buenos Aires, Argentina, and the group seemingly downed a passenger plane in Panama in 1994. Investigators believe it also carried out July 1994 attacks against Jewish targets in London and had plans to attack Israeli and American targets in Thailand and Singapore in the 1990s (Emerson, 2006). The *9/11 Commission Report* notes that the al-Qaeda operatives who carried out the 1998 East African embassy bombings developed their tactical expertise for the mission in Hizballah training camps in Lebanon (National Commission on Terrorist Attacks Upon the United States, 2004). Hizballah has also raised substantial funds through its involvement in criminal enterprises in the United States, Canada, and South America.

Hizballah has long received state sponsorship from Iran. Iranian representatives were present at the group's founding, and Iran continues to provide it with a great amount of financial support. This gives Iran the ability to exert a degree of control over Hizballah's actions, and thus introduces an extra element to negotiations with hostage takers linked to Hizballah. Negotiators will need to determine whether the operatives are trying to serve Iran's interests. If so, this information can help them navigate the negotiation process.

IMPLICATIONS FOR NEGOTIATION STRATEGIES

Understanding hostage takers' ideology and cultural context can assist negotiators in deploying a range of strategies because negotiators will be better able to explain and predict the hostage takers' behavior. Jihadist hostage takers can be particularly challenging because their religious and cultural contexts may be unfamiliar to negotiators. However, the background on jihadism that this chapter provides offers a number of strategic considerations that, if heeded, will increase the success of negotiators faced with a jihadist hostage-taking situation.

First, a sound understanding of Islamic radicalism will help negotiators to control the introduction of emotion into the negotiations. This chapter explores several areas that may present particular emotional triggers for the jihadist hostage taker. Because jihadist hostage takers will likely be strongly to moderately religious, and they view one of their primary goals as defending their faith, negotiators should be hesitant to engage in religious debate or discussion that may be seen as offensive or blasphemous. Some perceived insults may be subtle rather than obvious, such as asking a Muslim hostage taker if he wants a cigarette or food that is not *halal*. Similarly, Muslim hostage takers tend to have a common set of political grievances directed at the West. Contentious political discussions could rouse hostile feelings in the hostage taker and result in a loss of communication. This chapter also discusses certain kinds of negotiators who may present elevated risks, such as Muslim negotiators, Jewish negotiators, and female negotiators.

Second, a sound understanding of Islamic extremist beliefs may provide clues to the hostage takers' state of mind. For example, if a hostage taker who is determined to be formalistically pious asks for a cigarette, it may be a sign that he is rattled. Inversely, if a hostage taker does not present himself as pious, but suddenly begins reciting Qur'anic verses, that may signal that he is losing control.

Third, the principles introduced in this chapter can help negotiators assess hostage takers' intentions. This chapter examined the Holy Jihad Brigades, the previously unknown Palestinian group that claimed credit for the kidnapping of Steve Centanni and Olaf Wiig in August 2006. Unable to adapt when its demands were not met, the Holy Jihad Brigades ended up releasing the men after they converted to Islam at gunpoint. Their case can be contrasted with some of the more brutal established groups who beheaded their captives. Evaluating a group's connections and overall experience level can help in the critical task of assessing intentions.

Fourth, as negotiators build a deeper understanding of jihadist beliefs, ideologies, and history, unique opportunities may present themselves. This chapter discussed how the belief in history repeating itself can be seen in how Abu Musab al-Zarqawi modeled himself after Nur al-Din Zanki. If U.S. intelligence had understood this connection, a "Project Saladin" psy-ops campaign may have been able to exploit Zarqawi's probable fears of betrayal. Although it would require advanced knowledge, negotiators may be able to locate similarly unique strategies if they are attentive.

Being mindful of the intricacies of jihadist ideology and cultural mores will help negotiators attain greater success in situations involving Muslim extremists. The prior recommendations should provide a start.

CONCLUSION

As the "war on terror" progresses,[5] we will see more cases of Islamic radicals taking hostages. One important aspect of effectively handling such incidents is being able to understand Islamic extremists' culture and beliefs. This chapter provides a basic outline of Islamic radicals' understanding of the duty of jihad, as well as grievances that such men have against the United States and the West.

Ultimately, each jihadist hostage taker is an individual. Some will be more devout than others. Some may be driven by religion and others by perceived injustices. But as negotiators develop greater knowledge about the general worldview to which Islamic extremists subscribe, they will be more effective in dealing with these situations and less likely to be taken by surprise.

NOTES

1. There has been much terminological debate about what labels to use when referring to Islamic terrorists. In this chapter, we refer to them as *radicals* and *extremists* because their theological views do not represent the whole of Islamic thought and result in actions

that are properly regarded as extreme. We also use the term *jihadist*, which has the advantage of being organic: It is how participants in this violent movement refer to themselves. "'Jihadists' may be the most appropriate term for the adherents of the ideology. These are individuals for whom jihad has become the sole reason for existence," writes Brian Michael Jenkins (2006, p. 74), senior advisor to the president of the RAND Corporation.

Use of the term does not imply endorsement of their understanding of the Islamic theological concept of jihad.

2. The biographical material on Muhammad in this chapter reflects commonly held Islamic beliefs because the goal is to help the reader understand Muhammad in the same way that Muslims understand their prophet. Recently, "[s]ome Western scholars . . . have done ground-breaking work in researching which ahadith reflect what Muhammad really said and did, and which are pious legend—research which often deviates sharply from the received wisdom of Muslim scholars of the Hadith" (Spencer, 2006, p. 31). This chapter takes no position on the historical claims of this more recent scholarship vis-à-vis the traditional narrative.

3. Although Christians and Jews believe that Abraham was asked to sacrifice Isaac, Muslims believe that he was asked to sacrifice Ishmael.

4. Researchers do not know the relative percentage of terrorists for whom religious or political justifications for jihad are predominant. Marc Sageman (2008) downplays the role of religious ideology in contributing to terrorists' motivations, writing that "[t]he defendants in terrorism trials around the world would not have been swayed by an exegesis of the Quran. They would simply have been bored and would not have listened" (p. 157). Other researchers, such as Mitchell D. Silber and Arvin Bhatt (2007), place more emphasis on religious ideology. This scholarly debate underscores the need for negotiators to be familiar with both the theological and also political justifications in order to better understand jihadist hostage takers' motivations.

5. The formulation "war on terror" has always been both inadequate and inaccurate, and there are signs that Barack Obama's administration may abandon this phraseology (Isikoff & Hosenball, 2009).

REFERENCES

The Al Qaeda Manual. (n.d.). http://www.usdoj.gov/ag/manualpart1_1.pdf.

Alagha, J. (2006). *The shifts in Hizbullah's ideology: Religious ideology, political ideology, and political program.* Leiden, The Netherlands: Amsterdam University Press.

al-Banna, H. (n.d.). *The message of the teachings.* London: Ta-Ha Publishers Ltd.

Algar, H. (2002). *Wahhabism: A critical essay.* Oneonta, NY: Islamic Publications International.

Al-Mubarakpuri, S. (1979). *The sealed nectar.* Riyadh: Darussalam.

Al-Musnad, M. (1996). *Islamic fatawa regarding women.* Saudi Arabia: Darussalam Publishers & Distributors.

al-Zawahiri, A. (2006, December 20). *Realities of the conflict—between Islam and unbelief.* Retrieved at http://www.ict.org.il/apage/8215.php.

Arzt, D. (2002). The role of compulsion in Islamic conversion: Jihad, dhimma and ridda. *Buffalo Human Rights Law Review, 8,* 15.

Bergen, P. (2001). *Holy war, inc.: Inside the secret world of Osama bin Laden.* New York: The Free Press.

Blanchard, C. (2004). *Al Qaeda: Statements and evolving ideology.* Washington, DC: Congressional Research Service Report for Congress.

Calabresi, M., & Ratnesar, R. (2002, March 11). Can we stop the next attack? *Time Magazine.* p. 24.

Dao, J. (2004, May 26). Tracing a civilian's path to gruesome fate in Iraq. *New York Times.* p. A1.

Day, A. (1991). Morality, war: Do they mix? *Los Angeles Times,* p. A1.

Ellingwood, K. (2006). Fox journalists freed after 2 weeks in Gaza. *Los Angeles Times,* p. A4.

Emerson, S. (2006). *Jihad incorporated: A guide to militant Islam in the U.S.* Amherst, NY: Prometheus Books.

Esposito, J. (2002). *Unholy war: Terror in the name of Islam.* Oxford, UK: Oxford University Press.

Fields, L. (1988). The evolution of U.S. counter-terrorist policy. In C. Bassiouni (Ed.), *Legal responses to international terrorism: U.S. procedural aspects* (pp. 279–288). Dordrecht, The Netherlands: Martinus Nijhoff.

Fisher, I. (2007, March 22). Italy swapped 5 jailed Taliban for a hostage. *International Herald Tribune,* p. 1.

Freamon, B. (2003). Martyrdom, suicide, and the Islamic law of war: A short legal history. *Fordham International Law Journal,* p. 299.

Gold, D. (2003). *Hatred's kingdom: How Saudi Arabia supports the new global terrorism.* Washington, DC: Regnery.

Habeck, M. (2006). *Knowing the enemy: Jihadist ideology and the war on terror.* New Haven, CT: Yale University Press.

Hamidullah, M. (1969). *Introduction to Islam.*

Hamzeh, A. (2004). *In the path of Hizbullah.* New York: Syracuse University Press.

Hourani, A. (1991). *A history of the Arab peoples.* New York: MJF Books.

bin Humaid, A. (1996). The call to jihad (holy fighting in Allah's cause) in the Qur'an. In M. Al-Hilali & M. Khan (Eds. and Trans.), *Interpretation of the meanings of the noble Qur'an* (15th ed., pp. 945–966). Riyadh: Darussalam.

Hussein, F. (2005). *Al-Qaeda's second generation.*

Isikoff, M., & Hosenball, M. (2009, February 4). War on words: Why Obama may be abandoning Bush's favorite phrase. *Newsweek.*

Jackson, S. (2002). Jihad in the modern world: to 'Abd al-Karim Salabuddin. *Journal of Islamic Law & Culture,* p. 1.

Jenkins, B. (2006). *Unconquerable nation: Knowing our enemy, strengthening ourselves.* Santa Monica, CA: RAND Corporation.

Jorisch, A. (2004). *Beacon of hatred: Inside Hizballah's Al-Manar television.* Washington, DC: Washington Institute for Near East Policy.

Kabbani, R. (2006). Caligula's war. *Islamica Magazine,* pp. 37–39.

Khan, M. (1995). *Woman between Islam and western society.* New Delhi: The Islamic Centre.

Khan, M. (2003, June 9). The legacy of the prophet Muhammad and the issues of pedophilia and polygamy. *Ijtihad.*

bin Laden, O. (1996). *Declaration of war against the Americans occupying the land of the two holy places.* Available at http://www.pbs.org/newshour/terrorism/international/fatwa_ 1996.html.

Lawrence, B. (2005). *Messages to the world: The statements of Osama bin Laden.* New York: Verso.

Lia, B. (1998). *The society of the Muslim brothers in Egypt: The rise of an Islamic mass movement 1928–1942*. Reading, UK: Ithaca Press.

Lings, M. (1983). *Muhammad: His life based on the earliest sources*. Rochester, NY: Inner Traditions.

MacFarquhar, N. (2006, July 28). Tide of Arab opinion turns to support for Hezbollah. *New York Times*, p. A1.

Maududi, S. (1939). *Jihad fi sabilillah* [Jihad in Islam]. Birmingham, UK: Islamic Mission Dawah Centre.

Maududi, S. (1959). *Towards understanding Islam*.

Miniter, R., & Gartenstein-Ross, D. (2006, June 9). Zarqawi and his role model: The lessons of two parallel jihadist lives. *Weekly Standard Online*.

Mitchell, R. (1969). *The society of the Muslim brothers*. New York: Oxford University Press.

Nasr, V. (2007). *The Shia revival: How conflicts within Islam will shape the future*. New York: W.W. Norton.

National Commission on Terrorist Attacks Upon the United States. (2004). *The 9/11 commission report*. New York: W.W. Norton.

Pearl, M., & Crichton, S. (2004). *A mighty heart: The inside story of the al Qaeda kidnapping of Danny Pearl*. New York: Scribner.

Philips, A. (1990). *The fundamentals of tawheed* [Islamic monotheism]. London: Dar Al-Tawheed.

Pipes, D. (2001). The Muslim claim to Jerusalem. *Middle East Quarterly*.

Qutb, S. (1964). *Milestones*.

Raza, R. (1995, May 11). Pilgrimage a time to pray for the blessing of peace. *Toronto Star*, p. A29.

Sageman, M. (2004). *Understanding terror networks*. Philadelphia, PA: University of Pennsylvania Press.

Sageman, M. (2008). *Leaderless jihad: Terror networks in the twenty-first century*. Philadelphia: University of Pennsylvania Press.

Semple, K., & Filkins, D. (2006, March 30). Reporter freed in Iraq, 3 months after abduction. *New York Times*, p. A1.

Silber, M., & Bhatt, A. (2007). *Radicalization in the West: The homegrown threat*. New York: The New York City Police Department.

Spaeth, A. (2000, January 1). A risky precedent. *Time Magazine*, p. 14.

Spencer, R. (2006). *The truth about Muhammad: Founder of the world's most intolerant religion*. Washington, DC: Regnery Publishing.

Struck, D., & Dwyer, T. (2005, November 29). Virginia man among Iraq hostages. *Washington Post*, p. A14.

Weaver, G. (1997). Psychological and cultural dimensions of hostage negotiation. In R. Rogan, M. Hammer, & C. Van Zandt (Eds.), *Dynamic processes of crisis negotiation: Theory, research and practice* (pp. 115–128). Westport, CT: Praeger.

Westervelt, E. (2006). Video of kidnapped journalists lists demands. *All Things Considered* (National Public Radio).

Wright, L. (2006). *The looming tower: Al-Qaeda and the road to 9/11*. New York: Alfred A. Knopf.

Yakan, F. (n.d.). *To be a Muslim*.

Zino, M. (1996). *Islamic guidelines for individual and social reform*. Riyadh: Darussalam.

Negotiation Issues
with Terrorists

Wayman C. Mullins
Michael J. McMains

One statement we have often heard from negotiators is that terrorists cannot be negotiated with. Novice and experienced negotiators have made this statement. To them, any terrorist or extremist that takes hostages or becomes a barricaded subject has only one resolution—tactical. We strongly disagree with this attitude and believe that negotiators can have as much success with the terrorist and extremist as with any other hostage taker or barricaded subject. For negotiators, they must have the same positive mental outlook regarding success as they would with any other hostage taker. What is needed for the negotiator is an understanding of the terrorist/extremist milieu as it relates to the negotiated incident. This involves an understanding of who they are, why they may engage in this type of incident, and what the tactics/strategies are for negotiating with them. To make it easier for the reader, the term *terrorist* will be used to refer to both terrorists and extremists. Not all extremists are terrorists, but all terrorists are extremists. For the purposes of this chapter, we sum all together as *terrorists*. Also, unless the distinction needs to be made specifically, hostage takers and barricaded subjects will be referred to as HTs. Only where differences are important will they be separated. Again, that is a convention to assist the reader.

What type of terrorist incidents may negotiators be called on to resolve? In the United States, police experience is limited in dealing with terrorists. Of the few negotiated incidents in our history, the majority were handled by federal authorities. The FBI negotiated with Robert Mathews of an extremist group called *The Order* (December 8, 1984). Likewise, FBI negotiators (including one of the editors of this book) successfully negotiated with Randall Claude Weaver at Ruby Ridge (August 1992). Randy had ties with the Aryan Nations, another right-wing extremist group. At the Branch Davidian siege in Waco, Texas (February–April 1993), FBI and ATF negotiators were supplemented by local police negotiators. The FBI successfully negotiated with a militia organization in Montana called the Freemen (March–June 1996). In April 1997, the FBI and Texas Department of Public Safety Rangers successfully negotiated with another militia leader, Richard Lance McLaren of the Republic of Texas. McLaren and four other members of his group kidnapped a husband and wife and held them hostage in a 5-day standoff with authorities. In addition to these national incidents, there have been a few other isolated and non-national media situations to which local law enforcement has responded.

One significant note about these incidents, however, is that the incidents were negotiated because of the HTs criminal behavior, not because of terrorist ideology or activity. That is, none of these incidents was onset or negotiated because of a terrorist motivation or ideology. All of them revolved around criminal activity. Robert Mathews was wanted on an arrest warrant for armed robbery and murder, Randall Weaver for a federal warrant and murder of an ATF agent, David Koresch for a federal warrant, the Freemen for passing bogus checks and threatening to kill a federal judge, and Richard McLaren for kidnapping his neighbors. This is quite a different experience than that on the international stage, where there are hundreds of examples of terrorists engaging in hostage taking to advance their political agenda or recent experiences in the Middle East in negotiating with suicide bombers.

As with any criminal incidents, negotiations centered around the criminal behavior of the actor(s), and the incidents were ultimately resolved (with the exception of the Branch Davidian siege) by resolving the criminal aspects of the event. Granted, during the negotiation process, negotiators did have to deal with the terrorist ideology, psychology, and motivations of the actors. But these were handled as they would be with any negotiation. During a domestic incident, for example, negotiators will ultimately resolve the incident by resolving the criminal aspects of the incident, but during the process will have to deal with the actor's "storyline" and resolve those emotions as a corollary to the ultimate resolution.

Will the United States and local law enforcement remain largely immune from the same type of incidents and actors that have plagued the rest of the world? It is doubtful. It is probably only a matter of time until crisis negotiators here have to negotiate with the dedicated terrorist involved in an incident to further political goals, such as was the case in 1980, when Puerto Rican separatists took over the Republican and Democratic party headquarters, or the suicide bomber whose plan becomes interrupted, or the terrorist who takes a school hostage to force concessions from the government, as did Chechen terrorists in Beslan, Russia in September 2004 when they took over 1,200 hostages and held them for 3 days until Russian troops and police attempted to take the school by force, resulting in more than 300 dead. As the tentacles of international terrorism continue to spread and domestic terrorists become more determined, it is crucial that negotiators understand the terrorist threat and prepare themselves to respond to that threat.

Responding to a terrorist incident as a negotiator does not mean or imply that the negotiator needs a specialized body of knowledge, different set of skills, or different communication ability. What the negotiator does need is an understanding of terrorists—who the players are, why people become terrorists, what their psychological makeup and motivations are, and various negotiation strategies that are likely to be effective with terrorists. In a major international "scale" incident, the negotiators will also be swamped by a multitude of federal agencies, intelligence, suggestions, offers of help (and, in some cases, may lose control of the incident to federal agencies), and so on. Regardless of the magnitude, however, responding negotiators should do what they always do at a negotiated incident— set perimeters, evacuate the surround, start intelligence gathering, control the media, and so on. Accepted practices do not change because it is a terrorist incident.

DEFINITIONS

There is a lot of misconception as to what terrorism is and is not, so it is first necessary to define the phenomenon we discuss here. One of the remarkable issues in the study of terrorism is the number of varied ways that terrorism has been defined. There are literally hundreds of definitions of terrorism (Mullins & Thurman, in press). Schmid (1983), for example, identified more than 100 different definitions of terrorism that encompassed 22 separate areas of activity. Although seemingly a schematic issue, the problem becomes acute when trying to understand the person and deal with the act.

One of the more universally accepted definitions is the one used by the Federal Bureau of Investigation (2005), which states that terrorism is: "the unlawful use of force and violence against persons or property to intimidate or coerce a government, the civilian population, or any segment thereof, in furtherance of political or social objectives." Although agreeing in principle with that definition, terrorism does not have a social objective. Its sole purpose and goal is to effect political change. Even the Islamic terrorist who only wants to "kill" infidels, or the insurgents/militias in Iraq and Afghanistan, are attempting to ultimately cause political change. Neither does the terrorist have to actually use violence, the mere threat of violence from a known terrorist is generally sufficient to produce intimidation or coercion. Thus, a better definition of terrorism is: "the threat of violence, individual acts of violence, or a campaign of violence designed primarily to instill fear 'to produce political change' [added in 2007]. Terrorism is violence for effect; not for the victims (who may be totally unrelated to the terrorist's cause), but for the people watching. Fear is the intended effect, not the byproduct of terrorism" (Mullins, 1997).

The definition given by Mullins (1997) stresses four central themes important for the negotiator. One, violence may only be threatened; it does not have to occur. At one time, it was necessary for a terrorist to prove that they were capable of violence in order to threaten violence. Since 9/11 and in today's climate, it is no longer necessary for a terrorist to prove that he or she is capable of violence. Virtually any person or group who threatens violence is taken seriously and can produce panic and fear. In some cases, a mere suspicion is sufficient. For example, in January 2007, an advertising company caused panic in Boston, Massachusetts, by putting up a series of lighted boards advertising a cartoon. Two, violence is not the goal of terrorism; it is a tool of terrorism. The goal of terrorism is political change. Terrorists couch their philosophy in many disguises: religion, social movements, racial issues, and so on. These all serve to mask the true intent of the terrorist, producing political change. Three, any violence used by the terrorist is for the audience watching, not the victim of the violence (and this is a crucial point for negotiators). Thus, if terrorists take hostages and are threatening to kill them, the risk assessment is high because the hostages are being used as a platform for other viewers. Four, violence is used to produce fear in that watching audience because it is fear that produces political change. When citizens become dissatisfied and disillusioned with a government's ability to protect them, they force change.

Terrorism is about terror. It is the individual or small groups of individuals who use violence to control and change the behavior of a large group of people. The violence is used to produce fear, which is what ultimately leads to political change. That terror element is what makes the terrorist hostage taker extremely risky. Terrorist hostage takers are much more dangerous than other hostage takers (including the psychopath who enjoys killing) because, to them, the stakes are much higher. Their very act of taking hostages gives them a stage for the production of fear. Imagine the suicide bomber trapped in a busy restaurant with a room full of hostages. What is to stop the terrorist from detonating their explosives? They want that violence to produce fear in the audience watching. Compare that scenario with the criminal caught in the act of robbing the restaurant. What is his or her goal? Goals typically include freedom, not going to jail, and damage control. Each type of person has different outcome goals in this scenario.

Terrorists comprise a small percentage of the population. If the belief structures of any group of people are examined, they will fit into the normal, or bell, curve. For example, if one were to poll the public concerning beliefs on abortion, the beliefs of that population would fit within the normal curve. The pro- and anti-abortionists who use violence are at the very end, or extreme, of that curve. That is true for any belief structure, whether special interest, religious, racial, or political. In fact, many terrorists began in the center portion of the normal curve and, through time and circumstances, moved to the extreme end. One often-used definition of a terrorist, in fact, says that the terrorist is a person who desperation has overcome his or her fear of authority. The desperation is what moves the person to violence with no regard for the consequences or outcomes of that violence.

TERRORIST GROUPS THAT PRESENT A NEGOTIATION THREAT

There are a variety of terrorist threats facing law enforcement in the United States. Although every group presents the same threat, the means to the end may be different. The various terrorist groups operating in the United States can be classified into four general categories: international groups, left-wing groups, right-wing groups, and special interest terrorist groups. Although their goals may all be the same, their tactics, strategies, motivations, and personalities (including demographic characteristics) may be different.

INTERNATIONAL TERRORISM

In 1988, the New Jersey State Police stopped a van on a "routine traffic stop." The person driving that van was Yu Kikumura, a member of the Japanese Red Army. He had been purchasing components to construct homemade explosive devices (inside fire extinguishers) and was driving to New York City to a recruiting station to detonate those bombs. His bombings were to coincide with the 1988 bombing of a USO club in Italy that resulted in the deaths of four U.S. military members. In recent history, this was one of the first instances of a foreign terrorist being arrested while conducting an operation on U.S. soil. Since then, we have experienced many more attacks involving international terrorists. The two that all will be familiar with are the 1992 bombing of the World Trade Center by al-Qaeda members Abdul Rahman Yasin (still at large), Mohammad Amin Salameh, Mahmud Abouhalima, and cleric Omar Abdel-Rahman (aka The Blind Sheik), and the 9/11 attacks on the World Trade Center and Pentagon.

Hundreds of other international terrorist attacks have been thwarted and prevented by law enforcement. For example, the 1992 World Trade Center bombers also planned to attack the Holland Tunnel and several other targets in New York City. Since 9/11, numerous other al-Qaeda attacks have been prevented, including attacks against the Empire State Building, Seattle Space Needle, Mount Rushmore, and the *USS Arizona Memorial* at Pearl Harbor. But al-Qaeda is not the only international terrorist group operating in the United States. There are many others who have operatives and members inside our borders. The ultimate goal of all is the same, but the tactics and strategy are different. There are so many international terrorist groups that it is impossible to list all and give a brief synopsis of each. The best source of information for international terrorist groups is the U.S. State Department web page (see Table 11.1), which tracks all known groups, provides information about the group (including membership, size, headquarters, recent areas of operation, etc.) and the threat posed to U.S. citizens.

What is important for negotiators regarding international terrorist organizations is that, as the international threat has become more recognizable and we are doing more and more to prevent their attacks, it becomes ever more probable that

**Table 11.1 Sampling from the U.S. State Department List
of International Terrorist Organizations**

Level One Groups	Level Two Groups	Level Three Groups
Abu Nidal Organization	Armed Islamic Group (GIA)	Basque Fatherland and Liberty (ETA)
Abu Sayyaf	Gama'a al-Islamiyya (IG)	Kahane Chai (aka Kahane Lives)
Aum Shinriko	Japanese Red Army	Kurdistan Worker's Army
Hamas (Islamic Resistance Movement)	Palestinian Liberation Front (PLF)	Liberation Tigers of Tamil Eelam (LTTE)
Harakat ul-Mujadeen	Shining Path (Sendero Luminoso, SL)	Mujahedin-e Khalq Organization
Hizballah	Tupac Amaru Revolutionary Movement (MRTA)	Revolutionary Organization 17 Nov
al-Jihad		Revolutionary People's Struggle
National Liberation Army		
Palestine Islamic Jihad-Shaqaqi Faction		
Revolutionary Armed Forces of Colombia (FARC)		

law enforcement will have to deal with these people and groups. The intelligence gathered to prevent an attack also means there is a greater risk for the group to be caught in the planning, preparation, and onset of operations in an attack. Our proactive approach to the prevention of terrorist attacks from the international terrorist community also means a greater probability that crisis response teams will be responding to them. It is incumbent that negotiators understand and know their philosophies and goals and know where to go to obtain information about these groups.

The other threats posed by terrorists are from domestic groups. Historically, domestic terrorist groups have been the greatest threat to the United States. Our isolation and insulated borders have helped keep the international terrorist community at bay, but at the same time has led to a vast array of domestic terrorist groups free to operate.

LEFT-WING DOMESTIC TERRORISM

Less of a threat now than 10 to 15 years ago, the left-wing movement in this country is slowing rebuilding as opposition to our foreign policy increases. Groups such as the Weather Underground, SDS, M19Co, the United Freedom Front, and the Black Liberation Army are familiar names to the older readers. The most common tactics employed by these groups included bombings of government, military, and international businesses; robbery to obtain money; and murder (especially of law enforcement officers). Today, the leftist movement in the United States is a mere shell of what it was. There are few active persons or groups. It is expected that their presence will grow some as the war in the Middle East continues. Whether it will reach the level of activity of 30 to 40 years ago is questionable.

RIGHT-WING DOMESTIC TERRORISM

Of much greater concern is the presence of the far-right movement in the United States. For the past 25-plus years, this movement has been the largest terrorist movement in the country. Far-right extremists are characterized by racial/religious hatred and supremacy, and their hatred of the government, including law enforcement. There are literally hundreds of far-right groups in the United States, and they are continually changing (see Table 11.2 for some examples of past and current groups), but these groups can be loosely classified into five types. One type includes the Race Haters. These are groups that hate everyone who is different because they are different. Their attacks tend to be individualized against members of different races and are predicated on the fact that the victim is "different." The dragging death of James Byrd in Jasper, Texas, by three professed Klansmen is an example of this type of attack. Ambushes, drive-by shootings, lynchings, arson attacks against homes and businesses, and property vandalism have been common types of tactics by these groups. The most recognizable and notorious of these groups are the various Klan groups in the United States. One thing not a lot of people know, including law enforcement, but is a critical point for negotiators, is that there is not one Klan in the United States. There are hundreds! Several are national, such as the American Knights of the KKK, the Knights of the KKK, the United Klans of America, and the Invisible Empire, Knights of the KKK.

The neo-Nazi movement is typified by the philosophy and trappings of Hitler's old Third Reich in Germany of the 1930s and 1940s. They wear variations of the old Nazi uniforms, orate from Hitler's old Aryan supremacy philosophies (and not always accurately), and argue violently against the Nazi Holocaust as ever having occurred (as do many of the far-right groups). One of the common tactics employed by neo-Nazis has been to hold a rally and, while members were speaking, salt the audience with other members (out of uniform) to agitate and get the crowd riled enough to attack the speakers. When the crowd responds, the platform party can then attack the crowd, claiming "self-defense" (this tactic has often been used by KKK groups during rallies). Allied with the neo-Nazi movement is a small but dedicated skinhead element. In Europe, skinheads are a major extremist faction and are a force to be reckoned with. In the United States, a realistic estimate is prob-

Table 11.2 Very Small Sample of Some Far-Right Terrorist Groups That Have Operated or Are Operating in the United States*

Race Haters	Neo-Nazi	Militia	Christian Identity	Compound Dwellers
American Knights, KKK	National Alliance	Militia of Montana	Aryan Nations	Elohim City
United Klans of America	American Nazi Party	People's Court of Common Law	Aryan Brother-hood	Covenant, Sword, Arm of the Lord (defunct)
White Camilla, KKKK	Hammerskin Nation	United States Militia	Aryan National Alliance (new AN)	Christian Patriots Defense League (defunct)
Knights of the White Kamellia	Sacramento Area Skinheads	United States Militia	Women for Aryan Unity	
Knights of the KKK	National Socialist White People's Party/ New Order	13th Texas Infantry Regiment	World Church of the Creator	
White Aryan Resistance	National Socialist Movement	14 Word Press	The Christian Guard	
Southern Cross Militant Knights	SS Bootboys		Church of Jesus Christ Christian/AN	
National Knights of the KKK	White Revolution		The Christian Guard	
Confederate Knights of the KKK			Phineas Priesthood	
New Order Knights of the KKK				

*As of 2005 (the last year for which data are available), the SPLC identified 803 right-wing and hate groups operating in the United States (SPLC, 2005).

ably a couple thousand, if that. Skinheads are young, violent, and disenfranchised, and they have been taken in by senior members of the far right and given a place, a sense of purpose, and a sense of responsibility (e.g., the Aryan Nations used skinheads as security for the compound and as protection at gatherings).

Most of the militia groups in the United States fit the far-right typology. The mid-1990s saw the rapid rise of the militia movement, with hundreds of different militias across the country. The most famous of these became the Militia of Montana, when Timothy McVeigh claimed to have ties to that group. In fact, the leader and members of the Militia of Montana made numerous appearances on television news shows denying McVeigh's membership and relationship. Most militias established armed compounds, taught military tactics and survival skills, practiced military-type maneuvers, conducted training in armed defense, and openly preached anti-government philosophies. Many called for the overthrow of the government and claimed our government was part of a giant plot by the United Nations to establish a "one-world" government. Of course, the militias had many other conspiracy theories, including government extermination camps in the western part of the United States, secret surveillance technology to spy on "patriots," the training of Russian and other foreign troops within the United States, and doctors being given cancer-causing drugs to be used against "patriots." Militias also preached that the Oklahoma City Federal Building bombing was actually the work of the government and intended to get an anti-terrorism bill passed that would take away many of our constitutional guarantees. Following the turn of the new millennium (when the world did not end), many militias disappeared, only to reform and reappear following 9/11. Many militias now believe our government was responsible for 9/11 and was an excuse for the government to (a) remove constitutional liberties, (b) invade the Middle East, (c) take over international oil interests, and (d) ally as part of a United Nations one-world government. Today, several militias are "assisting" on the southern border to help the government "solve" the immigration problem.

By far the largest, most cohesive, and violent of all the far-right factions for the past 25 years or so has been the Christian Identity movement. A strange theology of Old Testament scripture, Nordic beliefs, and other mysticism, Christian Identity churches preach that the Bible is the history of the Aryan race and that the Second Coming of Christ cannot occur until the Zionist Occupational Government (ZOG) is overthrown. Christian Identity churches in the United States preach that the Second Coming is foretold in the Bible for the United States. Identity churches in England, however, say that the Bible indicates England as the site of the Second Coming. To most all, however, Identity churches believe other races and the Jewish religion are some mixture of space aliens and evolution, and that only Aryans are pure humans in God's vision of Earth. Although extremely bizarre, this specific belief has far-reaching ramifications and is one of the scariest beliefs of all. If all other races and religions are less than human, where is the moral prohibition against killing them? The Second Commandment, "Thou shall not murder," does not apply to "nonhumans," and thus it is not a sin to kill them.

Many Compound Dweller groups fit within the far-right ideology. These are groups that buy some land and construct a fortified camp for their members. Many of these groups see Armageddon at hand and need to protect themselves in the "end days." Typically, these groups share some ideology with other far-right factions. That is, there is another philosophy that combines with their Armageddon scenario, such as neo-Nazism, militia beliefs, and Christian Identity theology.

It is important to realize that, within the far-right movement, the types of groups discussed earlier are not discrete and independent. There is a significant amount of overlap in their belief structures. Within the Klan movement, for example, many elements of Christian Identity, neo-Nazi philosophy, militia conspiracy theories, and Armageddon scenarios have found a logical home. Do not assume that by labeling a group as one type or another, the other belief and philosophy elements do not apply.

When confronted with a situation involving members of the far-right movement, two excellent sources of intelligence information are the Southern Poverty Law Center (2005; *www.splcenter.org*) and the Anti-Defamation League (ADL) of B'nai B'rith (www.adl.org). The Southern Poverty Law Center (SPLC) publishes a quarterly magazine titled *Intelligence Report* that is free to law enforcement agencies. It is an excellent source of current information on the activities of the far right. They also sponsor Klanwatch, an intelligence resource that tracks Klan activities, events, persons, and attacks. Chapters of the ADL can be found in most major cities, and they will be glad to share intelligence information with law enforcement.

SPECIAL INTEREST TERRORISM

A third type of domestic terrorist group operating in the United States is special interest groups. Special interest terrorist groups do not necessarily want to overthrow the government or change the political system. They do want to change a set of laws concerning their interest area. The three primary types of special interest terrorism are the anti-abortionist movement, the animal rights movement, and the ecology protection movement. Richardson (2005) has pointed out that groups such as Animal Liberation Front (ALF) and Environmental Liberation Front (ELF) have been identified by the FBI as being the most serious domestic terrorist threats in America today. It is important to reemphasize that only a small number of people in these movements resort to terrorism to try and accomplish their goals. For example, the vast majority of Americans would be for saving the environment. Yet most would never dream of resorting to violence or terrorist tactics to save the environment. A very, very small percentage at the extreme end of the continuum, however, has become desperate enough to resort to terrorism to try and change the laws concerning the environment. Likewise, 99.9% of the millions against abortion would never consider the use of violence against abortion providers. The small, less than 1%, at the end of the continuum are the ones who bomb abortion clinics and kill doctors, nurses, and patients. The same is true for the animal rights and ecology extremists.

As mentioned, the anti-abortionist extremists have bombed abortion clinics and killed clinic staffs and patients. They have also engaged in mass protests and demonstrations. It is unlikely that negotiators would have contact with these persons unless they were committing a crime that went awry. For example, a person could be planting a bomb in a clinic or setting up for an ambush and get caught. Members of the other special interest movements are much more likely to do something that gets negotiators involved. For instance, one tactic of the *eco-terrorist movement* (which is a more accepted term for this extreme form of ecological activism) is tree sitting. At construction sites or logging forests, members of this movement climb trees and refuse to come down. The police are called, and, in some cases, negotiators are used to attempt to talk them down. They have also been known to chain themselves to trees, equipment, fences, houses, and so on. Eco-terrorists have sabotaged construction equipment, interfered with businesses, placed themselves in harm's way to prevent use of resources, and bombed/firebombed man-made items (houses, businesses, vehicles, etc.). In the western United States, some members of this movement have resorted to a tactic referred to as "monkey-wrenching" (the name used in a fictional novel by Edward Abbey), where members cut down power lines and billboards, sabotage equipment, and engage in other "nonviolent" activities.

Members of the animals rights movement who have resorted to violent tactics have attacked people, threatened aggression, destroyed property (i.e., burning animal labs), vandalized facilities (such as mass-releasing pent-up animals), and bombed people and facilities. As one example, people wearing fur or leather goods have been attacked with paint, spray paint, acids, chemicals, and other caustic substances. Most are familiar with the tactics of the anti-whalers who place themselves between the whales and harpoonists. They have also tried to prevent ships from leaving harbors (or docking). It is likely that negotiators will have to deal with these persons (and have in the past).

PSYCHOLOGY AND MOTIVATION

What kind of person becomes a terrorist? Is there a profile of the "typical" terrorist? Laqueur (1999) argued that a typology of terrorists cannot be developed because terrorists change over time and the terrorist profile is ever changing. Arena and Arrigo (2005) pointed out that terrorist group typologies are difficult to develop and that when dealing with the individual terrorist, it is almost impossible to develop a typology at that level. We tend to disagree. We believe that there are enough commonalities among terrorists and that there are certain personality types and characteristics that have been stable over time that some profiles can be developed. There are certain types of persons who enter the world of terrorism who share some common personalities, share some common characteristics, and whose actions have defined motivations. By understanding the personality typology, characteristics, and motivations, the negotiator can add to his or her knowledge/skill set and further increase the probability of a successful negotiation.

PERSONALITY TRAITS

Strentz (1981, 1988, 2006) said that terrorists have some common personality types: the possibly paranoid leader, the antisocial member, and the inadequate follower. Mullins (1997) presented a similar personality typology.

Leaders tend to be not only paranoid, but very rigid, seeing the world around them in absolutes. To the leader, there is no middle ground. Their way is not only the right way, it is the only way. To the leader, you are either with them or against them; there is no middle ground for compromise. To a terrorist leader who sees fault with the U.S. government, there are no positives about the government. If one thing about government is bad, all is bad. Leaders also have a high level of self-esteem. They are right, they are pure, they are true, they are unwavering, and they will give all to the cause. They see themselves as the only hope for the future and are the one true way. As part of this elevated self-esteem, leaders are quick to see injustice and are sensitive to injustices. In most cases, leaders are outsiders in society and have a background of humiliation at the hands of others. They are quick to accuse others of wrongdoing, and they see themselves as near perfect. In fact, taking all these qualities together, it can be said that most leaders have a messianic personality. They are a savior not only for their group, but for society, and in many cases for humankind. Leaders also have an inelastic personality. They are unwilling and unable to compromise and see another's view. They are right, period!

The implications of the leader personality are fairly obvious for the negotiator. It is imperative that the negotiator stay away from argument, debate, philosophy, pointing out errors or flaws in the leader's thinking, and taking an overt lead in negotiations. Instead, the negotiator should concentrate on using active listening skills, stress the leader's importance to the movement, and focus on concrete concessions that can lead to resolution. One common occurrence in the terrorist realm is that when the terrorist leader is taken away from the group (arrested, killed, or dies), the group generally dies. In terrorism, the leader is truly the head of the snake. With the head gone, the body dies. Stressing this in negotiations can focus the leader on staying alive to continue the fight another day.

In terms of personality, terrorists can be classified generally as antisocials and inadequates. For a more complete description of psychological traits of hostage takers, see Kris Mohandie's chapter (Chapter 9, this volume). The same guidelines for assessing and negotiating with these personality types apply to the terrorist and with any other hostage taker. The antisocial personality has an ongoing pattern of disregarding the rights of others (*Diagnostic and Statistical Manual of Mental Disorders, 4th edition* [*DSM—IV*]; American Psychiatric Association, 1994). Antisocials are characterized by early onset (before age 15), deceitfulness, inability to plan for the future, high irritability and aggressiveness, complete disregard for the safety of others, irresponsibility in their personal life, and no remorse for the suffering of others (McMains & Mullins, 2006). A subset of antisocial personalities are psychopaths (Hare & McPherson, 1984) and account for the majority of violence. Compared with other antisocials, psychopaths show even less remorse, are more self-centered, prey on others more, and have lower affect.

When negotiating with the antisocial, the negotiator should avoid confrontation or challenging the antisocial. Do not let him or her become bored because he or she will "create" something to do to keep stimulated. Do not use any tricks and promise only what you can deliver. The antisocial will try to make the best deal for him or herself. In addition, Bradstreet (1992) suggested three approaches to dealing with this personality: (a) a reasonable, problem-solving approach that is noncritical and rational, (b) a buddy approach that stresses the negotiator and hostage taker sharing criticism and blaming others, and (c) the Columbo approach that makes the negotiator seem caring but inept and is used when the hostage taker is angry ("I know it's taking a long time, but I am trying"). The bottom line is that the antisocial wants the best deal for him or herself, and it is the negotiator' job to convince the hostage taker that harming others is not in his or her best interests.

The inadequate personality (renamed the dependent personality in 1994 in the *DSM—IV*) is a person who has learned to be a loser or failure. These people try to find others to take charge of their life and become dependent on those persons. They have a hard time making any decisions on their own, do not take any responsibility for their actions (instead, they wait on others to do it for them), cannot take being alone, will go to extreme measures to get support from others and become a member of the group, and will follow whatever any significant other tells them to do. As Everly (1989) stated, the dependent's primary emphasis in life is to develop a caretaker and then prevent losing that caretaker, whatever that may take. In most respects, they are like a small child who needs a parent. To the terrorist, the group has become his parent, and he will do anything he can to maintain acceptance by the group.

The negotiator should focus on positive behaviors the hostage taker performs and reinforce those behaviors. The negotiator should not criticize nor make judgments concerning moral/value issues, but should wait and make positive comments about anything positive the hostage taker does. The negotiator should use active listening skills and use time as a tool. Over time, the negotiator can get the hostage taker to build a dependency on the negotiator. The negotiator needs to find a way for the hostage taker to surrender without having seemed like a failure again. Saving face, having the perception of winning, and having the perception of success are critical for resolving the incident peacefully. Do not use third-party intermediaries, and keep any friends and family away from the situation. These people may make the hostage taker act out, believing he or she has to do something "important" to prove him or herself (Fuselier, 1986).

Without making a personality assessment, another way to examine terrorist followers is as true believers and "wanna bes" (Mullins, 1997). True believers are persons drawn to the group because, for whatever reason, they believe in the terrorist cause and goals of the group. They have the same fervent zeal as to the leaders, and they see themselves as soldiers in a "good and just" fight. In many respects, the true believer is like a soldier. They engage in operations and actions designed to achieve the goals of the group, and their operations are mostly planned. Most important, they want to live to see their goals achieved. That is a critical point for anyone who must negotiate with them. Because their actions are goal-directed, they are motivated to see the "war" brought to a successful conclusion. These are generally not suicidal people.

"Wanna bes," in contrast, are very much like the inadequate personality (in fact, they are inadequates). They are lost in life and are looking for someone to accept them. The terrorist group makes a point of bringing them in and making them part of something important. As such, the "wanna be" will do anything to keep acceptance of the group, including becoming a suicide bomber or piloting a plane into the World Trade Center. The "wanna be" does not care about the goals of the group, does not care about any overriding political agenda or overthrowing a political system, or about systematically working toward the goal. All they care about is maintaining acceptance by the group. As such, they are often given the most dangerous assignments, made into suicide bombers, or given other tasks that are likely to result in their death. This may also be the most dangerous terrorist for the negotiator to deal with because the "wanna be" sees themselves as martyrs (the group will idolize their behavior). Killing a group of hostages, detonating the bomb, or "going out in a blaze of glory" are all likely scenarios with this type of terrorist. The best strategy for the negotiator is to treat them like an inadequate and downplay the significance of their act. All bystanders and media should be kept removed. No demands, involving media coverage, should be granted.

An example of this occurred in Jasper, Arkansas, in 1982, when two members of the Church of Fou (Father of Us) took hostage a busload of tourists. They parked the bus on an isolated bridge, and their only demand was to speak to the media. Authorities granted the demand in return for release of the hostages. The two hostage takers (husband and wife) spoke to the media and said their demand was for the media to televise their suicide and 3 days later to witness their resurrection. After speaking to the media and making sure the media was filming them, the two stepped off the bus, got on their knees, and committed suicide.

CHARACTERISTICS OF EXTREMISTS

George and Wilcox (1992) identified 22 characteristics shared by extremists. Table 11.3 lists those characteristics, along with a short descriptor of each. As can be seen from an examination of these characteristics, terrorist hostage takers will be unlike others, in that they cannot be persuaded by logic and rational thought. A husband, for example, who takes his family hostage will initially be emotional and hysterical. Over time, the negotiator can get him to calm down and think in a rational manner. The hostage taker will then usually surrender. Generally, most terrorists are not like this. Most terrorists operate less from an emotional spike.

Table 11.3 Terrorist Characteristics As Identified by
George and Wilcox (1992)

Characteristic	Descriptor
Character Assassination	Opponents are attacked on a personal level
Labeling and Name Calling	Shout, yell, curse, use racial/ethnic slurs rather than debate or discuss
Sweeping Generalizations	If part of something is wrong, all must be wrong
Motivated by Feelings, Not Facts	Do not support arguments with facts. Logical fallacy is norm
Live in a System of Double Standards	Opposition is morally corrupt, actions are illegal, and they are unenlightened and do not have "proofs"
Opponents Are Evil	All against them are evil, immoral, dishonest, etc.
Manichaean Worldview	World is either/or, and there is no room for gray area
Control Opponents	Because opposition is corrupt/immoral/and so on, they must be controlled/isolated/censored
Attribution to Opposition of What They Are Guilty of	Personality, motivations, attributes of terrorist are ones they accuse enemy of having
Argue by Intimidation	Opponents are judged by who they are more than by what they believe
Rely on Slogans, Buzzwords, Clichés	Do not feel they need to explain their position, that the slogan is sufficient
Morally Superior	Superiority based on political goals and leads to willingness for self-sacrifice
Engage in Doomsday Thinking	No change will lead to Armageddon
Harm Is Okay If Used to Produce Good	Any actions necessary to defeat opponents is legitimate
Emphasize Emotional Behavior and Deemphasize Reason and Logic	Propaganda is education and symbolism necessary for audience to have required emotional response
Hypersensitive and Overly Vigilant	Paranoia is extreme and everyone is an enemy
Political Agenda Becomes Religious	Religious Beliefs assume religious level and religion used to maintain emotions
Cannot Tolerate Ambiguity and Uncertainty	Laws to control enemy are necessary to bring order and predictability to the world
Engage in Group Think	Independent thought eliminated and not allowed to prevent equivocation of purpose
Hostility Becomes Personalized	Personalized Enemies deserve what they get
Political System Corrupt Because Terrorists Lost	Terrorists unjustly persecuted and citizens brainwashed by system in power
Conspiracy Theories Abound	Evidence is ignored and data fabricated to support these theories

Instead, they operate almost all the time from their emotions, so time is less of a tool for the negotiator. Time may calm some of the situational emotions, but it will not calm the overall emotional state of the terrorist. It will be difficult to ever get the terrorist to think logically and rationally. Notice that virtually all of the terrorist characteristics identified by George and Wilcox work to actively suppress logic and rational thought and increase emotions and reactionism. Even when terrorists use logic, the data used are fabricated or selectively filtered to support their position. Conspiracy theories claiming the U.S. government caused 9/11 use unsupported data, obviously fabricated data, nonscientific data, and data that are not complete enough to undergo scientific scrutiny. They ignore the solid and scientific data accepted by the mainstream.

An examination of Table 11.3 should make it obvious to the negotiator that attempts to argue the hostage taker's belief system is fruitless, will increase emotions, and will make the situation much more volatile. The negotiator must accept from the outset that he or she is the "enemy" and part of the problem, not part of the solution. Rapport-building will be difficult, and name-calling by the hostage taker will be the norm. Emotional outbursts should be expected, and the negotiator will often and regularly be shouted down. Instead, the negotiator should use active listening skills, the techniques of suggestion and persuasion, and should emphasize solving the immediate problem. Political discourses should be avoided, as should discussions of the HT's belief system. The negotiator must avoid arguing philosophy, religion, politics, and social issues. Recognize that these issues have already been resolved and decided on by the hostage taker, and any disagreement by the negotiator will further exacerbate the emotions and potential for violence on the part of the hostage taker.

TERRORIST MOTIVATION

Understanding the motivation behind terrorist acts will also assist the negotiator in resolving an incident. Terrorists engage in operations for specific purposes. In general, these are to: (a) make a government appear repressive; (b) get attention and publicity for their cause and gain world sympathy; (c) create a climate of uncertainty that will polarize a population, create economic discord, and ultimately erode support for the political system and power; (d) support their religious and/or racial fanaticism and supremacy; (e) reduce frustration because they have no legitimate means of redress; (f) liberate colleagues from jail; and (g) obtain money. Many times a terrorist operation may have multiple motivations, and at others may be for the simplest of reasons. It is important that the response team ascertain the true motivation behind the terrorist event and negotiate from that perspective. For example, terrorists armed with bombs inside a bank are likely there simply to rob the bank. It is rather trite, but the movie *Die Hard* is a classic example of this error. The police and response teams were attempting to discover what the terrorist wanted from a geopolitical standpoint (the police assumption was that the terrorist wanted some political concessions and never attempted to determine the true motivation), when he was merely robbing the business for bearer bonds (and many Hollywood movies are built around misidentification of true motives).

The terrorist's motivation does not change negotiation tactics and strategies. Negotiators still need to use the basic knowledge, skills, and abilities they would use in any incident. Negotiations with a terrorist progress through the same stages as with the criminal—the processes and negotiation issues are the same, the situational and team dynamics are the same, intelligence issues are the same, and the importance of time and dealing with demands are the same. The only potential difference is that active listening skills may be more important. They may be more important because the terrorist may take much longer to vent and validate because their act may have a political basis. But again, the negotiator should listen and not engage in debate, discussion, and argument. Negotiators respond because of the criminal act the terrorist has committed, not because of political philosophy. For example, with the Freemen standoff in Montana and the West Texas Republic of Texas standoff mentioned previously, negotiators were used because of the criminal acts committed, not because of the hostage taker's beliefs. These two situations lasted longer than most negotiations because the negotiators had to let the hostage takers vent and validate. Once that was done, the negotiation issues that resolved these incidents were the same ones as with any criminal negotiation.

THE SUICIDE BOMBER

One special type of terrorist needs discussion at this point—the suicide bomber. The United States has yet to experience this type of terrorist. We believe it is merely a matter of time until that occurs. Most readers will be familiar with the Japanese Kamikazi pilots of World War II. They were the most infamous examples of suicide bombers in history. They were a military unit that was specifically trained for one mission. They were given a plane with no seat (they sat on wooden crates), no machine guns, limited fuel (because it was a one-way mission), and a bomb. Their orders were to fly their planes into an American warship (preferably a Carrier). In the later stages of the war, they were responsible for an inordinate number of American casualties. But they were a military unit on a military mission. It has only been in recent years that the suicide bomber has become a terrorist tool. Prior to this, terrorists used bombs, not human bombs. In this century, suicide bombers were first active in the Middle East, mainly in Israel. On March 11, ten bombs ripped through four trains in Madrid, Spain, killing 191 people and wounding more than 1,700 (CNN, 2006). The mastermind of this attack, Serhane ben Abdelmajid Fakhet, blew himself up (along with four other suspects) when the police began a raid of his apartment. Fortunately, no police were injured. On July 7, 2005, fifty-two people were killed and more than 700 injured when a series of bombs struck three London subway trains and an overhead bus (CNN, 2007). All blasts were the result of suicide bombers. One of the suicide bombers, Mohammad Sidique Khan, a member of al-Qaeda, left a suicide note on a video. He said, "I and thousands like me have forsaken everything for what we believe. . . . Your democratically elected governments continually perpetrate atrocities against my people all over the world. Your support makes you directly responsible. . . . We are at war and I am a soldier. Now you too will taste the reality of this situation" (CNN, 2005). In the Middle East and England, hundreds more suicide bombers have been captured in the planning stages or operationally prior to them self-detonating.

Unlike the usual suicidal subject with whom negotiators may deal, a suicide bomber executes a unique form of suicide—one that Durkheim (1951) called an altruistic suicide. These are people who sacrifice themselves for a cause, such as the Kamikazi pilot, the soldier who throws himself on a grenade to save his buddies, the police officer who gets shot while pushing his partner out of harm's way, or the terrorist who enters a crowded bus and self-detonates. The person committing an altruistic suicide is operating for a greater cause, and self-sacrifice gives the terrorists' lives meaning (McMains & Mullins, 2006). They are not trying to end some personal pain (as is the case with other suicides); rather, they are trying to further a cause, provide some benefit to their identified group, and improve the general good (as they perceive it). Their self-concept is directed toward their group, not themselves as an individual.

The reason some cultures seem to produce suicide bombers while others do not is that some cultures emphasize the group—that the well-being of the person is tied into the survival of the group and that independence and self-survival are ways of caring for and bettering the group (Osterman, 2002). In the United States, the individual is emphasized. This is true from the federal legal system down to the earliest social teachings given the child. Our culture probably overemphasized the individual to the expense of the group. Other cultures are just the opposite. They stress the importance of the group, as well as the important of acting to serve, better, promote, and ensure survival of the group. It is from these cultures that the suicide bomber is born. Militarily, as in Japan in the 1940s, some members of the culture volunteered to become Kamikazi pilots (and man kamikaze submarines—a little-known part of the War in the Pacific) to best serve the group. Today, some join terrorist groups and volunteer to be a suicide bomber. Hoffer (1955), in fact, suggested that the group gives meaning to the person's life and that the only way for this person to have worth, meaning, and power in his or her life is to carry out group missions. To some, it may be becoming a soldier, sniper, maker, and placer of improvised explosive devices, vehicle borne improvised explosive devices, or instructor at a terrorist training facility. To others, it may mean self-detonating.

Hammer (2002) and Osterman (2002) contend that, in the Muslim culture, the suicide bomber has to be examined in the context of both the culture and religion. They argue that suicide bombers are acting out of a religious sense of purpose and that their religious training and interpretation of that training leads them to act. In their training, they have looked to a religious figure for guidance and instruction. This leader is the guidepost for their life, and they will not go against him. In order to act, they need a *Fatwa* (religious document that legitimizes their act and is issued by a high-raking religious figure and without which they cannot act). They are engaged in a Jihad, or a holy war sanctioned by the *Fatwa*. Once a course of action is set, they cannot go back on that course because to do so would shame the family. To them, what is important is the relationship, not the contract. That is, obligations made are based on the relationship they have with the other person. If they have a strong relationship, they will do what the other wants without question.

Negotiating with the suicide bomber is not hopeless or impossible. The negotiator should build rapport, raise doubts, and use indirect suggestions and problem-oriented questions to introduce alternatives to the suicide bomber (McMains & Mullins, 2006). Active listening, allowing ventilation and validation, and avoiding argument are all important negotiation strategies. In terms of validation, the negotiator should allow validation of the cause rather than the actions. That lets the negotiator deal with the person and increase rapport building while sending a message that the act is not appropriate. Unlike with other hostage takers, the negotiator should use emotions to support his or her statements. Allowing emotions to be heard shows that the negotiator is interested in the person as an individual and can keep the hostage taker focused on his or her cause. Allowing emotions also indicates to the hostage taker that the negotiator is serious about peacefully resolving the incident. Staying unemotional will make the hostage taker believe that the negotiator is not serious. Suicide bombing is an extremely emotional act, and emotions are driving the suicide bomber (perhaps more than for any other type of hostage taker). By allowing his or her emotions to show through communications, the negotiator is telling the suicide bomber that he or she understands the emotional depth of the hostage taker.

The negotiator should get the hostage taker to question his or her actions by using cultural issues. For example, the negotiator could ask how the family will be affected by the hostage taker's actions. The family is one of the most important groups within this type of culture. By focusing on how this act will bring shame to the family could help the negotiator make progress. The negotiator can focus on how innocents will be killed in this action. If the hostage taker is Muslim, he or she will be violating Muslim law by murdering innocents. Question the *Fatwa* and, if there is one, how this act fits within the Jihad authorized by that *Fatwa*. A Jihad can mean an actual physical war or a spiritual war inside the individual as he or she works to become more holy and religious. The lack of a *Fatwa* means that the hostage taker is acting unjustly and without spiritual authorization and could be punished in Heaven. For a more complete discussion of radical Islam, see the chapter by Gartenstein-Ross and Dabruzzi (Chapter 10, this volume). That chapter also has an excellent discussion of the religious and cultural factors that influence Islamic extremists, as well as a discussion of the *hadith* used by

Osama bin Laden to drive extremism. Recognize also that in most cultures that stress the group, communications are often indirect and metaphorical. That is, they use parables and stories to convey thoughts, ideas, learning, and so on. The negotiator using stories in this manner can build a lot of rapport, offer suggestions, suggest courses of action, and get the hostage taker to accept negotiator demands (McMains & Mullins, 2006).

In cultures that stress the group, promises are not as important as in individualistic cultures (Osterman, 2002). Informal promises and the relationships among individuals are much more important than are formal contracts. The negotiator may get the hostage taker to make some promises that will later be broken. If that occurs, the negotiator should not make the broken promises a significant issue. Doing so will result in the hostage taker moving away from the negotiator emotionally and become distrustful. Likewise, deadlines are not important to the hostage taker and will often be broken or ignored. Negotiations will likely be somewhat disjointed as the hostage taker will change topics often, jumping around into different areas on a whim. The negotiator should recognize that saving face is important. How others perceive the hostage taker is important and will be significant. The negotiator should structure negotiations so the hostage taker can save face and appear to "win."

SUMMARY AND CONCLUSIONS

As has been continually stressed, the terrorist can be successfully negotiated. In general, the negotiator should use the same skills as with any hostage taker. More critical than in most negotiated incidents, it is imperative that the negotiator understand the group associated with the hostage taker, the political philosophies and goals of that group, the past operational history associated with that group, and the areas of operation of that group. Additionally, it is critical that the negotiator understand the personality type of the hostage taker and the level of commitment to the group. Negotiate within the characteristics outlined by George and Wilcox (1992). Some strategies that a negotiator may use with a criminal, high-risk suicide, barricaded subject, domestic abuser, or addict may not be appropriate to use with the terrorist and may work in reverse of how they might work with the nonterrorist. For example, trying to shame the Klansman by asking what he will think when his family, neighbors, and friends see him splashed all across the evening news will likely bring on a diatribe about how the media is a Jewish-owned and Jewish-driven propaganda tool of all minorities, liberals, ZOG government, United Nations, and so on and will welcome the opportunity to be presented in the evening news as a "true patriot." The true believer will require a much different negotiation strategy than does the "wanna be." Although the negotiator will be dealing with the criminal aspects of the negotiated incident, it is important that the negotiator understand the motivations behind the particular act. Why is the hostage taker doing what he or she is doing? Understanding the motivation is crucial to a successful resolution.

In addition to using all the active listening skills, use good basic communication skills. Use advice, clarification, explanation, reassurance, reinforcement, self-disclosure, summation, and transition (V. Bazan, personal communication, January 10, 2006). Advice ("Have you thought about. . . ?") shows that you are interested and skilled and can direct the communications. Clarification ("Tell me more about that") encourages the hostage taker to continue talking and thinking. It demonstrates that the negotiator is interested and concerned. Explanation ("We should talk about this because . . .") indicates respect for the hostage taker and shows that the negotiator wants to be open-minded. Reassurance ("Together we can solve this") indicates skill and competence, builds trust and rapport, and can open cultural doors. Reinforcement ("I really appreciate you doing that. I know it was difficult for you") helps calm the hostage taker, decreases emotions, and keeps the hostage taker problem-focused. Self-disclosure ("My family, as well, had a profound influence on what I became") can help establish rapport and trust, shows you are honorable, and helps build a relationship. Summation (paraphrasing and summarizing) helps reduce mistakes and misunderstandings, encourages the hostage taker to continue talking and thinking, and helps build rapport. Transition ("Now that I know something about your family [since the hostage taker told about them], I would like to learn more about what's happening today") provides direction to the hostage taker, keeps the hostage taker problem-focused, and helps build trust. The negotiator should avoid being accusatory and confrontational in communications, avoid emotional labeling, not use reflecting/mirroring (may cause emotional arousal), and avoid silences and extended pauses (may be perceived as disinterest and can raise emotions) (see Table 11.4).

Always remember that, as a negotiator, a law enforcement/correctional officer, or federal official, you are the enemy and part of the problem and not part of the solution. With a criminal, he or she may initially perceive you as the enemy as well, but he or she will soon come to realize you are part of the solution and not part of the problem. This is not the case with the terrorist. You are part of the problem, and your solutions are a bigger part of the problem. The negotiator has to work to overcome this perception and present solutions that are not seen as worsening an already bad situation. Deal with the criminal element of the situation and ignore the political element. Negotiators dealing with Richard McLaren of the Republic of Texas concentrated on his shooting and kidnapping of his neighbors. They let McLaren vent and validate his political beliefs without arguing, debating, or disagreeing. They instead concentrated on problem solving his criminal situation.

As mentioned in the discussion with suicide bombers, understanding the hostage taker's culture is important. If negotiating with a right-wing supremacist from the south, for example, recognize that in the southern culture "macho" is im-

Table 11.4 Some Suggestions for Negotiating With the Terrorist

Negotiate from the perspective of the criminal activity, not the terrorist goal

Dangerousness is HIGH, and hostage taker is a desperate individual

Negotiator is an enemy, so rapport-building will be difficult

Gather good and plentiful intelligence

Use the Internet to help gather intelligence

Use a same-race negotiator with many terrorists (crucial with the far right)

Do not be confrontational, argumentative, or demanding

Present a unified approach among command, tactical, and negotiators

Do not threaten, but show force

Be aware of suicide potential with all terrorists

Be open to expressive demands (many terrorists will initially be grandiose, but the real issues to deal with is their welfare)

Do not unnecessarily provoke hostage taker

Do not argue politics, religion, or philosophy

Do not try and show the hostage taker the "error of their ways"

Help hostage taker find a way to save face

Use active listening and good communication skills

portant and saving face is critical. To many, women are of secondary importance and are responsible for home and family. The south is a gun culture, and gun ownership is a "God-given right." Saving face is important, and any deal must be structured with that in mind. Individualism and independence are important concepts that shape southern life. As discussed previously, the Arabic culture has a strong family component, and loyalty to family is a mainstay of daily life. Dignity and reputation are cornerstones of a person's life and must be maintained. A full elicitation of any culture is far beyond the scope of this chapter, but these examples serve to expose the negotiator to the importance of cultural understanding.

Religion is also important to many terrorists. The negotiator must understand religion and how it fits within the hostage taker's culture, family, and group. The religious belief structures must be understood in the context of political beliefs and the goals of the group. In most religions, humans do not control fate, God does, and so negotiation strategies must account for the role that God plays in the hostage taker's life. Do not argue religion, but ask for explanations. One mistake that negotiators can easily make in dealing with religious extremists is in trying to get into religious discussions, debates, and arguments. Extremist religious beliefs are not based on accepted philosophy and logic, and the extremist has been adequately prepared for assaults on their belief system. Trying to argue religion is virtually guaranteed to make negotiations go downhill and become much more contentious.

With the terrorist situation, intelligence is one of the keys to a successful resolution. In addition to situational intelligence negotiators would normally develop, intelligence concerning the group is critical. Intelligence gathering must focus on the size and level of sophistication of the group, recent group activities, known areas of operation, compound activity, and training curricula and sophistication. For the hostage taker, it is important to learn of the level of involvement in the group of the hostage taker, status within the group, specific orders from the group (or lack of orders), and overall history with the group. Richard McLaren established a Republic of Texas "embassy and headquarters" building in his trailer during his incident. At the same time, the Republic of Texas disavowed and disowned him and his actions. Although the Republic of Texas was distancing itself from McLaren, dozens of other militia persons were heading to West Texas to "assist" McLaren. Most were armed and were intent on interfering with the response teams. Likewise, at the Ruby Ridge incident involving Randy Weaver, members of the far right were on scene to offer support to Weaver and interfere with response efforts.

One excellent source of intelligence information for negotiators is the Internet. Numerous government sites can be used to uncover intelligence information. Some useful government sites include the FBI, CIA, State Department, Homeland Security, and Department of Defense. The Center for Disease Control, Health and Human Services, and United States Army Medical Research Institute for Infectious Diseases are excellent sites if a possible biological, chemical, or radiological weapon is in play. As mentioned previously, the ADL of B'nai B'rith and the SPLC are excellent sites when dealing with the right wing. News sites such as Fox, MSNBC, CBS, ABC, CNN, and Al Jazeer have information about terrorist groups and activities. Some information in this chapter concerning the Freemen and Republic of Texas was gleaned from Internet news sites years after the event. And do not neglect a Google search. Recognize that the Internet does not have the same control over accuracy as do other potential sources of intelligence. Finally, do not neglect terrorist sites. If negotiating with a member of the ELF, for example, go to the ELF website to discover information about that group. Many right-wing groups have websites (or find related-group websites).

Pay attention to bystanders, neighbors, and others who know the actor. They may be there less out of curiosity and more out a desire to learn more about law enforcement tactics and operations. The author was involved in an incident with a member of the Aryan Brotherhood (AB). A friend and neighbor was used as an intelligence source. It was learned after the incident that the neighbor was himself an AB and had an extensive arsenal in his house. Had he wanted, he could have caused significant problems for the negotiation effort by feeding the team false intelligence. He also could have caused problems for the entire response team by going to his house and starting a firefight.

REFERENCES

American Psychiatric Association. (1994). *Diagnostic and statistical manual of mental disorders* (4th ed.). Washington, DC: Author.

Arena, M. P., & Arrigo, B. A. (2005). Identity and the terrorist threat: An interpretative and explanatory model. In L. L. Snowden & B. C. Whitsel (Eds.), *Terrorism: Research, readings and realities* (pp. 11–48). Upper Saddle River, NJ: Pearson/Prentice Hall.

Bradstreet, R. (1992, September). *Communications: Getting on the right wavelength.* Presentation at a basic negotiations school, San Antonio Police Department, San Antonio, TX.

CNN. (2005, September 2). CIA: Bomber tape "appears genuine." Retrieved November 26, 2007, from http://www.cnn.com/200/WORLD/europe/09/02/london.tape.cia/index.html.

CNN. (2006, April 11). *29 indicted in Madrid train blasts.* Retrieved February 12, 2007, from http://edition.cnn.com/2006/WORLD/europe/04/11/madrid.bombings.

CNN. (2007). *Bomber target London.* Retrieved February 12, 2007, from http://www.cnn.com/SPECIALS/2005/london.bombing.

Durkheim, E. (1951). *Suicide: A study in sociology.* New York: The Free Press.

Everly, G. (1989). *A clinical guide to the treatment of the human stress response.* New York: Plenum Press.

FBI. (2005). Retrieved January 10, 2006, from http://www.fbi.gov.

Fuselier, G. D. (1981, revised 1986). A practical overview of hostage negotiations. *FBI Law Enforcement Bulletin, 50*(6), 12–15.

George, J., & Wilcox, L. (1992). *Nazis, communists, klansmen, and others on the fringe: Political extremism in America.* Buffalo, NY: Prometheus.

Hammer, M. (2002, May). *Cultural factors in negotiating with suicidal terrorists.* Presentation at the California Association of Hostage Negotiators Conference, Monterrey, CA.

Hare, R. D., & McPherson, L. M. (1984). Violent and aggressive behavior by criminal psychopaths. *International Journal of Law and Psychiatry, 7,* 35–50.

Hoffer, E. (1955). *The true believer.* New York: Harper Row.

Laqueur, W. (1999). *The new terrorism: Fanaticism and the arms of mass destruction.* New York: Oxford University Press.

McMains, M. J., & Mullins, W. C. (2006). *Crisis negotiations: Managing critical incidents and hostage situations in law enforcement and corrections* (3rd ed.). Cincinnati, OH: Anderson Publishing, a division of LexisNexis.

Mullins, W. C. (1997). *A sourcebook on domestic and international terrorism: An analysis of issues, organization, tactics, and responses* (2nd ed.). Springfield, IL: Charles C Thomas.

Mullins, W. C., & Thurman, Q. C. (in press). The etiology of terrorism: Identifying, defining, and studying terrorists. In B. Forest, J. Green, & J. Lynch (Eds.), *Security and justice in the homeland: Criminologists on terrorism.*

Osterman, B. M. (2002). Cultural differences make negotiations different: Intercultural hostage negotiations. *Journal of Police Crisis Negotiations, 2*(2), 11–20.

Richardson, V. (2005). FBI targets domestic terrorists. In T. J. Bradey (Ed.), *Annual editions: Violence and terrorism* (8th ed.). Dubuque, IA: McGraw-Hill/Duskin.

Schmid, A. (1983). *Political terrorism: A research guide to concepts, theories, data bases, and literature.* New Brunswick, CT: Transaction.

Southern Poverty Law Center. (2005). *Active U.S. hate groups in 2006.* Available from http://www.splcenter.org/intel/map/hate.jsp.

Strentz, T. (1981). The terrorist organizational profile: A psychological role model. In Y. Alexander & J. M. Gleason (Eds.), *Behavioral and quantitative perspectives on terrorism.* New York: Pergamon.

Strentz, T. (1988). A terrorist psychosocial profile: Past and present. *Law Enforcement Bulletin, 57*(4), 11–18.

Strentz, T. (2006). *Psychological aspects of crisis negotiation.* Boca Raton, FL: CRC.

12

Applying High-Reliability Organization Theory to Crisis/Hostage Negotiation

Anthony J. Hare
Karlene H. Roberts

The practice of law enforcement hostage and crisis negotiations is scarcely 30 years old. Despite their history of success, inasmuch as these techniques evolved trial and error from New York Police Department's initial efforts, it is unlikely they are fully perfected. This chapter reviews evidence and opinion that hostage and crisis negotiations practice has not continued to advance, that contributions from behavioral science research have not generated demonstrable improvements in performance, and that law enforcement negotiators and commanders would do well to follow the lead of disciplines that have adopted an innovative theoretical framework to examine their practice and guide safe and successful innovation.

This chapter identifies high-reliability organization (HRO) theory, a body of evolving analysis and practice that is particularly applicable to professionals who work in dangerous or critical environments. Researchers and practitioners in these critical settings report that similar concepts and practices increase safety and improve performance across a broad spectrum of industries and professions. Finally, as in the case of other social science contributions, this chapter argues the application of these high-reliability approaches to critical incident management and hostage and crisis negotiations will be best done by law enforcement personnel who study and adapt the analyses to their own practice and who work in concert with social scientists and mental health professionals to heedfully evaluate and incorporate innovations into their practice.

HRO THEORY

HRO Theory is a relatively new area of social science research concerned with organizational performance in settings where mistakes or poor practice can and do have disastrous consequences (Flin, 1996; Roberts, 1990; Weick, 1987). HRO researchers have identified common features that distinguish organizations that generally perform well in critical situations from organizations or agencies that do not. A growing number of organizations that work in dangerous environments have adopted HRO principles and use them to analyze and improve their performance and safety records.

A number of troubling incidents or unfortunate outcomes of negotiated critical incidents appear to illustrate HRO failures. This chapter is an introduction to HRO for negotiators and critical incident managers and an invitation to apply HRO findings to evaluate and improve our performance.

HRO theory recognizes two salient features of organizational performance: Some industries and organizations work in inherently dangerous contexts with notably safe and successful track records, and they manage unavoidable critical events with minimal consequences. An HRO is an organization that conducts relatively error-free operations over a long period of time and consistently makes good decisions resulting in high-quality and reliable operations (Roberts, 1990). After some 25 years of research, attention findings from HRO research are just reaching maturity. Recent findings deal with such issues as how organizations learn and unlearn (Madsen, 2007), how organizations need to pay attention to the interfaces within and among themselves (Roberts, Madsen, & Desai, 2005), and how organizations make sense of their internal processes and their environments (Weick, 1987; Weick & Roberts, 1993). These and other recent findings have exciting potential for application in various industries. However, their applications have not been fully worked out.

Two Bodies of HRO Research

Two streams of research have been applied to people working in potentially volatile situations. We believe they can be applied with positive outcomes in the hostage and crisis negotiations arena. One stream comes from an investigation in the financial industry of five high-performance organizations and five organizations under letters of understanding from the U.S. Office of the Comptroller of the Currency (Roberts & Libuser, 1993). This research highlights the differences between failing and succeeding organizations when the stakes are losing considerable money.

Without attribution to the research findings, the story of Long-Term Capital Management (LTCM; Lowenstein, 2000) is a perfect example of the failure side of the Libuser research. LTCM was a hedge fund founded in 1994 by John Meriwether (former vice chairman and head of bond trading at Salomon Brothers). On its Board were Myron Scholes and Robert Merton, who shared the 1997 Nobel Prize in Economics. In 1998, LTCM lost $4.6 billion, and the company went out of business in 2000. This case of the best and brightest researchers failing in practice sounds a cautionary note for the incorporation of academic research in high-consequence practice.

A complementary set of findings comes from an amalgam of research done in a variety of locations, including law enforcement (Roberts, Madsen, & Desai, 2006), the railroad industry (Frailey, 1998), health care (Kohn, Corrigan, & Donaldson, 1999), the nuclear power industry (Schulman, 1993), National Aeronautics and Space Administration (NASA; Vaughan, 1996), the U.S. Navy's carrier aviation program (Roberts, 1990), and so on. This and work in other industries is discussed by Weick and Sutcliffe (2001). These findings observe and label what successful organizations do well to succeed in these diverse fields.

The stories of NASA's loss of the space shuttles Challenger (Vaughan, 1996) and Columbia (Columbia Accident Investigation Board, 2003), and the many errors leading to hospital deaths (Kohn, Corrigan, & Donaldson, 1999), call on this body of research for explanatory principles and a common lexicon.

The Libuser work identifies five organizational processes that lead to highly reliable performance:

1. *Process auditing* or a system for ongoing checks and balances designed to identify expected as well as unexpected safety problems. Safety drills and equipment testing are in this category. Follow-ups on problems revealed in prior audits are critical.

2. The *reward systems* or the payoffs that people and organizations receive have powerful influences on what people will do. Interorganizational reward systems also influence behavior. One must avoid rewarding Behavior A while hoping for Behavior B (Kerr, 1975).

3. *Quality degradation* and developing inferior quality must be avoided. The quality standard in the industry might be examined for information about how to do this. The appropriateness of using the prevailing standard of care to evaluate performance is examined later.

4. The *perception of risk* must exist in the organization. Knowing risk exists is only one part of this process. Doing something about reducing risk is the other part.

5. Command and control elements must include *migrating decision making* to the person with the most expertise to make the decision (not the person with the most chevrons), ensuring that sufficient *redundancy* in people and/or hardware exists, making sure senior managers have the big picture (or "the bubble") instead of micromanaging, ensuring that formal rules and procedures are consistent with the desired organizational outcomes, and engaging in training-training-training.

These processes are relatively easy for organizations to adopt. An example of a successful adoption is discussed in Roberts, Madsen, Desai, and van Stralen (2005) and Madsen, Desai, Roberts, and Wong (2006), and an assessment of the existence of these processes in organizations is discussed in Gaba, Singer, Sinaiko, Bowen, and Ciavarelli (2003) and Desai, Roberts, and Ciavarelli (2006).[1]

Weick and Sutcliffe (2001) represent the second stream of research. They focus on managing the unexpected and on good management as a *mindful* activity. By *mindful activity,* Weick and Sutcliffe mean that organizations organize themselves in such a way that they are better able to notice the unexpected in the making and halt its development. If they have difficulty halting the development of the unexpected, they focus on containing it. If some of the unexpected breaks through the containment, they focus on resilience and swift restoration of system functioning.

Weick and Sutcliffe cite five hallmarks of organizations that persistently have less than their fair share of accidents. These HRO characteristics comprise what they term as *mindfulness* and are:

1. *Preoccupation with failure* in which HROs treat any lapse as a symptom that something that could have severe consequences is wrong with the system. HROs recognize that small errors may coincide at some awful moment and produce an accident similar to the Union Carbide plant accident at Bhopal in 1984 (Shrivastava, 1987).
2. *Reluctance to accept simplifications.* HROs try to create more complete and nuanced pictures of themselves than do other organizations. These organizations know the world is complex, unstable, unknowable, and unpredictable. In response, they try to avoid simplifying their pictures of the world and of themselves.
3. HROs are sensitive to operations. They are attentive to where the "rubber meets the road" or to where real operations are carried out. That is, they have well-developed *situational awareness* (Endsley, 1995).
4. HROs are committed to *resilience.* They develop capabilities to detect, contain, and bounce back from the unexpected, including the errors they make.
5. HROs defer to expertise and *cultivate diversity.* To accomplish this, they avoid deadly rigid hierarchies and push decision making down and around the organization.

Weick and Sutcliffe's (2001) mindful processes constitute a mechanism for assessing the reliability of an organization's internal processes. The mechanism is a good starter for organizations, but it has not been subjected to the rigorous psychometric norming required of perceptual and behavioral assessments. It follows from the mindfulness inherent in HRO that innovation in dangerous practice must proceed heedfully and with the analysis and measurement required in medicine or engineering.

A gentle stirring of the Libuser and Weick and Roberts processes should produce a set of conceptual boxes into which organizational practitioners can place their problems and challenges. For example, if we invent an "expertise" or a "migrating decision-making" box, we better understand that problems are best solved when we look through our organizations for the people who have the appropriate skills to solve them, rather than searching for the highest ranking person as the appropriate problem solver.

If we decide a "rewards" box, which includes "sensitivity to operations," is useful, we migrate toward thinking about the rewards we apply at the operational levels of our organizations. We may be rewarding negotiators for the wrong behaviors. Other boxes can be invented that address one or some combination of the concepts discussed.

Organizations That Subscribe to HRO Theory

Examining the agencies that have adopted HRO analyses suggests that law enforcement critical incident management is an appropriate application of HRO theory. Examples of HROs and industries that embrace HRO theory include United States Naval Aviation (Roberts, 1990); U.S. Marine Corps ground forces (Ciavarelli & Figlock, 1997; Ciavarelli, Figlock, Sengupta, & Roberts, 2001); petrochemical industries, including Shell and British Petroleum (Reid, 2006); the National Aeronautics and Space Agency (Columbia Accident Investigation Board, 2003); the Federal Aviation Administration (Hart, 2006), the U.S. Chemical Safety and Hazard Board (Merritt, 2006); pediatric emergency medicine (van Stralen & Perkin, 1997); the U.S. Department of Energy (Carnes, 2006); and the firm engaged in the assembly and disassembly of nuclear weapons in the United States. Accidents in any of these organizations or the failure to manage and mitigate the effects of weather, earthquakes, or human misbehavior on their daily operations can result in extreme consequences.

Implications of HRO Theory for Law Enforcement

Most critical incidents to which law enforcement negotiators and tactical teams respond meet the definition of an HRO challenge. These hometown incidents may not be as newsworthy as managing unexpected developments in a nuclear weapons plant or a space shuttle, but they are *low-frequency, high-consequence events* that threaten to overwhelm the resources and normal operations of the communities involved. They typically involve suicidal subjects, warrant suspects, armed and barricaded subjects, criminals interrupted in the course of a crime, domestic violence, persons under the influence of alcohol or drugs in a place where they cannot be safely detained by patrol units, and mentally ill persons who represent a threat to themselves or others. Law enforcement critical incidents that are not criminal in nature involve the response to fires, major accidents, natural disasters, and public events ranging from civil disorder to rock concerts and sports competitions (Flin, 1996). Failure to adequately manage any of these events can result in injury or death, property damage, or the disruption of essential services.

Law enforcement agencies that consistently successfully resolve diverse critical incidents can be demonstrated to practice similar sound generic approaches to these challenging situations. These approaches have been described and instructed as *critical incident management* (Flin, 1996; Sarna, 1984, 1996). Recognizing that dangerous negotiated incidents are critical incidents, advanced negotiations courses imbed their negotiation instruction in critical incident management principles (Hare, 1997a; Sarna, 1990). Critical incident management principles regularly practiced by effective law enforcement agencies include quickly establishing an *inner perimeter* to contain the problem and an *outer perimeter* to exclude the uninvolved, assembling a *critical incident management team* including the requisite variety of experts to advise the incident commander, and *introducing experts* to resolve the problem. The incident commander must also maintain effective and honest communication with the media to minimize intrusive behaviors on their part and to inform the public (that has an absolute right to know) how well their agencies are performing. An essential HRO element of effective incident management is *responsive and flexible command* that encourages the suggestions and frank criticism of all personnel on the scene. Failure to implement any of these incident management procedural steps as soon as possible can permit a negotiable incident to deteriorate. Like most containment and management techniques, these steps are both more effective and easier to implement before they are required than trying to accomplish them after a situation has gone critical.

Chief Peter Sarna was an early advocate of crisis and hostage negotiations in West Coast law enforcement. Consistent with the critical incident principles of flexible leadership and requisite variety, he applied crisis and hostage negotiations to a wide variety of situations. He incorporated negotiators and tactical subordinate commanders on his incident management teams, and he deferred tactical responses in many cases where lethal force was an option, demonstrating the efficacy of negotiations in challenging situations. His willingness to permit alternative approaches in intransigent cases where the traditional guidelines were not effective led to the development of more advanced negotiations and guidelines for how to deviate heedfully from guidelines that do not appear to be working (Hare, 1986).

THE CRITICALITY OF HUMAN BEHAVIORS

Avoiding and managing law enforcement critical incidents is complicated by problematic human behaviors—the behavior of the suspects as well as the behaviors and working relationships of the responding agencies. HRO scholars identified safety and organizational performance as cultural phenomena of the workplaces and work groups involved (Weick, 1987). Any major critical incident challenges the responsible agency's ability to contain, diagnose, and manage the outcome. The ability of an organization to rise to these challenges is significantly impacted by the attitudes and "culture" of responsible workers.

Despite the challenge of changing the attitudes and values of an organization, assessing and changing organizational attitudes and policies to improve safety and performance may be the most practical steps available to enhance an organization's performance, compared with the costs of increased manpower, extensive specialized training, or additional sophisticated equipment. The application of HRO assessments to the members of naval aviation squadrons has demonstrated a strong relationship to safety performance (Ciavarelli, 2005; Ciavarelli & Crowson, 2004).

Ciavarelli developed a detailed survey of attitudes toward aviation safety that is administered on a confidential basis to every member of naval aviation squadrons. As command interest in the assessment of personnel's attitudes toward safety has grown, this assessment tool has been administered to every active and reserve naval and marine aviation squadron in the U.S. Navy. A result of this examination has been a statistically significant increase in safety performance among units studied. Based on the impact of this HRO analysis of aviation safety, the U.S. Marine Corps elected to develop a similar HRO instrument for all Marine Corps ground forces.

NEGOTIATIONS GUIDELINES AND PRACTICE MAY NOT MEET HRO CRITERIA

Some accepted practices in negotiations may not meet the standards of HRO practice. Law enforcement agencies and the courts generally evaluate an agency's performance in a particular incident in terms of its adherence to the prevailing standard of care. It has been observed that crisis negotiations evolved trial and error from New York Police Department's original, innovative practice (Bolz & Hershey, 1979; Hare, 1997a; Schlossberg & Freeman, 1974). The basic guidelines pioneered by Schlossberg and Bolz, and subsequently adopted by the Federal Bureau of Investigation (FBI), were not organized into a coherent program, but as a compendium of dos and don'ts. Subsequent identification and consolidation of prevailing guidelines yielded a list of as many as 27 negotiations guidelines from different sources, some of which provide contradictory advice for similar situations (Hare, 1995). Every negotiations guideline has not been evaluated with the scrutiny of a novel surgical technique or a new drug in medicine. In fact, some guidelines that have been taught and subscribed to for years (e.g., avoid the use of civilian negotiators or "third-party intermediaries") have been modified or reexamined in recent years. Lanceley (1999) provides examples of tragic outcomes from the use of third-party intermediaries and discusses considerations that complicate or recommend their use. Lanceley's observations remind us that guidelines tend to be neither right nor wrong, but contingent rules that must be applied heedfully with close attention to early signals of progress or failure. The Oakland California Police Department had considerable experience with "civilian negotiators" and recognized both their efficacy and the problems they presented in many cases. They developed contingent guidelines for evaluating and controlling potential third-party negotiators (Hare, 1986, 1997b). The issue is not whether the FBI or the Oakland Police Department was more advanced. The issue is the failure of the practitioners of hostage and crisis negotiation to communicate and evaluate their experience as effectively as medicine, aviation, finance, or other critical industries. Simply perpetuating the standard of care may be legally conservative in a litigious society, but it will not advance or improve practice.

How Are We Doing: The Error Rate

A common feature of presentations at high-reliability conferences is the *error rate*. Presenters from diverse fields reviewing tragic accidents, discussing human factors research, or reviewing the efficacy of their industries' efforts to improve practice almost universally cite their error rates. Military and civil aviation, medicine, and financial institutions all recognize and publicize their error rates. Errors are ubiquitous and, at some level, unavoidable. What is an acceptable level of error, and how do we deal with errors and accidents when they occur?

Some error rate data show precipitous drops in deaths or accidents after the implementation of technological innovations. For example, one may take the replacement of internal combustion aviation engines with jet turbines in aviation (Boeing Company, 2006). If the turbine jet engine had precipitated an increase in accidents and deaths, this innovation would not have been embraced by the aviation industry.

Crisis and hostage negotiators do not know their error rate. They may not concur on what constitutes an error in a negotiated incident. Behavioral scientists and mental health professionals who study and report on negotiated incidents do not know the effects of their advice to practitioners. When researchers report the detailed analysis of a single suicide case (Rogan & Hammer, 1995) or observe that Stockholm Syndrome is reported to have occurred in a single incident in which skyjackers treated hostages well, negotiators may draw general lessons from these individual or small numbers of cases. It is not wise to adopt changes in practice or our understanding of these phenomena based on what may be anomalous cases.

In other dangerous fields, practitioners and researchers manage to work more in concert and with pragmatic metrics to save lives and improve performance. Rogan and Hammer (2006) review the relationship among crisis and hostage practitioners, mental health professionals, and researchers. They distinguish the divergent focuses and disparate bodies of knowledge developing among negotiators, researchers, and mental health professionals. A salient lesson from Hammer and Rogan's analysis is the failure of negotiators and behavioral scientists to bridge the gap between theory and practice to inform and advance negotiations. In HROs, practitioners enlist research closer to the operational or "deck plate" level to advance or validate practice.

Two Views of How Negotiations Work

In candid and confidential discussions, law enforcement and diplomatic observers from France, Greece, and the United Kingdom have characterized U.S. negotiations strategy as a rule-driven or "recipe" approach to assessing and resolving complex problems. Other nations' police and military forces with extensive experience with criminal and terrorist incidents contend they use a situational approach that is more reliable than U.S. practice (Combalbert, n.d.). Neither of these approaches has been objectively examined with the scrutiny of life and death practice in surgery or oil field firefighting; U.S. negotiators generally follow the principles from basic negotiations instruction, and negotiators from other nations believe they approach negotiated incidents from a different perspective. Absent a more definitive analysis, it is difficult to compare or appraise these perceptions.

The notion of a situational typology to guide complex negotiations does have precedents in the United States. Practitioners and researchers alike recognize common types or genera of negotiated incidents (Hacker, 1976; Miron & Goldstein, 1979; Schlossberg, 1984). Although there is not universal agreement on definitive categories of negotiated incidents, most basic crisis and hostage negotiations courses in the United States include a classification of commonly negotiated subjects (e.g., criminals, terrorists, mentally ill persons, domestic violence perpetrators, etc.). These courses recognize types of negotiated incidents, but do not prescribe different techniques for different types of negotiated subjects.

In the 1980s, abnormal psychology enjoyed a brief popularity as a key to understanding and conducting negotiations (Strentz, 1983, 1986). This psychological approach included training negotiators to recognize diagnostic criteria of psychopathology in the negotiations dialogue and suggested phrases for the negotiator to use (or avoid) with each disordered subject. The psychological approach to negotiations reflected an FBI observation that as many as half of all crisis negotiations involve mental illness (Fusilier, 1981), hence the optimistic expectation that social science, diagnostic techniques, or psychotherapy might guide the intervention in violent incidents.

The U.S. psychological typing approach to negotiations differs from the European typologies, in that U.S. negotiators were trained to identify types of *individual subjects* that corresponded to the disorders defined by the American Psychiatric Association (*Diagnostic and statistical manual of mental disorders, third edition* [*DSM–III*], 1980). European negotiators maintain they recognize types of *situations* (Combalbert, n.d.). With the exception of cases where there are salient indications of psychopathology, the U.S. reliance on psychological typing and diagnosis has been deemphasized; the prevalence of mental illness among negotiated subjects may not be as widespread as was thought, and even those cases shown to involve mentally ill subjects were diagnosed after the fact rather than during the incident (Rogan & Hammer, 2006).

The U.S. effort to use psychological typologies to inform negotiations with dangerous negotiated subjects was a hypothetical approach advanced without the validation that preceded the adoption of our basic repertory of techniques. Although Bolz and Schlossberg drew many of the New York Police Department techniques from 1970s crisis intervention counseling, the techniques were validated in trial-and-error practice before they were widely adopted as basic guidelines (Hare, 1997b). Contemporary advice from psychology derives from psychologists' or psychiatrists' experience of clients in psychotherapy. As Schlossberg observed in the first application of hostage negotiations by New York Police Department, the mental health professional's experience of a particular disorder or even a particular subject in the consulting office may not be as relevant to controlling a dangerous, armed gunman as a law enforcement negotiator's experience of many dangerous persons in crisis in negotiations and in street policing (Schlossberg & Freeman, 1974).

The psychological and psychiatric advice at the Branch Davidian standoff at Waco may be taken as an example. The various experts' advice was wide ranging and included a forensic psychiatrist's suggestion that the FBI turn the negotiations over to him (U.S. Department of Justice, 1993). Introducing academic, theoretical, or intuitively satisfying techniques into a crisis negotiation without careful testing and controls does not meet the standards of emergency medicine, hazmat response, or aviation safety.

The Evolution of Best Practices

Recent efforts to survey and consolidate the most widely accepted negotiations and management techniques nationwide have resulted in extensive and evolving lists of best practices (Kidd, 2005). Kidd's (2005, 2006a, 2006b, 2007) list of Peak Performance Standards has not been adopted as an integrated program, but it is well-received as a summary of the national standard of care by state-wide negotiator conferences. However, the use of the evolving standard of care in a field that is based on only 30 years of practice, and in which the sampled cases are defined by local jurisdictions' decisions to call out negotiators, is not a definitive analysis of the efficacy of the guidelines. Techniques that serve in commonplace, mediocre, or less challenging incidents will be retained; and techniques that are only attempted in more challenging incidents will not be used as frequently and may not succeed in the challenging cases to which they are applied. Consequently, they may not be included in the standard of care. Flin (1996) cites Sarna's observation that many agencies and most negotiators will never face a challenging case. These more routine experiences will shape our guidelines.

An alternative approach featuring the HRO attention to error would be to: (a) focus our analysis on the more challenging successes and failures we encounter, (b) withhold blame to encourage frank admission and examination of what worked well or badly, and (c) determine whether operational principles applied by reliable agencies in other fields discriminate the more and less reliable approaches and techniques. This is a broader based analysis than simply evaluating the present techniques against the prevailing law enforcement standard and less dangerous than evaluating prospective techniques by infrequent trial and error.

HROs draw on the experience of successful professions in diverse areas of specialized practice. The same observations that identify HRO practice in offshore oil drilling support successful treatment in pediatric emergency rooms and wild fire management. The techniques are different, but the overarching principles of successful organizations are similar.

APPLYING HRO LESSONS TO COUNTER TERROR PLANNING

Terrorist incidents directed against the U.S. homeland are classic examples of HRO interest. They are infrequent events with the potential for catastrophic consequences. Most of the agencies planning for homeland defense are designing strategies for their agencies to engage challenges they have never encountered. Most of the leaders, commanders, and personnel who respond to terrorist incidents will face these encounters with plans that have not been tested against real opponents. Detection, identification, and response to terrorist incidents will rely on the kinds of communication that have been the weak point in our response to critical incidents of all kinds. Clarke (1999) observed that many plans to contend with critical incidents and major accidents in dangerous environments are based on inadequate analogues. He calls these ambitious plans and comforting, but flawed, remedies "fantasy documents." Clarke attributes the fantasy plans he cites to the planners' deliberate intent to placate an anxious public, generally to obtain approval to conduct inherently dangerous operations.

Many plans to counter terrorist incidents in homeland defense do not meet the criteria of HRO practice and do not incorporate sophisticated negotiations in their response and analyses. These fantasy plans do not stem from ulterior motives, but from the limited direct experience of the planners with hostage and crisis negotiations.

> Under *highly* uncertain conditions rational planning becomes more difficult . . . when important aspects of the future are not or cannot be known, planning is shorn of its most functional aspects . . . when uncertainty about key aspects of a task is high, rationalistic plans and rational-looking planning processes become rationality badges, labels claiming that organizations and experts can control things that are, most likely, outside the range of their expertise. (Clarke, 1999, p. 4)

Terrorist threats are violent. Therefore, we invite the commanders of special weapons and tactics units to devise counterterror plans. The tactically trained planners develop plans to avert their worst tactical nightmares, or they plan to use the tactics they know best to neutralize terrorist subjects. The problem with these plans is that they overlook the fact that many police calls and most terrorist responses are false alarms. The confused, the mentally ill, and suspicious but innocent persons will trigger antiterror responses. Tactical bias or planning for an inevitable violent resolution may diminish the role of negotiation in the planned responses to suspected terrorist incidents and may fail to include adequate planning for winnowing out false alarms without tragic consequences.

Tacticians' plans for containing terrorist violence may not incorporate techniques for engaging and evaluating situations before resorting to deadly force because their plans are based on their particular law enforcement experience. By the time a law enforcement tactical team is called, an incident has already proved violent or beyond the first responders' capabilities. Hence, plans developed by tactical teams may emphasize tactical resolution at the expense of the engagement and assessment that should precede the application of force. Lanceley's (1999) comments on the failure to include negotiations as an option in the Ruby Ridge Siege may reflect the tactical commander's reliance on force options based on his personal experience or the Hostage Rescue Team's preparation to respond to tragic and violent situations.

Tactical plans may be based on a great deal of training, but little actual experience of violence. Most law enforcement snipers have never fired at a suspect, much less a terrorist. Tactical plans to counter terror will rely on the planners' favored responses and experience. Less lethal responses, like negotiations, may not be included in the tacticians' planning to the extent that they have been incorporated in European plans based on their greater experience of terrorist attack.

HRO TERMS AND CONCEPTS FOR LAW ENFORCEMENT

One of the greatest contributions of HRO theorists is the development of a lexicon of terms for the common principles they identify in diverse industries. This is significant because it suggests that there are universal principles that can improve safety and performance in different professions. Equally important, the existence of common terms permits the application of these concepts to the analysis of performance in industries and agencies that have not yet experienced a challenging incident that might result in failure. Common terms among HRO organizations are *leadership climate* or style, *closely coupled* versus flexible organization, *redundancy*, *safety culture*, *error reporting*, and *situational awareness*.

LEADERSHIP CLIMATE

An early finding about the culture of the dangerous workplace was the identification of particular styles of leadership that contributed to failure in critical incidents. In 1979, NASA conducted a workshop to address the number of aircraft accidents that resulted from avoidable human error (Cooper, White, & Lauber, 1980). As many as 70% of all air carrier accidents involve human error, and 60% to 80% of the incidents studied were associated with poor group decision making, ineffective communication, inadequate leadership, and poor management (U.S. Department of Transportation, Federal Aviation Administration, 1989). Researchers coined the term *cockpit resource management* (CRM) for the study of flight crew behavior, including leadership styles. They identified characteristic attitudes among junior and senior crew members that interfered with the ability to communicate important information in critical incidents. Styles of leadership and prevailing culture among flight crews contributed to this failure to communicate.

One style of leadership involves strict obedience to a highly directive leader who is expected to generate the advice and direction for normal and more critical circumstances. This style of leadership is rank based and is best portrayed by common perceptions of a "military commander." (Author's note: This attribution to the "military" style appears in quotations because of my own observation in combat that the most effective and extraordinary military leaders do not exercise command in this autocratic style.) In this directive style of leadership, more junior crew members might not share essential information or their alternative understandings of a critical situation with the first pilot. In particular, crew members might be reluctant to report apparent errors or criticize the work of the leader. Other more collaborative styles of command provide a climate that welcomes diverse views, even in critical events. The program to foster this leadership climate became known as crew resource management and evolved through several generations of increasingly sophisticated and more universally accepted practice in the airline industry (Helmreich, Merritt, & Wilhelm, 1999).

Roberts and her colleagues (Roberts, 1986; Tadmore, Roberts, & Yu, 2007) examined two accidents from an HRO perspective. They are the grounding of the USS Enterprise on Bishop's Rock in 1986 and the sinking of the Japanese fishing boat, the Ehime Maru, by the USS Greenville in 2001. These investigations relied on HRO analyses—examination of the workplace culture and the leadership climate. In both of these accidents, members of the respective U.S. crews had information that might have been used to avoid the collisions if it had been shared with the vessels' commanders.

Law enforcement leadership with its familiar military chain of command and rank structure is susceptible to autocratic or top–down management in dangerous situations. Rigid structure and overreliance on a single decision maker can be the least effective leadership approach in unpredictable and rapidly evolving situations. A more receptive style of command that assembles the requisite variety of experts and draws on the resources and insights of all personnel on the scene can be useful. Examples from pediatric intensive care units and aircraft carrier landings offer useful guidance.

Despite the command responsibility of an aircraft carrier's captain and the specific operational responsibilities delegated to other command officers (the Air Boss), a seaman on the flight deck can override the direction to land an incoming aircraft if he sees something amiss from his vantage point. This *decision migration* is accepted lifesaving practice in naval aviation, but might be considered an insubordinate and unacceptable violation of command authority in a law enforcement critical incident.

In the medical model, pediatric intensive care units face life and death critical incidents involving infants and children at risk who are unable to describe their own symptoms. A West Coast hospital implemented a number of HRO concepts to enhance their practice. They adopted a collegial team approach that recognized and achieved exceptionally high recovery and survival rates. Although traditional practice reflected the superior position of the physician who had the most formal training as an authority who should direct critical care, this unit recognized "the *authority gradient* that can occur between physician or surgeon and other team members can lead to tragedy" (van Stralen & Perkin, 1997, p. 53; italics added). They encouraged *decision migration*, recognizing that the attending nurse or charge nurse as the bedside caregiver may be the most qualified person to guide decisions in patient emergencies. They cultivated increased *risk awareness* to avoid the undetected instability that preceded rapid deterioration in several patients every month. Reducing blame and quilt, particularly after a bad outcome, encouraged more constructive examination of errors, with an eye toward learning from and reducing *normal accidents* (Perrow, 1984). These HRO changes in *command and control* reduced "consequential events" (accidents that can lead to cardiac arrest and death or brain injury) and decreased infant mortality (van Stralen & Perkin, 1997).

A negotiated incident is a low-frequency, high-risk event involving unpredictable human behavior. Although some negotiators argue that our basic guidelines and experience with prior incidents yield successful outcomes in most negotiations, an alternative observation is that most negotiated incidents are neither complex nor challenging, and guidelines developed from such incidents will not prevail in more dangerous incidents. In fact, the more challenging incidents may be identified by their failure to respond to traditional guidelines. An incident commander may only learn of the failure of the traditional techniques if he welcomes negative as well as positive reports.

RIGID STRUCTURE, CLOSELY COUPLED ORGANIZATIONS, AND REDUNDANCY

HRO theorists have adopted the term *closely coupled* to describe organizations whose structure is sufficiently inflexible that successive units will continue to pursue a failing course (Perrow, 1984). Uncritical adherence to guidelines, acceptance of questionable diagnoses, and continued application of failing courses of action are all dangerous approaches in unusual or rapidly evolving critical situations.

The traditional organization of negotiating teams recognizes several essential functions that are useful in negotiated incidents. Although there is some variation in team size and defined roles, most teams have a team leader, a primary, a secondary, an intelligence negotiator, and a liaison to command. Some teams designate technical experts, and some combine the liaison's and leader's roles. Most organizations fail to realize that these are critical *duties*, not *individual positions*. In some cases, there is little need for a telephone or equipment technician. In many challenging situations, having just the primary and a backup negotiator monitor the dialogue is inadequate; it is critical to have as many team members as possible listening carefully and contributing to the team's understanding of the situation and developing responses and countermeasures. Rigid organization based on the traditional roles may be inadequate and dangerous in more challenging incidents.

Another principal of HROs is *redundancy*. Their flexible organization allows for levels of backup or additional support in specific positions as critical needs evolve. Redundancy does not imply a luxurious surplus of reserves to replace injured, exhausted, or overcommitted personnel. It reflects the leader's willingness and the team members' ability to abandon their customary assignments to supplement critical skills. A sports analogy is the baseball pitcher's move to cover first base if the first baseman chases an infield fly ball.

We use an Oakland, California, negotiation with a multiple homicide suspect as an example of flexible organization. An estranged husband shot his wife, mother-in-law, and sister-in-law in the head when they came to collect court-ordered child support from him. He retreated to his apartment with his 9-year-old daughter and telephoned relatives in Guiana to tell them his plans to commit suicide and "not to leave his daughter in this godless country." Before these facts were known, the incident commander recognized that he was faced with three dead or dying victims on a busy street, a suspect at large, and a juvenile hostage at risk. The commander observed that his need for immediate contact and intelligence far exceeded the capacity of the negotiating team's designated intelligence negotiator.

The commander ordered the entire Criminal Investigation Division of the police department to respond to the shooting scene. Patrol units contained and isolated the population of a major thoroughfare for immediate questioning. Investigators quickly processed the crowd of bystanders to identify persons who had witnessed the shootings or who had possible knowledge of the suspect. Anyone with information was referred to the department's homicide investigators for a more in-depth interview. This unprecedented augmentation of the negotiating team exemplifies critical incident management, flexible organization, and redundancy of resources. The protracted negotiation was concluded successfully, and the suspect was prosecuted and convicted.

CRISIS DECISION MAKING—DECISION TREES OR ANALOGUE RECOGNITION

The understanding of how leaders manage accidents and critical incidents has undergone a watershed change in recent years (Klein, 1999). Historically, critical decision makers were thought to use a "decision tree" of sequential, logical choices to reach a course of action that would identify, mitigate, and resolve dangerous situations. This type of logical reasoning can be effective when practitioners face well-understood situations. Examples are the diagnosis of medical conditions, the identification of unknown chemicals in a HAZMAT, or distinguishing edible from poisonous mushrooms.

Critical incidents that respond well to the decision tree approach include mechanical failures in aircraft. Aircrews are trained to memorize an extensive body of information about the mechanical, electrical, and hydraulic systems of the aircraft they operate. Every failure of an aircraft is analyzed to diagnose what systems may have failed and to identify indications or symptoms of these particular failures. Aircrews experiencing system failures in flight analyze the problem from memory and using structured checklists, and then take definitive corrective action (Delta Airlines, 2002). More elusive or challenging problems may require the provisional implementation of corrective measures, followed by further analysis of their effectiveness.

When faced with a novel challenge whose parameters are not well known and which has not been replicated enough times to identify and delimit the types of incident that consistently respond to specific remedies, the decision tree of sequential analysis does not serve us well. A leader or incident commander facing a problem that is not well understood, and who improvises responses without a matrix to evaluate and, if necessary, retreat from his actions, is undertaking a pass–fail approach where failure can have terminal consequences.

A situational approach and identification by analogy can serve us better. Leaders who consistently manage novel, potentially overwhelming problems frequently report that they recognized how the problem was similar to other situations in entirely different contexts. This "naturalistic decision making," which distinguishes the most successful incident managers, is hard to dissect or train. When queried, the inspired problem solvers cannot reconstruct the logical steps they took to reach their decisions. These experts may report that they based their responses on techniques that prevailed in situations that may appear to be entirely unrelated. These successful problem solvers describe their recognition of the solution as an "a-ha phenomenon" (Reber, 1985). Ross (2006) provides a brief survey of this decision-making phenomenon in the word of *chess grandmasters*. Experts do not perform a sequential analysis of the evidence. They spontaneously recognize the situation as a whole from analogous situations. Experts in diverse crises recognize analogies that are not obvious. They may rely on only vaguely similar situations drawn from different contexts. This kind of problem solving may distinguish the best negotiators and incident commanders, but it is difficult to instruct. Challenging negotiated incidents, suicidal subjects, dangerous barricaded suspects, terrorist incidents, and unpredictable, extreme human behaviors present us with problems that exceed the known, well-understood, and predictable incidents that respond to our common repertory of techniques.

SITUATIONAL AWARENESS

Situational awareness (Endsley, 1995) is a psychological term used in HRO analysis of organizational performance. Although there is debate about the precise meaning of situational awareness across disciplines, a concise definition from naval aviation is the "degree of accuracy by which one's perception of his current environment mirrors reality" (Naval Aviation Schools Command, n.d.). A definition that more effectively captures situational analysis in a law enforcement critical incident is the "variety of cognitive processing activities that are *critical to dynamic, event-driven and multi-task fields of practice*" (Sarter & Woods, 1991, p. 49; italics added). In police events, situational awareness is not limited to the commander's perceptions and understanding of the situation, but includes all the responders' mutual understanding of the event. This is sometimes called *shared situational awareness* (SSA).

Situational awareness has several applications in law enforcement. A familiar example is the communications dispatcher's understanding and direction to units responding to a call for service. Communications division call takers take one or more calls from citizens to generate a call for service. The information provided by these callers is generally incomplete, may be delivered by emotional witnesses or traumatized victims, and sometimes contains deliberate inaccuracies, yet the call taker forms a reasonable understanding of the nature of the call and its relative urgency. A radio dispatcher broadcasts the call (or transmits a digital message) assigning an appropriate number of patrol units to respond. Field units may add their prior knowledge of a dangerous premise or subject and then continue to broadcast updates of developing information from the scene. The communications dispatcher and responding units form and share an understanding of the evolving incident. Based on their situational awareness, informed by experience of similar incidents, the dispatcher and field supervisors try to predict the likely course of the event and anticipate the need for additional resources (e.g., fire department, emergency medical technicians, tactical units, etc.).

Sometimes evolving information alters their understanding of the nature and urgency of the incident. It is not uncommon for communications dispatchers to receive citizen reports of stolen vehicles that have already been reported in hit-and-run accidents. Dispatchers are aware that hit-and-run drivers, particularly drunk drivers, may subsequently report their cars stolen to avoid responsibility for their offenses. The dispatchers frame their questions and the field officers' response on their informed, evolving understanding of the call.

Failure of responders to form accurate, shared situational analysis can lead to disastrous consequences. On October 12, 2006, a man climbed onto a rooftop in San Francisco. Onlookers called 9-1-1, and both police and fire units responded. The police secured the scene and engaged the subject in a dialogue using trained crisis negotiators (Noyes, 2006a). An off-duty fireman who accompanied the responding fire units climbed up to the roof, grabbed the subject from behind, and attempted to pull him to safety. The tile rooftop was precarious; the fireman worked alone and was not secured by ropes or safety gear. The subject and fireman struggled for balance, and the subject fell to the pavement.

The continuing controversy surrounding this tragedy would benefit from an HRO analysis. The police regarded the incident as a critical incident. They established a perimeter, recognized an incident commander and chain of command,

and designated experts (negotiators) to slow the pace of events and intervene to avert an apparent suicide in progress. The off-duty fireman who had personal experience with several rescues perceived the same event as a rescue and an opportunity for heroic action (Noyes, 2006b). The police and fire responses reflect their respective situational awareness, informed by their prior experience. Police negotiators and commanders understood the event as an incident to be managed, and the fireman reacted with his understanding of a desperate act in progress. However, he did not recognize or conform to protocols of chain of command or unified joint command, and he did not share the incident commander's evolving situational awareness, perhaps precipitating the unnecessary death of the distraught subject and imperiling his own life.

Situational awarenexx has been described as having "the big picture" or "having the bubble." This might describe the incident commander's "coarse-grained" view of the situation, compared with an entry team leader's more "fine-grained" view of all the details of the tactical approach. It also reflects the two most important and recurring questions the commander must answer throughout an incident: "What do we have here?" and "What if?"

The mischief of defining every situation to which negotiators respond as a negotiated incident is that it may unnecessarily commit an agency to a protracted siege and negotiation. A more enlightened situational analysis might recognize incidents that do not justify the resources of an extended siege. Lanceley (1999) observed that the dispatch of the FBI Hostage Rescue Team and their extensive resources to manage a barricaded suspect on a rural mountain top in the Ruby Ridge Incident was an overreaction. (He also observed that these resources and the commander's situational analysis and rules of engagement gravitated toward a tactical resolution, rather than a negotiated outcome.)

An Oakland case serves as an example of an incident "we can walk away from." A subject who was under the influence of alcohol discharged a gun into the air in his front yard and returned to his home. His wife fled from the house. Responding patrol units established a perimeter and called out negotiators and tactical responders. Units on the scene spoke to the subject's wife and other witnesses. They learned that the subject was "disagreeable" when he was drinking, but had no criminal record or history of violence. Approximately one half of the on-duty patrol force was involved in maintaining the perimeter and traffic control for this incident. Meanwhile, increasingly urgent and dangerous calls for service began to stack up around the city. The incident commander and supervisory personnel on the scene decided that, despite the commitment of negotiators and tactical specialists, this call was simply a dangerous misdemeanor, discharging a firearm within city limits. There was no evidence that it justified the overtime expense and depletion of resources from the rest of the city. The commander ensured that the suspect's wife had a place to stay, assigned two plainclothes officers to monitor the man's house, and dismissed all other units from the scene. The next day when the subject was sober, police investigators called him and invited him to meet with them. He surrendered his weapon and was cited and released.

This incident became a standard for evaluating whether the burdens outweigh the benefits of declaring a major critical incident and protracted siege.

EXTRACTING ANALOGIES FROM DIFFICULT CASES TO INFORM SITUATIONAL ANALYSIS

The most challenging cases we face and some of the most tragic outcomes we have suffered involve cases that clearly exceed the efficacy of our traditional negotiations guidelines. We have suggested "meta-rules" for heedful innovation when a case does not respond to our traditional techniques (Hare, 1986, 1997b; Hare & Weick, 2003), but these guidelines do not offer definitive guidance on when a particular case is beyond our traditional practice and requires us to apply special heedfulness and caution. Negotiators with extensive experience will recall numerous cases that dragged on interminably and showed no signs of progress. They have experienced briefing command on the apparent failure of negotiations, only to have the subject surrender without any salient indication of progress. Negotiator intuition, our generally accepted indicators of progress, and the analyses of psychological experts have not been effective predictors in intransigent cases. Challenging or dangerous cases are low-frequency, high-risk situations, in which the ability to recognize similarities to other extreme situations may better inform our decision makers than checklists or intuition.

We use a simplistic analysis of the Branch Davidian Siege at Waco as an example of decision making by analogy. During the course of the Branch Davidian siege, there were many efforts to assess the risk to the children within the compound. Law enforcement generally regards children who are held by their parents or who choose to accompany their parents in barricaded situations as potential victims. In this case, the FBI actually recognized the children as "hostages" and at risk (U.S. Department of Justice, 1993). Investigators have documented the FBI's efforts to solicit and assess expert opinions as to whether their containment might precipitate a mass suicide (U.S. Department of Justice, 1993; "Waco: The Inside Story," 1995). Incident managers considered David Koresh's statements to negotiators and the advice of psychiatrists, psychologists, and psychological profilers to form their analysis of the risk to the Davidian children (U.S. Department of Justice, 1993). Waco was clearly a situation that challenged or exceeded the experience of incident commanders, negotiators, profilers, and psychological experts. It was a low-frequency, high-consequence critical event with the potential for a catastrophic outcome.

In March 1993, an advanced negotiations class used the ongoing Waco standoff for an exercise in situational analysis. Several class members noted that David Koresh used the same Biblical allusions from the Book of Revelations as the suspects in the Jasper Arkansas Bus Hijacking. (The FBI distributes a training videotape of two subjects who hijacked a Greyhound bus in Arkansas to publicize their religious beliefs, including their belief in imminent death and resurrection.)

Another student pointed out similarities between the Davidians and William Chester Simpson and a follower who expressed their messianic religious beliefs, including death and resurrection, and cited similar apocalyptic allusions in another training videotape distributed by the FBI under the generic title of "Mentally Ill and Mobile." The class cited similarities between the Davidian community and Jim Jones' Peoples Temple sites in Oakland, San Francisco, and Guyana. The most chilling comparison was with the 1988 Philadelphia Move siege, which began with a shootout with police and ended in a conflagration that killed members of this movement and their children and burned blocks of row houses.

Each of these bizarre incidents ended tragically. The advanced negotiations class (and a San Francisco Police Department negotiators class that replicated this exercise) identified salient common features among these and other violent incidents. The list developed by San Francisco Police negotiators included many local (California) incidents that did not rise to the level of national attention. In each case, participants in the exercises recognized the similar cases first and then parsed out the several objective similarities presented in Table 12.1.

This exercise was not intended to criticize or replace the decision-making process at Waco. But it does illustrate the process by which an incident commander and incident management team lacking the resources of the FBI at Waco might assess a challenging incident using their knowledge of superficially similar cases. Clearly, it signaled the possibility of mass suicide, including the deaths of children in similar incidents that are well known to most negotiators. It also reinforces the value of the training tapes distributed by the FBI Academy. Finally, the entire tragic incident reminds us that social science and law enforcement specialists cannot give definitive answers in individual cases. Our most reliable analytical and predictive measures yield probable outcomes rather than certainty.

THE ROLE OF ERROR REPORTING IN HROS

HROs ranging from airlines to hospitals rely on the careful examination of errors and "near misses" to enhance their performance (Helmreich, Merritt, & Wilhelm, 1999; van Stralen & Perkin, 1997). Error reporting establishes a quantitative baseline for evaluating performance and provides qualitative data to inform how we might improve performance. For error reporting to work, there must be positive incentives for the voluntary and full disclosure of mistakes and performance failures, and there must be a reasonable, accurate standard for the analysis of performance. Success and failure are not adequate standards for evaluating agencies' performance in the face of diverse challenges.

There is a danger of creating a blaming or adversarial climate in the examination of error. There is also the liability of admitting blame in a litigious society. Law enforcement is the frequent target of litigants alleging our inadequate performance denied individuals their civil rights or caused harm; the admission we might have done things better in a dangerous incident may invite lawsuits. More

Table 12.1 Analogous Incidents and Identifying Characteristics

	Jasper Arkansas	William Simpson	Peoples Temple	Philadephia Move	Branch Davidians
Messianic Leader or Prophet	Yes	Yes	Yes	Yes	Yes
Life After Death (personal resurrection)	Yes	Yes	Yes	Yes	Yes
Surrendered Personal Possessions	Yes	Unknown*	Yes	Yes	Yes
Imminent Cataclysmic Conflict	Yes	Yes	Yes	Yes	Yes
Sexual Submission to Leader	Unknown	Unknown	Yes	Unknown	Yes
Prior Criminal History	Unknown	Unknown	No	Yes	Yes
Prepared for Extended Siege	Unknown	No	Yes	Yes	Yes
Preparations for Suicide	Yes	Yes	Yes	Unknown	Yes

*William Simpson publicly gave his savings to strangers in the days before his death. It is unknown whether his followers turned their assets over to him, as did the believers in the other cases cited.

universal and candid examination of every critical incident may offset the liability of admitting error. Error and accidents are ubiquitous, and most do not lead to tragic consequences. Establishing a body of expert knowledge of the extent and variety of errors and countermeasures in critical incident management may provide expert defense against lawsuits that focus on our admitted errors. It will certainly improve practice and reduce the frequency of error as has been done in other fields. There is no better protection from litigation than improved practice.

CONCLUSION

Crisis negotiation, critical incident management, and specialized tactical responders are relatively recent innovations in law enforcement, yet it is universally acknowledged that these specializations have saved many lives. Developments in the technology, organization, and training of tactical responders have clearly advanced their practice. Efforts to advance negotiations and incident command have not yielded a comparable increase in sophistication. In fact, efforts to quantify negotiations or streamline incident command may have reduced flexibility and the sophistication demanded by more challenging incidents. Some agencies have adopted organizations that make negotiations team leaders subordinate to tactical elements. This may increase the likelihood of a tactical resolution. Critical incident management and HRO practice would endorse the London Metropolitan Police approach of assigning equally high-ranking tactical and negotiations coordinators to advise the incident commander of the capabilities and obstacles facing each of these resources (J. Boocock, Chief Detective Superintendent, London Metropolitan Police, personal communication, May 23, 1992).

This chapter is an invitation to students of negotiation to adopt the concepts and approaches of HROs in other fields to improve their ability to recognize and manage our most challenging cases. Readings in the areas of decision theory, crew resource management, safety culture, and HROs are the first steps in this process. We look forward to the day when negotiators and police commanders join medical personnel, the nuclear power industry, commercial air carriers, military commanders, and the petrochemical and maritime industries at international conferences, where they will learn and adapt HRO principles to improve the safety and sophistication of law enforcement management of critical incidents.

NOTE

1. For more information about this organizational assessment instrument, see http://www.HFA-OSES.com

REFERENCES

American Psychiatric Association. (1980). *Diagnostic and statistical manual of mental disorders* (3rd ed.). Washington, DC: Author.

Boeing Company. (2006). *Statistical summary of commercial jet airplane accidents worldwide operations 1959–2005.* Chicago, IL: Author.

Bolz, F., & Hershey, E. (1979). *Hostage cop.* New York: Rawson Wade.

Carnes, W. E. (2006, April). *Research and theoretical approaches to high reliability.* A panel presented to Grouping for Solutions: Increasing Organizational Reliability by Bringing Academicians and Practitioners Together, the annual meeting of the Coalition for High Reliability Organizations, Ontario CA.

Ciavarelli, A. P. (2005, September). *Assessing safety climate and culture: From aviation to medicine.* Paper presented to Safety Across High-Consequence Industries, St. Louis University, MO.

Ciavarelli, A. P., & Crowson, G. (2004, March). *Organizational factors in accident risk assessment.* Paper presented to Safety Across High-Consequence Industries, St. Louis University, MO.

Ciavarelli, A. P., & Figlock, R. (1997). *Organizational factors in naval aviation accidents.* Proceedings of the International Aviation Psychologists, Columbus, OH.

Ciavarelli, A. P., Figlock, R., Sengupta, K., & Roberts, K. H. (2001, March). *Assessing organizational accident risk through survey questionnaire methods.* Paper presented at the 11th annual International Aviation Psychology conference, Columbus, OH.

Clarke, L. B. (1999). *Mission improbable: Using fantasy documents to tame disaster.* Chicago, IL: The University of Chicago Press.

Columbia Accident Investigation Board. (2003). *Report, Volume 1.* Washington, DC: U.S. Government Printing Office.

Combalbert, L. (n.d.). *Interview negociateur.* Retrieved June 6, 2005, from http://raid.admin .free.fr/negociateur.htm.

Cooper, G. E., White, M. D., & Lauber, J. K. (1980). *Resource management on the flightdeck.* Proceedings of a NASA/industry workshop (NASA CP-2120). Moffett Field, CA: NASA-Ames Research Center.

Delta Airlines. (2002). *Boeing 767 operations manual quick reference handbook.* Atlanta, GA: Author.

Desai, V., Roberts, K. H., & Ciavarelli, A. P. (2006). The relationship between safety climate and recent accidents: Behavioral learning and cognitive attributions. *Human Factors, 48,* 639–650.

Endsley, M. R. (1995). Toward a theory of situation awareness in dynamic systems. *Human Factors, 37,* 32–64.

Flin, R. H. (1996). *Sitting in the hot seat: Leaders and teams for critical incident management.* Chichester: Wiley.

Frailey, F. (1998, January). Union Pacific's Texas traffic jam. *Trains,* p. 6.

Fusilier, G. D. (1981). A practical overview of hostage negotiations (part I). *FBI Law Enforcement Bulletin, 50*(6), 2–6.

Gaba, D., Singer, S. J., Sinaiko, A. D., Bowen, J. D., & Ciavarelli, A. P. (2003). Differences in safety climate between hospital personnel and navy aviators. *Human Factors, 45,* 173–185.

Hacker, F. (1976). *Crusaders, criminals and crazies.* New York: W.W. Norton.

Hare, A. J. (1986, September). *Hostage negotiation: An introduction to advanced concepts.* Paper presented to Federal Bureau of Investigation Special Seminar on Hostage Negotiations, Quantico, VA.

Hare, A. J. (1995, September). *A summary of guidelines for negotiators.* Presented to U.S. Park Police seminar: Hostage negotiations for public areas, Presidio of San Francisco, CA.

Hare, A. J. (1997a). *Dealing with critical dispatch Incidents: Incorporating advanced negotiations in communications dispatch.* Seminar presented to Greater Harris Co. 9-1-1 Network, Houston, TX.

Hare, A. J. (1997b). Training crisis negotiators: Updating negotiation techniques and training. In R. G. Rogan, M. R. Hammer, & C. R. Van Zandt (Eds.), *Dynamic processes of crisis negotiation* (pp. 151–160). Westport, CT: Praeger.

Hare, A. J., & Weick, K. E. (2003, August). *Unfolding processes and error evolution.* A panel presented at the meeting Getting It Right: The Science Behind Solving the Unsolvable,

High Reliability Organization Theory and Practice in Medicine and Public Safety, Crafton Hills College Press, Yucaipa, CA.

Hart, C. (2006, April). *Implementing and sustaining change.* A panel presented to Grouping for Solutions: Increasing Organizational Reliability by Bringing Academicians and Practitioners Together, the annual meeting of the Coalition for High Reliability Organizations, Ontario, CA.

Helmreich, R. L., Merritt, A. C., & Wilhelm, J. A. (1999). The evolution of crew resource management training in commercial aviation. *International Journal of Aviation Psychology, 9*(1), 19–32. Retrieved October 28, 2006, from http://homepage.psy.utexas.edu/homepage/group/helmreichLAB/publications/publications/html.

Kerr, S. (1975). On the folly of rewarding A while hoping for B. *Academy of Management Journal, 47,* 469–483.

Kidd, W. F. (2005, August). *Hostage crisis negotiation team training 201.* Paper presented to the Kansas Association of Hostage Negotiators, Olathe, KS.

Kidd, W. F. (2006a, September). *Peak performance survey.* Paper presented to Rocky Mountain Hostage Negotiators Association annual conference, Estes Park, CO.

Kidd, W. F. (2006b, December). *Peak performance standards.* Paper presented to Chico Police Department/Butte County Sheriff's Department, Chico, CA.

Kidd, W. F. (2007, January). *Peak performance standards.* Paper presented to annual Southwest Negotiators' Seminar, Texas State University–San Marcos, San Marcos, TX.

Klein, G. (1999). *Sources of power: How people make decisions.* Cambridge, MA: MIT Press.

Kohn, L. T., Corrigan, J. M., & Donaldson, M. S. (Eds.). (1999). *To err is human: Building a safer health system.* Washington, DC: National Academy Press.

Lanceley, F. L. (1999). *On-scene guide for crisis negotiators.* Boca Raton, FL: CRC Press.

Lowenstein, R. (2000). *When genius failed: The rise and fall of long term capital management.* New York: Random House.

Madsen, P. M. (2007). *Organizational learning from direct and vicarious experience with catastrophic and minor accidents.* Working paper, Marriot School of Management, Brigham Young University, Salt Lake City, UT.

Madsen, P. M., Desai, V., Roberts, K. H., & Wong, D. (2006). Designing for high reliability: The birth and evolution of a pediatric intensive care unit. *Organization Science, 17,* 239–248.

Merritt, C. (2006, April). *Lessons learned from catastrophe: How organizations responded to Hurricane Katrina.* A panel presented to Grouping for Solutions: Increasing Organizational Reliability by Bringing Academicians and Practitioners Together, the annual meeting of the Coalition for High Reliability Organizations, Ontario, CA.

Miron, M. S., & Goldstein, A.P. (1979). *Hostage.* Elmsford, NY: Pergamon.

Naval Aviation Schools Command. (n.d.). *Situational Awareness (SA).* Retrieved September 20, 2006, from http://wwwnt.cnet.navy.mil./crm/crm/stand_mat/seven_skills.

Noyes, D. (2006a). *Firefighter to blame for man's fall?* Retrieved January 6, 2007, from http://abclocal.go,com/kgo/story?section=i_team&id=4677423.

Noyes, D. (2006b). *Family sees video of botched rescue.* Retrieved January 6, 2007, from http://abclocal.go,com/kgo/story?section=i_team&id=4691876.

Perrow, C. (1984). *Normal accidents: Living with high-risk technologies.* New York: Basic Books.

Reber, A. S. (1985). *Dictionary of psychology* (2nd ed.). New York: Penguin Books.

Reid, C. (2006, April). *Changing organizations following a major catastrophe.* A panel presented to Grouping for Solutions: Increasing Organizational Reliability by Bringing Academicians and Practitioners Together, the annual meeting of the Coalition for High Reliability Organizations, Ontario, CA.

Roberts, K. H. (1986). *Bishop Rock dead ahead: The grounding of the USS Enterprise.* Unpublished manuscript, University of California at Berkeley.

Roberts, K. H. (1990). Some characteristics of one type of high reliability organization. *Organization Science, 1,* 160–176.

Roberts, K. H., & Libuser, C. (1993). From Bhopal to banking, organizational design can mitigate risk. *Organizational Dynamics, 21,* 15–26.

Roberts, K. H., Madsen, P. M., & Desai, V. (2005). The space between in space transportation: A relational analysis of the failure of STS 107. In M. Farjoun & W. Starbuck (Eds.), *Organization at the limit: Lessons from the Columbia disaster* (pp. 81–98). Malden, MA: Blackwell.

Roberts, K. H., Madsen, P. M., & Desai, V. (2006). Organizational sense-making during crisis. In C. Pearson, C. Roux-Dufort, & J. Clair (Eds.), *The international handbook of organizational crisis management* (pp. 107–122) London: Sage.

Roberts, K. H., Madsen, P. M., Desai, V., & van Stralen, D. (2005). A case of the birth and death of a high reliability healthcare organization. *Quality and Safety in Health Care, 14,* 216–220.

Rogan R. G., & Hammer, M. R. (1995). Assessing message affect in crisis negotiations: An exploratory study. *Human Communication Research, 21,* 553–574.

Rogan, R. G., & Hammer, M. R. (2002). Crisis/hostage negotiations: A communication-based approach. In H. Giles (Ed.), *Law enforcement, communication, and community* (pp. 229–254). Amsterdam, The Netherlands: John Benjamins.

Rogan, R. G., & Hammer, M. R. (2006). The emerging field of crisis/hostage negotiations. In J. G. Oetzel & S. Ting-Toomey (Eds.), *The Sage handbook of conflict communication* (pp. 451–478). Thousand Oaks, CA: Sage.

Ross, P. E. (2006, August). The expert mind. *Scientific American, 295*(2), 64–71.

Sarna, P. C. (1984). Training police commanders and supervisors in the management of critical incidents. *Washington Crime News Services, Training Aids Digest, 9*(12), 1–6.

Sarna, P. C. (1990). *Critical incident management lesson plan guide.* Pittsburgh, CA: Los Medanos College.

Sarter, N. B., & Woods, D. D. (1991). Situation awareness—a critical but ill-defined phenomenon. *International Journal of Aviation Psychology, 1*(1), 45–57.

Schlossberg, H. (1984). *Basic hostage negotiation course.* San Jose: CA: San Jose State University Administration of Justice Bureau.

Schlossberg, H., & Freeman, L. (1974). *Psychologist with a gun.* New York: Conan, McCann & Geoghegan.

Schulman, P. S. (1993). The negotiated order of organizational reliability. *Administration and Society, 25,* 353–372.

Shrivastava, P. (1987). *Bhopal: Anatomy of a crisis.* Cambridge, MA: Ballinger.

Strentz, T. (1983). The inadequate personality as hostage taker. *Journal of Police Science and Administration, 11*(3), 363–368.

Strentz, T. (1986). Negotiating with the hostage taker exhibiting paranoid schizophrenic symptoms. *Journal of Police Science and Administration, 14,* 12–16.

Tadmore, C. T., Roberts, K. H., & Yu, K. F. (2009). *Structural failures and the development of an organizational breakdown: The tragedy of the USS Greeneville.*

U.S. Department of Justice. (1993, February 28–April 19). *Report to the attorney general on the events at Waco, Texas.* Retrieved November 10, 2006, from http://www.usdoj.gov/ 05publications/waco/wacothree.html.

U.S. Department of Transportation, Federal Aviation Administration. (1989). *Advisory circular: Cockpit resource management training.* Washington, DC: Author.

van Stralen, D., & Perkin, R.M. (1997, June). *Pediatric critical care as a high reliability organization.* Paper presented at the meeting of the Center for Risk Management, University of California, Berkeley, CA.

Vaughan, D. (1996). *The challenger launch decision: Risky technology, culture, and deviance at NASA.* Chicago: University of Chicago Press.

Waco: The inside story. (1995). *Frontline.* Retrieved on December 12, 2006, from http:// www.pbs.org/wgbh/pages/frontline/waco/timeline.html.

Weick, K. E. (1987). Organizational culture as a source of high reliability. *California Management Review, 29,* 112–127.

Weick, K. E., & Roberts, K. H. (1993). Collective mind and organizational reliability: The case of flight operations on an aircraft carrier deck. *Administrative Science Quarterly, 38,* 357–381.

Weick, K. E., & Sutcliffe, K. M. (2001). *Managing the unexpected: Assuring high performance in an age of complexity.* San Francisco: Jossey-Bass.

13

Concluding Thoughts and Future Directions in Crisis and Hostage Negotiation

Frederick J. Lanceley
Randall G. Rogan

When organizing this book, it was our intent to pull together the most recent findings and ideas from academics in the fields of communication and psychology, as well as former law enforcement professionals with years of crisis and hostage negotiation experience. We believe that we were successful in realizing this objective. Each of the final contributors is internationally recognized as a leading expert in his or her discipline and his or her work in crisis negotiation.

Clearly, the content and focus of the chapters presented in this volume vary, with some of the chapters providing a historical perspective about the genesis and development of crisis and hostage negotiation. Several chapters present and review findings from specific research of various aspects of negotiation dynamics, others present scholarly based models and theories for application in incident management, and still other chapters discuss critical and emerging issues that affect crisis negotiation dynamics. Uniformly, every chapter functions to advance our current knowledge and understanding about the essential conditions of crisis and hostage negotiation and to demonstrate the potential translational integration of academic research and practice. Taken together, the chapters offer hope for peaceful resolutions to potentially violent interactions.

REFLECTIONS ON THE CHAPTERS

In the late 1970s, Bob Louden and his team of negotiators with the New York Police Department (NYPD) an inspiration to other hostage negotiators around the United States, especially to a young Fred Lanceley, who had just joined the Federal

Bureau of Investigation's (FBI's) Special Operations and Response Unit as a new negotiator. Louden and his group of negotiators further developed the hostage negotiation procedures and policies that were first introduced by his predecessors, including Harvey Schlossberg and Frank Bolz (Bolz & Hershey, 1979; Schlossberg, 1979). In those early days, the prevailing mentality within law enforcement tended to be that of engaging the suspect in a confrontational manner (Hammer & Rogan, 1997; Rogan & Hammer, 2002) and waiting until sniper response units could secure a "clear shot" at the suspect and an attitude on the part of many law enforcement personnel that "he (the suspect) is not going to screw with us." A great deal of commitment, courage, and a conviction that there must be a better way to resolve such incidents was required of those early negotiators who advocated for trying to talk to the subject first. Bob Louden and his team had that commitment, courage, and conviction. Undeniably, the field of crisis and hostage negotiation would not be what it is today without the work of the negotiators and their commanders at NYPD. Louden (Chapter 2), therefore, provides an essential historical perspective on the early development of crisis negotiation and some of its evolution over the past several years. Appreciating where we came from and how the practice of crisis negotiation has advanced, due principally to the innovative thinking of a cadre of individuals who questioned the existing customary morality of crisis negotiation and who were open to new ideas, serves as an important model to continued evolution and translational interaction between research and practice.

In Chapter 3, Mitchell R. Hammer focused his attention on the role of communication and the concept of framing for seeking resolution in critical incidents. He presented a summary of the S.A.F.E. model of crisis negotiation that was developed to assist hostage and crisis negotiation teams more effectively deescalate and peacefully resolve critical incidents. Hammer argues that the core premise of the S.A.F.E. model approach is grounded in the belief that the evolution of crisis interactions is based on whether the negotiator successfully attends to the germane S.A.F.E. frames—that is, whether Substantive demands are negotiated or ignored, Attunement (relational closeness) enhanced or diminished, Face honored or threatened, and/or Emotional distress empathically transformed or intensified. From the perspective of law enforcement, it is a step in the right direction to see researchers investigate the applicability of such theory-based models within actual interactions. Field negotiators need and should welcome innovations that can improve their effectiveness.

In the early 1980s, Lanceley did an extensive literature search and spoke to authorities on the topic of persuasion techniques, with the idea of implementing some of those concepts into the FBI's hostage negotiation in-service. In Chapter 4, Ellen Giebels and Paul J. Taylor impressively demonstrate how far the fields of social influence and persuasion have progressed in the last 25 years. Giebels and Taylor focused their attention in this chapter on the use of persuasive messages and influence tactics. They began the chapter by discussing the significant role of influence tactics in contemporary crisis negotiation research and practice. They followed with a theoretically derived set of 10 influence tactics and discussed how and when these tactics shape the development of a negotiation. The chapter was concluded with a discussion of how the effectiveness of influence tactics can differ across cultures and negotiation contexts.

Of particular interest is Geibels and Taylor's "Table of Ten," which provides a structure for thinking about the ways in which a negotiator's objectives may be presented in a persuasive fashion. According to Geibels and Taylor, negotiators have stated that the Table of Ten has helped them in their efforts to expand their use of influence strategies and has assisted in their efforts to employ the most effective tactic for the situation. The Table of Ten may also assist negotiators in making a more deliberate selection of the most appropriate influence tactic based on what is known about the type of incident, the incident phase, and the cultural background of the perpetrator. An exciting prospect to this book is that many of the chapters have the potential for developing skills that officers, not just negotiators, may find themselves using on a daily basis.

In Chapter 5, William A. Donohue focused on the communicative dynamics by which negotiators and suspects manage the dialectical tensions of their relationship. According to Donohue's Relational Order Theory (Donohue & Roberto, 1993, 1996), all relationships, and in particular conflictual relationships, are constantly being negotiated along two essential relational parameters of affiliation and interdependence, and that these parameters define four contextual orientations that individuals negotiate during their interactions. These four conditions include collaboration, cooperation, coexistence, and conflict. Drawing on several research studies, Donohue asserts that crisis bargainers must learn to address and even make explicit these inherent paradoxes as they strive to deescalate the cycle of destructive conflict interaction and move the situation from one of crisis negotiation to that of more normative bargaining. Similar to Hammer, Donohue contends that linguistic cues function as framing devices for communicators, reflecting the dominant relational condition during a specific episode of interaction, and that attending to these cues can assist negotiators in effectively managing the various paradoxes that present themselves during the course of an incident.

In Chapter 6, Randall G. Rogan presents the findings from an investigation of facework dynamics present within actual negotiation incidents. As noted in the S.A.F.E. model that he and Mitchell Hammer developed, Face is one of four core frames to conflict interaction generally, and crisis negotiation specifically. Rogan and Hammer (1994) conducted a similar investigation comparing the facework of suspects and negotiators in three incidents and reported that suspect behavior was markedly unique in the one suicide incident, leading them to suggest follow-up research with more incidents. In his chapter, Rogan reports that results indicated that barricaded subjects employ mostly self-directed face-defending and face-restoring behaviors, whereas police negotiators use mostly other-directed face-defending and face-restoring strategies. His findings are generally consistent with the earlier investigation, suggesting that facework frames may function as potentially critical linguistic markers for determining a suspect's potential suicidality during the course of a crisis negation.

In Chapter 7, Wolfgang Bilsky, Beate Tebrügge, and Denise Weßel-Therhorn reviewed the dynamics of conflict escalation and deescalation. In particular, this chapter described a multilevel analysis of communications between a hostage taker and a negotiator during a single hostage incident. The authors hypothesized that communications differ substantially depending on whether the specific incident demonstrated features of escalation or deescalation. Four discrete studies were carried out, each of them focusing on a different aspect of communicative behaviour: emotionality, face issues, motivation and interaction, and tactics. Transcripts of 53 phone calls between hostage taker and negotiator were analyzed by means of content analysis using five different instruments. Emotions, face concern, and goal-directed behaviour varied depending on the current conflict dynamics as indicated in escalative and deescalative telephone calls. Bilsky and his colleagues conclude that negotiations are complex interactive dynamics in which negotiators strive to make sense out of the messages of hostage takers as they work toward nonviolent resolution. This is no easy feat. They argue that educating negotiators about the multiple dimensions of concurrent information contained in linguistic messages is an important step toward thoughtful and responsible negotiation. Although interaction-based research on crisis negotiation is still scarce, they encourage using the few existing models that do exist as templates for training of law enforcement negotiators.

In Chapter 8, Frederick J. Lanceley presented the findings from a research project that he conducted into the behavior of suicidal persons in the last moments of their lives. He was concerned with a number of issues regarding an apparent disparity between what he had been taught in the area of suicide intervention and what law enforcement negotiators were reporting to him during seminars. Of particular significance, Lanceley concluded that perturbation during interaction does not seem to be a reliable indicator of suicide enactment. Perhaps of particular noteworthiness, Lanceley's nonscientific study highlights the challenges of direct transferability of scholarly and clinical research to the context of crisis negotiation and how context-specific research investigations are necessary.

In Chapter 9, Kris Mohandie presented extant knowledge about the various psychological traits and personality conditions associated with subjects in negotiated incidents. Often an early question to police officers from a plaintiff's attorneys in a lawsuit following the outcome of a crisis negotiation incident is about the officer's knowledge of bipolar disorder, depression, suicide, and other psychological characteristics. When a person suffering from a mental illness or personality disorder dies in a confrontation with the police, the public response is often one that asks whether something could have been done better or whether something was done wrong. The public is often partially correct. When someone dies during a negotiated incident, few would argue that police could have done something better because they failed to achieve the ultimate goal of a nonviolent resolution for everyone involved, including the suspect. Therefore, a basic understanding of personality disorders, affective disorders, and psychosis is extremely important for all law enforcement officers, particularly negotiators. With such knowledge, responding officers and negotiators are better equipped to more effectively understand and possibly predict the subjects' moods, thought processes, delusions and hallucinations, and ultimate behavior.

In Chapter 10, Daveed Gartenstein-Ross and Kyle Dabruzzi provide a thoughtful and revealing explanation of radical Islam and the jurisprudence undergirding jihadi terrorism. Although dealing with terrorist-based hostage taking is not new to the field, jihadi terrorism represents a potential significant threat for Western Europe and the United States. Their chapter offers the reader a glimpse into the theology and philosophy that drive this terrorism. Unfortunately, limiting them to a chapter in this volume means that they could only provide an overview to the myriad issues associated with radical Islam. Yet Gartenstein-Ross and Dabruzzi provide an excellent introduction for us that we think is essential knowledge for all negotiators for the next decade. Gartenstein-Ross and Dabruzzi have amply demonstrated in their chapter how difficult achieving any kind of accord with radical Islam can be and the challenges that negotiators will likely face during terrorist-motivated incidents.

In Chapter 11, Wayman C. Mullins and Michael J. McMains have reminded us of the wide diversity of groups and persons that have been described as "terrorist." There are left-wing groups, right-wing groups, and special interest groups all composed of individuals with different personalities and motivation. Mullins and McMains have emphasized the importance of knowing the group and the use of skills already known to negotiators across the United States, such as active listening and other communication skills for attempting to negotiate terrorist-based incidents. They further emphasize the importance of knowing the individual with whom one is negotiating—his or her motivation and the various psychological factors associated with the suspect's behavior. They conclude that it is critical to remember that, although suspects are often members of groups, we negotiate with individuals, not the group.

The more avenues one has in approaching a problem, the higher the probability that problem will be successfully resolved. One of the exciting aspects of this book is that it presents some ideas and approaches to managing high-risk situations. In Chapter 12, Anthony J. Hare and Karlene H. Roberts presented a new theoretic perspective that they argue can help advance the practice of crisis and hostage negotiation. Their chapter reviewed High-Reliability Organization (HRO) theory as a framework for continual performance analysis and practice implementation that has significant application for professionals who work in dangerous or critical environments and argue for its potential for application in crisis and hostage negotiation. The authors note that various researchers and practitioners of HRO report similar conceptual frameworks and procedural practices across diverse technological contexts that arguably enhance practitioner safety and improve performance. Hare and Roberts contend that the application of HRO approaches to critical incident management and hostage and crisis negotiation will be most effectively realized by law enforcement personnel who study and adapt the analyses to their own practice and who work in concert with social scientists and mental health professionals to heedfully evaluate and incorporate innovations into their practice.

FUTURE DIRECTIONS AND FINAL THOUGHTS

Each of the chapters included in this volume provides compelling evidence of the interest and concern that practitioners and scholars have for increasing our knowledge, understanding, and practice of crisis negotiation. For researchers, more studies need to be conducted of actual negotiation incidents that build on and investigate the various dimensions presented here. Human interaction and communication is a complex interplay of relational dynamics, nonverbal symbols, and features of linguistic cues (Watzlawick, Bavelas, & Jackson, 1967). Striving to understand precisely how these dialectics play out in crisis negotiation demands a larger body of research and more sophisticated analyses. To date, scholars have generally only been able to explore one aspect at a time.

Equally important, researchers will need access to more incidents. This requires greater interaction and support from negotiators. Law enforcement officers work with people in their "natural habitat" every day—people under stress. Deputies, police officers, FBI agents, and many others have built an invaluable level of experience and, perhaps more important, have extensive records of these events that could and should be shared with researchers. Through 36 years of experience in law enforcement, Lanceley has seen the academic and law enforcement communities attempting to understand some of the same problems, but on distinct and parallel paths. These two professions need to increase their collaboration for the good of humankind. Today's negotiators need to demonstrate the same kind of courage and conviction to advance knowledge and practice as did the early negotiators of NYPD.

We were eager to collaborate on this book because we viewed this project as an opportunity to further promote this interaction of scholar and law enforcement officer. It is our sincere hope that this book serves that purpose and that an increased synergy can evolve through the sharing of information. Saving lives is something that we can all agree and collaborate on in order to help make nonviolent resolutions to crisis and hostage negotiation incidents a reality.

REFERENCES

Bolz, F., & Hershey, E. (1979). *Hostage cop*. New York: Rawson Wade.
Donohue, W. A., & Roberto, A. J. (1993). Relational development in hostage negotiation. *Human Communication Research, 20*, 175–198.

Donohue, W. A., & Roberto, A. J. (1996). An empirical examination of three models of integrative and distributive bargaining. *The International Journal of Conflict Management, 7,* 209–229.

Hammer, M. R., & Rogan, R. G. (1997). Negotiation models in crisis situations: The value of a communication based approach. In R.G. Rogan, M. R. Hammer, & C. R. Van Zandt (Eds.), *Dynamic processes of crisis negotiation: Theory, research, and practice* (pp. 9–23). Westport, CT: Praeger.

Rogan, R. G., & Hammer, M. R. (1994). Crisis negotiations: A preliminary investigation of facework in naturalistic conflict. *Journal of Applied Communication Research, 22,* 216–231.

Rogan, R. G., & Hammer, M. R. (2002). Crisis/hostage negotiations: Conceptualization of a communication-based approach. In H. Giles (Ed.), *Law enforcement, communication, and community* (pp. 229–254). Amsterdam, The Netherlands: John Benjamins Publishing.

Schlossberg, H. (1979). Police response to hostage situations. In J. T. O'Brien & M. Marcus (Eds.), *Crime and justice in America* (pp. 209–220). New York: Pergamon.

Watzlawick, P., Bavelas, J. B., & Jackson, D. D. (1967). *Pragmatics of human communication: A study of interactional patterns, pathologies, and paradoxes.* New York: W.W. Norton.

Author Biographies

Dr. Wolfgang Bilsky is Professor at the Westfälische Wilhelms-Universität (WWU) in Münster, Germany, and head of the department of Personality and Differential Psychology. He received his academic degrees from the Technische Universität Braunschweig (Dipl.-Psych. and Dr.rer.nat.) and from the Albert-Ludwigs-Universität Freiburg i.Br. (Dr.habil.). Before changing to Münster, he served as Assistant Professor and Lecturer at the University of Freiburg and as Senior Researcher at the Criminological Research Institute of Lower Saxony (KFN) in Hannover. In recent years, he was a member of the Crime Prevention Council of North Rhine-Westphalia (NRW) and Visiting Professor at UFPB in João Pessoa, and Universidade Presbiteriana Mackenzie in São Paulo, Brazil. His main research interests focus on psychology and law, and on cross-cultural values research. He has published on helping behavior, conflict resolution, fear of crime and victimization, crisis negotiation, lay theories of criminal behavior, facet theory, and values and motives.

Kyle Dabruzzi is a summer fellow at the Foundation for Defense of Democracies (FDD), where he is a member of the research division. Before joining FDD, he served as a terrorism analyst for Daveed Gartenstein-Ross' consulting firm. His writing has appeared in publications that include *Middle East Quarterly* and the *Daily Standard*. Dabruzzi graduated from Wake Forest University in 2006, where he received a BA in political science with a minor in Middle East and South Asian politics. While at Wake Forest, he served in Army ROTC.

Dr. William A. Donohue is currently a Distinguished Professor of Communication at Michigan State University. He received his PhD in 1976 from The Ohio State University in Communication. Bill's work lies primarily in the areas of mediation and crisis negotiation. He has worked extensively with several state and federal agencies in both training and research activities related to violence prevention and hostage negotiation. He has more than 70 publications dealing with various communication and conflict issues, and he has won several awards for his scholarship from national and international professional associations. Bill is an active member of the International Association for Conflict Management and its current president. He is on the editorial board of several journals in the areas of conflict management and communication.

Daveed Gartenstein-Ross is the Vice President of Research at the Foundation for Defense of Democracies and author of *My Year Inside Radical Islam*. He has testified before the U.S. Senate's Homeland Security and Governmental Affairs Committee and Georgia's state legislature, and he has appeared on academic and policy panels at the LAPD's Joint Regional Intelligence Conference, the Cato Institute, and the Conservative Political Action Conference. His writings about terrorism have appeared in *Reader's Digest, Middle East Quarterly, The Wall Street Journal Europe, Commentary, The Weekly Standard,* and *The Dallas Morning News.* Gartenstein-Ross earned a JD from the New York University School of Law, where he was a member of the Law Review, and a BA from Wake Forest University, where he won the 1997 National Debate Tournament.

Dr. Ellen Giebels (PhD, University of Groningen, 1999) is Associate Professor in the Department of Psychology at the University of Twente, The Netherlands. Her research focuses on conflict, negotiation, and mediation, particularly in a crisis context. Ellen has worked with Dutch and other European police forces since 1996 (research, training, and on-scene advice), and she spent a year with the Belgian Federal Police in Brussels. She is co-author of numerous peer-reviewed articles and several books, including *Crisis Negotiations: A Multiparty Perspective* (with Sigrid Noelanders). Three of these papers received a best paper award, including her work on cultural differences in crisis negoations (with Paul J. Taylor), which won the 2007 Best Applied Paper award of the International Association for Conflict Management conference.

Dr. Mitchell R. Hammer is President of Hammer Consulting, LLC. In 2006, Dr. Hammer was awarded Professor Emeritus from the American University in Washington, DC. In addition to his work on the S.A.F.E. model for hostage/crisis negotiation, Dr. Hammer has developed the Intercultural Conflict Style Inventory and the Intercultural Development Inventory. Dr. Hammer has gained an international reputation as a leader for numerous projects involving critical incident management, hostage/crisis negotiation, conflict resolution, intercultural communication, and cultural diversity. His new book, *Saving Lives* (2007, Praeger Press), presents a comprehensive explanation of the innovative S.A.F.E. approach for resolving crisis situations. His earlier book (co-authored with Randall Rogan and Clint Van Zandt), *Dynamic Processes of Crisis Negotiation: Theory, Research and Practice* (1997), was honored with the Outstanding Book Award in 1998 by the International Association of Conflict Management. In 1992, Dr. Hammer was given the Senior Interculturalist Award of Achievement by the Society of Intercultural Education, Training, and Research.

Anthony J. Hare is a visiting scholar at the Center for Catastrophic Risk Management of the Institute for Business and Economic Research at the University of California at Berkeley. He earned his BS in psychology from the University of California at Berkeley and his PhD in psychotherapy from the Wright Institute. Dr. Hare is a postdoctoral intern with Pacific Forensic Psychology Associates. He served as a hostage negotiator, negotiations team leader, and incident commander with the Oakland Police Department, where he retired as a captain and continues to serve as a reserve officer. Dr. Hare's advanced and innovative techniques for hostage and crisis negotiation have been adopted by major U.S. law enforcement agencies, the FBI, the U.S. Department of State, and military and law enforcement negotiators around the world. He has written U.S. Military doctrine on the incorporation of mental health professionals into negotiated incidents and on the integration of negotiations and tactics in challenging incidents. He served as an infantry commander in Vietnam and as Aide de Camp to the Chief of Staff, U.S. Army, Vietnam. He was recalled to active duty for Operation Desert Shield/ Desert Storm.

Frederick J. Lanceley, MSAJ, retired from the Federal Bureau of Investigation after 26 years of government service. While in the FBI, he worked in New Orleans, Los Angeles, and at the FBI Academy in Quantico, Virginia. At the Academy, he was the FBI's senior negotiator and principal director of their internationally acclaimed crisis negotiation course for 13 years. He has worked several hundred hostage, barricade, suicide, aircraft hijacking, and kidnapping cases. With the University of Louisville, he conducted a major study of aircraft hijacking that included the interview of 21 hijackers. Mr. Lanceley has trained officers from every major law enforcement agency in the United States and more than 50 foreign countries. He is the author of *On-Scene Guide for Crisis Negotiators*, now in its second edition. Mr. Lanceley is currently the Director of Crisis Negotiation Associates in Canton, Georgia, where he writes, conducts seminars, and provides expert witness testimony.

Dr. Robert J. Louden is Professor and Program Director, Criminal Justice, at Georgian Court University, Lakewood, NJ. Before this appointment, Dr. Louden was Professor of Public Management at John Jay College of Criminal Justice,

NYC, where he taught graduate and undergraduate students in Criminal Justice and Protection Management. He also created graduate and undergraduate course work in Hostage Negotiation. Prior to his academic appointments, Dr. Louden was a career police officer with the NYPD (1966–1987). His last assignment was as Commander of Detective Squad and Chief Hostage Negotiator. During his 13 years as a hostage negotiator, Louden actively participated in several hundred hostage, siege, kidnap, and extortion incidents and investigations, including inside three missions to the UN in NYC. He has received numerous awards for bravery and outstanding police work. His academic pursuits include research, writing, and teaching about hostage negotiation, police organization and training, and terrorism. Dr. Louden earned his PhD from the City University of New York.

Dr. Michael J. McMains currently consults with local, state, and federal law enforcement agencies, as well as private/public entities on crisis management issues, workplace violence, hostage and crisis negotiations; family violence; crisis intervention skills for first responders; suicide intervention; hostage survival strategies; and traumatic stress. He is co-author of *Crisis Negotiations: Managing Critical Incidents and Hostage Incidents in Law Enforcement and Correction* (3rd ed., co-authored with Dr. Mullins). He has been involved in more than 400 crisis/hostage incidents. From 1982 to 2004, he was Chief Psychologist and Director of the Victims Advocacy Section of the San Antonio Police Department. He developed the Victims Advocacy Section and co-founded the Crisis Intervention Team training program for officers. Prior to working with the police department, Dr. McMains served as a Psychologist in the U.S. Army for 9 years. He was on the Board of Directors of the Texas Association of Hostage Negotiators, the Society of Police and Criminal Psychology, the Bexar County Psychological Association, and the Applied Division of the Texas State Psychological Association. He holds a Doctor of Philosophy in Clinical Psychology from Vanderbilt University in Nashville, Tennessee, and a Diplomate in Police Psychology from the Society of Police and Criminal Psychology.

Dr. Kris Mohandie is a police and forensic psychologist with more than 17 years of experience in the assessment and management of violent behavior. He has worked in field responses and case investigations for local, state, and federal law enforcement organizations, including LAPD's Threat Management Unit and SWAT/Crisis Negotiation Team. He responded on-scene to the O.J. Simpson barricade and the North Hollywood Bank Robbery Shootout. Dr. Mohandie assisted the Los Angeles County District Attorney's prosecution of the stalker of Steven Spielberg. He regularly consults on workplace violence, extreme violence, stalking, and threat cases in the private and public sector through his company, Operational Consulting International, Inc. His book, *School Violence Threat Management,* came out in 2000 and is now in its second printing. He is the lead author (with Meloy and others) of the largest published study of more than 1,000 North American stalkers, which appears in the January 2006 volume of the *Journal of Forensic Sciences*. He is lead researcher (with Meloy & Collins) of a large ($N = 707$) ongoing study of police shootings, with an emphasis on suicide-by-cop cases. Dr. Mohandie has conducted extensive trial-pending and prison interviews of violent offenders, including a number of notorious stalkers, hostage takers, workplace and school violence perpetrators, and multiple murderers.

Dr. Wayman C. Mullins received his PhD in Psychology from the University of Arkansas at Fayetteville. He is Professor of Criminal Justice at Texas State University in San Marcos, Texas (1984–present). He is a commissioned officer with the Hays County Sheriff's Department and is on their crisis negotiation team. Prior to that, he served for more than 10 years as a reserve officer with the San Marcos Police Department. Dr. Mullins has published extensively on crisis negotiations, terrorism, stress, and posttraumatic stress disorder. He has served as a consultant to law enforcement and correction agencies at the federal, state, and local levels. Dr. Mullins has authored several books, including *Crisis Negotiations: Managing Critical Incidents and Hostage Situations in Law Enforcement Corrections*, 3rd edition (co-authored with Dr. Michael McMains; Anderson Press, 2006), and *A Sourcebook of International and Domestic Terrorism*, 2nd edition (Charles C Thomas, Publisher, 1997). In Fall 2006, Dr. Mullins served in Iraq as Advisor to the Center for Ethics and Human Rights under the Multi-National Security Transition Command–Iraq (MNSTC–I) in the Civilian Police Assistance Training Team section.

Dr. Karlene H. Roberts is a Professor at the Walter A. Haas School of Business at the University of California at Berkeley. Roberts earned her BS in Psychology from Stanford University and her PhD in Industrial Psychology from the University of California at Berkeley. She also received the docteur honoris causa from the Universite Paul Cezanne (Aix Marseilles III). Roberts has done research on job attitudes, cross-national management, and organizational communication. Since 1984, she has been investigating the design and management of organizations and systems of organizations in which error can result in catastrophic consequences. She has studied both organizations that failed and those that succeed in this category. Some of the industries in which Roberts has worked are the military, commercial marine transportation, healthcare, railroads, petroleum production, commercial aviation, banking, and community emergency services. She has consulted in the areas of human resource management, staffing policies, organizational design, the development of cultures of reliability for the military, the health care industry, software development, and the financial industry. She testified before the Columbia Accident Investigation Board.

Dr. Randall G. Rogan (PhD, Michigan State University) is Professor of Communication and currently serves as Associate Dean of the Graduate School for Arts and Sciences at Wake Forest University. Professor Rogan's research is in forensic discourse analysis of crisis negotiations and author identification. In particular, his research focuses on the affective and framing features of conflict communication, for which he has received scholarly awards. His 1997 book (co-edited with M. R. Hammer & C. Van Zandt), *Dynamic Processes of Crisis Negotiation: Theory, Research and Practice,* was awarded the "Outstanding Book Award" in 1998 by the International Association of Conflict Management. Professor Rogan is also co-editor on the forthcoming book by Donohue, Kaufman, and Rogan (Eds.), *Framing and Conflict.* Dr. Rogan is recognized as an international expert and leading researcher in crisis negotiation. Dr. Rogan has consulted with various law enforcement agencies on crisis negotiation and threatening communication. Of particular note, his analysis of written documents assisted in the investigation that resulted in the arrest of the Unabomber.

Dr. Paul J. Taylor is Senior Lecturer in Forensic Psychology at Lancaster University, UK, where he leads a team of forensic psychologists and directs the Department's postgraduate course on investigation and expertise. His team collaborates with academics and professionals from Europe, the Middle East, and North America, and Dr. Taylor is an honorary research associate of the Police Research Laboratory at Carleton University and the Laboratory for Bounded Rationality and the Law at Memorial University, Canada. Dr. Taylor has published more than 30 peer-reviewed journal and conference papers on behavior in crisis environments, particularly in relation to negotiation, where he and his colleagues have addressed issues such as effective strategy use and the prediction of outcome. This work has received the Earl Scheafer Best Research Paper award and, more recently, the 2007 IACM best applied paper award.

Beate Tebrügge received her psychology degree from the Westfälische Wilhelms-Universität (WWU) Münster in 2006. Her interest in hostage negotiation first awoke during a research-oriented course on crisis negotiation. Since then, this area has become one of her main fields of work. She familiarized herself with the practical experience of police pscyhologists during internships at the Landeskriminalamt (LKA; State Office of Criminal Investigation) in Düsseldorf and at the Institut für Aus- und Fortbildung der Polizei (IAF; Institute for the Vocational and Advanced Training of the Police) in North-Rhine Westphalia. The focus of her diploma thesis was on structural patterns of negotiation behavior. At present, she is working as a qualified clinical psychologist in the counselling and therapy of mentally ill clients in Münster.

Denise Weßel-Therhorn studied psychology at the Westfälische Wilhelms-Universität (WWU) in Münster, Germany. Her diploma thesis dealt with strategies and tactics in crisis/hostage negotiation. She completed her studies at the WWU in 2006 with a diploma in psychology (Dipl.-Psych.). In addition to her university courses, she worked as a student assistant at the Center of Criminology (KrimZ) in Wiesbaden. In 2007, she received a doctoral scholarship from the

German National Academic Foundation. Since then, she has been a doctoral student at the Department of Personality and Differential Psychology of the WWU. The working title of her dissertation is "Multilevel Analysis of Communication Behavior in Hostage Negotiation." Her research interests lie in conflict management and crisis negotiation.

Author Index

Subject Index

279

CPSIA information can be obtained at www.ICGtesting.com
Printed in the USA
LVOW050218190812

294904LV00002BB/44/P